The Rise of Western Christen...

THE MAKING OF EUROPE

Series Editor: Jacques Le Goff

The Making of Europe series is the result of a unique collaboration between five European publishers – Beck in Germany, Blackwell in Great Britain and the United States, Critica in Spain, Laterza in Italy and le Seuil in France. Each book will be published in all five languages. The scope of the series is broad, encompassing the history of ideas as well as societies, nations and states, to produce informative, readable, and provocative treatments of central themes in the history of the European peoples and their cultures.

Published

The European City
Leonardo Benevolo

The Rise of Western Christendom
Peter Brown

The Search for the Perfect Language
Umberto Eco

The Distorted Past:
A Reinterpretation of Europe
Josep Fontana

The Origins of European
Individualism
Aaron Gurevich

The Enlightenment
Ulrich Im Hof

Europe and the Sea
Michel Mollat du Jourdin

The Culture of Food
Massimo Montanari

The Peasantry of Europe
Werner Rösener

The European Revolutions,
1492–1992
Charles Tilly

In preparation

Democracy in European History
Maurice Agulhon

Migration and Culture
Klaus Bade

Women in European History
Gisela Bock

The European Renaissance
Peter Burke

Europe and Islam
Franco Cardini

Literacy in European History
Roger Chartier

Nature and Culture
Robert Delort

The Family in European History
Jack Goody

The Law in European History
Peter Landau

The University in European History
Jacques Le Goff

The Population of Europe
Massimo Livi-Bacci

The First European Revolution,
900–1200
R. I. Moore

The Frontier in European History
Krzysztof Pomian

The Birth of Modern Science
Paolo Rossi

State and Nation in European History
Hagen Schulze

The Rise of Western Christendom

Triumph and Diversity
AD 200–1000

Peter Brown

BLACKWELL
Publishers

First published 1996
First published in paperback 1997

Blackwell Publishers Inc
350 Main Street
Malden, Massachusetts 02148, USA

Blackwell Publishers Ltd
108 Cowley Road
Oxford OX4 1JF, UK

Library of Congress Cataloging in Publication Data
Brown, Peter Robert Lamont
The rise of Western Christendom: triumph and diversity.
AD200–1000 / Peter Brown
p.   cm. — (The Making of Europe)
ISBN 1–55786–136–6 (Hbk) — ISBN 1–57718–092–5 (Pbk)
1. Church history—Primitive and early church, ca. 30–600.
2. Church history—Middle Ages, 600–1500.
I. Title. II. Series.
BR162.2.B76   1995   95–11589
274—dc20   CIP

British Library Cataloguing in Publication Data
A CIP catalogue record for this book is available from the British Library

Typeset in 10 on 12pt Sabon
by Grahame and Grahame Editorial, Brighton, East Sussex
Printed and bound in Great Britain by T. J. Press Ltd, Padstow, Cornwall

This book is printed on acid-free paper

Contents

v

List of Maps

Preface

This book hopes to tell in its own way a story that is already well known in its general outlines. It is the story of the role of Christianity in the last centuries of the Roman empire, of its adjustment, in western Europe, to a post-imperial age and of the formation of a distinctive western Christendom through the slow joining of the former heartlands of the western Roman empire to the non-Roman territories of northwestern Europe, Germany and Scandinavia. Its principal theme is the Christianization of western Europe, from the emergence of the Christian Church in the Roman empire and the conversion of Constantine, in AD 312, to the adoption of Christianity in Iceland, in AD 1000.

To handle so large a topic in so short a compass has imposed deliberate renunciations at every turn. I can only hope that readers will perceive the central preoccupations of my narrative and that, in the light of these, they will pardon me for the many omissions which the pursuit of this preoccupation has forced upon me. Let me be clear, at least, on some of these. Although this is a book in which Christianity is central, it is not a book about the Christian Church. It is, rather, an attempt to study late antique and early medieval Christianity as it encountered and adjusted to changing situations and to changing environments. Hence the geographical range of the book. I have attempted, in many chapters, to reach far beyond

viii

the boundaries of Europe, to touch on the Christianities of Byzantium and Asia, if only to highlight, by way of contrast and comparison, the very different destinies of the forms of Christianity that emerged, nearer home, in the west.

In Europe itself the narrative, as it proceeds, concentrates largely on the establishment of Christianity in Atlantic Europe. Given my theme, I trust that this emphasis will be considered a defensible one. It is agreed that the shift of power and culture away from the ancient Mediterranean to northwestern Europe, which culminated in the new empire of Charlemagne, is crucial to the end of the ancient world and the emergence of a medieval form of Christianity. I have, therefore, lingered by preference on Ireland, Britain, northern Gaul, Germany and, even, on Scandinavia because they were the frontiers of that new Europe. The process by which a Christianity, which had grown up around the Mediterranean, adjusted to local conditions took place in those regions at a considerable distance from the certainties inherited from the Roman past, and on terms largely set by the local populations. Precisely for this reason, these regions can tell us most about the uncertainties, the ambiguities and the compromises which lie behind the seemingly inexorable development by which western Europe came to speak of itself as "Christendom."

The early medieval history of western Europe has attracted, in recent decades, scholarship of the highest quality. Archaeologists and historians from all over Europe have done nothing less than ensure that the period between the end of the Roman empire and the emergence of medieval Europe proper can no longer be described as "The Dark Ages" – as an obscure and fragmented interregnum between two periods of high achievement. If this book brings to the attention of the average reader at least the outlines of the new view of the history of Europe implied in this recent revolution in scholarship, it will have achieved no small part of its purpose.

The books which I cite in the bibliographies to each chapter were chosen so as to do justice to the impressive changes in scholarship on this period, by providing up-to-date guides to further reading on a variety of topics. I myself owed much to them, and trust that they will have the same effect upon the reader. But they remind me, also, of my friends and mentors, without whose inspiration and friendship over so many years I would not have dared to venture beyond the late antique Mediterranean and the Middle East, where I had lingered by predilection, to wander a little in the exciting new territories into which the theme of the Christianization of Europe must inevitably lure the curious scholar.

The reader should also know that no small part of the excitement of this period is the manner in which the written sources themselves change in character, as Christianity came to establish itself in different regions. We begin with the relatively familiar writings of the Fathers of the Church, in Latin and in Greek. Like other "classical" texts of the Greco-Roman world, these are now available in standard editions, abundantly translated into all modern European languages. But these writings were sooned joined, in eastern Christendom, by texts in Coptic, Syriac and Armenian, eventually Georgian, Soghdian and even (as in the great inscriptions at Hsian-fu and at Karabalghasun) in Chinese and Old Turkish. The rise of Islam added Arabic and classical Persian. In the West, Latin was joined, after 600, by Old Irish, Anglo-Saxon, Old High German and Old Norse. Along the northern frontiers of Byzantium, by 900, Greek texts became available also in Old Church Slavonic. I have used frequent citations from all such sources throughout this book, in no small part in order to convey the surprising diversity of so many voices, in so many languages, from a distant Christian past, whose richness and variety we tend to forget. I trust that they speak – and speak vividly – for themselves, each in its own context.

My wife Betsy has journeyed with me, with undeterred good cheer, from northern Iceland to the Gulf of Aqaba. She has shared throughout, and bears much responsibility for, the joy which comes from the opportunity to rethink long-accustomed knowledge and to open the heart to new horizons – an opportunity that was made possible to me through the invitation of my distinguished colleague Jacques le Goff, to contribute to a series planned to stretch the mind

of all of us, who wish to think, once again and in this present
time, on what constitutes "The Making of Europe."

Peter Brown
Princeton

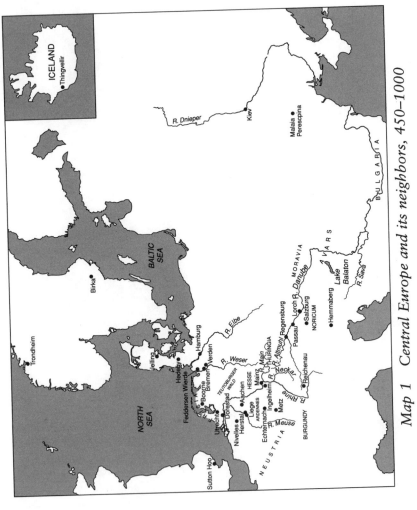

Map 1   Central Europe and its neighbors, 450–1000

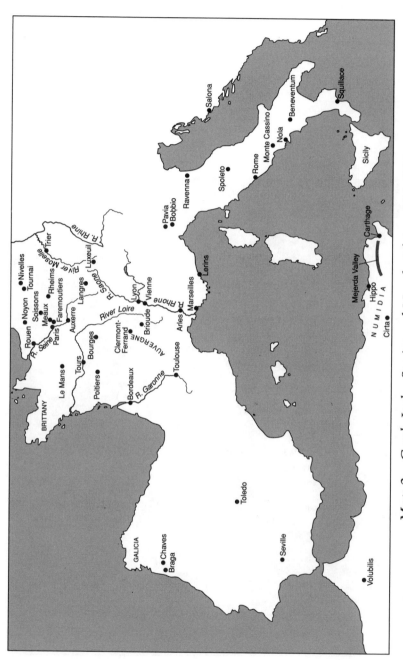

Map 2 *Gaul, Italy, Spain and North Africa, 200–700*

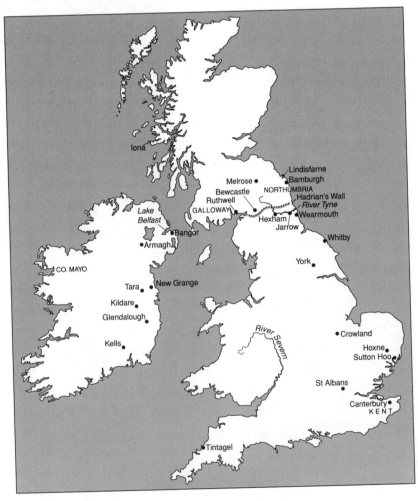

Map 3   The British Isles

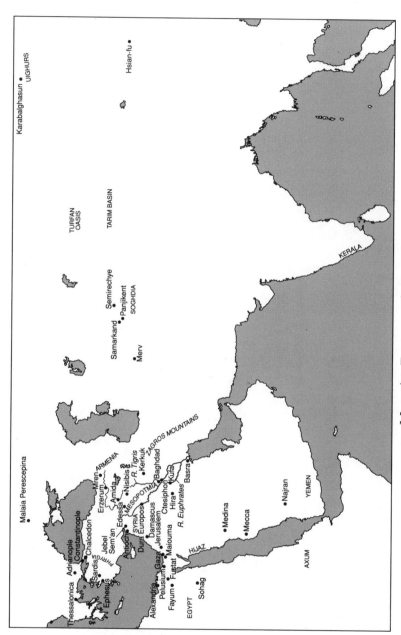

Map 4 Eastern Christendom

Part I

Empire and Aftermath
AD 200–500

1

"The Laws of Countries"

In the early third century AD, at Edessa (modern Urfa, Tur-key), a disciple summarized the views of Bardaisan, a learned figure at the court of the kings of Osrhoene, in a treatise on determinism and the freedom of the will. At that time, Osrhoene was still an independent kingdom: its ruler was a client of the Roman emperors. As befitted a nobleman from a region open at either end to Rome and to Persia, Bardaisan (154–ca.222) was a man of complex culture. Greek visitors to Edessa were impressed by his skills as a Parthian archer. As a philosopher, however, he was entirely a Greek. The treatise began with a Platonic dialogue between two Edessene friends, Shemashgram and Awida. Yet it was written in Syriac, soon to become the major literary language in the Christian Churches of the Middle East.

Furthermore, Bardaisan was a Christian. He wrote to prove that all persons in all places were free to follow the commands of God. Christians observed "the laws of the Messiah" – of Christ – wherever they were:

> in whatever place they may find themselves, the local laws cannot force them to give up the law of the Messiah.

The treatise was appropriately named *The Book of the Laws of Countries.* The disputants scanned the Eurasian landmass from the North Atlantic to China. They described the caste-dominated society of northern India, the splendidly caparisoned horses and fluttering silks of the Kushan lords of Bokhara, Samarkand and northern Afghanistan, the solemn brother–sister marriages of Zoroastrians on the Iranian plateau, the Arabs of the Euphrates and of Petra, with their savage codes of sexual honor, the impenitent polyandry of the Celts of Britain and, of course, "the Romans," whom no power of the stars had ever stopped "from always conquering new territories."[1]

The extent of his panorama marks Bardaisan as the inhabitant of a city placed at the cross-roads of western Asia. Edessa lay at the northernmost stretch of the Fertile Crescent. Less than fifteen days of easy travel westward from Edessa led to Antioch and to the eastern coastline of the Mediterranean – the sea that formed the heart of an empire that stretched as far to the northwest as Scotland and the estuary of the Rhine. Fifteen days to the southeast of Edessa, where the Tigris and Euphrates came closest, lay the heart of Mesopotamia, a zone of intensive irrigation that would support a succession of world capitals. A little south of modern Baghdad, Ctesiphon emerged, soon after Bardaisan's death, as the Mesopotamian residence of the Sasanian King of Kings of Iran. The Sasanian empire joined the rich land around Ctesiphon to the Iranian plateau and the trading-cities of Central Asia, and so to the chain of oases that led the traveller, over perilous distances, to the legendary empire of China.

This was the world that Bardaisan scanned, from Edessa, in around AD 200. Any book on the role of Christianity in the formation of western Europe, between AD 200 and 800, must begin with the sweep of Bardaisan's vision. What is being studied in this book is the emergence of one form of Christendom only, among the many divergent Christendoms which came to stretch along the immense arc delineated in Bardaisan's treatise. We should always remember that the "making of Europe" involved a set of events that took place on the far, northwestern tip of that arc. Throughout the entire period covered by this book, Christianity continued to exist and to be active over the entire stretch of "places and climates" that made up the ancient world of the Mediterranean and western Asia. Like identifiable beads, found scattered from a single, broken necklace, archaeologists have discovered fragments of Christian texts that speak of basic Christian activities pursued from the Atlantic to the edge of China. Both in County Antrim, in Northern Ireland, and in Panjikent, east of Samarkand, fragmentary copy-books – wax on wood for Ireland, broken potsherds for Central Asia – contain lines copied from the Psalms of David. In both milieux, in around AD 700, something very similar was happening. Schoolboys, whose native languages were Irish and Soghdian, tried to make their own, by this laborious method, the Latin and the Syriac versions, respectively, of a truly international, sacred text.[2]

Less innocent actions, also, betray the workings of a common mentality. The combination of missionary zeal with a sense of cultural superiority, backed by the use of force, that became so striking a feature of early medieval western Europe, was not unique to that region. In around 730, Saint Boniface felled the sacred oak at Geismar and wrote back to England for yet more splendid copies of the Bible, written "in letters of gold . . . that a reverence for the Holy Scriptures may be impressed on the carnal minds of the heathen."[3] At much the same time, Nestorian missionaries from Mesopotamia were waging their own war on the great sacred trees of the mountain slopes that rose above the Caspian, laying low "the chief of the forest." The Nestorian bishop, Mar Shubhhal-Isho',

made his entrance there with exceeding splendor, for barbarian nations need to see a little worldly pomp and show to attract them to make them draw nigh willingly to Christianity.[4]

Even further to the east, in an inscription set up in around AD 820 at Karabalghasun, on the High Orkhon river, the Uighur ruler of an empire formed between China and Inner Mongolia, recorded how his predecessor, Bogu Qaghan, had introduced new teachers into his kingdom in AD 762. These were Manichaeans, who, as bearers of a missionary faith of Christian origin, shared with the Nestorians a similar brusque attitude towards conversion. The message of the inscription is as clear and as sharp as that which Charlemagne would adopt, between 772 and 785, when he burned the great shrine of the Irminsul, of the "Column that supports Heaven," and outlawed paganism in Saxony:

> We regret that you were without knowledge, and that you called the evil spirits "gods." The former carved and painted images of the gods you should burn, and you should cast far from you all prayers to spirits and to demons.[5]

These events, of course, had no direct or immediate repercussions upon each other. Yet they do bear a distinct family resemblance. They show traces of a common Christian idiom, based upon shared traditions. They remind us of the sheer scale of the backdrop against which the emergence of a specifically western Christendom took place.

The principal concern of this book, however, will be to characterize what, eventually, would make the Christendom of western Europe different from that of its many, contemporary variants. In order to do this, let us look, briefly, at another aspect of Bardaisan's geographical panorama. The vivid gallery of cultures known to him appeared to stretch from China to Britain along a very narrow band. Bardaisan was oppressed by the immensity of the unruly, underdeveloped world of the "barbarians," that stretched to the north and south of him. Grim stretches of sparsely populated land flanked the entire civilized world.

> In the whole regions of the Saracens, in Upper Libya, among the Mauritanians . . . in Outer Germany, in Upper Sarmatia . . . in all the countries North of Pontus [the Black Sea], the Caucasus . . . and in the lands across the Oxus . . . no one sees sculptors or painters or perfumers or money changers or poets.

The all-important amenities of settled, urban living were not to be found "along the outskirts of the whole world."[6]

It was a sobering vision, shared by most of Bardaisan's Greek and Roman contemporaries. It was appropriate in a man bounded by two great empires – the Roman and the Persian. These two great states controlled, between them, most of the settled land of Europe and western Asia. Each was committed to sustaining the belief, among their subjects, that their costly military endeavors were directed towards defending the civilized world against barbarism. In the words of a late sixth-century diplomatic manifesto, sent by the King of Kings to the Byzantine emperor:

> God effected that the whole world should be illuminated from the beginning by two eyes [the Romans and the Persians]. For by these greatest powers the disobedient and bellicose tribes are trampled down and man's course is continually regulated and guided.[7]

To a human geographer of the western hemisphere, there is a certain degree of truth in this statement. From the intensely cultivated grain fields of Andalusia and coastal North Africa, through Egypt, the Fertile Crescent and the vivid, if less extensive, flecks of cultivation that flanked the mountains of Iran and Central Asia, settled life – as a man such as Bardaisan would have recognized it – was grouped as if in a series of vast oases, separated from each other by desolate steppelands. The great empires of the time strove to control as many as possible of these oases. The political history of Europe and western Asia in this period was dominated by that struggle. In AD 200, at the time of Bardaisan, Rome had joined the western to the eastern basin of the Mediterranean, and then absorbed the western side of the Fertile Crescent. Mesopotamia, however, remained largely out of reach for the Romans, although Bardaisan's own city of Edessa was soon annexed to their empire. Northern Mesopotamia, including Edessa, though from the military point of view a frontier region, fought over by the armies of Rome and Persia, formed an undivided cultural zone. It was the clamp that held east and west together. As the center of a region of shared high culture, the horizons of the inhabitants of northern Mesopotamia reached from the Mediterranean to Central Asia. After AD 240, the Sasanians joined southern Mesopotamia to Iran and Central Asia. After AD 410, the western provinces of the Roman empire slipped, with surprising ease, out of the control of the Roman emperors. For the emperors had already found a "new Rome" in

Constantinople. The eastern Mediterranean, the Black Sea and the western Middle East proved more than sufficient to support a "Roman" empire which found that it could manage very well without Rome. Finally, after AD 640, the Arab conquests joined the regions previously divided between Rome and Persia, so as to form the largest empire ever created in ancient times. Made up of a galaxy of ancient lands, that stretched from Andalusia to Turkestan, the Islamic empire of the Calif Harun al-Rashid (788–803) dwarfed the empire of his contemporary, Charlemagne (768–814), recently established at the northwestern extremity of Eurasia.

Yet, when it came to relations with the "barbarian" world that flanked the settled lands, the fate of western Europe differed significantly from that of North Africa and the Middle East. We must always remember that "barbarian" meant many things to Bardaisan and his contemporaries. It could mean nothing more than a "foreigner," a vaguely troubling, even fascinating, person from a different culture and language-group – by which criterion, Persians and even, to a man such as Bardaisan, Romans, were "barbarians." But "barbarian" in the strong sense of the word meant, in effect, "nomad." Nomads were human groups placed at the very bottom of the scale of civilized life. The desert and the sown were held to stand in a state of immemorial and unresolved antipathy, with the desert always threatening, whenever possible, to dominate and destroy the sown.

In North Africa and the Middle East, of course, the reality was profoundly different from this melodramatic stereotype. For most of the time, pastoralists and peasants lived side by side, in a humdrum and profitable symbiosis. Compared with the solid structures of towns and villages, the nomads were demographically and socially as light as driven dust. They blew in and out of the interstices of the settled world at periodic moments of the year. They were a despised but useful underclass, condemned, by the merciless conditions of the ecological niche that they controlled, to remain as if on another planet, locked into a distinctive culture and life-style. It was assumed that this debris of humanity, though often irritating, could never constitute a permanent threat to the great empires of the settled world, much less that it could replace them. The Arab conquests of the seventh century, and the consequent foundation of the Islamic empire, took contemporaries largely by surprise.

This could not be said, however, of the cold plains of the north, that stretched from the *puszta* of Hungary, across the southern Ukraine, to Central and Inner Asia. Here conditions favored the intermittent rise of aggressive and well-organized nomadic empires. Fast, sturdy horses bred rapidly and with little cost on the thin grass of the steppes. These overabundant creatures, mounted for war, gave to the nomads the terrifying appearance of a nation in arms, endowed with uncanny mobility. One such confederacy penetrated the Caucasus into the valleys of Armenia, in the middle of the fourth century:

> no one could number the vastness of the cavalry contingents [so] every man was ordered to carry a stone so as to throw it down . . . so as to form a mound . . . a fearful sign [left] for the morrow to understand past events. And wherever they passed, they left such markers at every crossroad along their way.[8]

The sight of such cairns was likely to stick in the memory. Unimpressed by the nomads of Arabia and the Sahara, the rulers of the civilized world scanned the nomadic world of the north with anxious attention.

Yet, terrifying though the nomadic empires of the steppes might be, they were an intermittent phenomenon. Effective nomadism depended on the maximum dispersal of families, each maintaining the initiative in maneuvering its flocks towards advantageous pasture, with a minimum of interference from a central authority. To change from herding scattered flocks to herding human beings, through conquest and raiding, under the leadership of a single ruler, was an abnormal and, usually, a shortlived development for most nomads. In any case, even a mighty war-lord such as Attila (434–453) found that his ability to terrorize the inhabitants of the settled land was subject to an automatic "cut off." The further from their native steppes the nomads found themselves, the less access they had to those pastures that provided the vast surplus of horses on which their military superiority depended.

As a result, the nomadic confederacies of the Huns, in the fifth century AD, and of the Avars, in the seventh and eighth centuries AD, tended to settle down, after a few decades of spectacular sabre-rattling. They lay like cold fog-banks on the eastern horizon of Europe. What they brought, in the long run, was not the end of the world, as many feared, but a hint of the immense spaces that lay behind them. They stood for an international world whose vast horizons the great settled empires to their south could barely rival. Garnets from northern Afghanistan, set in intricate gold work that echoed the flying beasts and coiled dragons of Central Asia and China, flowed into the Danubian court of Attila. By the mid-fifth century, such jewelry formed an international "barbarian chic," a sign of high status sported alike by Roman generals and by local kings. Hunting with hawks entered western Europe from Central Asia at this time; and, in the eighth century, the crucial development of stirrups spread to western horsemen as a result of Lombard–Avar contacts in the region between the Danube and Friuli. Up to almost the end of our period, the Avar governor commanding the regions bordering on Vienna still bore a name that was a distant echo of the official title of a Chinese provincial governor.

Yet, in western Europe, the nomad world remained a remote, if imposing, presence. Relations with "barbarians" evolved in a significantly different manner. The juxtaposition of "settled" and "barbarian" regions was charged with great weight for a man of the Near East. It was not appropriate when applied to the Roman frontiers of Britain and the Rhine. The ideology of the settled world made it appear as if a chasm separated the populations contained within the frontiers of the Roman empire from the barbarians gathered outside. Their life was portrayed as incommensurable with that of civilized persons, as if it was the life of the nomads of the steppes and the deserts. But these populations were not nomads. Northwestern Europe had no place for the stark ecological contrast between the desert and the sown that made the settled populations of North Africa and the Middle East feel so different from their "barbarian" neighbors. Rather, Roman and non-Roman landscapes merged gently into each other, within a single temperate zone.

Despite certain contrasts of terrain, which struck Roman observers, most notably, the somber, primeval forests of Germany, the lands outside the Roman frontiers were inhabited by peoples who shared with the provincial subjects of the Roman empire, in Britain, Gaul and Spain, the same basic building-blocks of an agrarian society. They, also, were peasants. They, also, struggled to wrest their food from the heavy, treacherous earth, "the mother of men." Their overall population was low. It was more dispersed. They lived in isolated farms and hamlets, cut off from each other by stretches of forbidding forest and moorland. The villages excavated by archaeologists rarely seem to have contained more than three hundred inhabitants. Yet, as in the case of the village excavated at Feddersen Wierde, near Bremerhaven on the north German coast, these could be stable settlements, laid out with care; large barns and buildings hint at increasing social differentiation over the centuries. Along the North Sea coast of Frisia, beyond the last Roman garrisons, the inhabitants defended the arable land against the salt-water tides with the same skill and tenacity as did their neighbors across the sea, the nominally "Roman," British peasants of the Fenland. Crucial skills of metal-working were practiced; but such skills were virtually invisible to Roman eyes, taking place as they did in the smithies of tiny villages, unconnected by the over-arching political and commercial structures that enabled the Romans to bring so much metalwork together, with such deadly effect, in the armaments of their legions.

Livestock played a prominent role among such peoples. It promoted more dispersed patterns of settlement. It was the focus of intense, upper-class competition for mobile wealth, as in the great cattle raids of Irish epic and in the solemn cattle-tributes that expressed the power of chieftains in Germany. Pastoralism on this scale seemed rootless to Romans. It certainly gave greater access to protein, in the form of meat and dairy-products, than was common among the disciplined but under-nourished peasants of the Mediterranean. Hence the pervasive sense, among Romans, of the "barbarian" north as a reservoir of mobile and ominously well-fed young warriors. Germans, wrote a doctor in fifth-century Constantinople, eat large quantities of meat. As a result, they have more blood in their veins, and, consequently, are not afraid of losing it: no wonder, he adds, that they make such admirable soldiers! Yet, the moment Germanic villagers and ranchers found themselves confronted by true nomads, such as the Huns, they had no illusion as to which world they belonged: they were agrarian peoples, a northern extension of a peasant economy that stretched, without significant interruption, from the Mediterranean to the southern Ukraine. When the Visigoths of Moldavia and the Ukraine began to be subjected to Hunnish raids, in 374, their first reaction was to seek permission to enter the Roman empire. What has been grossly misnamed as a "barbarian invasion" was, in fact, the controlled immigration of frightened agriculturalists, seeking to mingle with similar farmers south of the border.

The ideology expressed by a writer such as Bardaisan was widespread among educated persons in the Latin- and Greek-speaking worlds. "I expect no more to have Germans among my readers," wrote the famous Greek doctor, Galen of Ephesus, an older contemporary of Bardaisan, "than I would expect to have bears and wolves."[9] Despite such views, no unbridgeable social or ecological chasm stood between the Roman frontiers of Britain, the Rhine and the Danube and the "barbarians." The reality was more complex than Roman stereotypes of the "barbarians" would suggest. The arrival of the Roman empire in northwestern Europe set in motion a process which reached its inevitable (but largely unexpected) culmination in our period. The well-known history of the Roman empire in the west was flanked by an alternative history. This was the slow creation of a "new" barbarian world, very different from the bronze-age societies of an earlier period. By the fifth century AD, this new world would find itself the master of those frontier zones that had been intended, according to Roman ideology, to mark the outer limits of the civilized world.

In the first and second centuries AD, the establishment of

large Roman armies on the frontiers and the foundation of Roman-style cities behind them, brought wealth and demands for food and labor that revolutionized the countryside of Gaul, Britain and the Danubian provinces. At the mouth of the Rhine, a population of less than 14,000 had to find room for legionary garrisons of over 20,000. The garrisons of Northern Britain ate enough food to keep 30,000 acres of land under permanent cultivation. The skins of 12,000 cattle were regularly used in the leather tents of the Roman army in Britain. A new "Romanized" society grew up to meet these constant, novel demands.

Across the frontier, nucleated settlements remained small. Barbarian societies were "state-less" by Roman standards. Apart from the occasional warrior-confederacy, forms of authority above the level of the village were fragile in the extreme. Even the villages, in many regions, were little more than contiguous groups of farmsteads. The family and its land, grouped in individual farmsteads, were the basic, and exiguous, units of society. On the Roman side of the frontier, by contrast, hitherto unimaginable coagulations of human population were gathered into the newly founded towns. Trier, London, Paris and Cologne, cities of up to 20,000, were echoes, in the north, of an urban life around the Mediterranean that supported human groups of unprecedented density: Rome had a population that reached a million; the populations of Alexandria, Antioch and, later, of Constantinople could be counted in hundreds of thousands.

An average population of around 5,000 was more normal for most towns in the Roman provinces of the west. They were mere "agrotowns" by modern standards; but those who lived in them found themselves caught in a mesh of interlocking communities. The power of a distant, semi-divine world ruler was represented by provincial governors and their staffs. Apart from his soldiers, the emperor had few servants. Compared with a modern state, the Roman empire remained surprisingly undergoverned: even in a fiercely controlled province such as Egypt, the proportion of imperial officials to the overall population was one in ten thousand. The fact of empire was mediated, rather, on a permanent basis, by the *ordo*, the legally constituted town-council of each city. A formal body, recruited from thirty to a hundred or so of the richest families in the region, the *ordo* was held responsible for running the city and for collecting the taxes of the territory assigned to it. In peaceful (or less-provident) times, such elites exercised virtually unimpeded control over their locality, in exchange for maintaining peace in the cities and a regular supply of taxes for the armies. Taxation, therefore, was not simply a recurrent event imposed from above: it was delegated in such a manner as to become a way of life for the leading members of every locality. In Egypt, in the fourth century AD, one out of every three inhabitants of the large villages were involved, in some way or other, in the administration of taxes and the maintenance of law and order. Roman government was not strong, by modern standards, but, by modern standards, it was remarkably pervasive.

These towns were not as impersonal as modern cities. Their inhabitants were grouped into relatively small cells, provided by a honeycomb of neighborhoods and of voluntary associations – funerary clubs, cultic groups, fan-clubs of circus artists and dining clubs formed by fellow-tradesmen. These voluntary groups, the *collegia*, rarely included more than a hundred members. They turned up in public on all ceremonial occasions. Their loyalism was expected to be effusive. Along with well-organized urban neighborhoods, the *collegia* played an essential role as a means of social control in an otherwise studiously under-governed urban population.

Life in the countryside remained simpler. But all over western Europe, the huge fact of empire slowly settled its vast weight on the land. Agrarian society was congealed into solid structures, designed to aid the permanent extraction of wealth from the tillers of the land. Behind the frontiers, in northern Gaul, great, grain-producing villas (whose owners even experimented with primitive harvesting machines) came to dominate an increasingly subservient peasantry. The new provinces of the west joined the Mediterranean and the Middle East in a single imperial system, where, since time immemorial, life's miseries had been summed up in the double affliction of rent and taxes:

> When a man goes out into the fields and he meets a bailiff, it is as if he met a lion. When he enters the city and meets a tax-collector, it is as if he met a bear. When he enters his house and finds his sons and daughters suffering from hunger, it is as if he was bitten by a serpent.[10]

Despite unceasing complaints, the tax-loads of the Roman empire were not, in themselves, excessive: they amounted to no more than about 10 percent of the agrarian yield. But they were unflinching. They came every year. They came to be assessed in fifteen-year cycles, called *indictions*. Time, even the time of distant hamlets whose inhabitants still lived as they had done in the Bronze Age, was measured out by Roman time, the time of taxes.

What contemporaries failed to perceive was the other side of this development. The Roman frontier, set in place to separate the Roman world from the squalid lands to its north, became the unwitting axis along which the Roman and barbarian worlds converged. Like a wide depression formed by the weight of a glacial ice-pack, the frontiers of the Roman empire, maintained at the cost of such crushing expenditure of wealth and settlement, created a catchment area, into which the economic and cultural life of the lands beyond the frontier tended to trickle. Roman garrisons along the estuary of the Rhine came to purchase grain and cattle in the non-Roman territories. The first lines of Latin written from beyond the Roman frontiers take the form of a purchase-order for a Frisian cow, discovered near Leeuwarden in northern Holland. Written in the ungrammatical Latin of a provincial, this wooden tablet is the direct forerunner of the simple copy-book, filled with the Christian Psalms, made, five centuries later, in Ireland. The spread of Latin loan words in German and Old Irish; the recurrence of Roman motifs in the gold-work of Jutland; the fact that *ogham*, the archaic script cut along the edge of wooden tallies and on standing stones in Ireland, followed a categorization of the consonants propounded by Roman grammarians: these details show a barbarian world slowly changing shape under the distant gravitational pull of the huge adjacent mass of the Roman empire.

What we have tended to call the "barbarian invasions" was not the battering down by primitives from a totally other world of the frontiers that guarded Roman civilization. What occurred at that time, rather, was the emergence into ever greater prominence of regions where Romans and non-Romans had long been accustomed to meet as equals to form a social and cultural "Middle Ground." This development did not happen without suffering and bloodshed. To take one example from the middle of the fifth century AD: Saint Patrick did not first visit Ireland of his own free will. He was brutally swept away from northern Britain in a slave raid. A young man who might have gone on to polish his Latin in the Roman schools of Britain, he was set to herding pigs on the rain-lashed coast of County Mayo. But his subsequent return to Ireland and the slow implantation of Christianity in what had been an entirely non-Roman island was due to the emergence of the Irish Sea as a Celtic "Mediterranean of the north," where the Romanized coasts of Wales and northern Britain were joined to Ireland and the western isles of Scotland in a single zone that ignored the former Roman frontiers. In exactly the same period, the Frankish kingdom created by Clovis represented a return to the days before Julius Caesar, when successful warrior-kings had straddled the Rhine, to join Germany with the "Belgic" regions of northern Gaul.

From AD 500 onwards, the spread of Christianity along the former Roman frontiers of western Europe took place against the backdrop of an ever-widening "Middle Ground," formed by the convergence of "Roman" and "barbarian" regions. By AD 700 there was nothing strange in the fact that some of the most polished Latin scholarship of the age was produced in monasteries founded by Saxon kings and aristocrats in the former frontier zone between York and Hadrian's Wall. For the Jarrow and Monkwearmouth of the Venerable Bede (died 735) and the spectacular foundations of bishop Wilfrid (died 709), far from being miraculous oases of "Roman" culture perched at the furthest ends of the earth, lay, rather, close to the center of a whole new world of their own – a northwestern world, where the Irish and the North Seas came closest, around the slender neck of northern England. They stood out as centers of learning in a new cultural zone that stretched from Mayo to Bavaria. By AD 800, the emergence of Frankish power under Charlemagne joined this new "Middle Ground" to Italy and the Mediterranean. For good or ill, a peculiarly determined form of Catholic Christianity became the mandatory common faith of all the regions, Mediterranean and non-Mediterranean alike, that had come together to form a post-Roman western Europe. Compared with the process by which large regions of northwestern and central Europe came to be joined, slowly but irrevocably, to the former territories of the Roman empire, in a shared Catholicism, that would soon stretch as far as Scandinavia and into parts of eastern Europe, the contemporary successes of Nestorians and Manichees in China and Inner Asia were transitory ripples, a mere flick of wind across the surface of the vast, still ocean of non-Christian Asia. It is this process that we shall follow, as, indeed, a crucial stage in the "Making of Europe."

But this is to anticipate. In the next two chapters, we must turn to the nature of Christianity as it developed within the territories of a changed Roman empire in the period between AD 200 and 400.

2

Christianity and Empire

Bardaisan died in around AD 222. The *Book of the Laws of Countries* had defended the possibility of change. The seemingly immovable mass of local custom might give way to the free choices of individuals (especially when, as Christians, they embraced the universal "law of the Messiah") and to the forceful policies of rulers, who frequently changed the customs of their lands. The subsequent century proved him right. It was an age of dramatic change and reorganization. After 224, the Sasanian kings of Iran turned the loose-knit Parthian kingdom into a formidable empire. The Roman empire, also, emerged with the power of the emperors greatly strengthened after a period of crisis.

Renewed warfare along all its frontiers, and the emergence, in the Middle East, of the Sasanian empire, as a military equal and persistent rival, revealed the inadequacy of the previous structures of the Roman empire. It was no longer possible to delegate the powers of local government, throughout the Roman world, to traditionally minded elites, in return for taxes that touched little more than 5 percent of the agrarian surplus. This system had, in effect, allowed a small group – 3 percent of the population, who owned a quarter of all the land of the empire and 40 percent of its liquid wealth – to control the cities and to take on themselves the role of representing, in their locality, the benevolent rule of a distant emperor.

Modern readers, following the well-satisfied and articulate opinion of the elites of the first and second centuries AD, tend to identify this uncharacteristically indirect form of government with the apogee of Roman imperial civilization. It was, if anything, a fortuitous suspension of the normal condition of imperial systems. After AD 238, all classes in the Roman world had to face up to the more unpleasant, day-to-day realities of empire. Between 238 and 270, bankruptcy, political fragmentation and the recurrent defeats of large Roman armies laid bare the superb nonchalance on which the old system of government had been based. What was remarkable was not so much this collapse, but the speed and determination with which a new system was put in place, after a generation of humiliating uncertainty. The Roman empire over which the emperor Diocletian reigned, from 284 to 305 – ensuring yet closer control over each of its regions by delegating these to a coalition of co-emperors, known as the "Tetrarchy" – was an empire in the true meaning of the term. The emperor and his servants took over responsibilities that had been delegated, in previous centuries, to local interest groups.

The restored Roman empire was a badly shaken society, anxious for the return of law and order. *Reparatio* and *Renovatio* were the slogans of the day. It was not, however, an irreparably impoverished society. Despite an expansion of the army and of the imperial bureaucracy, the overall tax-load was no more than 10 percent of the agrarian surplus – a load that was within the capacities of most peasant communities. In Anatolia, for instance, tax-loads reached under Diocletian continued, largely unchanged, until the last days of the Ottoman empire. What had changed was the presence of empire itself. The elites lost their unique advantages of wealth and local status. The imperial court became the direct and ever-present source of honor. Cities throve only if they remained centers of government. Constantinople, founded in 327 by the emperor Constantine, was nothing less than a "new Rome:" it was Rome, the "ruling city," made present to the entire eastern part of the empire. In each province, a *metropolis*, a "mother city," became the permanent capital of the region, leaving other cities in the shade. In many significant regions – as in the Danubian provinces – it became only too obvious that the imperial government could even do without cities. Imperial power might rest directly on the land. In Pannonia, around Lake Balaton, great imperial villas dominated the countryside as "ruling cities" in miniature, surrounded by towers and high walls that were forbidding symbols of authority and security in a world restored, for a moment, to order.

The extension of the Roman state drew top and bottom closer together. Aurelius Isidore was a canny farmer of the Fayum, in Egypt. Between 297 and 318, he was constantly involved in the annual spasm of activity connected with the collection and distribution of the imperial taxes. Isidore was illiterate, yet he kept his tax-documents carefully – lists of assessments, constant petitions to "Your Magnificence" (the local representative of the central government), and even an edict of the emperor Diocletian, which spelled out, with high-flown rhetoric, the advantages of the new tax-system. Such documents only survive in the dry sands of Egypt. But they must have been everywhere, in the homes of relatively humble provincials throughout the empire. They show a political system forced to mobilize the interest and the loyalty of all its subjects.

Societies under strain are usually reassured if one aspect, at least, of their accustomed life remains unchanged. The inhabitants of the Roman empire and its adjoining territories felt that they could still contemplate a long-familiar religious landscape. Diocletian's empire was an overwhelming polytheist society. It was assumed, as a matter of common sense, that there were many gods, and that these gods demanded worship through concrete, publicly visible gestures of reverence and gratitude. The gods were there. They were invisible and ageless neighbors of the human race. Knowledge of the gods and of what pleased and displeased them tended to be a matter of local, social memory, kept alive by inherited rites and gestures. *Religio*, the apposite worship of each god, stressed (even idealized) social cohesion and the passing on of tradition in families, in local communities, and through the memories of proud cities and nations bathed in centuries of history. Nor were the gods airy abstractions. Vibrant beings, their lower orders shared the same physical space as human beings. They touched all aspects of the natural world and of human settlement. Some gods were considerably higher than others. The *religio* that these high gods received depended, to a large extent, on the self-image of their worshippers. Mystical philosophers yearned for the higher gods and, beyond them, for union with the One, the metaphysically necessary, intoxicating source of all being. Such high love lifted the soul out of the body, in a manner that made all earthly cares fall silent. But the other gods were not replaced by this experience. They were demoted, not denied. Philosophers were superior souls. They did not share the coarse concerns of the multitude. But no one denied that average gods existed, also, for average persons. It was believed that such gods hovered that much closer to earth. They "stood close by" their worshippers, ready to maximize and to maintain, in return for due observance, the good things of life.

What mattered were *religiones*, "religions" in the plural, the many, traditionally accepted ways of paying respect to a multitude of gods whose invisible presence lent warmth, solemnity and a touch of the immemorial to the honeycomb of overlapping communities in which, as we have seen, the inhabitants of the Roman empire (and especially those who lived in the complex society of its cities) found themselves embedded.

Diverse *religiones*, very much in the plural, did justice to the perceived diversities of human fortune and to a heavy sense of obligation to diverse communities, some of which, such as the empire of Rome, seemed as all-embracing and as immovable as nature itself. *Religio*, therefore, could consist of a graffito scratched on a wall at Ostia: "Hermes, good fellow, bring me profit." It could be a command to an Egyptian priestess to go to the village temple,

> to perform the usual sacrifices on behalf of our lords the emperors and their victories, and the rising of the Nile, and the increase of the crops, and the healthy balance of the climate.[1]

And, for a man such as Diocletian, as he celebrated the crowning mercy of twenty years of stable rule, on a monument set up in the Roman Forum, in AD 303, *religio* still meant appearing at a smoking altar, flanked by the ever-present gods and surrounded by the animals deemed, from time immemorial, to be appropriate for a major sacrifice. As Diocletian had declared, some years earlier:

> The ancient religion ought not to be censured by a new one. For it is the height of criminality to reverse that which the ancestors had defined, once and for all, things which hold and preserve their recognized place and course.[2]

Nine years later, on October 29, 312, the emperor Constantine entered Rome, having defeated his rival, Maxentius, on the previous day, at a battle near the Milvian Bridge, outside the city. The altars of the gods stood ready, on the Capitol, to receive the sacrifice appropriate to the celebration of his triumph. But Constantine, instead, went straight to the imperial palace. He later let it be known that he had received a specific and unique sign from the One God of the Christians. Writing to Christians, he made plain, in subsequent years, that he owed his successes to the protection of that High God alone. Over a decade later, he wrote to the young king of kings, Shapur II: "this (One) God I invoke with bended knees and recoil with horror from the blood of sacrifice."[3]

In 325, Constantine gathered together all the Christian bishops of his empire at Nicaea (modern Iznik, in Turkey, a city set on a quiet lake equally close to the sea of Marmara and to the imperial roads that led up from the east) for an "ecumenical" – that is, a "world-wide" – council, that included, even, a token party of bishops from Persia. In so doing, he allowed the Christian Church to see itself, face to face, for the first time, as the privileged bearer of a universal law. Constantine died in 337. He had ruled far longer than Diocletian, and longer, even, than the emperor Augustus. His choice of a new god as protector of his empire, much less the impenitent success of his reign, could not have been predicted in AD 300. We must now look at the Christian churches of the Roman empire to understand the meaning of Constantine's decision to worship their God.

In 312, Christianity was not a new religion. It had been in

existence for over 250 years. The world of Jesus of Nazareth and of Saint Paul was as far distant from older contemporaries of Constantine, as is the age of Louis XIV from ourselves. Christians presented their Church as having been locked in unchanging and continual conflict with the pagan Roman empire. In reality, the period after AD 250 represented a new situation. Both Church and empire had changed. The empire came home to the localities. Emperors involved themselves more directly in local affairs. Christianity became an empire-wide problem. Sporadic local violence and condemnations by local governors gave way to imperial edicts against the Church as a whole. The first of these was issued in 250. A final set of measures, known to Christians as the Great Persecution, was instituted by the emperor Diocletian in 303, and continued, in parts of Asia Minor, Syria and Egypt, for eleven years. The Great Persecution marked the coming of age both of the new empire and of the Christian Church.

The Christian Church, also, had changed. It now had a recognizable hierarchy with prominent leaders. In 303, as in 250 and 257, the government attacked Christian bishops, priests and deacons. Bishops were singled out as authoritative figures. Cyprian of Carthage, for instance, was executed in 258, as "the standard-bearer" of the Christian "faction." If the bishop yielded, the loyalty of a whole Christian community might be broken.

The Church also possessed its own, universal code of law. This also was attacked. The Christian Scriptures were taken out of the churches and burned. They were known to be the jealously guarded, holy writings of the sect. Even the format of these Scriptures spoke of the urgency of a new age. They were no longer the unwieldy scroll of the classical era. They were *codices*, books as we now know them, such as had developed rapidly in an age of organization. They were compact and easy to carry. They were bound in such a way as to make their contents final and easy to refer to. They were appropriate vehicles for a new "Law," that came from a source even more exalted than the emperor. They could be consulted anywhere, and were applicable everywhere. While the *religio* of the gods was subject to the vagaries of local memory, it was only necessary to open a *codex* of the law of God to read that *He that sacrificeth to other gods shall be utterly destroyed.*

Last, but not least, the authorities destroyed Christian churches. Contemporary Christians spoke of their churches as if they were already highly visible places of worship – "vast assemblies that crowded together in every city." Such views were tinged by wishful thinking. Christian churches of the third century may have been relatively humble affairs, assembly-rooms created within the existing structures of houses.

The church at Dura Europos, on the Euphrates, had been constructed, in this manner, in the 230s, to house a congregation of barely more than seventy. A hundred yards down the street, the Jewish synagogue of Dura was a large building, resplendent with frescoes that showed the deeds of Moses and of other heroes of Israel, and with seats for at least 120 worshippers. The later Christian basilica at Aquileia was 37.4 by 20.4 meters, and could house a congregation of 750. At the same time, the synagogue of Sardis was a magnificently built building of 80 by 20 meters, with room, that is, for at least 1,500. It spoke of a long-established Jewish community, to which the Christians were no more than estranged, poor relatives. What mattered, however, is that, in the Christian image of themselves, the Christian churches were "growth points." They welcomed converts, and expected them to remain loyal. To level these walls, therefore, was to halt an institution that was not only cohesive and exclusive, but that was widely perceived to be capable of "runaway" growth.

The Church to which Constantine brought peace, in 312, was a complex body. It is impossible to know how many Christians there were in the empire at this time: up to 10 percent of the population has been suggested, grouped more heavily in Syria, Asia Minor and the major cities of the Roman Mediterranean than in any other region. What is certain is that there is no room for the later romantic myth of Christians as a perpetually hounded minority, literally driven underground by unremitting persecution. Nor is there much more truth in the modern myth that presents the advance of Christianity as the rise of a religion of the under-privileged.

The third century, indeed, was an age of surprising Christians, of whom the emperor Constantine was only the last. Marcia, the influential concubine of the emperor Commodus, had been a Christian and a protector of the bishops of Rome. Bardaisan was both a courtier and a Christian. His king, Abgar VIII of Osrhoene, was believed to have been a "pious man," even a "believer." Julius Africanus, a Greek polymath from Palestine, was a Christian. He visited Bardaisan, wrote to the great Christian theologian, Origen of Alexandria, and then went to Rome to help the emperor to set up a library in the Pantheon. Newly discovered inscriptions show a more lasting phenomenon: a Christian gentry already established in Asia Minor. In the Upper Tembris valley (southwest of Ankara, Turkey) gentleman-farmers, complete with plough-teams, and wives bearing the conventional woman's distaff, speak of themselves, on large gravestones, as "Christians for Christians." One city of the area even boasted a Christian wrestler, known as "the Creeper," who returned to an honorific seat on the town-council, having won prizes from as far afield as Brindisi. In around AD 300, in Andalusia, a council of bishops at Elvira made rulings on Christian town councillors whose honorific role as "priests" of the imperial cult caused them to be present at sacrifices offered out of loyalty to the emperors; on their wives, who donated robes for the local processions of the gods; on landowners who received consecrated first-fruits from their peasants, as part of the rent; and on women who had beaten servants to death. It could not be said that Christians, in the early years of the reign of Constantine, were totally innocent of wealth, of slave-owning or, even, of power.

Altogether, unlike the many trade associations and cultic brotherhoods – most of which were class- or gender-specific – the Christian Church was a variegated group. In that respect, it was not unlike the new empire in miniature: high and low met as equals because equally subject, now, to the overruling law of one God. Those who entered such churches were encouraged to find in them an orderly assembly. Grown men, married women and children, widows and unattached women: each group was carefully separated, and seated in their appropriate place. Deacons watched the doors to scrutinize incoming strangers:

and let the deacon also see that no one whispers, or falls asleep, or laughs, or makes signs.

Social differences were not expunged in such gatherings. They were, rather, handled with an elaborate and pointed courtesy. If a "man of worldly honor" entered a crowded church, the bishop must on no account rise to receive him, lest he be thought to be a "respecter of persons." But the deacon should tell one of the young men to move over: "that they also may be trained and learn to give place to those more honorable than themselves." If a poor man or a destitute stranger should come in, however, it was an entirely different matter:

do thou, o bishop, with all thy heart provide a place for them, even if thou hadst to sit upon the ground.[4]

These rulings, first written before the Great Persecution, continued to be operative for many centuries in Syria. They provide a glimpse of the workaday moral and social horizons within which most Christians of the age of Constantine were content to live.

The Christian churches of the third century AD were not, in any way, places where the world was turned upside down. What mattered for contemporaries was the message that was preached in them, and achieved through them. This was about salvation and about sin. It was in this respect that Christianity emerged as an unusually democratic and potentially wide-reaching movement. It takes some leap of the modern imagination (saturated as it is by later centuries of Christian language) to understand the novelty of seeing every human being as subject to the same universal law of God and as equally capable of salvation through the triumphant or the studious conquest of sin, brought about through permanent and exclusive membership of a unique religious group.

Salvation meant, first and foremost, salvation from idolatry and from the power of the demons. "The unity of God and the refutation of the idols" were themes which any Christian lay man or woman was free to expound to outsiders. All past tradition was re-interpreted by such teaching. In polytheist belief, the lower ranks of gods had been treated as ambivalent, moody creatures, capable of being spiteful and manipulable on some occasions and generous and powerful on others. The Christians attacked the gods, not by denying their existence: they existed; but they were all equally evil. All gods, even the highest, were malevolent and unreliable. The demons, faceless invisible powers, past-masters of the art of illusion, merely used the traditional rites, myths and images of polytheism as so many masks, with which to draw the human race ever further away from the worship of the one true God. Polytheism existed for the sole purpose of denying the existence of the true, Christian God. Seen with Christian eyes in the age of Constantine, the immemorial worship of the gods throughout the Roman world was a grand illusion. The ancient rites to which the emperor Diocletian paid such heavy reverence were no more than a tawdry stage-set, that stood between mankind and its rightful God.

Nor was this God a distant reality. Christian communities encountered the polytheist world along a front that crackled with demonstrations of divine power. Exorcism, for instance, was a well-known form of religious drama. Cures were effected by driving disruptive spirits from the human body, which they had entered and possessed. Christians used this common practice to teach nothing less than a condensed lesson in the direction of world-history. Christ had already broken the power of the demons in the invisible world. Now His servants could be seen to drive them from their last hiding places on earth. Exorcism rendered palpable the pre-ordained retreat of the gods, as the demons, screaming the names of traditional divinities, withdrew violently from the bodies of the possessed, when challenged by the name of Christ.

Even at the height of the Great Persecution, martyrdom was not an everyday occurrence in any region. But those who died for Christ made the power of God overwhelmingly present among believers. Even when in prison, the potential martyr was the special joy of the Christian community:

Let him be esteemed by you a holy martyr, an angel of God or God upon earth . . . For through him you see the Lord our Savior.[5]

In a world where execution was a form of public spectacle, witnessed by the entire community, martyrdom was seen, by Christians, as an unmistakable sign of salvation, offered by God in the very center of every great city:

You could see a youth not twenty years of age, standing unbound and stretching out his hands in the form of a Cross . . . while bears and leopards almost touched his flesh. And yet their mouths were restrained, I know not how, by a divine and incomprehensible power.[6]

This happened in the circus of Caesarea in Palestine. The ancient story of Daniel, delivered by God in the lions' den, merged with the figure of Christ and with the victorious power of His Cross, in a setting vibrant with popular associations of contest and victory. It took place in 308, only four years, that is, before the armies of Constantine, a man already accustomed to looking to heaven for help from "a divine and incomprehensible power," converged on the Milvian Bridge.

For the average Christian, the one triumph that was always possible was the triumph over sin and, eventually, over death. The Christian funeral was a triumphal progress, an affair of white robes and radiant lamps. The grave was a place of rest, a *koimétérion* (this Greek, Christian usage is the source of our word "cemetery"), where the dead, and those gathered around the tomb, enjoyed a foretaste of the *refrigerium*, the joyous refreshment of God's paradise. For the community of the living, however, sin was the more present concern. And, in the Early Church, sin (despite modern prejudices against the notion) was a precise and helpful concept. It gave contemporaries a largely novel, and clearly focussed, language with which to talk about change and about their relations with a new religious community.

Elements of the new language of sin and conversion already lay to hand. Christians did no more than sharpen the assertion of ancient philosophers that philosophy was a skill of self-transformation. Christianity, they claimed, was a God-given "philosophy," a "school of virtue" open to all. They propounded a potential for discontinuity in the human person, that shocked austere pagans as light-headed and irresponsible. But the prospect of total transformation through conversion and baptism delighted Christian authors in an age of heady change:

> The few commands of God so change the whole man and render him new when the old has been put off, that you do not recognize him to be the same . . . For with one washing, all malice will be wiped out . . . Here is that which all philosophers sought in their whole life . . . He who wishes to be wise and happy, let him hear the voice of God.[7]

"Sin," for some Christians, could be seen as a part of the person, an inert mass of ancient, demonically inspired habits built up over time within the self. It could be put in the past, by a trenchant and dramatic act of conversion. For Christians of less euphoric temperament, "sin" was a reminder of how much of that past still lingered in every person. It was upon "sin" that the Christian community was supposed to work with unremitting vigor.

Unlike the ferociously individual self-grooming of the philosopher, the handling of "sin" in Christian circles was a communal concern. Sin could be changed into righteousness through reparation to God. And reparation was not a purely personal matter. It was the small Christian community, gathered frequently within the narrow walls of its churches, which interceded, before God, for each individual with its prayers, and which decided, in effect, how, when and, even, whether such reparation was possible. A Christian gathering was expected to include gripping scenes of moral "exorcism," through the penance of notable sinners. An adulterer might be

> led in to the midst of the brethren and prostrated all in sackcloth and ashes, a compound of disgrace and horror . . . suing for everyone's tears, licking their footprints, clasping their knees.[8]

Rare though such spectacles might be, they showed that,

in the matter of sin, the Christian community meant business.

In most churches, the handling of sin devolved, by default, on the person of the bishop. The Christian notion of moral change, applied to diverse communities, whose members came from so many different pasts, heightened the need for a single judge and arbiter of sin. Aided by his clergy, this was what the bishop did. He was the searching mercy of God personified:

> first of all judge strictly and, afterwards, receive . . . command the sinner to come in . . . examine him . . . and appoint him days of fasting.

Judged by the bishop and supported by the prayers of fellow-believers, individual Christians were able to pace themselves in making due reparation to God for the many frailties that still tied them to "the world" – that is, to that potent presence, outside the Church, of a society that still lay in the dark shadow of the demons. *Thy repentance shall be with thee and thou shalt have power over it.*[9]

Repentance invited concrete and fully visible reparatory actions. Christians had inherited from Judaism the practice of giving alms "for the remission of sins." The notion of almsgiving accompanied by the notion of repentance harnessed the use of wealth to a new system of religious explanation, thereby ensuring that wealth gained in "the world" flowed, without undue inhibitions, into the Church. Even the most humble members of the Christian community were involved in this mobilization of wealth. The average adherents of Judaism and Christianity were industrious townsfolk. Their hard-won coins "gathered sweat in the palm of the hand," before they were given to deserving causes.[10] But every believer was obliged to give. As a rabbi said, the "breastplate of righteousness," associated with almsgiving, was made up, like the round scales of the scale-mail armor of third-century cavalry, of innumerable small coins, given frequently by ordinary believers.[11] Thus, unlike the cities and their proud temples, the Christian churches were never entirely dependent on the generosity of a few wealthy donors, who might, at any moment, go bankrupt

– as happened to many pagan shrines in the course of the crisis of the third century.

Far from being a cold, cash transaction, almsgiving triggered, at the time, deep-laid imaginative structures, that made it seem an entirely appropriate penitential gesture. By giving to the destitute, at the furthest edge of the community, the act of almsgiving made present on earth a touch of the boundless care of God for all mankind. The utter pointlessness of giving to those who, as beggars, could offer nothing in return highlighted the magnificent transcendence of God: "They who are useless to men are useful to God." [12] The gesture of reaching out the hand in mercy to the poor was held to echo (and so to provoke) the gesture that the sinner hoped, above all, from God Himself – that His hand, also, would stretch out to offer the supreme gift of forgiveness. Such alms were made regularly, because sin occurred regularly. For both wealth and sin were seen in the same terms: both represented the silent growth of superfluities. Surplus wealth gathered round the Christian, in the course of ordinary duties in "the world," in a manner almost as imperceptible as the gathering of dust in the corners of a house. Such a surplus was held to be best dispersed by making amends for those "sins of the flesh," which also grew in a barely perceptible manner, like stubble on the chin, by reason of the frailties of human nature.

Altogether, as a result of imaginative structures that made the act of giving a central part of the day-to-day practice of the Christian community, the churches of the late third century emerged as remarkably cohesive and solvent bodies. Christians were known to look after their own. The churches had created systems for the care of unprotected and afflicted fellow-believers that grew like thick layers of bark around every Christian community. The relatively small Christian church at Cirta (Constantine, Algeria) was revealed, by the imperial commissioners, in 304, to have a storeroom with 16 shirts for men, 38 veils, 82 dresses and 47 pairs of slippers for women, as well as 11 containers of oil and wine. By placing so much emphasis on the act of giving to persons on the very margins of their own community, Christian almsgiving implied, in theory at least, that the Church might reach out to embrace an entire local society – strangers, beggars and all. In AD 251, the Christian church in Rome supported – from the gifts of the faithful – 154 members of the clergy (of whom 52 were exorcists) and took care of 1,500 widows, orphans and destitute persons. The destitute alone were more numerous than the entire membership of all but the largest professional association in the city; and the clergy formed a body as large, and as self-conscious, as the *ordo*, the city-council, of any small town.

It is in this one, crucial respect that the Christian Church had already gained a prominence far out of proportion to the relatively small number of Christians, as a whole, within the empire. A polytheist society had been made up of innumerable small cells. Though supported by immemorial custom, it was as delicate and as brittle as a honeycomb. The Christian Church, by contrast, brought together activities that had been kept separate under the old system of *religio*, in such a way as to form a compact, even massive, constellation of commitments. Morality, philosophy and ritual were treated as being intimately connected: all were part of "religion;" all were to be found in their only true form in the Church. In the polytheist world, by contrast, these were separate spheres of activity. Self-grooming and the search for truth had taken place in a clearly defined social niche: they tended to be what gentlemen did. Neither philosophy nor morality owed much to the cult of the gods. They were human activities, learned from and enforced by human beings. In the Christian churches, philosophy was dependent upon revelation and morality was absorbed into *religio*. Both commitment to truth and moral improvement were held to be binding on all believers, irrespective of their class and level of culture. Both were inescapable consequences of having accepted the Law of God.

The circulation of wealth, also, was harnessed to a strictly religious process of sin and reparation. It was channelled, on an unprecedentedly wide basis, to the building up of a single religious community. It was distributed along the margins of the Church in such a way as to suggest that the Christian community was capable of expanding into the furthest reaches of Roman society.

Thus, when a continuous spate of laws and personal letters in favor of Christians issued from the palace of Constantine after AD 312, they were received and exploited to the full by a religious group which knew how to make the best of its good fortune. If, in the words of the English proverb, "God helps those who help themselves," the Christian Church, as it had developed in the course of the third century, more than deserved the apparent "miracle" of the Milvian Bridge.

3

Tempora Christiana: Christian Times

The religion of the (pagan) Greeks, made dominant for so many years, by such pains, by the expenditure of so much wealth, and by such feats of arms, has vanished from the earth.[1]

Thus wrote a Christian priest, Isidore of Pelusium (an Egyptian seaport, close to modern Suez) in around AD 420. All over the Roman empire, articulate Christians, such as Isidore, enjoyed the inestimable advantage, in a time of rapid change, of being a group convinced that history was on their side. They looked back on the century that followed the conversion of Constantine as an age of triumph. For they saw the changes of that time against a majestic, supernatural backdrop. Long ago, Christ had broken the power of the gods. The invisible empire of the demons had crumbled the moment that Christ had been raised on the Cross on Golgotha. What happened, on earth, in the fourth century, merely made plain that pre-existent victory. It was a "mopping up" operation. The dislodging of the demons from their accustomed haunts – from sacrificial altars, from temples, from so many alluring statues – was the grandiose, and satisfactorily swift, equivalent, on the public level, of the widespread, more individual drama of exorcism, by which the self-same gods had often been driven from the body of the possessed by the victorious power of the Cross.

A sense of history moving swiftly to its preordained conclusion runs through much Christian preaching and most Christian narratives of the period. In 404, a group of pagan notables in the small North African town of Boseth (in the Mejerda valley of Algeria) entered the Christian basilica to listen to a sermon by a famous visiting bishop, Augustine of Hippo. What they heard was an exhortation to wake up, to listen to the *strepitus mundi*, the roar of the Roman world, as it rushed, like a *wadi* in full flood, towards Christianity.[2]

The inhabitants of the newly organized Roman empire had come to expect change in many aspects of their life. In giving their support to the Christians, however, Constantine and his successors had chosen a group that positively gloried in change at the expense of the traditional beliefs of the majority of the population. After 312, Constantine, his devout son, Constantius II (337–361), and, finally, Theodosius I (379–395) progressively forbade public sacrifices, closed temples and colluded in frequent acts of local violence against major cult-sites – of which the destruction of the gigantic Serapeum of Alexandria, in 391, was the most spectacular.

A vocal body of Christian opinion invested these sporadic governmental actions with an aura of inevitability. Paganism was never treated, by contemporary Christians, as a living religion. It was deemed to be an obsolescent faith, a *superstitio*. In the sharp words of an early edict of Constantine, polytheists might, if they wished, "celebrate the rites of an outmoded illusion," provided that they did not force Christians to join in them.[3] Even when polytheism was tolerated, it was allowed to exist only on condition that it was seen to be an empty shell, drained of supernatural power, and characterized by the increasingly dilapidated state of its once-glorious temples.

In the later fourth century, the word "pagan," *paganus*, began to circulate among Christians, in order to emphasize the marginal status of polytheism. Originally, *paganus* meant "second-class participant" – civilian as opposed to regular soldier, lower as opposed to high official. The Spanish priest, Orosius, who wrote his *History against the Pagans* at the behest of Augustine, in 416, added a further touch to this language of exclusion. Cultivated polytheists, urban notables and even members of the Roman Senate, were told that theirs was the religion of countryfolk, of men of the *pagus*, of *paysans, paesanos* – that is, a religion worthy only of a stolid core of peasants, untouched by the mighty changes that had swept through the cities of the Roman empire.[4]

Nor was this simply a matter of clerical preaching. In 436, the lawyers of Theodosius II (408–450), the grandson of Theodosius I, met in Constantinople to bring together the edicts of his Christian predecessors in a single, bound book, a *codex* (from which, significantly, our word "Code" derives). The subsequent *Theodosian Code* appeared in 438. It was the most compact and the longest-lasting monument of this great age of organization. The *Code* ended with a book *On Religion*. This was to be its grand finale. From Constantine to Theodosius II, extracts from the laws on religion communicated a rising sense of governmental certainty: there was to be little place, in the new Roman order, for heresy, schism, or Judaism, and no place at all for "the error of stupid paganism."[5]

This hurried mood, though it played an essential role in maintaining the morale of the Christian churches, was not necessarily shared by the majority of the inhabitants of the Roman world. Sometime in the fourth century, Annianus, son of Matutina, an aggrieved Romano-Briton, from whom an unknown person had stolen a purse with six silver coins, visited the temple of the goddess Minerva Sulis at Bath, so as to place a curse-tablet in the sacred spring of the goddess. The curse contained a conventional list of potential suspects: "whether male or female, boy or girl, slave or free." But it opened with a novel antithesis: "Whether a Christian or a gentile, whomsoever." In late Roman Bath, Christians existed; but they were no more than one category of persons among many; and they were held to be equally subject to the avenging power of an ancient, and still powerful, deity.[6]

In Hippo and Carthage, at the very heart of Mediterranean Christianity, sophisticated persons who attended the sermons of Augustine, and considered themselves to be good Christians, carried in the backs of their minds a model of the supernatural world that was not polarized in the dramatic manner proposed by their leaders. Their monotheism was that much less clear-cut. Their belief in the Highest God of the Christians was sincere. But this belief in a new high God did not apply to all aspects of their lives:

> There are those who say, "God is good, He is great, supreme, eternal and inviolable. It is He who will give us eternal life and the incorruptibility which He has promised at the resurrection of the dead. But these things of the physical world and of our present time belong to the *daemones* and to the invisible (lower) Powers."[7]

To Augustine's hearers, the lower powers were by no means impotent beings. Distinguished parishioners reminded their bishop that the gods had, after all, foretold their own withdrawal from their temples, in widely circulated oracles. For such persons, the venerable religious past of Rome was not, in its entirety, a demonically manipulated illusion. In their universe other, more familiar powers, the protectors of more humble activities, had not been pushed aside by the austere and exclusive presence of the One God of the Christians.

It takes a considerable effort of the modern imagination (which has inherited from strict Christian monotheism an inability to enter into the highly compartmented view of the universe held by late antique persons) to realize that, in the fourth and fifth centuries, a large number of believers, in all regions and of all levels of culture, thought very much as Augustine's congregation thought. For so widespread a mentality to change, to any significant degree, so as to share the intransigence of more "advanced," more strict, Christians, the society and culture of the Roman empire itself had to change. This is what happened in the generations which separated the affluent and surprisingly self-confident age of Constantine and Constantius II from the less-secure period that began with the reign of Theodosius I. In this sense, the Latin Christianity of the early Middle Ages goes back directly, not to the conversion of Constantine, but to the troubled, but immensely creative generation – a generation of barbarian invasion, civil war and weakened imperial authority – that coincided with the mature years of Saint Augustine, who was baptized at Milan in 387, became bishop of Hippo Regius on the coast of North Africa (modern Annaba/Bone, Algeria) in 395 and who died, in AD 430, at the age of 76, having come to witness a world very different from that in which he had grown up.

What Constantine and his successors had brought to the Christian churches was peace, wealth and, above all, the ability to build up, at a surprising rate, a strong local position. Constantine faced an institution that had already shown itself able to mobilize and redistribute wealth for religious causes. He emerged as a Christian donor of overpowering generosity. The great basilica churches (true "royal halls," as the name *basilica*, from *basileus*, "king," implies) that he set up in Rome (Saint Peter's and San Giovanni in Laterano), at Antioch (a large, golden-domed octagon opposite the newly built palace-quarter across the Orontes), and, above all, the Church of the Holy Sepulchre at Jerusalem, were sermons in stone. They spoke more loudly of the providential alliance of Church and Empire than did any imperial edict or the theorizing of any bishop. They left visitors amazed:

> The decorations really are too marvelous for words [wrote Egeria, a Spanish pilgrim, on the church at Golgotha]. All you can see is gold and jewels and silk ... You simply cannot imagine the number and the sheer weight of the candles, tapers, lamps and everything else they use for the services ... They are beyond description, and so is the magnificent building itself. It was built by Constantine and ... was decorated with gold, mosaic and precious marble, as much as his empire could provide.[8]

They were gigantic assembly halls, with room for up to 4,000 worshippers. In them, Constantine made real the Early Christian dream of each local church as a united "holy people," grouped frequently in vast assemblies, around their one leader, the bishop.

And they did not stand alone. What we call a "church" was not an isolated building. It usually stood in a complex of buildings, that included a *secretarium* – an audience-hall – an extensive bishop's palace, warehouses for supplies for the poor, and, above all, an impressive courtyard, of the sort that stood in front of a nobleman's town house – for charitable banquets, distributions of alms, or, simply, for the faithful to meet and catch up with the news of the town. Augustine's basilica at Hippo, for instance, had room for around 900. It was not one of the largest; but it stood in a "Christian quarter" 5,460 square meters in area, with 120 separate rooms.

Such buildings made palpable the emergence of a new style of urban leadership. Bishops and clergy received immunities from taxes and from compulsory public services. In each city, the Christian clergy became the one group to expand rapidly, at a time when the strain of empire had brought other civic associations to a standstill. Bound by oath to "their" bishop, a whole hierarchy of priests, deacons and minor clergy formed an *ordo* in miniature, as subtly graded as any town-council, and as tenaciously attached to its privileges. Constantine expected that the bishop would act as exclusive judge and arbiter in cases between Christians, and even between Christians and non-Christians. Normal civil litigation had become prohibitively expensive. As a result, the bishop, already regarded as the God-like judge of sin among believers, rapidly became the *Ombudsman* of an entire local community. Imperial supplies of food and clothing turned the ferociously inward-looking care of Christian fellow-believers for each other, that had characterized an earlier age, into something like a public welfare system, designed to alleviate, and to control, the urban poor as a whole. In a world where, as we have seen, the business of administration had always been delegated, at a local level, in such a manner as to mobilize a wide variety of participants, the emergence of the Christian clergy as a privileged and ambitious local group was a decisive change: for it took place in an area that affected the entire structure of the Roman empire.

For, stunning though the vast basilicas founded by the emperors at Rome – and, a little later, at Trier and Milan – might be, they were dwarfed by the sheer number of churches, of more moderate size, that reflected the ability of the clergy to mobilize local loyalties and to appeal to local pride. As far apart as northern Italy and Syria, the mosaic floors of new churches were covered with carefully itemized squares, each bearing the name of a local family. Christian villages pooled their resources to cover the Algerian plateau (to name only one region) with solid little "houses of the righteous." In Roman Britain, the church at Water Newton, a small community, nonetheless had a solid silver chalice, given by a Publianus – "Dependent on Thee, I honor Thy holy altar" – and a collection of silver *ex voto* plaques, marked with the Cross, that do not differ from those offered in the non-Christian shrines of Britain.[9] These were churches built, from the ground up, as it were, by local initiatives. They were not invariably amenable to control by a distant emperor.

Christian bishops were not the sort of decorous grandees to whom the emperors had once been content to delegate control of the cities. The career of the great patriarch of Alexandria, Athanasius (296–373) showed this clearly. In the eventual opinion of Constantine's son, Constantius II, Athanasius was

> A man who came from the lowest depths of society and obtained authority . . . His flatterers . . . applauded, and most of the simple folk took their cue from them . . . The man who led the crowd was no different from a common artisan.[10]

Athanasius was the portent of a new age. He combined an ability to provoke the unrelieved suspicion that his local power, as bishop, was based on peculation and violence, with a gift (a sincere gift, but one that he put to use with great political acumen) for presenting himself as the representative of a timeless and universal Christian orthodoxy, declared, forever, in 325, at the Council of Nicaea. He persistently denied legitimacy to his accusers by labelling their views as "Arian" – as those of the followers of Arius (250–336), a learned Alexandrian priest. In this way, Athanasius defended his own growing local power in Alexandria by appealing to all that was most majestically non-local in the Christian notion of a universal "law."

Athanasius' career included five periods of exile. On one occasion, he escaped at midnight from his fellow-bishops, who had gathered at Tyre to judge him, perched on a raft, so as to avoid detection by the harbor-guards, and turned the tables on his enemies by appearing in person, totally unannounced, before an astounded Constantine. Such bravado baffled most of his contemporaries and alienated many. It was far from clear at the time what was "orthodox" and what was not. It was only later agreed, by the victorious "Nicene" party, that Athanasius had been the hero of a Christian orthodoxy laid down at Nicaea. But the story gained in the telling – and especially in the Latin West. By the end of the fourth century, the "Arian Controversy" was narrated in studiously confrontational terms: "orthodox" bishops had defeated "heretics;" and, in so doing, they had even offered heroic resistance to the cajolery and, at times, to the threats, of "heretical" emperors. Such *ex post facto* narratives masked the reality of the situation. Western Christians have come to see the Arian controversy as the beginning of the problem of Church and State. At the time, however, it took the form of a series of trials of strength, in which determined local leaders, the Christian bishops, found out how far they could go in testing the basic structural weakness of the Roman empire – the continued reliance of distant emperors on local interest-groups, in this case, on the expanding power of the churches.

Not every city was as turbulent as Alexandria, nor, fortunately, was every bishop an Athanasius. The cities remained the spoiled children of the Mediterranean Roman world. They depended on the favor of the emperor for much of their food supply and amenities. A civic-minded, secular aristocracy still resided in them. They could be controlled. It was, if anything, the countryside that tended to slip from the orderly embrace of the new Christian empire. It was an ebullient countryside. In northern Syria and in Numidia, in North Africa, population had risen and new forms of village life throve. It was in the countryside that many of the most radical forms of Christianity took root. In 270, in the year that Constantine was born, Anthony (250–356), a comfortable farmer of the Fayum, made his way out into the desert, to re-emerge, around 310, as a famous *erémétikos*, a "man of the desert," the model Christian "hermit" of all future ages. The roads of Syria had long been travelled by bands of charismatic preachers who owed nothing to the "world." Pointedly celibate, and, so, entirely open to the power of the Holy Spirit, they had to be advised not to burst into chanted psalms when passing through non-Christian villages – lest they be mistaken for travelling musicians! They were the "unique ones," the "lonely ones." In Egypt, the Greek word *monachos*, "lonely one," "monk" soon became attached to such persons.

Beyond the territories of the empire, in a village south of Ctesiphon, Christian religious ferment led to the foundation, by a visionary, of the first new religion to emerge out of Christianity. The religion of Mani (216–277), known as Manichaeism, made plain, if in an exotic form deeply hated by other Christians, the immense potential of an ascetic, "apostolic" missionary movement. Mani had outdone the previous founders of the great religions of Asia:

> The Lord Zoroaster came to Persia . . . The Lord Buddha, the wise, the blessed one, came to the land of India and of the Kushans (to Central Asia) . . . Jesus the Christ, in the Western lands of the Romans, came to the West.[11]

The "Church of Mani," by contrast, would spread to all these regions. And it did. Manichaeism would later span the entire length of that sweep of settled life, from the Mediterranean to China, that had once been surveyed, from Edessa, by Bardaisan.

Manichaeism was a religion carried by ascetic missionaries. The Manichaean "Elect" depended entirely on the laity, the "Hearers," for food and lodging. Thus supported wherever they went, they travelled far and wide. Manichaeism, also, was a religion of the book. Manichaean manuscripts from as far apart as Middle Egypt and the Turfan Oasis of western Sinkiang show the unmistakable power of the *codex* as the bearer of a universal religious law. A Manichaean Psalmbook from Egypt even has a five-page index of contents at the back; and a recent, astonishing discovery, a *Life of Mani*, was exquisitely produced in a miniature format, so as to fit, discreetly, into the robes of a traveller.[12] It was through Manichaean missions that ordinary inhabitants of the Roman empire might glimpse the immensity of Asia, through references to "the blessed one," the "Lord Buddha."

Checked by savage persecution within the Christian empire, the public appeal of Manichaeism soon waned in the west. This could not be said of the monks of Egypt, Palestine and Syria. In the west, monasticism existed, as yet, in the eye of the beholder – and, largely, of the upper-class beholder. Only such persons could read, could travel to the Holy Places and could receive, in their spacious town-houses, visitors from the east. In Syria and Egypt, monasticism was a complex and, in many ways, a humdrum movement. But, seen from the Latin west, it spoke, in a melodramatic manner, to the disquiets of a new Christian upper class. The *saeculum*, "the world" – seen very much in terms of their own upper-class culture and their own vast wealth – stood condemned by the lives of these distant, miraculously authentic, Christians. Seldom had *codices* containing the history of obscure foreigners provoked such moral landslides in the lives of influential Romans. The *Life of Anthony* appeared immediately after the great hermit's death in 356. It was ascribed to none other than Athanasius of Alexandria. It was soon available in a Latin translation. In 386, an imperial official from Gaul met Augustine, now a teacher of rhetoric in Milan:

> He told how . . . on one occasion [two well-placed friends had gone for a stroll in the countryside] – it was at Trier, when the emperor was at the chariot races in the circus . . . They came to a certain house, the dwelling of some servants of God . . . There they found a book in which was written the life of Anthony. One of them began to read it, marvelled at it, was set on fire by it.

Augustine reacted instantly:

> What is wrong with us? What is this we have heard? The unlearned rise up and take heaven by force, while we, with all our culture, remain stuck fast in flesh and blood.[13]

Augustine was only one of many successful persons in the west who had been touched by tales of the desert. A decade previously, Martin (335–397), a retired member of the Imperial General Staff who became bishop of Tours, had created a monastery on the cliffs overlooking the Loire outside his episcopal city. His monks were men of good family. They were careful to wear, not the local wool, but camel's hair imported directly from Egypt! Martin combined, significantly, the role of an exorcist with that of a destroyer of country temples. He re-enacted, in the countryside of Gaul, the victorious rout of the demons, that formed, at that time, the basic Christian narrative for the spread of the faith. He did so with the collusion of a circle of landed aristocrats. They welcomed the appearance, in their own province, of a *vir apostolicus*, of a "truly Apostle-like man," endowed with miraculous powers. A disaffected man of culture, Sulpicius Severus (363–425), produced a *Life of Martin* in 396, that soon proved to be a classic of Latin hagiography. Here was a saint for new, less quiet times: a prophet raised up by God in the west, to warn a generation of tepid Christians of the swift approach of the Last Days.[14]

When, in 399, the senatorial lady, Melania the Elder (342–411), returned to Campania from Jerusalem, where she had lived among monks for over twenty years, she came to a world that now needed her presence. Her upper-class relatives flocked to her:

> They thought they were cleared from the pollution of their riches if they succeeded in gathering some of the dirt from her feet.[15]

These dramatic scenes were orchestrated and relayed to each other by a relatively small group of influential and highly articulate persons. They reflected a growing dissatisfaction in the Christianity of the Latin West. Many Latin Christians had come to feel that, despite the conversion of the emperors, their world had not yet become Christian enough.

The vivid religious history of the fourth century has tended to divert attention from the fact that the religious revolution associated with the reign of Constantine went hand in hand with a social revolution – the creation and stabilization of a new, and self-confident, upper class. The splendid late

Roman villas, that dominated the countryside in every province of the western empire, spoke of a world restored. Their occupants – part landowners and part government servants – embraced the new order with enthusiasm. For them, conversion to Christianity was a conversion, above all, to the almost numinous majesty of a Roman empire, now restored and protected by the One God of the Christians. Constantine's *labarum* – the victory-giving sign associated with the battle of the Milvian Bridge, and, so, with the new, Constantinian order – came to be placed on every kind of object associated with their affluent way of life. To take one recently discovered example: in Pannonia, near Lake Balaton (western Hungary), a hoard of magnificent silverware shows Sevso, a provincial aristocrat – possibly a military man of non-Roman background – at ease in his world. With his favorite horse – carefully marked "Innocentius" – and his fortified villa, Sevso was there to stay. The main serving dish was made of 2½ kilograms of solid silver, and bore the inscription:

> May these, o Sevso, for many ages be,
> Small vessels, fit to serve your offspring worthily.

And in Sevso's world, Christianity, also, had come to stay. The *labarum* appears at the beginning of the inscription, directly above Sevso's head, as he presided at his ease over the huntsmen's banquet.[16]

Such persons were prominent, also, in the cities of the empire. To celebrate their power, they drew upon ceremonies, art-forms and literary styles that reached back into the non-Christian past. Large areas of the public life of the upper classes of the Roman empire remained magnificently opaque to the confessional definitions of identity, which claimed to divide the world neatly between Christians and *pagani*. In this public culture, Christians and non-Christians could meet on neutral ground. Men of different *religiones* could collaborate to maintain a Roman world restored to order.

But the maintenance of a neutral public culture depended on a studied ambiguity. Constantine's new city, Constantinople, for instance, was hailed by Christians as a city without temples.

Certainly, blood-sacrifice was avoided. But it was not a city without gods. Constantine had deliberately made it an astonishing, open-air museum of the art of the classical world, by filling its public spaces with statues taken directly from temples all over Greece. A post-pagan world was not, by any means, necessarily a Christian world. In this period, for instance, the Feast of the Kalends of January gained in importance.[17] It owed nothing whatsoever to Christianity. It was a feast that celebrated with ancient, religious fervor (although without blood-sacrifice) the unflagging vigor of a Roman order, mysteriously renewed at the start of every year. It coincided with the yearly naming of the consuls. It involved lavish exchanges of gifts between patrons and their dependents, and competitive banqueting, that displayed – and predicted for the coming year – the affluence of individual households. Christian bishops preached against it all over the empire. On one occasion at Carthage, Augustine spoke for over two and a half hours on end, to divert the attention of the congregation, by a stunning display of rhetoric, from the murmurous jubilation that surrounded them.[18] He preached in vain. His congregation, though good Christians, were also loyal members of their city: they would not forgo that great moment of euphoria, in which the fortune of the city, and of all within it, was renewed. As long as urban life survived in the west, the feast of the Kalends continued. It was, indeed, so closely identified with the urban life of the Roman Mediterranean that, when, centuries later, Muslim Arabs came and took over the great cities of North Africa and the Levant, they found the Kalends still celebrated: it was, they said, "a great feast of the Christians."[19]

But a strong, religiously neutral public culture depended on the continued stability of west Roman society. Constantine had exploited brilliantly the prosperity that had followed the establishment of a stable empire under Diocletian. But this stability did not last. In 363, the pagan emperor Julian lost a large part of the Roman armies in Mesopotamia. In 378, further legions were annihilated by the Visigoths at Adrianople (Edirne, Turkey-in-Europe). Sevso's Pannonia, to name only one region, became a far from secure place. The late fourth century was an age of renewed civil wars, which involved the stripping of frontier garrisons. In 406, Gaul experienced a major barbarian raid. In 410, Rome was sacked by Alaric the Visigoth. Neither of these were definitive disasters; but public morale was badly shaken. Pagans began to speak of *tempora Christiana*, "Christian times;" and by "Christian times" they meant, not the stability of the Constantinian order, but a new age of anxiety, overshadowed by a crisis of authority that led to renewed barbarian raids throughout the Roman provinces of the west.

Public disasters provided many Christians with a convenient alibi. They enabled restless persons to embark on drastic courses that they would not have contemplated in more peaceful times. The career of Pontius Meropius Paulinus (355–431), later bishop of Nola, in Campania (where he had once served as a provincial governor) showed that, for some Christians, at least, the age of consensus could be publicly declared to be at an end. Paulinus was an Aquitanian senator, whose inflamed eye had once been touched by none other than Saint Martin. A withdrawal to his estates in northern Spain, at a time of civil war, in 389, rapidly hardened into an uncompromising ascetic conversion. Challenged by his friend and former tutor, the poet Ausonius of Bordeaux, Paulinus now presented himself, in powerful verse, as the classic convert:

And absolutely, with a master's right,
Christ claims our hearts, our lips, our time.[20]

It was as Ausonius had feared. "The golden tissue" woven by shared office and by friendships based on a shared high culture had become unravelled. Ausonius was unable to summon Paulinus back to take up his duties as a public figure in Aquitaine. For Paulinus had redefined *pietas*, the essential Roman virtue of loyalty to friends and to one's homeland, in starkly Christian terms. Piety to Christ was all that mattered for him. His loyalties lay with a new group of like-minded friends: "slaves of God, insurgents against the world." These included Sulpicius Severus, the biographer of their shared hero, Martin, the formidable Melania, and, last but not least, a man the same age as himself, a recent fellow-convert, who had become bishop of Hippo in 395 – Augustine. Augustine's *Confessions* appeared in 397. It was the story of the beginning of a new life, now made fully public, and presented with as exquisite a literary sense as that shown, a decade previously, by Paulinus, in his poems to Ausonius.

Augustine's *Confessions* looked back on the youth and vivid adulthood of a successful provincial. But they did so in the light of a new resolve. Augustine now served God as Catholic bishop of Hippo. His past – the flowering of his talents under a traditional, non-Christian system of schooling, his contact with strange doctrines (first, with the Manichees and, later, with the writings of the pagan Platonists), his mother, Monica, his friends, his concubine, the strains of a career driven by "the hope of the world:" all this had come to an end, in the summer of 386, with a decision to adopt a life of continence, as a preliminary to seeking baptism at the hands of Ambrose, bishop of Milan. Now Augustine was like Ambrose – he was a leading bishop in his own province. Conversion from "the world" had not meant a retreat into obscurity. In one way or another, all the great Latin converts to the ascetic life ended up in positions of prominence in the Catholic Church – their behavior was watched, their books were read, their ideas were hotly discussed. Whether they wished it or not, they had moved from one style of public life to another.

Augustine wrote his *Confessions* in such a way as to invest surprising new departures, such as his own, with an overpowering sense of God-given agency:

> For *He hath made us and not we ourselves* . . . indeed, we had destroyed ourselves, but He who made us made us anew.[21]

The grace of God worked on the heart, "as if it were a speck of gold in the hands of a master craftsman," hammering the fragile, discontinuous will into an ever-firmer, finally victorious resolve. This was no abstract doctrine for Augustine. The life of the Catholic Church, as he saw it, was made up of countless, small victories of grace. To those who had learned to pray with a humble heart, God would always give the grace that fired the will to follow His commands.

Not every ascetic Christian was comfortable with such a view. When the *Confessions* were read out, in the company of Paulinus, Pelagius, a devout layman from Britain, walked out of the room. For Pelagius, and his many supporters, the "grace" of God did not work in this manner. God's "grace" had been to create human nature in such a way that human beings could follow His commands with ease, once that original, good nature had been stripped of the accretion of evil habits, through the transformative rite of baptism. For Pelagius, every baptized Christian was free to be the master craftsman of his or her own soul.

From 413 to Augustine's death, in 430, the various phases of the Pelagian controversy revealed to an attentive (and not always sympathetic) audience of educated Latin Christians, which stretched from Britain to Jerusalem, successive layers of the message condensed, with such persuasive power, in the *Confessions*. The controversy placed human agency at the center of attention; and the qualified acceptance of the views of Augustine in preference to those of Pelagius placed God at the center of that agency. By this decision, Latin Christians of the fifth century made plain that they needed heroes, not self-improvers; and heroes, as many late Roman persons knew (including the emperor Constantine, whose sense of imperial mission had been fuelled by frequent great visions), were made by God. In the words of a fervent supporter of Augustine, Prosper of Aquitaine, the Church gained nothing from "a fickle will, that is not ruled by the changeless will of God;" for "the elect receive grace, not to allow them to remain idle . . . but to enable them to work well." [22]

In Augustine's world, the "elect," the "predestinate," were reassuringly visible. They were the heroes of the faith, whose memory was now celebrated in every city of the Mediterranean in massed festivals, shot through with a sense of collective triumph and delight. They were the martyrs, whose overriding love of God had led them past all other loves, past even the tenacious love of life itself. They were the great bishops, spectacular converts, whose love of God, as

Truth, had caused them (like Augustine) to bring a whole pre-Christian culture out of their stormy past into the service of the Catholic Church. This was what grace was for: grace gave

> a liberty . . . protected and made firm by the gift of perseverance, that this world should be overcome, this world in all its deep loves, in all its terrors, in all its countless ways of going wrong.[23]

What made Augustine particularly acceptable, at this time, was that he emerged as far more consequentially egalitarian than was Pelagius. Pelagius had wished to break down the growing compartmentation of the church into first-class and second-class believers. He insisted that all Christians were capable of being perfect and, so, should set about becoming perfect. He wished to blur the distinction between lay person and monk by making every Christian a devout ascetic.

Augustine, by contrast, accepted that the Christian church had become a bafflingly differentiated institution. Not every Christian could be perfect. Yet each Christian was equal to every other, because each was equally – and totally – dependent on the grace of God. For him, the doctrine of election was a source of comfort to the humble, and a stern warning to the proud. He wrote, for instance, with lyrical fervor in support of the virgins of the Church – the communities of dedicated women who had sprung up in every Christian community. Virgins mattered vastly to contemporaries. In many churches, they stood behind a chancel screen of glistening white marble, that seemed to condense the rock-like purity which their gesture of sexual renunciation had brought to themselves and to the Christian community. But he also reminded these virgins that some of the greatest martyrs in the North African church had been married women and the mothers of children. Their festivals marked them out, unambiguously, as members of the "elect." Nuns should constantly bear this fact in mind. It was not their virginity that would bring them to heaven, but only their love of Christ, inspired by the same grace which had led *matronae*, married housewives, such as Perpetua and Crispina, to scorn death. That same grace was still at work, if in a more humble manner, in each married member of his congregation.[24]

Indeed, the Catholic Church was a united community precisely because it was a community of sinners. In Augustine's writings against the Pelagians, we can glimpse the Catholic laity of his own, and of many subsequent centuries:

> who indulge their sexual appetites, although within the decorous bonds of marriage, and not only for the sake of offspring, but, even, because they enjoy it. Who put up with injuries with less than complete patience . . . Who may even burn, at times, for revenge . . . Who hold to what they possess. Who give alms, but not very lavishly. Who do not take other people's property, but defend their own: but do it in the bishop's court, rather than before a worldly judge . . . But who, through all this, see themselves as small and God as glorious.[25]

What was truly glorious on earth, for all the imperfections of its individual members, was the Catholic Church. For without Catholic baptism, Augustine was convinced, it seemed impossible (to human minds, at least) that God would grant forgiveness of the original sin that made all human beings equal because equally estranged from God. For this reason, the Church had to be truly universal. It was the only resting place, on earth, in which a sorely wounded humanity could hope to recover its lost health.

Augustine was at his most disagreeably impatient when faced by groups whom he saw as self-regarding enclaves, deaf to the universal message of the Catholic Church. He insensibly presented the Church not only as the true Church, but as the Church of the majority. He saw no reason why the normal pressures by which any late Roman local community enforced conformity on its members should not be brought to bear against schismatics and heretics. He justified the exile and disendowment of rival Churches. As for pagans, they were simply told to "wake up" to the fact that they were a minority. For the entire world had been declared, millennia previously, by the prophets of Israel, to belong only to Christ and to His Church:

Ask of Me, and I shall give you the uttermost parts of the earth for Thine inheritance.[26]

Hence the supreme importance, for Augustine, of the *City of God*, which he began to write in 413, as an answer to pagan criticisms and to Christian disillusionment, provoked by the news of Alaric's sack of Rome. The disaster provided Augustine with an excuse to expatiate on a theme dear to his heart. It was summed up in the title of the book, *On the City of God*. For, as in Psalm 87, Jerusalem was the "City of our God," of which "glorious things are spoken." Jerusalem stood for Heaven, the distant home of the saved. Like the Jerusalem of the Psalms (as Augustine read them) the Heavenly Jerusalem claimed those born in all other nations as potential citizens. A common sin had made all men and all women, quite irrespective of race, of class and of level of culture, equally aliens from that Heavenly Jerusalem, equally potentially damned. All were summoned, with stark impartiality, to return to their true homeland. Displaying his command of pagan literature and philosophy to its fullest extent, Augustine deliberately created a common ground with his readers, precisely so that, all obstacles removed and all arguments vanquished, they might have no excuse not to slip across that shared ground into the Catholic Church, and so to become potential citizens of heaven.

Of course, not all did so. We have a recently discovered letter that Augustine wrote, at the end of his life, to Firmus, a notable of Carthage. Firmus had attended afternoon readings of the *City of God*. He had even read as far as Book X. He knew his Christian literature better than did his wife. Yet his wife was baptized, and Firmus was not. Augustine informed him that, compared with her, Firmus, for all his culture, even his sympathy for Christianity, stood on dangerous ground as long as he remained unbaptized:

> For what was the purpose of this book? Not so that people might delight in its style, nor learn from it things they had not known before, but that they may be convinced about the City of God – that they should enter into this city without further delay and persevere within it to the end:

beginning first with rebirth (in baptism) and continuing within it with rightly ordered love.[27]

One thing was certain, Augustine's "Glorious City," and its entrance-point on earth, the Catholic Church, was not a small place. It was a "city" for all ages and for every region:

> in a wide world, which has always been inhabited by many differing peoples, that have had, in their time, so many different customs, religions, languages, forms of military organization, and clothing, there have, however, only arisen two groups of human beings [those destined for the "City of God" and those who were not] – groups we call "cities," according to the special usage of the Scriptures.[28]

It was a notion whose sweep and clarity took on new weight and intensity as the Churches of the west settled down, as best they could, to face the increasing possibility of a world without empire.

4

Virtutes Sanctorum . . . Strages Gentium: "Deeds of Saints . . . Slaughter of Nations"

In AD 418, Augustine received a letter from Hesychius, bishop of Salona (Solun, on the Dalmatian coast of Croatia). Hesychius had written to ask Augustine, in faraway Africa, if the end of the world was at hand. Augustine reassured him. The Roman empire had experienced worse disasters in the course of the third century AD:

> For, to cut a long story short, under the emperor Gallienus [253–268], when barbarians from all over the world were overrunning the Roman provinces,

many Christians had thought that the end of the world had come. They were proved wrong. In any case, Augustine added, a wide world still stretched beyond the Roman frontiers. Christ would not come again until His Gospel had been preached to distant, pagan nations:

> The Lord did not promise [to the Catholic Church] the Romans only, but all the nations of the world.[1]

Augustine's calm detachment from the present troubles of the empire may not have comforted the bishop of Salona. Like many Christians who had grown up in the post-Constantinian age, for Hesychius a world without empire was no world at all.

Yet, in Britain, Gaul and Spain, the prospect of a world without Rome became ever more real. After the raids that began in 406, the age of peace was over. By the 430s it was already obvious that, in marked contrast to the age of Diocletian and Constantine, if dislocation was to be followed, yet again, by an age of recovery, this recovery would owe nothing to the Roman state. The military and fiscal apparatus associated with the reformed empire of the fourth century failed, ingloriously, to protect the frontiers. The west fell apart. It became a patchwork of separate regions. Southern Gaul, around Marseilles and Arles, Italy and Africa (up to its catastrophic conquest by the Vandals, in 429–439) remained "imperial" provinces. For three-quarters of a century, until the undramatic resignation of the last emperor, Romulus Augustulus, in 476, Italy and Provence were an extension, into the western Mediterranean, of the old order of things – of an imperial stability that was still taken for granted throughout the eastern parts of the empire. If Constantinople was "New Rome," Ravenna, the north Italian capital of the western emperors, was very much a "little Byzantium."

Elsewhere in the west, a very different state of affairs emerged. Intense provincialism had always characterized the western provinces. For centuries, the local elites had profited by identifying themselves with an over-arching imperial system. But once this system ceased to defend them, local loyalties, made all the more secure by centuries of Roman peace, were what counted for most. But if the local elites of Britain, of Gaul and of the vast sub-continent of Spain were to remain *Romani* – that is, if they were to maintain something of the position that they had enjoyed under Constantine and his successors – then they would have to learn to adjust to a world without Rome, and to do so with the despised "barbarians" as partners, even as masters.

What is truly remarkable about the history of the fifth-century west is the tenacity with which the *Romani* of so many regions re-established their own position in a post-imperial situation. The end of the world may not have come, as bishop

Hesychius had feared. But *a* "world" – a specific religious and social order which many articulate Christians had come to take for granted – came to an end, in many regions, in the course of the fifth century. What emerged, instead, was a world where the Roman provincial aristocracies strove to maintain their local power in uneasy collaboration with non-Roman warlords.

What were lost irrevocably were the wide horizons associated with the post-Constantinian Christian empire. To take one example: Hydatius (*ca.*397–470) came from Galicia. He had visited Jerusalem with his mother at the age of ten. The little boy had even been presented to Saint Jerome. But that had been in AD 407. When he wrote his *Chronicle*, in 455, Hydatius had been Catholic bishop of Chaves, near the Atlantic coast of northern Spain, for almost twenty years. He had seen the end of an age. He was now caught

> within Gallaecia, at the edge of the entire world . . . not untouched by all the calamities of this wretched age . . . [faced with] the domination of heretics, compounded by the disruption brought by hostile tribes.

Only a few travellers from the Holy Land now passed his way. They could not even tell him when Jerome had died. Hydatius could record, however, that neighboring Braga had been sacked by a Visigothic army in search of quick plunder: "although accomplished without bloodshed [this cynical shakedown of a Roman city] was lamentable enough." It was, he added, a "partial reliving," in his own sad land, of the tragic destruction of ancient Jerusalem.[2]

The end of Roman peace, and the loss of the wide horizons associated with the Christian empire, were troubling enough to a man such as Hydatius. But what was more painful still was the increasing recognition that regional societies, cut loose from the empire, could maintain a level of order, even of prosperity, provided that a *modus vivendi* of some kind was reached with the barbarians.

But this in turn meant that the *barbari*, the stereotypical "outsiders" of the Roman imperial imagination, had to be allowed to become, in some way or other, "insiders."

This was difficult to accept. Romans preferred to speak of barbarians in terms familiar to readers of classical literature. Gallic landowners wrote of Visigoths and Burgundians as men "in unkempt clothes, with furs piled high upon their shoulders" – men dressed, that is, not like Romans, in woven silks that were the fruit of civilization, but in raw products of the wild. Their followers were lifelong warriors. The intricate cloisonné gold-work of their shield-bosses, "showed, at one and the same time, their wealth and [war], their ruling passion."[3] The descriptions implied that the barbarians were total aliens who had arrived from nowhere: they could never have a role in the traditional fabric of Roman life; or, if they did, it would be only as subordinate "allies" of Rome, not as partners and potential masters. It was easier to see the barbarians in such old-fashioned terms than to face the fact that many of them were, simply, *potentes*, new "men of power" – alternative Romans, who had already become more than half Roman by the rough standards of a post-imperial age.

In reality, the barbarians with whom the inhabitants of the west had to deal were as much a product of the achievements of the new empire of Constantine and his successors as were the local aristocracies themselves. The fourth-century empire had needed loyal servants. It had tended to prefer those who did not share the values and inhibitions of the traditional land-owning aristocracy. Soldiers, in particular, were positively encouraged to be a class apart – to remain alien and abrasive. For over a century, imperial armies had been recruited from frontier areas, where "Romans" and "barbarians" were largely indistinguishable. What mattered was loyalty – an overriding loyalty to the Roman state, summed up in the solemn soldier's oath to the emperor, "as to a god, present in human flesh."[4] As *viri militares*, men of war, "Romans" and "barbarians" met as equals in the Roman armies. They were equally distinctive and equally privileged servants of a powerful state. Both derived their entitlement to wealth and status from the *cingulum militiae*, the heavy, golden belt (often produced in the imperial workshops of Constantinople, in a style that captured the barbaric splendor of the art of Central Asia and the Danube), which distinguished them from all civilians.

Even after the invasions, "barbarian" groups continued to be treated as if they were soldiers of the emperor. The Visigoths were settled by the imperial authorities around Bordeaux in 418. The Burgundians were given garrisons in the middle Rhône and Saône in 443. Detachments of Alan cavalry were stationed along the Loire, within striking distance of the restless coasts of Brittany. As far as we can see, even the Saxon pirates settled in enclaves around the Thames had arrived as the result of an agreement to defend Britain. All were recognizable avatars of the *viri militares* of an earlier age. They were not invaders from "outer space." They did not hold their lands through outright conquest. Their settlements were the last legacy of a policy of divide and rule, bequeathed by a failing empire to its provincials.

Thus, the so-called "barbarian settlements" did not involve great upheaval. The Visigoths of the Garonne valley, for instance, were never more than one-sixtieth of the overall population of the region. Barbarian settlers, in fact, were no more prominent than military personnel had been when stationed on the frontiers. And they were settled in such a way as to make them look, as much as possible, like Roman soldiers. Their families received lands, as if they were veterans. They had access to the produce of estates, as if they were regular soldiers billeted on the civilian population. Elsewhere, local garrisons collected a share of the region's taxes for their own use.

But there was one crucial difference. These settlements now recreated, in the most fertile heartlands of the Mediterranean, where the Roman landowning aristocracy was most firmly entrenched, conditions that had been normal only in the militarized provinces of the extreme north. Over large areas of Gaul, Spain, and, eventually, after 476, in Italy, military men of non-Roman origin became prominent members of local society. They were in a position to compete with the *Romani* on their own terms. They turned their military privileges into solid, Roman gains – in land, clients and slaves – displayed in a Roman style of life. Far from remaining the fur-clad leaders of roving warrior bands, Visigoths and Burgundians rapidly became indistinguishable from their civilian Roman neighbors. They owned villas with identical mosaic floors, were buried in identical marble sarcophagi, rode to the hunt in identical clothes – with flowing cloaks and trousers and with the Cross branded on their horses' rumps. Their poorer fellows, on whose military man-power the leaders depended, may have retained certain folk-ways: the man who stole a dog in a Burgundian hamlet had to make amends by kissing its backside in public.[5] But such persons were largely indistinguishable from Roman peasants. In the words of king Theodoric (493–526), an Ostrogothic successor, in Italy, to Romulus Augustulus: "An effective Goth wants to be like a Roman; only a poor Roman would want to be a Goth."[6]

But these "barbarians" were no longer defined in Roman society by loyalty to a distant emperor. A Visigoth or a Burgundian drew his privileges from serving in the army of his king. Visigothic Toulouse, acclaimed as "a new Rome," and Burgundian Vienne were power bases for local militias, who claimed to be the armies of separate *gentes*, of separate tribes, loyal to separate kings.

Life would have been easier, in the post-imperial west, if these *gentes* – these so-called "tribes" – had been what modern scholars once imagined them to be: compact, clearly defined groups, nothing less than the ancestors of the modern European nations. In reality, active membership in a specific army – and not ethnic origin in and of itself – defined membership in a specific *gens*. And the kings needed soldiers. They were not fastidious as to who served in their armies. Each barbarian group may have predominated in the army to which it gave its name. But the forces of most barbarian rulers were like the "Free Companies" of the Hundred Years War – diverse bands, brought together by ambitious impresarios of violence.

This was a troubling prospect. The barbarian armies were places where a Roman might lose his identity entirely, through serving a "barbarian" king. Like the Ottoman armies, or the Cossacks of southern Russia, the militias of the fifth century were a haven for renegades of every sort – from escaped slaves to Roman country gentlemen whose taste for violence was not satisfied by the excitements of the hunt. Disloyalty to the traditional civilian values of the Roman elites was in the air, fed by countless stories of *Romani* who found that the "barbarians" were not a problem, but an opportunity.

It was, indeed, when barbarians were at their least alien that they posed the greatest threat to influential segments of the Roman population. For they, also, were sincere Christians. As befitted military men, the Visigoths, in particular, had received the faith in the glory days of the empire, in the reigns of Constantius II and Valens. They were committed to what had been the current orthodoxy of the Danubian provinces at that time. It is only in retrospect that we call it "Arianism." But times had changed. Arianism went out of fashion. The Visigoths arrived in Gaul already labelled as "Arian" heretics, unacceptable to "Nicene," Catholic Christians.

Most barbarian rulers tended to keep their beliefs to themselves. They rarely victimized Catholics. But they shared the same religious language. Far from being simple sons of the wild, the Visigothic, Burgundian and Vandal kings felt that they knew "correct" doctrine when they saw it. Articulate, Latin-speaking Arian clergymen frequented their courts. The Visigoths proudly ascribed the victories of their armies to their own, "Arian" orthodoxy. The Vandals went one further. They applied to Catholic bishops the same laws exiling "heretical" bishops that Augustine had justified, at great length, in the interests of the Catholic Church!

The constant irritant presented by such alternatives ensured that the Catholic Christianity of the western Mediterranean came to see itself, in exceptionally stark terms, as a religion on the defensive. Looking back, from the end of the sixth century, a Catholic bishop, the descendant of a Roman senatorial family from the Auvergne, Gregory of Tours (538–594), saw the fifth century as a time of dramatic confrontations. As in the days of ancient Israel, the *virtutes sanctorum,* "the deeds of the saints," took place against a background characterized by *strages gentium*, by "the slaughter of warring nations."[7]

Christianity had not been long established in Gaul. But it had already obtained a foothold in the towns; and, in the fifth century, the towns emerged in Gaul, as also in much of Spain, as the nodal points of contested regions. For they were fortified. Solid walls, many of them built in the insecure days of the third century AD, surrounded the compact nucleus of once-sprawling classical cities. The walls of Clermont, for instance, enclosed only three hectares of what had been an open town of 200 hectares. Apart from the occasional re-use of pre-Roman hill forts, the rural villas that formed the power-base of the aristocracy remained undefended. Walled cities stood out, in contrast to an exposed countryside, as enduring symbols of Roman security and authority.

Walls and bishops went together. The *virtutes*, the miraculous deeds, most appreciated in fifth-century saints were those in which city walls had held. In 451, Attila's Huns headed for the Loire. The inhabitants of Orleans turned to their bishop, Annianus:

> He advised them to prostrate themselves in prayer and with tears to implore the help of the Lord . . . "Keep a watch on the city walls [he said] to see if God, in his pity, will send us help." . . . When their prayers were finished, they were ordered by the old man to look for a third time. Far away they saw what looked like a cloud of dust [the Roman cavalry of Aetius, along with a Visigothic army, were on their way to relieve the city] . . . "It is the help sent by God." The walls were already rocking under the shock of the battering rams.[8]

But it was essential that not only the walls should hold. The fate of each region depended on the morale of its urban centers. Apart from the occasional, chilling grand raid (such as that associated with Attila), most warfare, in fifth century Gaul, was a small-scale affair. The control of whole regions was decided by a war of nerves, not by massive engagements. Small bands would march through the countryside, "destroying the fields, spoiling the meadows, cutting up the vineyards and ruining the olive groves." The aim was to inflict just enough damage to persuade the local leaders to think twice about offering further resistance: they would pay tribute or open their gates to a new overlord.[9]

The townsfolk were particularly vulnerable to such scare tactics. They needed leaders on whom they could rely, to maintain their spirits and to mitigate the disruptive effects of small, vindictive raids. They found these in the Christian bishops. The intensely communal quality of the Christian churches, which we have seen developing in the cities of the fourth century, now stood out in pointed contrast to a divided and easily dispersed secular aristocracy. The local church became the "fixative" that held whole populations in place. The Church's charitable activities palliated the effects of famine and siege. They even kept peasants in their place, through the ransoming and return to their owners of captured serfs – many of whom may well have profited from the disorders of the time to run away. As bishop of Arles, Caesarius (470–542) ransomed and relocated thousands of uprooted peasants. The silver decorations of his cathedral were melted down to pay for his charities:

> Even today, the marks of the axes can be seen on the pillars and screens of the sanctuary where the silver ornaments of the columns were stripped off.[10]

More important still, the buildings of the church spoke of the day-to-day determination of cities to survive and to be seen to survive. The bishops of Gaul vied with each other to place splendid basilicas in the fortified enclaves of their cities, and along the urban peripheries, where the Roman roads passed through venerable tombs. Five churches were built in Lyons in this period. The bishops of Tours and Clermont competed to construct cathedrals with room for over a thousand worshippers. At a time when secular building had come to a standstill, these churches represented a coagulation of wealth and collaborative energy that amounted to a flat denial that the end of the world had come to Gaul. Given a minimum of security, it was plain that a Roman province could still fill its cities with new structures, as opulent as giant jewel cases. In these churches, daylight was trapped in the unearthly shimmer of gold mosaic and multicolored marbles. To all who entered them, they brought to earth a glimpse of Paradise. As Gregory of Tours wrote of the basilica of his native Clermont:

> In it one is conscious of the fear of God and of a great brightness, and those who pray are often aware of a most sweet and aromatic odor wafted towards them. Round the sanctuary it has walls which are decorated with mosaic work and many varieties of marble.[11]

An age of great basilicas fostered a piety of great assemblies. The mechanisms of reparation for sin, that were long familiar to all Christian communities, took on a distinctively communal meaning in Gaul and Italy. Group penance, linked to penitential forms of intercessory prayer, was a discipline that curbed the widespread mood of *sauve qui peut*. Penitential supplications assembled a whole local population in one place, and kept them there for hours on end. The Rogation processions instituted by bishop Mamertus of Vienne, in the 470s, were swiftly adopted by his colleagues. They gathered an entire urban population, and flattened the differences between rich and poor – thereby, it was hoped, inhibiting the reflex of the rich to emigrate to safer locations. They made of small cities "a single fellowship of sighing supplicants."[12]

Collective ventures were not invariably successful. In Paris, Saint Genovefa (Sainte Geneviève) was almost drowned in the Seine as a "false prophet," as a witch and diviner, for urging the citizens to stay where they were as the Hunnish army swept across the plains of Champagne. She and the married ladies of the city kept a lonely vigil in the city's principal baptistery.[13] It was more usual to rally round a bishop who could claim to speak in the name of the city's ancient dead. The saintly dead represented collective loyalty at its most familiar and most intense. Local martyrs and holy persons, whose graves were visited on a regular basis and whose death-days were celebrated with a regular festival, were "fellow-citizens." For the saints had once stood in the local church praying for the Christian people of "their" city. It was assumed that they still did so: that their spirit remained present at their tomb.

This image of solidarity, based on the loving concern of holy persons for the "family of God," was enhanced by the use of terms that carried weighty, public overtones. The saints, also, were leaders. They were *patroni*, "patron saints." They were "the boss" – *le patron, il padrone*. They were thought of as persons with power and influence. Their *suffragia*, their "suffrages," – the words that they spoke on behalf of their clients – counted for much in the distant courts of Heaven. Members of a "celestial Senate house," the saints were invisible aristocrats. They demanded *reverentia*, fully public tokens of respect, from their loyal clients.

It was in the 460s, when imperial rule was perceived to have no further chance of asserting itself north of the Rhône valley, that the somewhat unprepossessing tomb of Saint Martin at Tours was given increasing prominence by bishop Perpetuus. Tours stood in a no-man's-land, in a privileged but uncertain political vacuum between the Visigothic kingdom to the south and the rudderless frontier provinces of northern Gaul. It now received a gigantic pilgrimage basilica. The inscriptions on the mosaics that showed the miracles of Martin told visitors from all over Gaul what Martin had once done and, so, what his *potentia*, his ever-present power to heal and to punish, might yet do. It was a reassuring message. In the courtyard outside the tomb, the possessed roared, their voices rising at times to a howl of garbled Greek and Hunnish. They were a reminder of a perilously wide world, where the *virtutes*, the effective power of "patron" saints, coexisted with the unquiet movements of alien races.[14]

In the fifth century, the landed aristocracy of Gaul (many of whose grandfathers had been pagans) took over the government of the Church. Of all the experiments in leadership that characterized this fluid century, the "aristocratization" of the Church in Gaul was the most enduring. It placed the cities in the hands of men used to exercising power in a Roman manner. Compared with the tenacious episcopal dynasties of *Romani*, who regarded the major sees of southern Gaul and Spain as their unchallenged appanage for another two centuries, the barbarian kingdoms were an evanescent phenomenon. The real map of post-imperial Gaul and Spain was drawn by its network of episcopal cities.

As a result, Gaul became very different from Italy, North Africa and the eastern empire. Its bishops tended to come into their city "from on top." They had not risen through the ranks of the clergy. It was not always a popular development. But at least it placed the churches in the hands of men who knew what they wanted and what others wanted of them. To take one well-known example: Sidonius Apollinaris (430–480) became bishop of Clermont in 470, after a long career as a politician and a writer. When called upon to justify the choice of an aristocratic bishop for the vacant see of Bourges, he did so with gusto. A bishop drawn from the clergy would only lead to jealousy. A monk, of course, would be an admirable candidate; but a monk was accustomed to praying to God for the salvation of souls, "not to earthly judges for the safety of our bodies." Simplicius, the son and son-in-law of former bishops, was the ideal choice. He had built a church for the city. He had stood up to the Visigoths:

> Time and again . . . he has acted as spokesman of the city, before skin-clad kings and purple-robed emperors.

Bourges needed such a man. "A few priests twittered in holes and corners," Sidonius added; but that was only to be expected.[15]

Sidonius was a particularly flamboyant representative of this class of persons. He stood at the end of a generation. What made Gaul unique was not so much that it had an aristocratic episcopate: the *Katholikos*, the head of the Armenian church, was taken from one noble family alone, and would even appear at the altar, celebrating the Eucharist in the fox-fur robes of an Armenian magnate![16] It was, rather, that this development coincided with a religious revolution. Many of these aristocratic bishops had also become monks. A group of persons who had been placed in high office largely so as to reassure their flock that nothing had changed in Roman Gaul, acted as bishops by claiming that, in themselves, everything had changed.

Hence the decisive role of the monastic communities established at Marseilles and Lérins. In the fifth century AD, Marseilles became again what it had been at the time of its first foundation in the fifth century BC. It was a bridgehead of Mediterranean-wide commerce, perched on the edge of the uncertain hinterland of Gaul. John Cassian (360–435), a Latin-speaking monk from the Dobrudja, who had lived for decades in Egypt, arrived there in 415. His writings placed an entire world in the hands of Gallic readers. Once again, the *codex* helped to bring the furthest frontiers of the eastern Christian world close to the west. His *Institutions of the Monastic Life*, written in 420, provided reports of the monastic life in Egypt, with which to correct over-enthusiastic local experiments. His *Conferences*, of 426, disseminated spiritual guidance, in the form of interviews granted to him, while in Egypt, by the great old men of the desert.[17]

Even more important, at the time, was the island monastery of Lérins, opposite Antibes, founded in 400 by Saint Honoratus. Lérins was an outpost of the wilderness of Egypt placed within sight of the sun-beaten slopes of the Alpes-Maritimes. It was a Circe's Isle from which young men of noble family emerged transformed. Many of those who came to the island did not stay there for long. They re-emerged, after a spell of searching ascetic discipline, to become bishops all over Provence. A succession of bishops of Arles, most notably Hilary (430–449) and, later, Caesarius, made Arles, the center of continuing Roman rule in Gaul, a colony of Lérins. By 434, eight sees in southern Gaul were already in the hands of men from Lérins. Spiritual "capital" acquired on the island was "lent out at interest" to an ever-increasing number of churches.

The monastic discipline of Lérins was designed to break forever, in young men of noble family, the springs of worldly pride. Like the drastic Jesuit novitiate of later times, Lérins sent out into the world zealous thirty-year-olds, from old families, fully capable of deploying the old skills of rhetoric and government, but in a new manner, for a new, high cause. The transformation of the old order began with the body. A body changed in every detail from its previous aristocratic ease

– luxuriant hair cut short, the flush of high living drained by penitential fasting, the proud eye and haughty step of the "natural-born" leader of Gallic society curbed by a monastic discipline of humility: this was, now, a body ready for new, fully public action.

Germanus, bishop of Auxerre from 407 to 437, had been an imperial servant. On becoming bishop, "he instantly changed in every manner." He showed this change through his body. A hair shirt, a bed made of piled cinders, above all, a leather bag of relics of the saints tied across his chest – Germanus' body was touched, at every point, by suffering and by the sacred. His mortification brought down around him a sheath of unfamiliar privations that cut him off from his past. Yet, once cut off in this drastic manner, Germanus' past became innocent. It flowed in a pre-ordained manner into his episcopal present:

> The study of eloquence prepared him for preaching, legal doctrine for works of righteousness, marriage to a wife to set off his [future] chastity.[18]

From then onwards, the life of Germanus was presented in terms of meteoric energy. His biographer showed him moving from one end of the Roman west to another, always bringing relief and order. In Britain, he baptized a Romano-British army, before it sallied forth to rout the Saxons to the chant of "Alleluia." On the Loire, he grabbed the bridle of king Goar of the Alans, bringing to a dramatic halt the column of mailed cavalry despatched, by the Roman authorities, to crush a tax-revolt. He became the cynosure of the imperial palace at Ravenna. The *Life of Germanus* was written by a friend of Sidonius, at an anxious time, when Sidonius knew that his native Clermont might have to stand siege. It was a stirring assertion of the faith that, once chastened by spectacular ascetic effort, the old skills of public life might come again, in higher form, to serve the Catholic Church.

Bishops even looked their part. A new aesthetic, a Roman gravity made luminous by renunciation, determined the representation of the saints on the walls of the great basilicas. It was echoed in their earthly representatives. One had only to look at Epiphanius of Pavia to know that he would be a bishop:

> His cheeks smiled . . . Well-formed lips made doubly precious the sweetness of his words . . . His brow was like white, translucent wax . . . well-rounded hands with tapering fingers made it a delight to receive a gift from him . . . His voice was sonorous, not harsh or rustic . . . nor was it lacking in manly vigor.[19]

Decisive though such images of the bishop would prove to be in later ages, not everyone regarded the Gallic bishops as paragons. The bishop of Rome, pope Leo (440–461) regarded the high-handed dealings of a man such as the austere Hilary of Arles – who had carved out a wide metropolitan diocese for himself through the influence of powerful secular friends – as nothing less than the "balkanization" of an immemorial Church order. Leo professed to be appalled: "inflated by his own pride, he buries himself in Hell."[20]

Even after the Gothic sack of 410, Rome had remained a city with a population of some 200,000. It was ten times larger than Paris. Each of its major basilicas was four times larger than any Gallic cathedral. Carefully nurtured memories of the Roman martyrs reached back for all of four centuries. The Roman clergy were a faceless group of men, buoyed up by immense corporate confidence in the absolute rightness of all things Roman. Their bishop, drawn from their ranks, was the last person to appreciate experimental forms of leadership. The bishop of Rome was a *papa* – a Grand Old Man. He liked to play the Elder Statesman to less-experienced regions. Throughout the fifth century, the *papa*, the pope, of Rome could be relied upon to provide authoritative, reassuringly old-fashioned (and, for that very reason, largely inapplicable) advice on how a well-run church should function:

> Let novelty cease to afflict antiquity, let unease cease to upset the peace of the church.[21]

Individual bishops and clergymen travelled frequently to Rome to seek a ruling from its bishop. Many of them were tenacious malcontents. For a Gallic bishop, to appeal to Rome was usually a face-saving alternative to exile. The churches of Africa, just across the water from Rome, produced a stream of enterprising ne'er-do-wells who appealed to the popes against the judgements of local councils. One was a country bishop, deposed by Augustine and his colleagues for having, among other things, built his episcopal palace from the ruins of houses that he had seized and looted.[22] Such visitors did little to increase the respect of the pope and the Roman clergy for the way in which churches in the western provinces managed their affairs.

It would be a serious anachronism to see the bishops of Rome as being, at this time, central to the Latin churches of the west. They themselves looked eastwards. The imaginative geography of a man such as Leo was determined by the vast fact of a technically undivided empire. He owed his peculiar position to being the bishop of the westernmost Christian *metropolis* of a united Roman empire, whose power had weakened only in the distant west. Far from being peripheral to the Greek east, Leo's position as the bishop of the only major non-Greek city in the empire gave him considerable advantages. The participation of the bishop of Rome was essential to maintaining the constantly threatened balance of power among the churches of the eastern Mediterranean.

For the churches of the east, the single most dramatic and destabilizing event of the entire century had not been the emergence of local pockets of disorder in the west. It was the meteoric rise in their midst of Constantinople as a new world capital. The city now had a population of almost half a million, over four thousand upper-class town houses, and a mile and a half of wharves, to dock the grainships that fed its inhabitants. Nobody could know where the ambitions of the bishop of "New Rome," the patriarch of Constantinople, might not lead.

Faced by this novel threat, the patriarchs of Antioch and Alexandria, ancient Christian cities as large as Rome itself, vied with each other to secure the election of their own candidates to the bishopric of Constantinople. Each attempted to discredit the one set up by the other. Each attempted, at different times, to bring the bishop of Rome into the struggle on their side. Last but not least, the emperors themselves – who were "Romans" in a real sense, in that Latin remained the language of the law and was even spoken at court (much as Spanish continued to be used at the Habsburg court of Vienna) – were anxious to invoke the safely distant prestige of Saint Peter as a counterweight to the all-too-present, ever-insistent claims of the bishops of Antioch and Alexandria.

If, in Leo's eyes, *ambitio*, hard-driving politics, was the besetting sin of the Gallic bishops, the *ambitio* of his eastern colleagues took place at the very highest level and on a scale that made the activities of a Hilary of Arles seem trivial. The patriarchs of Alexandria were very much the heirs of the unruly Athanasius. They were a whole century richer. On one diplomatic mission to Constantinople alone, Cyril of Alexandria (412–444) was believed to have distributed to the officials of the imperial court bribes to the value of 2,500 pounds of gold – enough, that is, to feed 45,000 poor persons for one year, and twenty-five times as much money as Caesarius of Arles had been able to raise for the ransom of captives in Gaul. The pope's representative to a Church council, presided over by Cyril's successor, the heavy-handed Dioscorus, in 449, arrived back in Rome so shocked by the violence he had witnessed – he had been forced to flee to the sanctuary of the church in which the council took place, shouting in Latin, to no effect, over the heads of a riotous mob of oriental monks, "*Contradicitur,*" "I object" – that he set up in the Lateran baptistery an *ex voto* plaque to celebrate his deliverance!

The grand maneuvers set in hand by men such as Cyril and Dioscorus exacerbated and exploited what had become a burning theological problem. The Council of Ephesus (431) and the Council of Chalcedon (451) were successors to Constantine's grandiose experiment at Nicaea. In them, the emperors hoped to obtain the consent of the entire Christian Church to a formula that would resolve a hotly contested issue: how close to man had God drawn near, in the person of Jesus Christ?

On this issue, fifth-century Christians felt that they had entered exciting new territory. The ancient imaginative model of the universe (to which we referred in the last chapter) no longer helped them. This model had stressed the chasm between the higher and the lower reaches of the universe. It gave the human soul a steep upward glimpse, very much from the bottom up, of the hierarchy of ever more exalted spiritual beings which it must ascend in order to reach a distant God. The Incarnation of God in Jesus Christ, by contrast, brought the top of this universe down to the bottom. It placed the ancient model of the universe on its head: "It is far less amazing [Leo said] that human beings should progress upwards towards God than that God should have come down to the human level."[23] It mattered less, now, how to get from the lowest to the highest, from man to God. What truly preoccupied Christian thinkers was how to understand the unique manner in which the highest had been joined to the lowest – God joined to man – in the person of Christ. It was how to discern, in the person of Jesus, a figure whose actions and utterances were known in detail from the narratives of the Gospels, the God in the man and the man in the God.

Large Christian congregations needed to know this. They needed to feel that God was with them on ground level, as it were. It was not enough that God should make His will known to a distant human race through a series of special representatives. This was a weakness in previous Christian theology that Athanasius had already spotted and exploited with unrelenting, narrow clarity, in his conflict with the supporters of Arius. Christ was not simply a privileged messenger of God, as Arius seemed to suggest. He was not to be seen only as "a kind of Prefect of the Supreme Sovereign," governing the material universe on behalf of a still distant High God.[24]

Such views had seemed natural to a thinker of the age of Constantine, such as Eusebius of Caesarea (263–340). It was an age where it seemed as if the victory of monotheism had, indeed, been the victory of a High God, who had reached down to earth, to make his commands plain through a series of privileged representatives of His will, of which Christ had been the greatest and Constantine, on a lesser plane, the most recent. This view was dominant for much of the fourth century. But it made of God a remote monarch, Who acted through agents who were, by definition, different from Himself. Emperors were like that. God did not have to be so distant. Athanasius realized that the Christian people needed to be able to say

"*Emmanuel*," "God is with us." Christ's life on earth, he had insisted, had not been like "an official governmental visit from on high:" it had been the "blazing forth on earth of God Himself."[25]

Throughout the fourth and fifth centuries, the patriarchs of Alexandria, the master-politician Cyril and the fatefully over-confident Dioscorus (444–451), rode the tide whose strength, in Christian piety, Athanasius had already sensed. Because Christ had come down to earth among men, it was that much more easy to turn directly to Him. The intermediate powers of the *mundus* did not have to be invoked for help in earthly matters. In regions such as Egypt, monotheism became real, not through denying the reality of the lower powers – not through stripping the universe of its shimmering layers of angelic and demonic beings – but through pushing them to one side. All powers were subject to Christ; and Christ, because He had become a human being, was present to His worshippers on all levels of experience. The unspoken barrier that had separated those high, unearthly things with which Christ, as God, had always been associated – spiritual salvation and the afterlife – from the humdrum, earthbound cares of the average Christian, was lifted. It was possible to call on the name of Jesus in all situations, knowing that He had known them all, and that His power was available, as it had once been, to overcome them all. In the words of Shenoute of Atripe (385–466), the great abbot of the White Monastery, at Sohag in middle Egypt:

> Try to attain to the full measure of this Name, and you will find it on your mouth and on the mouth of your children. When you make high festival and when you rejoice, cry Jesus. When anxious and in pain, cry Jesus. When little boys and girls are laughing, let them cry Jesus. And those who flee before barbarians, cry Jesus. And those who go down to the Nile, cry Jesus . . . And those whose trial has been corrupted and who receive injustice, let them cry the Name of Jesus.[26]

Backed by such passions, it is not surprising that the great patriarchs of Alexandria acted with such high-handed confidence. But nor is it surprising that each side feared the worst in its opponents. For this worst was nothing less than the fear that God and man would drift apart again, separated by the unbridgeable spaces implied in the ancient model of the universe.

For Nestorius, who was patriarch of Constantinople from 428 to 431, the Alexandrian solution was repugnant. It brought God so close to humanity as to implicate an all-powerful and deathless being in the dishonor of suffering. Christ, rather, must be thought of as a man who became progressively linked to God, by a bond of the same quality, though of infinitely greater intensity and permanence, as that which had linked God to any other of His prophets. God's power and majesty were not affected by the crucifixion of Christ: for it was His chosen human Son and servant, not God Himself, who had suffered on the Cross.

When his views were condemned at the Council of Ephesus, Nestorius observed bitterly that the ignorant populace of Constantinople danced around bonfires, chanting, "God has been crucified. God is dead." A God thought, in this manner, to be exposed to weakness would prove to be weak the next time His misguided worshippers turned to Him in distress. It came as no surprise to Nestorius that, a few years later, the Huns flooded into Thrace, looting up to the walls of Constantinople.[27]

For the Alexandrians, it was a very different matter. It was vital for them that the Incarnation had made of God and man a single, indissoluble whole – a single "nature." For this reason, the intransigent followers of the theology of Cyril came to be known as Monophysites (from *monos*, single, and *physis*, nature). It was not a title they would have accepted. What counted for them was a more urgent matter. To speak of God as having been, indeed, crucified, in the person of Jesus, was to remind Him of the shared suffering that bound Him indissolubly, almost organically, to the human race. He could not forget those with whom He had once shared the universal taste of death. When earthquakes struck northern Syria in the 470s, the patriarch of Antioch added to the current form of the litany, "Holy Powerful One, Holy Deathless One," the *risqué* phrase, "Who was Crucified for us." It was a gloriously contentious addition. Attached to a chanted, public prayer, it involved Christians of all classes. In the main courtyard of the Great Church of Antioch, sympathetic crowds gathered round a street-artist who had trained his parrot to squawk the litany, with the all-important "Crucified for us" at its end.[28] In a time of affliction, no matter how cruelly distant God might seem to be, Monophysites believed that He could be summoned by these words, that spoke to Him of His own sufferings as a human being.

The cult of the Virgin Mary as *Theotokos*, as "she who gave birth to God" – a formula adopted by the Council of Ephesus so as to exclude the views of Nestorius – throve in an atmosphere that demanded one thing of God: that His relations with mankind should rest not on a mere partnership with mankind but on the tender, wordless kinship of shared flesh. "The bond of the womb" was the strongest tie of all between human beings. Pleas for mercy to the powerful, at this time, stressed the fact that even the most miserable and undeserving east Roman was a fellow human being, some mother's son, cradled in a human womb and suckled at human breasts. As a result, Mary came to be shown, in the art of the late fifth and sixth centuries, as holding Christ enthroned on her lap, as if He were still tied to her womb. Christ was spoken of, in hymns sung by whole congregations, as drawing His human flesh from sucking the breasts of Mary. For a mother's milk, to ancient persons, was interchangeable with her blood: it was liquid flesh, transferred to the child by suckling. Christ must listen to those who prayed to His mother; for it was she who had rendered Him fully human. Only she could remind Him, with the authority of a mother, of what He shared with the afflicted human flesh of those who turned to Him in distress.

These issues came to divide the Christians of the east in a manner that no emperor could hope to solve. But it was not for lack of trying. The Council of Chalcedon was summoned by the emperor Marcian in 451. It was the greatest council ever assembled. Over 600 bishops met at Kadiköy, just across the water from Constantinople. The emperor was taking no chances. But, unlike his predecessor, Theodosius II, Marcian was a newly installed, military man. Like most weak monarchs, he needed to show, as soon as possible, that he was powerful. He did not wait for a consensus to emerge. He opted heavily for a careful statement drawn up by Leo – the famous *Tome* presented by the pope's representatives. Later legend (circulated in Constantinople by none other than pope Gregory the Great) liked to believe that Leo had placed his *Tome* upon the tomb of Saint Peter himself, to have it proof-read by the saint. To Latin theologians, it was a perfect statement of the faith. This was not what the Egyptian followers of Cyril of Alexandria thought. To them, Leo's careful balancing of the divine and the human in the person of Christ seemed to lead straight back to Nestorius. It threatened to open, once again, a crevasse between the divine and the human. The opponents of Leo insisted that divine and human had been joined in Christ in a manner that transfused the human person of Christ with the divine, to such an extent that even the touch of His fingers was sufficient to bring healing to the sick. In Egypt, in much of Syria and for many thinking persons elsewhere, the council of Chalcedon, summoned so as to be the council to end all councils, came to be known as "The Great Prevarication."

In the west, however, much of this would soon become irrelevant. The Christological controversies were fought out most fiercely within the territories of the eastern empire. Soon a Roman empire no longer existed in the west. In 476, Romulus Augustulus was pushed aside, and barbarian kings became the rulers of Italy. It was not until 536, in very different circumstances, that the troops of the east Roman emperor Justinian entered Rome, making it once again an "imperial" city. By that time, however, the Roman empire had become little more than a memory along the frontiers of the west. It is to the rapid changes in that crucial frontier-zone, that lay at many weeks' journey to the north of Marseilles and Rome, that we must now turn.

5

On the Frontiers: Noricum, Ireland and Francia

Throughout western Europe, in the fifth century, the military frontier of the Roman empire came to an end. Along the Danube, in Noricum (western Austria) the life of a holy man, Severinus, provides a series of vivid close-ups of this process:

> At the time when the Roman empire was still in existence, the soldiers of many towns were supported by public money to guard the frontier. When this arrangement ceased, the military formations were dissolved and the frontier vanished. The garrison of Passau, however, still held out. Some of the men had gone to Italy to fetch for their comrades their last payment. But nobody knew that they were killed by barbarians on the way. One day, when saint Severinus was reading in his cell, he suddenly closed the book and began to sigh . . . The river [he said] was now red with human blood. And at that moment, the news arrived that the bodies of the soldiers had been washed ashore by the current.[1]

Severinus was a saint of the open frontier. A mysterious stranger, he came to Noricum as a hermit in around AD 454. Some thought he was a fugitive slave; but he spoke the good

Latin of an upper-class *Romanus*. Until his death, in 482, he moved along the Danube, from one small walled town to another, preaching collective penance, organizing tithes for the relief of the poor, denouncing grain-hoarders in times of shortage.

Along the Danube, city-walls defined the *Romanus*. These were small towns, with small Christian congregations. The church at Lorch, for instance, held some 200 worshippers – it was a fifth, only, of the size of a Gallic cathedral. For the townspeople, the Roman empire was already a distant affair. The empire whose fall had truly altered their lives was the fall of the empire of Attila. For Hunnish power had controlled the tribes north of the Danube. The disintegration of Hunnish domination north of the Danube left small barbarian tribes free to infiltrate the "Roman" territories on its southern banks.

The relations of the *Romani* to the new groups from across the Danube were ambivalent. Much as the mountain chieftains of nineteenth-century eastern Anatolia were said (in an unceremonious but apposite phrase) to "eat" the villages of the plain, so tribes – such as the Rugi, in the region around Lorch – settled down to "eat" the Roman cities. They had no wish to destroy them. Instead, they offered the inhabitants high-handed and unpredictable protection in exchange for tribute and occasional levies of skilled manpower. The city-dwellers were "their" Romans. At least no other, rival tribe would "eat" them.

Severinus was remembered for the manner in which he ensured that this rough compact was observed. He moved with authority among competing kings. Gibuldus of the Alemanni quailed before him:

> the king declared to his armed men that never before, either in battle or in any peril, had he been shaken with such violent trembling.[2]

The uncanny hermit was held to control their fortunes. He predicted the rise to power of one local warrior, Odoacer; he would eventually, as a general, oust the last emperor, Romulus Augustulus, and so come to rule Italy from 476 to 493:

at the time [Odoacer] was a young man, tall and clad in poor clothes. He stooped for fear of hitting the roof of [Severinus'] cell . . . "Go to Italy [the saint said]. Go, now covered with mean hides; soon you will make rich gifts to many."[3]

On the frontier, religious boundaries that meant so much for the civilian populations of the Mediterranean counted for little: Severinus extended his blessing to all tribal leaders, Catholic, Arian or pagan. What mattered more was security. Always short of manpower, and particularly of skilled craftsmen, the barbarians across the frontier absorbed *Romani* at an alarming rate. Slave-raiding was a grim feature of life on the frontiers. To use *Romani* that one "ate," by selling them as slaves or relocating them among the wood-villages of Moravia, was the most heinous breach of all in the tacit compact between the Danubian townsfolk and their protectors. Queen Giso of the Rugians did just that. She was swiftly punished. Her son, Friderichus, wandered by mistake into the blockhouse in which skilled foreign slaves were kept, set to work producing royal jewelry. They seized him and held him as hostage for their own release.[4]

It is a grim glimpse of the human cost, for many, of the brittle new societies that came into being once the "Roman" and the "barbarian" sides of a frontier region "imploded," as it were, to form new cultural and social units. In the case of the *Life of Severinus*, it was a glimpse from a safe distance. His biography was written in 511, by Eugippius, a refugee from Noricum who had become the abbot of a monastery that overlooked the Bay of Naples. A distinguished neighbor and patron of the monastery was none other than the former emperor, Romulus Augustulus, who was now living on a comfortable pension in a villa that still bore the name of its former owner, Lucullus, the famous Roman gourmet of the time of Augustus! A story of the end of Roman urban life on the distant Danube merely served to heighten the sense of security that still reigned in Italy.

In fact, only the upper classes of the cities had emigrated to Italy. The Christian graves of humble *Romani* continued, for centuries, to cluster around Severinus' church at Lorch. Their Christianity, largely deprived of clerical leadership, became a folk religion – to such an extent that memories of distinctive Early Christian, late Roman practices, such as public penance, survived into modern times in the folk songs of Slovenia. In the Alpine hinterland of Noricum, away from the dangerous banks of the Danube, large basilicas, modelled on the churches of northern Italy, flanked by hospices and pilgrimage-shrines containing exotic relics, continued to be built long after the death of Severinus. On the Hemmaberg, that rose above the river Sava (in Kärnten), the narrow plateau was covered with no fewer than five large churches. It was a thriving pilgrimage center similar to the many others that stretched right across the Christian world of the late fifth century, from Saint Albans in Britain, through Saint Martin's at Tours, to the new sanctuaries of Symeon Stylites, in northern Syria, and that of Saint Menas in Egypt. Romans and barbarians, even, one suspects, Catholics and Arians, came together at such a center, to visit relics placed above ancient healing springs.[5]

What happened in Noricum happened also in Britain. The withdrawal of the Roman armies, after 406, left a power vacuum on the island. An entire governmental elite vanished. The buried treasures that lie in such numbers beneath the soil of East Anglia speak of the sudden loss of an imperial order. In one such hoard, recently discovered at Hoxne, 14,600 gold and silver coins had been stowed away in wooden chests. The tableware alone included 78 silver spoons. A woman's golden body-necklace weighed 250 grams. A collection of heavy armbands, of the cosmopolitan "barbarian" workmanship sported by Roman officers all over the empire, indicates the hasty departure of a *vir militaris* of the old style.[6]

Yet, in a province with twenty-eight walled cities, "castellated towers and gatehouses . . . reared menacingly skyward," the surviving elites of Britain felt that they could look after themselves, without an empire to protect them.[7] But things did not happen as in Gaul. The settlement of Saxon pirates as billeted "guests," in the traditional late Roman manner, proved a failure. Small Saxon bands settled permanently, and with no governmental control, where the English Channel met the North Sea. These Saxons participated, along with other soldiers of fortune (such as the Irish chieftain, Cunorix MacCullen, who was buried, with an Ogham commemorative stone, at Wroxeter, near the Severn), in the civil wars in which local leaders of Roman background fought each other for control of the island. But it was not until the 570s that Saxon kings entered as conquerors the walled cities of western Britain. They were impressed by what they saw:

> Wondrously ornate is the stone of this wall, now shattered by fate. The precincts of the city have crumbled. The work of giants has rotted away . . . There were bright city buildings, many bathhouses, a wealth of lofty gables.[8]

Only at that time (and not in the 440s) did the Saxons weave for themselves a more flattering narrative to justify their unexpected rise to dominance. They now claimed to be the lineal descendants of heroic shiploads whose leaders had sailed direct from the North Sea coast of Jutland to seek, in Britain, their Promised Land.

As far as we know, no Severinus intervened as the Saxons settled down to "eat" the Romano-British cities of the Midlands. Christianity was that much less securely established in Britain. Large Celtic hill-shrines, dating from prehistoric times, dwarfed the small churches of the cities. Nor did the Christian clergy play the "representative" role that it took up, so rapidly, in Gaul. Many British bishops were suspected of Pelagianism. "Old Christians" in a largely pagan province, they may well have resembled the first supporters of Pelagius at Rome: they saw themselves as a self-chosen group of "saints," proud to remain a morally superior minority in a pagan land.

Power, in Britain, fell, by default, into the hands of men of war. "Tyrants," successful local chieftains, and not bishops, as in Gaul, dominate the history of fifth-century Britain. Many of these came from the under-Romanized, highland zone of northwest Wales and northern Britain. Their ancestors might have borne Roman names such as Tacitus; but they now spoke of themselves in Welsh. In the Y *Gododdin* of Aneirin, the sub-Roman princes of the north appear, by AD 600, as epic heroes, in a long Celtic tradition. It is the chieftain's mead, "yellow, sweet, ensnaring," and not the solemn oath of the professional soldier to his emperor, that now sent young men to their deaths, among "the war horses and the blood-stained armor."[9]

Yet the British princes still held court, if now in timber halls, within the framework of the stone forts on Hadrian's Wall. They celebrated their power by lavish gift-giving on the *Ddyw Calan Ionawr*, the high, imperial day of the Kalends of January, denounced, throughout the Roman world, by Christian bishops. They thought of themselves as Christians. They gave "gold to the altar" before each campaign, as well as "gifts to the bard." If they perjured themselves, they did it on Christian altars; just as, when they murdered their kinsmen, they did so in the sanctuary of Christian monasteries. West of the Severn, at least, these hard men defended what had remained a recognizably "Roman" provincial landscape: estates were organized around Roman villas, documents were drawn up in Roman form, and the small cities maintained their Roman walls.

Not surprisingly, they were not greatly concerned that the Saxons should have remained pagans. Despite the wide vision of a man such as Augustine, most old-fashioned *Romani* still felt that Christianity was too precious a thing to waste on mere barbarians. Saxons could be expected to continue their unsavory pagan ways – much as the Christian Visigoths of Gaul were not expected to be other than Arian heretics. Only when the nature of the frontier itself changed would a common Christianity emerge, of a sort that would embrace Romans and barbarians alike.

Hence the most significant development of all took place on the northwestern frontier of Britain. Hadrian's Wall ceased to be an effective boundary. The northern and western parts of Britain and the hitherto utterly non-Roman eastern coast of Ireland came together, once the barrier of Roman control was removed, to form a single "Celtic Mediterranean" of the north. The settlements of the Dalriada Irish (the *Scotti*, the "freebooters," of our texts) linked Ulster with Galloway and the coast of Scotland as far north as the Isle of Skye, in an Irish hegemony maintained by fleets of seven-benched row-boats. Wales and the estuary of the Boyne faced each other: Irish kings took British wives, and new coins of the most Christian emperor, Theodosius I, appear as votive offerings in the Irish center of New Grange. On the western tip of Cornwall, Tintagel became a fortress city, heavily supplied with wine, oil and lamps from Africa, even from Egypt. Ogham stones, signs of extensive Irish settlement, appeared throughout southwestern Wales. Latin terms of trade and military status, borrowed from the sub-Roman society of western Britain, now seeped into Old Irish.

Not all aspects of this discreet flow of persons and ideas were peaceful. Sometime in the 420s, Irish raiders fell on an unknown city of northern Britain. A well-to-do sixteen-year-old, Patricius, the son of a deacon, from a family of town councillors, was among the captives. He served as a slave on the Atlantic coast of County Mayo. Yet Patricius emerged from this experience as very much the Severinus of the north. In his exile, he turned to an ascetic brand of Christianity to which he had given no thought when a young man from a clerical family in Britain:

> My faith grew and my spirit was stirred, and as a result I would say up to one hundred prayers in one day and almost as many by night . . . and I would wake to pray before dawn in all weathers, snow, frost and rain; and I felt no harm . . . as I now realize, it was because the Spirit was fervent within me.[10]

Patricius escaped from slavery, returned to Britain and, once ordained, decided to go back to Ireland. It was a hotly contested step for a British bishop to take. Patricius did not enjoy the support of a unified "Roman" community, as Severinus and the bishops of Gaul had done. Yet his career in Ireland was dominated by the same concerns as theirs – above all, by the terrible movement of persons connected with the slave trade. When Coroticus, a British war-lord, raided a Christian community in Ireland, the letters sent by Patricius, asking for the return of all baptized Christians, were rejected: Coroticus and his warriors "roared with laughter at them." To Coroticus, Irish "barbarians," whether baptized or not,

could never hope to count as "fellow citizens of Romans."[11]
Patricius was disowned by his British colleagues as a charismatic maverick. He was accused of having made a profit from
his mission – collecting, for his own purposes, the splendid
jewelry that high-born Irish women piled, as votive offerings,
on his altar.

Patricius' *Letter to Coroticus* and his subsequent *Confession*
are so well known, as coming from the pen of Saint Patrick,
the patron saint of all Ireland, that we forget what remarkable
documents they were. They are the first, extensive pieces of
Latin to survive that were written from outside the frontiers
of the Roman world. Their tone is startlingly universalist.
Patricius took on the full *persona* of Saint Paul. He was a
Spirit-filled man; "a stone, lying deep in the mud," God had
set him on high for one purpose only:

> Look, we are witnesses that the Gospel has been preached
> to the point beyond which there is no one.

Summoned by his colleagues to Britain, he would stay among
the Irish,

> to serve a people just now coming to the faith and which
> the Lord has chosen from the ends of the earth.[12]

Patricius was an older contemporary of Severinus, in faraway Noricum. He also was a saint of the open frontier. His
letters show him as an old man, on the defensive. When he
died, perhaps around 490, it was far from certain that his
mission would survive. What made the Christian communities
in Ireland permanent was the quickening pace of exchanges
around the "Celtic Mediterranean." Yet, despite their eventual
success, the Christian churches along the east coast of Ireland,
in Antrim, County Down, Kildare and Munster, remained
unusual. For the first time in centuries, Christianity was, once
again, a minority religion. It had few of the grandiose ambitions and collective intolerances that characterized the post-
Constantinian Christian empire and that continued to characterize the large urban centers of Gaul and Italy. It tended to
spread family by family, *túath* by *túath* – small tribe by small
tribe. Christians, therefore, had to fit into a society made up

of tightly interlocking, but separate, groups, many of whom remained pagan.

The religion of some families, but not of others, the Christian churches enjoyed an almost total absence of persecution. Christians were considerably less concerned with how they might Christianize their neighbors than with how to preserve their own identity. An early synod, the so-called *First Synod of Saint Patrick*, forbade Christian clergymen to act as guarantors for pagans. Christians were not to swear oaths before a druid. The kilt, also, and the heroic, flowing hair of a chieftain were deemed unsuitable in a bishop:

> Any cleric . . . who is seen without a long tunic and does not cover his private parts [was condemned, as were those] whose hair is not cut short as a "Roman" should.[13]

As a result, the great narratives of the expansion of Christianity around the Roman Mediterranean meant little in this northern land: no violent persecution by the heathen, no dramatic exorcisms, no conversions of great rulers, no spectacular destructions of pagan temples. Instead, with a few exceptions, later Irish legends of Saint Patrick lingered by preference on problems that were dear to the heart of a resolutely non-Roman society. His mission had to be explained in other terms. What reserve of "natural goodness" must have led the first householder in a given region to offer hospitality to Patrick, a total stranger, with no previous claims upon him? How was it that, in exchange for no more than a few Latin words, written on pages of white parchment, this stranger had charmed from so many hard-fisted chieftains so much solid wealth – land, gold, cattle, even their own daughters, as nuns given to Christ? In a society held together by gift-giving, this was the ultimate feat of the trickster. Hardly surprisingly, the legends that concerned Patrick's imagined progress through Ireland gravitated, insensibly, over time, towards identification with the great annual festival of the *Lughnasa*. For at the *Lughnasa*, Lugh, the archetypal trickster god of Celtic mythology, had, like Patrick, tricked out of grim winter, in return for mere words, the solid riches of the next year's harvest.[14]

We only know of Patricius' mission from his own writings. No one mentioned Patricius at the time. This was not the case with the formation, in northern Gaul and along the Rhine, of a new-style kingdom of the Franks – soon known by the all-embracing term of *Francia* – in the reign of king Clovis (481–511).

After the 460s, northern Gaul resembled Britain. It was a land without empire. Its leading inhabitants had begun to accept this fact. This is shown, even, by their burial customs. *Romani* and barbarians alike, whether Christian or pagan, came to be buried bearing arms. For weapons, fine brooches and heavy belts, the former insignia of the *viri militares*, were what now distinguished any leader of local society.

In this increasingly militarized world, the Franks were not newcomers. Many had served in the high command of the imperial armies of the fourth century. One such Frank, Bauto, became consul in 385 and received a panegyric on that occasion, in Milan, from none other than the young Augustine. He took care to have his daughter brought up at Constantinople, in the palace of a Roman fellow-general. She married the emperor Arcadius: thus, their son, Theodosius II, was at least one-quarter Frankish! Franks such as Bauto were already honorary Romans. They were said to be descended, like the Romans, from the Trojans. Priam had been their first king. They had only recently – so Franks close to the Rhine frontier tended to believe – come to Germany from ancient Troy!

Not every Frank was like Bauto. The Franks who were led by king Childeric, in the 470s, were wilder men. Childeric drew his family origins from the back country – from as far east as Thuringia and Weimar. He was a Merovingian, a descendent of Merovech, which meant "Sea Warrior." Merovech had been conceived when the first Frankish queen had coupled with a sea monster while swimming in the North Sea, the legendary home of heroes. Childeric's own career as a war-lord in northern Gaul is obscure. But, when he died in 481, the burial that he received at Tournai left a studiously composite image of his power. Discovered in 1653, Childeric's grave is the most splendid barbarian burial yet known in Europe. But it was also, in part, Roman. It lay near a Christian basilica, outside a

Roman city. Childeric carried a Roman official signet ring, with which to seal his documents. It bore his portrait. The magical long hair of a Merovingian "long-haired king" fell over the folds of the robe of a Roman official. Only in 1983 was a further trench discovered, filled with horse skeletons. Lavish horse-sacrifice had taken place at the funeral of Childeric the Frank.

Childeric's son, Clovis – Hlodovech, "Pillaging warrior" – inherited the many strands of his father's authority in Gaul. He was a pagan; yet he received a letter from Remigius the Catholic bishop of Rheims: "May justice proceed from your mouth." From the very beginning, Clovis wished to be king of the Franks in a new, more forceful style. When Soissons fell, in 486, and the Franks divided the booty, Clovis wished to please the Catholic bishop by setting aside the sacred vessels plundered from Christian churches. One such item was a precious ewer, probably used to pour wine into the Eucharistic chalice. The manner in which booty was usually divided can be seen in the many exhibits, in modern museums, of what is now known as "hack-silver" – exquisite late Roman silverware summarily chopped into equal squares, as a warband drew its dividends at the end of a raid. Such careful hacking implied a strictly egalitarian code, appropriate to violent young men. Not surprisingly, a warrior objected to Clovis' high-handed suggestion that he reduce the pool of precious metals available to his companions, by setting aside Christian plate:

> [he] raised his battle-axe and struck the ewer: "You shall have none of the booty," he said, "except your fair share."

A little later, Clovis made the man stoop, on parade, to pick up his axe:

> King Clovis raised his own battle-axe in the air and split his skull with it. "This is what you did to my ewer at Soissons." [15]

It was a sharp lesson in the new prerogatives of royalty.

At the same time, Clovis may have issued, in Latin, a law-code for his Franks. The *Lex Salica*, the *Laws of the Salian*

Franks, took the paganism of the Frankish inhabitants of the Rhine estuary for granted. It protected with special penalties the great gelded boars – bristling, magical guarantors of the wild, waving growth of golden cornfields – that were set apart for sacrificial banquets. The law was particularly concerned to regulate the legal status of humble Frankish farmers, over against the neighboring *Romani*. As *Franci*, from *Frekkr*, "the fierce ones," weapon-bearing Franks, even the poorest, could stand high in Gaul. But they were told so in a Latin text, from a king who used Latin advisers and intended to rule Romans and Franks alike as firmly as had any *Romanus*.[16]

By the end of his life, in 511, Clovis had altered the entire nature of Frankish kingship. He eliminated a confederation of Frankish "royal" chieftains, and ensured that the kingship was held by his own, Merovingian family alone. Later generations of Franks relished the violence and cunning that went with every move of Clovis' rise to dominance. To take one example: Clovis bought out the war-band of Ragnachar of Cambrai with arm-bands of fake gold:

> This is the sort of gold [he replied, when they discovered the trick] which a man can expect when he has lured his lord to his death.

In old age, he wished to finish the job:

> he is said to have made the following remark about the relatives he had destroyed. "How sad a thing it is that I live as a stranger like some solitary pilgrim, and that I have none of my own relatives left to help me when disaster threatens." He said this, not because he grieved for their deaths, but because in his cunning way he hoped to find some relatives still alive whom he could kill.[17]

Forceful kingship on such a scale may well have required some change, or some novel elaboration, of cult to mark its inauguration. The tradition initiated by Constantine would have been totally intelligible to any Germanic warrior: decisive battles, preferably with hereditary enemies, were expected to be associated with a show of divine power. Yet Clovis moved slowly. He took a Christian wife from the Burgundians, in around 490 – queen Chlothilde. Yet he did not take the obvious further step. He did not join the "family of princes," formed by the barbarian rulers of the western Mediterranean. For them, Arian Christianity was the truly universal religion. It linked the Visigoths of Toulouse, the Vandals of Carthage and the Ostrogoths, now firmly established under Theodoric, at Ravenna, in a single faith, different from that of their Catholic subjects.

Clovis may have sensed that he could hold out for yet more undivided loyalty on the part of his *Romani*. The continued, tacit segregation of "barbarians" from the Catholic civilian population, as *ex officio* Arians and military men, echoed the highly compartmented structures of the late Roman state. These structures had survived in the more settled Mediterranean provinces; but they were out of date in a northern Gaul where the distinction between soldier and civilian had been eroded. There was no reason why all the inhabitants of a region should not share the same religion, and, even less, why a ruler should be excluded from the faith of his subjects.

Troubled by the rise of an incalculable new power in northern Gaul, the Arian Visigoths were prepared to do everything, barring an official conversion to Catholicism, to enlist the whole-hearted loyalty of their own Catholic subjects. In 506, the Visigothic king, Alaric II, issued an abbreviation of the *Theodosian Code* – the *Breviarium Alaricianum*. It bore his own name. It was ratified by Roman provincial aristocrats and by Catholic bishops. In the same year, he summoned the Catholic bishops to Agde, for the first kingdom-wide council of the Catholic Church ever to be held in Gaul. The bishops were delighted:

> and then, with our knees bent to the ground, we prayed for the kingdom [of Alaric] . . . so that the Lord might expand the realm of him who had permitted us the opportunity to meet.[18]

For Clovis, it was now or never. Such loyalty from Catholic bishops, if once consolidated within the Visigothic kingdom, would have blocked forever the road to the south. A previous victory over the pagan Alemanni had already convinced Clovis of the power of Christ. At some time before 500, he may have declared himself a Christian – and a Catholic Christian at that. He was baptized with his entire army by Remigius, Catholic bishop of Rheims. A force of up to 3,000 men, these soldiers were the effective "people of the Franks." Many of them may have been renegade Romans. They had wider horizons than did the boar-sacrificing peasants of their northern homeland. They were easily persuaded to follow their king. It was a memorable occasion:

> The public squares were draped with colored cloths, the church was adorned with white hangings, the baptistery was prepared, incense gave off clouds of perfume, sweet-smelling candelabra gleamed bright, and the holy place was filled with divine fragrances . . . [all those present] imagined themselves transported to some perfumed paradise.[19]

But that had been a local affair. Now was the time to turn south against Alaric II. In 507, Clovis deliberately sought an oracle from Saint Martin at Tours, and did so as a Catholic king:

> He loaded [his messengers] with gifts to offer to the church . . . "Lord God," said he, "if you are on my side . . . deign to show me a propitious sign as these men enter the church, so that I may know that you will support your servant Clovis." . . . As they entered the church, it happened that the chanter was just beginning to intone the antiphon: *For thou hast girded me with strength unto battle; thou hast subdued under me those who rose up against me* [Psalm 18:39].[20]

It was blessing enough for the coming war. Clovis' campaign only became an anti-Arian crusade in retrospect. It was a show of force, ostensibly to collect arrears in tribute, in fact, to test the loyalty of the southern *Romani*. Far from welcoming the Franks, the Catholic nobility of the Auvergne, including the sons of Sidonius Apollinaris, turned out in force to support the Arian Visigoths against these fierce interlopers from the north. A whole southern society, Catholics and Arians alike – along with their king, Alaric II – died together, at the fateful battle at Vouillé (or, possibly, at Voulon), south of Poitiers, in the early summer of 507.

Clovis knew how to celebrate his triumph in a suitably Roman and Catholic style. He brought part of the spoils to the altar of Saint Martin at Tours. There he was met by ambassadors from the eastern emperor, Anastasius, who saw in this northern upstart a counterweight to the new barbarian rulers of Italy. He sent to Clovis scrolls of appointment as an honorary consul. Like the great imperial generals of an earlier age, Clovis rode on horseback from the basilica into the city, scattering gold coins. Some even remembered that he had been acclaimed as an "Augustus."[21]

Though the best known to western historians, the Frankish kingdom was not the only Christian state to emerge along the edges of the Roman world in this period. Far to the south, in what is now Morocco and western Algeria, Moorish chieftains of the High Atlas absorbed the Roman cities of the plains. They emerged as common "kings of the Moorish and Roman peoples." The symbiosis of Berber warrior highlanders with Latin-speaking townsfolk ended only with the arrival of Islam. A Roman-style town council, recorded in Latin inscriptions, survived at Volubilis, near the Atlantic coast of Morocco, up to the 650s. Moorish kings adopted Latin names. The Berber ruler who held the Arab armies at bay in the late seventh century bore the name Caecilius, a common Latin name in Africa, once borne by none other than Saint Cyprian! Through their influence, knowledge of Christianity penetrated the oases of the deep Sahara, so that, in the Touareg language, the word for any sacrifice, *tafaske*, was derived from the Christian high festival of Pascha/Easter.[22]

At the southern end of the Red Sea, also, where the trade of the entire Indian Ocean came within easy reach of Alexandria, the warrior-kingdom of Axum straddled the straits, joining the highlands of northern Ethiopia (a formidable reservoir of warlike tribes) to the Yemen, in southern Arabia. This remarkable forerunner of the later Christian kingdom of Ethiopia had long identified Christianity with strong kingship. Since the reigns of Constantine and Constantius II, the solid coins of Axum, minted from local gold, bore the sign of the Cross. Whatever the religion of the majority of the population, Christianity was very much the religion of a court of conquering overlords, whose campaigns, ranging as they did from Aden to the Blue Nile, were as vigorous as any undertaken by Clovis. They were celebrated on inscriptions associated with stupendous granite *stelae*, higher than any Egyptian obelisks, and with memorial thrones, set up in the mountain redoubt of Axum, at a distance from the Red Sea coast. Ella Atsbeha (*ca.*519–*ca.*531) was a younger contemporary of Clovis. His inscriptions, and those of his successors, echo the same warlike verses of the Psalms as were heard by the messengers of Clovis when they first entered the basilica of Saint Martin at Tours:

> The Lord strong and brave, the Lord mighty in battle ... in Whom I believe, who has given me a strong kingdom ... I trust myself to Christ so that all my enterprises may succeed.[23]

What is remarkable about these Christian kingdoms of the periphery is that, despite extensive borrowings from local Roman practice and occasional diplomatic relations with the court of Constantinople, they did not wish to see themselves exclusively as miniature Romes. Because they were Christian, they could belong, also, to a non-Roman past – to the Old Testament. The *Kebra Nagast*, "The Glory of the Kings" (the foundation-legend of the medieval empire of Ethiopia, whose nucleus may go back to the age of Ella Atsbeha), treated the Byzantine emperors as no more than accommodating, northern partners of an Ethiopian imperial dynasty, that claimed to be descended from Menelik, the son of Solomon and the queen of Sheba.[24] Gregory of Tours' account of Clovis advanced no such claims for the Franks. But when Gregory wrote his *Book of History*, in the 580s – a full seventy years, that is, after the events he described – it is surprising how little attention he paid to Clovis' relations with the east Roman emperors. Instead, he placed great emphasis on Clovis' supposed hatred of Arian heretics, and he recorded, without a hint of moral condemnation, the king's unsavory rise to power among the

Franks. For Gregory, the Catholic bishop, it was a career worthy of the morally flawed energies of king David. It was better to be remembered as resembling a king of the long-past ancient Israel than as having once been an ally of the still-existing east Roman empire.

When, in 520 or later, the British cleric, Gildas, wrote the only surviving description of his war-torn island, his *On the Ruin of Britain*, Rome, again, is peripheral to his story. He sees the Britons as an erring people of Israel, and himself as their Jeremiah, threatening divine punishment for their sins at the hands of foreign nations, especially the Saxons. As a sinning Israel, Britain now had a history of its own. The Romans, for Gildas, were no more than the "worthy allies" of the ever-fickle Britons. They were admirable and orderly, but, essentially, foreigners. Gildas identified them almost exclusively with their army. They were now gone forever, leaving mighty walls across the island as a testimony to their military genius.[25] Though he wrote in Latin and had lived in the recognizably sub-Roman world of western Britain, Gildas, as a Christian writer, evidently felt that the Old Testament did better justice to his stormy times than did fading memories of a Roman empire. From Hadrian's Wall to the Atlantic coast of Morocco and the Horn of Africa, the idea of Rome had shrunk to ever smaller dimensions, to be replaced by a different past – a past brought close through Holy Scriptures that described, so vividly and so appositely, the turbulent warrior-kingdom of ancient Israel.

Part II

Divergent Legacies
AD 500–750

6

Reverentia, Rusticitas: Caesarius of Arles to Gregory of Tours

On February 15, 495, despite previous warning from the pope, Gelasius, a group of Roman Senators initiated, once again, the annual purifying ceremony of the *Lupercalia*. Naked youths dashed through Rome, as they had done since archaic times. The senators concerned were public figures and good "sons of the Church." But they also knew what Rome needed after an anxious year of epidemics and bad harvests: in their rowdy run-around, the "Young Wolves" cleansed the city once again in preparation for another year.[1] In the city with the longest Christian tradition in the Latin west, collective memory still looked past the great basilica-shrine of Saint Peter to the world of Romulus and Remus. A sense of the vast antiquity of Rome was matched by a sense of the proximity of a numinously radiant universe. On reaching the top of the flight of steps that led up to the courtyard of Saint Peter's, many Catholic Christians would still turn their backs to the saint's basilica, to bow, with a reverential gesture, to the rising sun.[2]

All around the Mediterranean, the Christian Church had emerged, by AD 500, as the sole public religion of the Roman world. We know of the successes that led to that situation from abundant, and largely celebratory, Christian sources. What we can only glimpse, out of the corner of our eye, as it were, is the muted landscape that stretched far beyond our Christian evidence. For Christianity had remained very much a religion of the Roman towns. In a poem of around AD 400, Gallic peasants could still be presented as speaking of the sign of the Cross as if it was to be found only "in great cities." Even at a later time, the first concern of most bishops was to build up an imposing Catholic order in their own cities. By 573, the bishops of Tours had built twenty-four churches in the villages of their diocese; but thirteen churches had sprung up in Tours itself in the same period. The countryside was no religious desert. Great landowners built churches for themselves and their peasants. Even the serfs on royal estates in Spain pooled their meager resources to house an altar and to pay a priest. But the countryside remained the Cinderella in a recognizably "Roman" Christian order that still looked to the bishop and his city as the center of "high density" Catholicism.

Even if the countryside had been less isolated, the problem would have remained: having driven the demons from their temples in and around the cities, Christians of the late fifth and sixth centuries now had to face the problems posed by the diffused sacrality which all ancient persons, townsfolk quite as much as peasants, tended to see all around them in the natural world. The natural world absorbed the energies of over 90 percent of the inhabitants in any Christian region, as farmers and as pastoralists, who depended every year on the erratic fortunes of the weather and the harvest. Far from being a neutral space, the world of nature was thought to be shot through with supernatural energies. It was not enough to have placed a single, exclusive God at the head of the *mundus,* nor even to have brought that God down to its lowest level, to move among human beings in the person of Jesus Christ. Christianity had to make sense to populations who had always thought of themselves as embedded in the natural world, and as being able to impinge upon that world, to elicit its generosity and to ward off its perils, by means of rites that reached back, in most parts of Europe, to prehistoric times.

We should not under-estimate the sheer range and complexity of the pre-existent sacred landscape against which the

Christian churches came to perch in western Europe. From Roman Britain to southern Italy, deserted temples with their time-worn idols stood out as foreboding, uncanny presences: "stark as ever . . . outlines still ugly, faces still grim."[3] Nor were these shrines always inactive. As late as the 690s, in parts of Spain, votive offerings made to idols had to be publicly transferred to the local churches. They were put on show, to persuade the population that idolatry was finally at an end (three centuries after the laws of Theodosius I!) and that only the altar-spaces of Christian churches, and not trees, springs, cross-roads and hill-tops, should be marked by little piles of *ex votos*.[4]

In Gaul holiness still oozed from the earth, in the form of 6,000 holy springs. In Egypt, the spectacular rise of the Christian Church at the expense of the temples merely blocked the view of the humble, day-to-day relation between man and the sacred along the valley of the Nile. When a crow alighted on a wall beside a Christian layman, who had come to consult Shenoute of Atripe, the layman instinctively turned to greet the bird, whose prophetic, cawing song was held to speak about the secrets of the invisible world quite as clearly as did the words of the great abbot.[5] To Shenoute, the prospect seemed endless:

> Even if I take away all your household idols, am I able to cover up the sun? Should I build walls all along the west [the Egyptian *Amente*, the land of the gods and the dead], so that you do not pray towards the sunset? Shall I stand watch on the banks of the Nile, and in every lagoon, lest you make libations on its waters?[6]

Different Christian regions faced the situation in very different ways. The Christians of the Greek east tended to see their world in terms of the triumphant narrative that had emerged in the age of Constantine. For them, the present was a bright new age. The power of Christ on earth had brought about a mighty transformation. Christian holy men now perched on mountains once sacred to the gods; Christian churches rose triumphantly from the foundations of levelled temples; the names of the gods were forgotten, while those of saints and martyrs were on everyone's lips. Even when churches were not built on top of temples, they were spoken of, in self-confident inscriptions, as if they had been:

The dwelling place of demons has become a house of God.
The saving light has come to shine, where shadows covered all.
Where sacrifices once took place and idols stood, angelic choirs now dance.
Where God was angered once, now God is made content.[7]

Considered to have been conquered, so suddenly and in so total a manner, the pre-Christian past was free to live on in the Christian present without causing further disquiet. With the sign of the Cross neatly engraved on their foreheads, the statues of Augustus and Livia, that had stood for centuries in the civic center of Ephesus, now gazed down serenely on the Christian bishops assembled by Theodosius II – the most orthodox, direct successor of Augustus – to the momentous council of 431.

This did not mean, in fact, that many regions of the eastern empire were Christianized any more rapidly than those of the west. The Greek intelligentsia continued to include distinguished pagans: Christians called them "Hellenes," upholders of the culture and the gods of the Greeks. Athens remained a university city, in which known "Hellenes" taught Christians with full public support until AD 529. Perched at a safe distance from major cities, in the prosperous mountain valleys of Anatolia, Lebanon, and northern Mesopotamia, pagan villages looked down, largely untroubled, on the disciplined plains, where the new religion had been declared, at least officially, to have triumphed.

Despite the occasional outbursts of a man such as Shenoute, the leaders of the eastern churches were less consistently preoccupied than were their western colleagues with the weight of the pagan past within their own congregations. The fact that they still lived in a successful and stridently Christian empire was enough to persuade them that they lived in a basically Christian world. By contrast, from Augustine onwards, a succession of Latin preachers and legislators tended to stress the fact that the idols, though broken in public, lingered tenaciously in the hearts of all too many Christians. Paganism was not simply a *superstitio*, a bankrupt dispensation that lay outside the Church: paganism lay close to the heart of all baptized Christians, always ready to re-emerge in the form of "pagan survivals." The master narrative of Christianization, as it was explicitly propounded in many circles in the Latin west, was not one of definitive triumph. It was one in which an untranscended past perpetually shadowed the advancing footsteps of the Christian present.

Caesarius, who was bishop of Arles from 502 to 542, was the Christian preacher who provided for future generations a classic statement of this distinctive mood. Devoted to Augustine (he even died, reassuringly, on the same day of the year as had the great bishop of Hippo), Caesarius adapted Augustine's own sermons, preached a century before at Carthage and Hippo, to the townsfolk of Arles and the peasants of Provence. When it came to a scenario as timeless as the Devil's long, sly siege of Christian souls, the Mediterranean was a narrow lake, and the entire century in which the western Empire had fallen was a mere flicker of time. Far from seeming second-hand, Caesarius's sermons struck his contemporaries as speaking directly to each hearer of his or her own condition. He was remembered for his "unceasing voice." On one occasion, he even closed the doors of the basilica, lest members of his congregation walk out before the sermon: when they stood at the Last Judgement, he reminded them, they would not be free to leave the room![8]

What Caesarius accomplished in such sermons was a pastoral *tour de force*. He domesticated the daunting immensity of the pre-Christian spiritual landscape of Provence. Much as he had once locked his congregation into the basilica, so that they should hear him out, so he enclosed paganism within the Christian community. Paganism, for him, was not a set of independent practices, shimmering still with the allure of a physical world shot through with mysterious, non-Christian powers. Rather, paganism was presented as being no more than a fragmented collection of "survivals" – "sacrilegious habits," inert "customs," "dirt from the gentiles" (to use the language of a slightly later Gallic council), inadvertently brought into the Church on the feet of so many average believers.[9]

Caesarius did not mince words on those who indulged in such practices. Beneath the deliberate simplicity of his preaching style, he was very much a Gallo-Roman noble, and a product of the austere monastic discipline instilled at Lérins. To fall back into pagan ways was, quite frankly, to lack grooming. It was to behave like *rustici*, boorish peasants, devoid of reason, unamenable to culture, driven by passion and, so, especially prone to collude with the earthy errors of the past. And in bed (he reminded even sophisticated urbanites) anyone could be a *rusticus*. To make love on Sundays, or when one's wife was menstruating, was to act no better than a peasant; and the result, in the grim folk-lore of Gaul, would befit such indecorous tumblings – deformed children, lepers, epileptics.[10] The pruning of *rusticitas* among baptized Christians, and not the eradication of paganism itself, was the proper object of a bishop's pastoral care.

But to prune *rusticitas* meant far more than to destroy the occasional country shrine or to denounce the occasional festive occasion as "dirt from the pagans." It meant nothing less than an attempt to change an entire mentality. Caesarius and those who followed him had to dethrone the ancient image of the world. In the preaching of a man such as Caesarius, the *mundus*, the physical universe, was drained of its autonomy. It had no life of its own apart from that given to it by the will of God. Christian time, for instance, did not register directly the organic throb of nature, shown in the changing seasons. It registered the great acts of God, in which He had brushed aside the *mundus*, to deal directly with mankind. The swaggering birth of the year, at the Kalends of January, meant nothing compared to the divine humility of Christ's birth at Christmas. Since imperial times, the days of the week had borne the names of the gods, who ruled the earth from their thrones on the ominous, unblinking orbs of the planets. Such names, associated with the powers that controlled the *mundus* should go. Ideally, Christians should count the days of the week from the Lord's Day, as *prima feria, secunda feria*. (By which high standards, Portugal would count as the only fully Christianized country in Europe!)[11]

Above all, human beings were denied the possibility of active participation, through ancient rituals, in the workings of the *mundus*. To think that human wills could intervene to change the course of nature in a material world where all events depended on the will of God, was, in the opinion of Caesarius, the height of stupidity. During an eclipse of the moon, the citizens of Arles would join in, with loud hurrahs, to "help the moon in her distress." Shouts of "*Vince luna*," "Up with the Moon," encouraged the bright neighbor of the human race to shake off the engulfing powers of darkness. To Caesarius, the moon hung above Provence, untouched by such "sacrilegious sounds." It was as distant, as opaque to human hopes and as unaffected by human rituals, as it is today. Only its darkened face, on such occasions, might be read as a "sign," given to remind mankind of what truly concerned them, and of what they had the power to change – of the sins that had brought upon them the frown of an angry God.[12]

It would be a long time (perhaps not until the death of peasant Europe in the nineteenth century) before the mentalities denounced by Caesarius changed greatly. More revealing, for the eventual spread of Christianity, are the scattered hints in Christian sources that show a process of compromise at work. These are not mindless "pagan survivals," as bishops such as Caesarius said that they were, so much as carefully considered attempts by sixth-century Christians to find some "fit" between their present religious skills and the patterns of an earlier time. In this process of adjustment, Christianity often held the initiative: pagan communities borrowed Christian signs and rites. The sign of the Cross would be made at sacrificial banquets. The names of Christian angels and saints would be shouted at the solemn toasts around the table. Monks and clergymen, many of whom came from learned, even from former priestly families, and not non-Christian diviners, were now the principal source of amulets and remedies. Christianity gave its own distinctive flavor to fundamental agrarian rites. The splashing of sacred water, that had fortified the harvest in the drought-prone climates of North Africa and Provence, was postponed slightly to the day of Saint John the Baptist. By this small change, the ancient powers of water were reinforced by the vast new potency ascribed to Christian baptism. In late sixth-century Spain, an exuberant urban clergy merely added the Christian chant of *Alleluia* to the general euphoria of the Kalends.[13]

It would require a measure of poetry, such as the plain-spoken Caesarius did not possess, to bring about the imaginative Christianization of the *mundus*. The Christian cult of the saints did this more effectively in the long run than did the "unceasing voice" of any preacher. For it aimed to create enduring religious habits, associated with Catholic *reverentia* – a reverential attention to the saints, directed primarily to major shrines, that became pilgrimage-sites at this time, but applicable also to any number of places and situations. *Reverentia* was the one sure answer to *rusticitas*. For when approached with *reverentia*, Christian saints might, indeed, prevail on their God to touch the *mundus* at every level. Their interventions could infuse phenomena and places in the natural world, in which people had always sought the sacred, with a new quality. They brought to their shrines and to the landscape itself a fragrant touch of Paradise.

The man whose vivid and abundant writings were devoted to maintaining this view, Gregory of Tours – Georgius Florentius Gregorius, bishop of Tours from 573 to 594 – came from a different region and from a very different generation from that of Caesarius.[14] Caesarius had been a southerner. Roman emperors had still ruled at Ravenna when he was a child. Gregory's family, by contrast, came from further north, from Langres, Lyon, and the Auvergne. His elevation to Tours took him yet closer to the northern heartland of *Francia*. He was born in 538, a few years before Caesarius died. Much had happened in western Europe before he became bishop of Tours. The emperor Justinian had attempted to reconquer the western Mediterranean, ruining the Roman social order in Italy by his failure. Between 542 and 570, bubonic plague had burned out the heart of the once-formidable eastern Roman empire. Even in Gregory's Gaul, it had left tragic gaps between the generations, as wide as those created in modern Europe by the slaughter of the First World War. By the end of Gregory's life, power and, with it, cultural confidence had begun to tilt insensibly away from the Mediterranean and towards northwestern Europe.

Gregory was a loyal, if occasionally critical, subject of the Frankish kings. He expected them to be powerful defenders of the Catholic Church, and not to waste their energies on unnecessary family feuds. Even though Gaul was now divided between potentially conflicting kingdoms, it had remained, in reality, a confederation of regions, whose frontiers were defended by a viable state. Foreigners noticed this basic stability. When the poet Venantius Fortunatus came to *Francia* from Ravenna and Treviso in 566/7, he immediately presented himself as an Orpheus fallen among northern barbarians, a refined representative of southern grace among harp-twanging *leudes*, the "strong men" of a barbarian court. It was a flattering self-image. He soon learned, as he sailed along the Moselle and visited great bishops in their country estates, from Trier to Bordeaux, that a larger measure of old-world solidity existed in Gaul than in his native Italy. He was more than happy to end his life as bishop of Poitiers.[15]

From the Rhine to Aquitaine, old Roman families had survived in Gaul. They were joined by a new class of *potentes*, "men of power" of mixed Frankish and Roman descent. United by the tenacious bonds of a shared Catholicism and a shared avarice, these people were firmly in the saddle in every region. Those who survived the occasional feeding-frenzies of the great, occasioned by the plots of rival Merovingian brothers, could expect to thrive – and none more so than the Catholic bishops.

The 110 bishops of Gaul had changed over the generations. From being the upholders of the morale of beleaguered Roman populations, in the dangerous fifth century, they had become eminently "representative" figures within the new Frankish kingdom. Each, in his own way, was law and order incarnate in his region. When consecrated, the bishop would be carried into his city on the high sedan chair, once reserved for Roman consuls. He would act as judge and peacemaker. He would conduct solemn ceremonies in basilicas and baptisteries that were maintained in a constant blaze of light, heavy with exotic perfumes.

Whether they came from old families, or were royal servants, many of these bishops were fabulously rich. To take one example: bishop Bertram of Le Mans – the bearer of a Frankish warrior-name, "Glorious Raven," from the great bird that pecked at the bodies of the dead on the battlefield – controlled a private fortune of 300,000 hectares, scattered all over western Gaul. Wealthy in their own right, the bishops presided over the distributive system connected with almsgiving and pious donations. They made visible the alchemy by which gold – flickering, flame-red gold, that stood, in the imagination of contemporaries, for all that was most cruel, most labile, and, ultimately, most rigid and "dead" in this world – was brought alive by being offered to the sacred. The great gold-encased, jewelled shrines that covered the bodies of the saints in Gaul spoke of a magical transfer effected by the bishop. By spending the measureless wealth of the church upon the saints, the bishop had sent it on to heaven. Heaven had allowed a representative part of that wealth to return to earth, in shrines that shone like frozen drops of supernatural splendor. The shimmer of the tomb was a guarantee of the further "blaze" of miraculous power that a saint, especially if he was a famous bishop, was expected to show from beyond the grave. The tomb of Saint Eligius (Saint Eloi), bishop of Noyon from 641 to 660, throbbed with such splendor that it had to be covered with a linen cloth during Lent, throughout which time it sweated with veiled miraculous power! Not surprisingly, the poor clustered round such shrines, the congealed symbols of the wealth of the Church from which they were fed.

In the course of the sixth century, the cities of Gaul lost much of their Roman shape and ebullience. They became, instead, ceremonial centers, carefully maintained oases of the holy. Bertram's Le Mans had eighteen churches, Paris as many as thirty-five. Cities were no longer enclosed, regularly organized spaces, as Roman towns had been. They blended into the countryside. Each was surrounded by a galaxy of shrines, and, beyond these, by the administrative villas and hunting lodges of a largely rural aristocracy. Yet they were still dominated by the castle-like Roman walls of what had become, very much, the bishop's "inner city."

As a "lover of the poor," the bishop did not merely support the indigent. He poured wealth and energy into maintaining an entire community. Formed in the sixth century, the image of the good Catholic bishop as a "father" of his city became what was, perhaps, the most long-lasting institutional ideal in western Europe. It changed little until the end of the *Ancien Régime*:

> With all his social grace and his appearance of worldliness, [he] fulfilled his duties as a bishop as though he had no other cares to distract him. He visited hospitals, gave alms generously but judiciously, attended to his clergy and religious houses. He found time for everything yet never seemed busy. His open house and generous table gave the impression of the residence of a governor. Yet in everything it was becoming to the Church.[16]

This could be the description of any Merovingian saint-bishop. It is, in fact, Fénélon, bishop of Cambrai, in 1711, as described in the *Memoirs* of Saint Simon! The criteria for a good bishop had changed so little in a thousand years.

Gregory came from a group of families who had helped to build up such a world in southern Gaul: he was the great-grandson, the grandnephew, and the nephew of bishops. He grew up a grave child, surrounded by grave relatives. *Reverentia* was a family tradition. His father always carried a gold medallion full of relics round his neck: they protected him from

> the violence of bandits, the dangers of floods, the threats of turbulent men, and attacks from swords.[17]

Gregory himself made his first "remedy" as soon as he could read. A good Catholic boy, he had alleviated his father's gout with a supernatural recipe described in the *Book of Tobit*. The *codex* of the Holy Scriptures, not the whispered lore of *rustici*, was to be his guide. Not for him, the fluid, homespun world of the mystical healer, who

whispered chants, cast lots, tied amulets around the neck.[18]

Gregory was no *rusticus*. When struck by frequent illnesses, he knew how to approach Saint Martin as a friend and as a great *patronus*, a stern protector. His hopes and fears had been molded over the years by the vast ceremoniousness that characterized the relation of late Roman persons to their lord:

I approached the tomb, knelt on the pavement, wept.[19]

Bishop of Tours by the age of 34, Gregory expected all Catholic Christians to show the same deep reverence for the saints. It was, indeed, essential for his position as bishop that they should do so. Tours had all the disadvantages of being an "open city," a pilgrimage center that lay at the joining point of rival kingdoms. In the twenty years of Gregory's episcopate, Tours wavered in and out of different kingdoms, being governed, in turn, from Metz, from Soissons and from Burgundy. His diocese was ravaged by punitive raids, in which the militias of neighboring cities took part with gusto. The basilica of Saint Martin was filled, at regular intervals, with high-placed persons, who sought sanctuary at his tomb. Gregory had a unique opportunity to watch the *potentes* of Gaul at their worst and at their most vulnerable.

Gregory wrote his *History*, in large part, from the viewing point of that sanctuary. He wrote deliberately in a "rustic" Latin. But this was not so as to address peasants. It was to warn the *potentes* of future ages, Frankish and Roman alike, for whom an unpolished Latin, well on the way to becoming French, was the common language. To call it a *History of the Franks* is seriously misleading. As a bishop, sin and retribution for sin, not ethnicity, was Gregory's all-consuming interest. In writing the history of his own times, Gregory ensured that the misfortunes of well-to-do sinners, Frankish and Roman alike, would be long remembered. He did not lack material: he describes, often in memorable detail, the violent deaths of some thirty politicians. Those who came to a bad end did so because they had offended God and His saints. The

Frankish general, Guntram Boso, for instance, died so stuck through with spears that he could not even keel over. Gregory knew why. Spasmodically pious, Guntram had also consulted a pagan prophetess. It had done him no good. Gregory made sure that contemporaries would remember Guntram for what he was:

> an unprincipled sort of man, greedy and avaricious, coveting beyond measure the goods of others, giving his word to all, keeping it to none.[20]

But Celsus, the Roman, was no better:

> a tall man, broad of shoulder, strong of arm, haughty in speech, quick in his reactions, and learned in law. He would often seize the possessions of the Church . . . One day in church he heard a passage being read from the prophet . . . *Woe unto them that join house to house, that lay field to field.* He is said to have replied: "This is a poor look out! Woe then to me and my children!"

He was right. His son died childless,

> bequeathing the greater part of his possessions to the Church from which his father had stolen them.[21]

As the guardians of a moral order represented on earth by the bishops, the saints drew themselves up to their full height in the cities of Gaul. The world of Gregory's *History* is a largely urban world, that cried out for justice and peace. Yet Gregory also wrote further books of *Wonders* – wonders at the tomb of Saint Martin, at the tomb of Saint Julian at Brioude, the wonders that made up the *Glory of the Confessors* and the *Glory of the Martyrs*, a *Life of the Fathers*, and even a treatise on the stars, that included a catalogue of the wonders of nature. These books of *Wonders* are as extensive as his *History*. Their sheer size and loving circumstantiality mark a new departure. It is as if Gregory had reached out with his pen to catch the infinitely varied spiritual landscape of his region in a fine web of Christian words.

It was important for Gregory that he should do this. He gave the impression of living in a fully Christian region. He refers to paganism only in connection with the "barbarian" regions of northern Gaul, with the hills and forests that flanked the Rhine and the Moselle. What concerned him far more was the ease with which alternative versions of Christianity sprang up whenever Catholic bishops such as himself relaxed their vigilance. Wandering preachers, bearing relics and claiming to represent none other than Saint Peter himself, even had the impudence to visit Tours when he was absent! Prophetesses attracted large crowds and gathered much wealth through their ability to seek out thieves and to divine the sins of others. When the bubonic plague struck Berry, in 571, the hermit Patroclus, whom Gregory admired, found himself faced by a rival, a woman called Leubella who claimed to have been visited

> by the devil, falsely appearing to her as Saint Martin . . . bearing objects which, so he said, would save the people.[22]

Unpredictable stirrings of a "vernacular" Christianity, whose vigor we can barely estimate, other than in terms of the anxieties which it inspired in men such as Gregory, caused greater anxiety to the bishops of Gaul, in the sixth as in later centuries, than did the survival of paganism. Such phenomena seemed to them to herald nothing less than the coming of Antichrist to earth. There were only too many figures like Leubella, of whom Gregory had heard, in Gaul and Spain.[23] He wrote, in part, as an attempt to counter an alternative Christian religiosity that was disquietingly prevalent. His *Life of the Fathers* ensured that, even in distant country regions, the memory of true, Catholic hermits would be remembered, in a world quite prepared to admire less-reliable figures. The reverence for the saints, in its correct Catholic forms, must be seen to touch every aspect of the countryside of Gaul, to account for every local legend and to explain every beneficent manifestation of the sacred.

As a result, the natural world regained some of its magic. It was now presented by Gregory, no longer as throbbing, of course, with a spiritual life of its own, but, rather, as if it were a heavy, silken veil, whose rustling surface betrayed the hidden presence, behind it, of the countless saints of Gaul. For early medieval persons, a "relic" was a physical fragment, an enduring "trace," left in the material world by a fully redeemed person, a saint, who now dwelt in God's Paradise. Gregory had few illusions as to how rare such persons must be. Yet, on this point, his optimism prevailed. Over the centuries, the Christian churches of Gaul had produced, and still produced, a number of such holy persons, of both sexes and of every class, race, and region. Their relics were everywhere, scattered throughout the entire Christian world. In every region, there were specks of dust unlike all other specks of dust, fragments of bone unlike other fragments, tombs unlike other tombs. Some were already clearly visible: among the late Roman sarcophagi piled up in a family vault, one might be covered by a silk embroidered veil, with a lamp burning before it – it was a tomb whose miraculous powers proved that it housed a holy person. Others lay at vanishing point. They were tantalizing hints of the riches that God might yet reveal to the faithful: a fragment bound in a silken ribbon that had emerged, unscathed, from a bonfire; sweet voices singing among the dark lanes of tombs outside Autun; an intermittent glow and a whiff of heavenly fragrance among the brambles of a deserted hilltop in the Touraine, that betrayed the presence of a "place of Christians," long deserted and taken over by secondary forest after the raids of AD 406. These were intimations of the "presence" of holy men and women, waiting patiently to receive reverence from Catholic worshippers, and ready to help them, in return, in their many needs.

Relics were called, appropriately, *pignora*, pledges. They were guarantees of the proximity of loving and efficacious persons who now dwelt in the exuberant and aromatic Paradise of God. They brought into this world not only the touch of a human hand, but the touch of a place. Through the saints, Paradise itself might ooze into the world. Nature itself was redeemed.

The great shrines of Gaul were incessantly lit and fragrant with the permanent presence of aromatic substances. Each stood out, in an ill-lit and malodorous world, as a "fragment of Paradise."[24] Not all of this, Gregory thought, was due to human artifice. Walking at night, Gregory had seen empty churches filled with mysterious light. The priest of the shrine of Saint Julian at Brioude once entered the sanctuary in the depths of November, to find the tomb of Julian and the floor around it strewn with gigantic red roses:

> their fragrance was overpowering. These roses were so fresh that you might think that they had been cut at that very moment from living stems.[25]

To be healed at the tomb of Saint Martin was not merely to experience justice and amnesty at the hands of a great patron. It was to experience a sudden flowering of the body. Gregory lingers, in gripping detail, as much on the physical rhythm of each cure as on its outcome. Like a sponge, "intensely soaking up liquid . . . the skin [of a withered hand] became red as a rose." "You might see his pale countenance become rose red." A child crippled by malnutrition "blossomed again," as if re-entering, for a moment, the Paradise from which Adam had been cast out and into which Saint Martin had already entered.[26]

Because of the proximity of Paradise, sacrality seeped back into the landscape of Gaul. The countryside found its voice again, to speak, in an ancient spiritual vernacular, of the presence of the saints. Water became holy again. The hoof-print of his donkey could be seen beside a healing spring, which Saint Martin had caused to gush from the earth at Nieul-les-Saintes. The tree that Martin had blessed beside the road at Neuillé-le-Lierre, in Touraine, was still standing, though now dead; for its bark had been entirely stripped away for medicinal remedies. All over Gaul, great trees bloomed profusely over the graves of saints. Gregory looked on such trees with happy eyes. They no longer spoke to him of pagan rites – of bright rags fluttering from branches that drew their strength from the dark and questionable powers of the earth. Rather, they brought down from heaven to earth a touch of the unshackled, vegetable energy of God's own paradise.[27]

Gregory's unflagging pace as a *raconteur* tends to lull us into believing that he has told us everything that we ever need to know about Frankish Gaul. This is not so. He was fiercely regional in his interests. He looked back deep into the past of the small Roman towns of southern Gaul. He tells us less than we would like to know about the countryside outside the cities. In this sense, he remained very much an old world *Romanus*. He took for granted that he belonged to a wider Christendom, defined by cities and their saints. In the late sixth century, Gregory's Tours was one Christian city among many, placed at the northwestern corner of a vast parallelogram, covered by similar cities, each with its bishop, that reached southwards as far as Volubilis, near the Atlantic coast of North Africa, and eastwards to the foothills of the Zagros and the frontiers of Arabia. Let us now turn to the eastern half of the Christian world, in the sixth century – a century dominated by the reign of the great emperor Justinian – before returning, once again, to the west, to men who had entered middle age when Gregory of Tours completed his *History* – to the Roman pope, Gregory the Great, and to the Irishman, Columbanus.

7

Bishops, City and Desert: East Rome

In August 452, only ten months after the fateful council of Chalcedon, Peter the Iberian, a former Georgian prince, was elected bishop of Maiouma, the harbor city of Gaza on the southern coast of Palestine. He was faced by a fervent congregation, which threatened to burn down the basilica, with himself inside, if he did not celebrate for them at once the Great Liturgy as their bishop. When he reached the solemn prayer of consecration and broke the sanctified bread of the Eucharist, blood gushed from the loaf and covered the entire altar. He turned, to see Christ at his side:

> Break the bread, bishop . . . I have done this for my glory, that everyone may know where the truth is and who are they who hold the orthodox faith.[1]

Peter, in fact, was an uncompromising opponent of the council of Chalcedon. Not everyone (certainly not pope Leo!) would have considered him "orthodox." Yet all sides agreed. A bishop was the high-priest of his city. The bishop's solemn celebration of the Eucharist at the Great Liturgy was a public rite, that ensured God's favor for the entire community. When a bishop first entered "his" city, he would bless the chapel at its gate with clouds of incense, and would lead his clergy in loud supplications. He would do the same at the Tetrapylon – the four-columned monument that marked the center of the city. After the Great Liturgy, he would retire to his palace, to receive the town-council and the representatives of the imperial government.[2]

The public rituals performed by the bishop and his clergy made the city holy. His presence as honorary chairman of the town-council, assisted by the local notables, made the city orderly. Altogether, as in the Gaul of Gregory of Tours, bishops were their cities. The wealth of the patriarchs of the great cities of the eastern Mediterranean was legendary. In AD 610, the patriarch of Alexandria had 8,000 pounds of gold in his church's treasure. He supported 7,500 indigent persons on his poor-roll (when Gallic bishops barely supported more than a hundred). The trading fleets of the patriarch sailed from Alexandria as far as Morocco and Cornwall.[3]

But the great patriarchs were an exception. Unlike the aristocratic bishops of Gaul and Spain, the average bishop in the east Roman empire was a careworn and humdrum person: he was a glorified town-councillor, not a potent magnate. Across an area almost as vast as the later Ottoman empire, the imperial system created by Diocletian and Constantine had remained in place. Bishops were the heirs of the many tribulations which a fiercely intrusive and centralized government had brought upon the cities. By AD 500 the Christian bishop and his clergy had taken over many of the duties that had once been performed by the town councils. Local notables would buy their way into the clergy, simply so as to enjoy the privilege of being seen in public "in the robes of a clergyman."[4] The Church was the new avenue to local status and prestige. It provided new opportunities for display. Bishops and clergymen decorated their cities with new churches, whose floors were covered with exuberant mosaics containing inscriptions that praised their own generosity and intelligence. They dedicated to the altars large pieces of silverware, that bore their names and those of their family.

The imperial government, for its part, used the clergy as local watchdogs. Bishops were commanded to use "sacerdotal freedom" to report to the emperor governors guilty of graft or incompetence. They represented the emperor to their cities. Imperial mandates were now read aloud to the local notables in the bishop's audience-hall. They were then posted for the entire city to read in the porch outside the local church. The bishop of Bosra "performed a service to his city" by building his own jail, to house and feed criminals awaiting trial. Bishops validated the weights and measures used in the market-place. They ensured that the city's walls were maintained. At times of crisis, they even blessed and discharged the catapults that lined its battlements – as did the bishop of Theodosiopolis (Erzerum, eastern Turkey), killing a Hunnish chieftain with a stone thrown from the catapult "of the church," named the "Saint Thomas."

> It is the duty of bishops [wrote the patriarch of Antioch to a subordinate] to cut short and restrain the unregulated movements of the mob . . . and to set themselves to maintain good order in the cities and to keep watch over the peaceful manners of those who are fed by their hand.[5]

Thus, the Christian life of the largest political unit in the Mediterranean was firmly based on the conscientious mediocrity of almost 2,000 such bishops. It was not surprising that the imperial government at Constantinople thought that, given the right mixture of command and persuasion, a strong imperial line on Christian dogma would create a united, "orthodox" Church. Yet the course of the sixth century and, especially, the reign of one of the most self-confident rulers ever produced in the Roman empire, the emperor Justinian (527–565), proved that this would not be the case. In the vastly extended and complex Roman empire of the east, neither the state nor the cities through which it ruled proved to have sufficient coercive force or moral authority to impose religious unity.

In heading the cities, the bishops were implicated in all that was most impenitently profane and least Christian in east Roman society. The triumphal narratives of "instant" Christianization through victory over the gods had left much of the past intact in the east Roman cities. All over the empire, the monumental decor of the cities remained standing. Many statues retained sinister associations with the pagan past. A statue of none other than Julian the Apostate, for instance, was still standing in Oxyrhynchus, in Middle Egypt. It had the reputation of descending from its base at night, to stalk unwary strollers through the darkened streets of the city.[6]

Outside the Church, the city as a whole and its lay governing classes remained deeply attached to symbols of power and prosperity that owed nothing to Christianity. One might now enter a theater through a gate on which the Cross surmounted the traditional invocation of the *Tyché*, the numinous good fortune, of the city. But in the theater itself, little had changed. Clouds of incense still gave an air of mystical solemnity to the spectacular ballets of the pantomime dancers, whose miraculous leaps and sinuous gestures took place against a backdrop of mythological friezes that dated from classical times. Those who attended paid little attention to the warnings of their clergy:

I do not go that I may believe, but I go that I may laugh. It is a game; it is not paganism.[7]

Even in the long-Christian city of Edessa, the arrival of a troupe of Greek dancers was a major event:

there came round again the time of that festival at which the heathen tales were sung; and the citizens took even more pains about it than usual. Lamps were lighted [before the dancers], and they were burning incense and holding vigils the whole night, walking about the city and praising the dancers until morning, with singing and shouting and lewd behavior . . . they neglected also to go to prayer [and] . . . they mocked at the modesty of their fathers, who, quoth they, "did not know how to do things as we do."[8]

In the late fifth century, the youth culture of the east Roman cities changed, with dramatic eventual consequences. Young men – and especially the privileged sons of the civic elites – had always supported competitive activities in their cities. Now this competition became both more clear-cut and more uniform throughout the empire. Each city was now officially divided between two principal "factions" – the "Blues" and the "Greens." These groups were encouraged to vie with each other in supporting rival performers of all kinds. The competition was particularly fierce between the rival teams of "Blue" and "Green" charioteers. The frequent bloody clashes between rival gangs of supporters of each faction were tolerated because the rivalry itself ensured that, in all cities, all heads remained turned towards the emperor and his representatives. Gathered in their separate benches in the hippodromes and theaters of all great cities, assembled at the center of the city on state occasions, the young men of the "Blues" and the "Greens" actively competed to show loyalty to the distant emperor. They would rival each other in chanting loyal acclamations and in denouncing his enemies.

These factions were utterly profane and unusually inclusive. As young men of the "Blue" or "Green" factions, religious outsiders, such as Jews, had exactly the same rights as did "orthodox" Christians. All had a place on the benches of their local hippodrome. And what was celebrated, in the chariot races, was, quite frankly, *Tyché*, Lady Luck. The Hippodrome was both a public Wheel of Fortune and a public Victory Parade: it celebrated the heroic skills of the charioteers, who turned blind fortune into victory, as they whirled at headlong speed around the race course. Everyone was involved, from the emperor downwards. It was from the imperial box at the side of the gigantic Hippodrome of Constantinople that the emperor met "his" people. And he did so by sharing the same passions as themselves. He also was the supporter of a faction. Though denounced by Christian writers as the "Church of Satan," the Hippodrome summed up a mystique of empire that reached back far behind Constantine: for, in the hard-driving east Roman state of the sixth century, good fortune and victory had remained the stuff of life in a "Roman" empire.

Hence a paradox of east Roman society. In the west, the bishops felt increasingly secure in their control of the surviving towns. They tended to look out from these oases of carefully maintained Christian propriety, to confront a spreading countryside where Christianity seemed less securely rooted, certainly less easy to control. In Syria and Egypt, by contrast, it could appear as if the cities, the centers of imperial government, were enclaves of profane living in the midst of a population made up of God-fearing farmers. Along the Nile, villages that had once cohered around their pagan temples now found a new cohesion in their Christian clergy and a new identity in their fervent loyalty to the Monophysite patriarchs of Alexandria. It was through the activities of clergymen that Syriac and Coptic became major literary languages. Though both languages had deep roots in the pre-Christian past, they were identified with a triumphant Christian present.

The agrarian society of northern Syria, around Antioch and Aleppo, was, indeed, new and thriving. Since the fourth century, expanding population had taken over marginal lands. By AD 500 northwestern Syria was a populous landscape, dotted with villages. The remarkable churches that were built by the villagers have survived to this day. Spectacular hoards of silverware have recently emerged from the area. They give an impression of the wealth that local landowners were prepared to lavish on local churches. An entire new Christian world had come into existence to one side of the cities.

Prosperous and ostentatiously pious, the world of the countryside, in northern Syria and elsewhere, expressed its cohesion through great pilgrimages to spectacular holy men and to the monasteries associated with them. Thousands would stream out from the new villages, to gather every year at the shrine of Saint Symeon Stylites. Symeon was the first "column saint." (He derived his name from *stylos*, Greek for "column.") He had stood in prayer for some thirty years, until his death in 459, on top of a sixty-foot column, on the edge of the limestone massif that still bears his name, the Jebel Sem'an, close to the main road that led from Antioch to the Euphrates. A new, dramatic form of Christianity had emerged, in a new Christian landscape that occupied the vital defensive zone between Antioch and the eastern frontier.[9]

The most significant divide of all in the Christian imagination of the east Roman empire, however, was not that between town and countryside: it was between the "desert" and the "world." It was a notional chasm. It separated two closely juxtaposed spaces: the "desert" was associated with the "angel-like" life of the ascetic, the "world" with the more hesitant Christian behavior of the *kosmikos*, of persons "in the world" – men and women, and clergymen quite as much as lay persons, who were caught in obligations to society, and, for that reason, were not free to give all of themselves to Christ.

In the west, a strong current of opinion, that went back to Augustine, expected that the triumphant grace of God would show itself within society, in the form of holy persons who were, more often than not, called to be leaders of the Catholic Church: it was such persons who had "overcome the world," and many did this as bishops, rulers of cities and embodiments of law and order in Gaul and in other western regions. Holiness and ecclesiastical office tended to converge. In Syria and elsewhere, the Holy Spirit was thought, rather, to have raised up holy men and women in great numbers so as to make them active outside society, in the desert. This "desert" was no impenetrable wilderness. It often lay within easy walking distance of towns and populous villages. But only in the "desert" – that is, in a place to one side of settled life – could a few great ascetics bring back, through long penance and hard labor on their own bodies, a touch of the angelic glory that Adam had enjoyed in the garden of Eden.

A western bishop, such as Gregory of Tours, for all his admiration of living saints, tended to look for the most potent traces of Paradise among the holy dead, as at the tomb of Saint Martin. In the eastern Mediterranean, by contrast, living persons were thought capable of regaining Paradise on earth. In Egypt, farmers would run up to scoop the sand from the footprints of Apa Apollos, as he walked near his cell, on the edge of the desert. They would take this sand back to sprinkle on their fields in the valley below. The holiness of Apollos had turned the dead sand, the antithesis to the green valley of the Nile, into the richest earth of all – the earth of Eden.[10] Clouds of heavenly incense regularly surrounded the column of Symeon the Younger (521–592), the precocious imitator of Symeon Stylites. At the age of seven, Symeon had settled in the mountains near Antioch. He was believed to have played with mountain-lions, calling them "pussy." He brought back to earth the sweet smell of Paradise, and a hint of Adam's innocent mastery of the animal kingdom.[11]

"Angelic" holy men did not abandon the world, in the sense of severing all relations with it. Rather, in the imagination of contemporaries, they transformed its wild edges. They ringed a careworn society with the shimmering hope of Paradise regained. They effected a symbolic exchange on a deep imaginative level. Having drained from themselves all hint of the world, they validated that world by constantly praying for it:

> assistance flows from their bones to all creation.
> Civilization, where lawlessness prevails,
> is sustained by their prayers.
> And the world, burdened by sin,
> is preserved by their intercession.
> The earth, heaving with controversy,
> is upheld by them.
> Troubled with speculation,
> their vigil fills it with calm.[12]

The spectacular lives of a few great saints validated the role of innumerable, less-famous ascetics whose reputation for holiness led them to be sought out by persons "in the world." Holy persons – men, in the desert, and women, more usually in the safer seclusion of the towns and villages – were the true democrats of eastern Christendom. They met the deep longing for solidarity and for spiritual guidance which the official leaders of the Church – bishops and clergy now deeply implicated in a world of power and status – could not provide. Paradoxically, it was the awesome austerity of such ascetics that enabled them to do so. Seen with the eyes of a great monk, all persons of all ranks and status, vocations and levels of culture were equal. Clergy and laity were alike. Both equally caught in the "world," each, in their different manner, limped slowly towards the kingdom of Christ. Emperor or peasant, bishop or lay person, monk or prostitute, each needed the advice of holy persons and the constant support of their prayers.

We possess a precious record of the spiritual guidance offered by two major holy men in this period: the *ostraka* – the inscribed shards of pottery – that record the requests sent to Apa Epiphanius in his cell among the empty temples of Thebes, in the late sixth century, and the remarkable collection of *Questions and Answers* associated with the Great Old Man, Barsanuphius (470–547), an Egyptian recluse settled outside Gaza. Both holy men moved with ease from providing exacting spiritual direction to a small group of disciples to offering firm and humane advice to married persons "in the world."

An elderly priest asked Epiphanius how he should spend the last years of his life:

> broken, lying abed, carried in and out . . . A great grief is in my heart, night and day . . . be so good as to appoint to me prayers and a regime of fasting convenient to my sickness and old age, and even if it be lying down, I will fulfill them.[13]

As for Barsanuphius, he supplied the notables of the region with moral counsels that upheld, from the awesome darkness of his permanently closed cell, ancient standards of grace and courtesy. Should a landowner allow a Jewish neighbor to use his winepress?

> If, when it rains, God causes the rain to fall on your fields and not those of the Jew, then you can refuse to press his wine. But He is full of love for all mankind . . . why should you, then, wish to be inhumane rather than merciful?[14]

On one thing, however, Barsanuphius was firm. *Kosmikoi* and monks alike should avoid contact with heretics. They should never be drawn into debate with them. "Heretics," for Barsanuphius, included Monophysites, who opposed the Council of Chalcedon. This was the problem. A remarkably unified empire did not possess a unified Church. The forceful reign of Justinian witnessed the failure of the most energetic attempt yet made to reassert, from Constantinople, a single imperial faith.

It is easy for the historian, with hindsight, to foresee Justinian's failure. Contemporaries, however, face their world generation by generation. The generation that came into its prime in Constantinople in the 520s was characterized by a quite exceptional combination of anxiety and high purpose. They knew that they lived in a changed world. The Roman empire of the west had fallen. In Constantinople, this was an ominous event. Pagans ascribed it to the suppression of sacrifice to the gods, Monophysites, predictably, to the Council of Chalcedon. No longer simply a "new" Rome, a replica of Rome offered to the east, Constantinople now stood alone as the sole surviving capital of the "true" Roman empire. To call this empire "Byzantium," and its subjects "Byzantines" (from Byzantium, the former site of Constantinople), is a modern practice that denies the continuity with the Roman empire to which the men of the sixth century were fiercely attached. They thought of themselves as members of "the fortunate race of the Romans." Learned folklore, treasured in government departments, insisted that the Praetorian Prefect's court used the plural form, "we," because it had been used by Romulus and Remus, when they sat together in judgement. It was also believed that the uniforms of the guards of the imperial bedchamber had been designed by Romulus, who had received the pattern from Aeneas![15] Latin remained the language of the law. Though mediated by serviceable Greek and Syriac translations, Latin, "the Roman tongue," continued to be used as the sacred language of a "Roman" state – as opaque but as redolent of uncanny continuity with the distant past as was the Latin of the former Catholic Mass.

In Constantinople, the opinion was that if the west fell, it had been because the western emperors had not been "Roman" enough. They had failed to flex the muscles of empire that were still so very present to those who governed in New Rome. The yearly budget of the east Roman empire was 900,000 gold pieces. Eighty thousand tons of grain arrived each year at Constantinople as part of the tax-levy of Egypt alone. The emperor Anastasius (491–518) had left 320,000 pounds of gold (23 million gold pieces) as an unspent surplus in the imperial treasures. No state west of China could mobilize such sums on a regular basis.

Petrus Sabbatius Justinianus – the emperor Justinian and

his unprepossessing uncle, Justin (who reigned from 518 to 527, under the shadow of his forceful nephew) – came from the upper Vardar valley, near Skopje, from a Latin-speaking periphery of the empire, half way, as the crow flies, between Constantinople and Rome. Like that other outsider, the Corsican Buonaparte, Justinian threw himself headlong into a burgeoning new myth. He was convinced that he knew more clearly than did any of his predecessors what a Christian Roman empire should be like.

Justinian had an outsider's intolerance for the compromises and anomalies that had made possible the smooth running of a splendid, but slow-moving, system. Theodosius II, for instance, had been content to declare that pagans no longer existed in his empire. This meant, in fact, that many men of skill and high culture who were loyal to the old religion were allowed to play a public role as long as they kept their beliefs to themselves. Not so Justinian. In 528, all pagans were given three months in which to be baptized. In 529, the pagan professors of philosophy at the Academy in Athens were forbidden to teach in public. All knowledge was Christian knowledge: it could not be taught by "persons diseased with the insanity of the unholy Hellenes."[16]

Justinian also knew what it was to have an up-to-date code of Roman law. The *Codex* of Theodosius II appeared to him to have been a half-hearted effort. Justinian set the lawyer, Tribonian, to work with a team of experts, to compile a *Digest* of the entire corpus of Roman law: 1,528 law-books were read through and condensed into 800,000 words. The *Institutes*, prepared at the same time, provided a streamlined new text-book for the law schools at Beirut. The *Codex Justinianus*, a *Justinianic Code*, brought the *Theodosian Code* up to date. The *Codex* appeared in 529; the *Digest* and the *Institutes* in 533. The Roman law that was later revived in medieval Europe, and that became the basis of all subsequent codes of "civil" law, as well as the imperial law of Russia, which remained valid up to 1917, were neither of them a direct legacy of ancient Rome. They all came from Justinian. They drew upon the works produced by a team of lawyers in Constantinople, driven, for five hectic years, by a man determined to test to its limits the possibilities of the empire he had come to rule. Justinian had done

> what no one else had dared to hope to achieve and to decide on ... But we stretched out our hands to Him, Who can, by His mighty power, grant ultimate success to quite impossible enterprises.[17]

The reform of Roman law set the brisk tempo for a further decade. For a time, it seemed as if Justinian could do anything. Then, on January 13, 532, Constantinople exploded. For the first time ever, the Blue and the Green factions united, under the common rallying-cry of *Nika*, "Conquer." They wished to replace Justinian's advisers, and eventually to overthrow Justinian himself. Thirty thousand citizens died in a massacre carried out by Justinian's troops of a panic-stricken crowd trapped in the Hippodrome. For days after, the huge roar of the firestorm that consumed the entire center of Constantinople drowned every other noise. Yet recovery came quickly. Characteristically, Justinian used the destruction to go beyond his predecessors. The city's main basilica was replaced by the stupendous new church of the Hagia Sophia, the Aya Sofya, the Church of the Holy Wisdom.

Hagia Sophia was dedicated only five years after the *Nika* riot. For all future ages, it became the enduring symbol of Justinian's piety and of Constantinople's position as the center of the orthodox world. The Hagia Sophia was also a symbol of empire. It was, indeed, so powerful a symbol that the great Ottoman architect of the sixteenth century, Sinan, strove to rival it, in a series of stupendous domed mosques. As a result, Justinian's great church lives on, in Muslim form, in the imposing Ottoman mosques that stretch from Mostar to Damascus.

At the time, however, the new church was a prodigious gamble. A structural engineer's nightmare, the piers that supported one main arch began to sway outwards under the weight of masonry piled ever higher upon it, and the columns beneath others began to flake from the strain. Justinian was said to have urged the builders to continue. Sure enough, the completed arches settled under their own unimaginable weight. As he first entered the completed building, Justinian was believed to have exclaimed: "Solomon, I have outdone you!"[18]

In the years in which the Hagia Sophia was being built, between the summer of 533 and 540, Carthage, Sicily, Rome and, eventually, Ravenna, fell to Justinian's armies. It was a seemingly effortless demonstration of imperial power. A large navy landed small, highly professional contingents, supplemented by deadly Hunnish horse-archers. Divided among themselves, the armies of the Vandals and most of the Ostrogoths crumbled. Once again, it seemed as if Justinian had brought off the impossible:

> We have good hope . . . that God will grant us to rule over the rest of what, subject to the ancient Romans to the limits of both seas, they later lost through their easy-going ways.[19]

A large part of the coastline of the western Mediterranean, from Carthage to Volubilis and from Sicily to Istria (including, for a time, a strip of the southern coast of Spain around Cartagena) fell back into the imperial order after no more than a century of barbarian rule. Carthage remained an imperial city until 698, Ravenna until 751. The present-day name of the hinterland of Ravenna, the Romagna, marks it as former "Roman" land – a little *Romania*, overlooking the Adriatic sea, down which ships sailed frequently to Constantinople. Throughout the early Middle Ages, the popes were subjects of the east Roman emperors. Up to AD 800, every papal document sent to western bishops and to western rulers was dated by the regnal year of the emperor in Constantinople, the pope's true lord and master.

The bubonic plague, however, is nature's rare, but deadly, comment on the creation of an Asia-wide economy. Justinian had created such an economy. A revived empire, anxious for goods, east Rome lay at the northwestern end of the trade routes of the Indian Ocean. Justinian's gold pieces, the imperial *solidi*, were admired in Ceylon as those of the greatest empire in the world. Justinian's navies reunited the western to the eastern basin of the Mediterranean. Ceramics of unusual uniformity circulated throughout the eastern Mediterranean.

They betray a surprisingly homogeneous consumer economy, driven by the demands of a unified empire. When the bubonic plague escaped its deadly pocket in the African Lakes, it moved swiftly west. By the summer of 542, it was in Pelusium, the port at which the Indian Ocean trade of the Red Sea entered the Mediterranean. It emptied the coastal cities, and left an uncanny swathe of deserted villages and unattended harvests along the principal highroads of Asia Minor.[20] The plague soon reached Constantinople, instantly killing a third of its population. It almost killed Justinian himself, leaving him with appreciably less energy. His laws shrank to a trickle. Theological negotiations occupied an increasing amount of his time. In 563, at the age of 81, Justinian left the capital for the first time in over fifty years. He crossed the highlands of Anatolia as winter approached, in an unexpected pilgrimage to the shrine of the Archangel Michael at Germia (Yürme, near Ankara). The shrine was noted for its immemorial fish-pond, a source of miraculous healings. The old emperor needed yet more life. But he died only two years later, in November 565. But the empire he had once ruled with such high hopes had as good as died two decades earlier.

Societies can regain momentum after the first dislocating impact of the plague, as happened in Europe after the Black Death of 1348. But a vast empire, already stretched to its limits, had less chance of recovery. Plague remained endemic in the Middle East until the middle of the eighth century. Periodic outbursts of plague continued to erode the human resources of the great empires that struggled to control the region. The Middle East remained an area characterized by great empires. But after the arrival of the plague, the empires in the region rested on a far less secure basis than they had done previously. Only when the plague finally burned itself out, after the middle of the eighth century, were two great states, the newly founded Califate of Baghdad and the revived Byzantine empire, able to emerge in their final, more stable medieval forms.[21]

After 542, distance, which had once placed such huge fiscal resources at his disposal, now became Justinian's most unrelenting enemy. Each distant frontier had to compete with every other for the allocation of diminished resources. Italy and the Danube lost out to the most formidable emergency of all. Under Khusro I Anoshirwan (530–579) the Persian bid to join Mesopotamia to the Mediterranean coast was on again. The head of a vast empire that stretched across the Iranian plateau to Central Asia, the Persian King of Kings enjoyed a perpetual military advantage. From 540 to 628, the "running ulcer" of war with Persia dominated the politics of the east Roman empire.

Italy was neglected. Reduced to a military side-show, imperial rule could not be securely established throughout the peninsula. An entire, old-world provincial society died in Italy, as the Po Valley and the Apennines became an uncertain frontier region defended by a handful of imperial troops, first against the remaining armies of the Ostrogoths and, a decade later, against the newly arrived war-bands of the Lombards.

Along the Danube and as far south as the Aegean, great gashes began to appear in the imperial structure. After 550, Slavic tribes penetrated the mountainous hinterland of the Balkans as far as Greece and the Dalmatian coast. Small groups of farmers and pastoralists, stolidly indifferent to imperial pretensions, the Slavs welcomed Roman runaways and captives. They incorporated them with ease into their own tribal system. For that reason, they grew at a rapid rate. The *Sklaviniai* of Greece and the Balkans were an ominous sign. They signalled the end of an imperial order. They were stateless zones, whose inhabitants no longer paid taxes or provided soldiers for the emperor. If they identified with an imperial system at all, it was with the new nomad confederacy of the Avars, an avatar of the empire of Attila, that formed along the Danube in the 580s.

Despite so many violent discontinuities, Justinian maintained the momentum of his quest for religious unity. Authoritarian as only a Roman emperor could be, he was not a violent man. He simply expected those around him to be swept into sharing his own, terrifying certainty on matters of belief. He was determined to persuade the Monophysite dissidents to accept the Council of Chalcedon. In so doing, he concentrated, not on Egypt, a monolithically Monophysite province, but on Syria. Syria was more divided, and, in any case, Syria and the highlands to its north were the frontier provinces that had to face continuous attack from the revived Persian empire.

When Justinian thought it necessary, he could be a good listener:

He sits unguarded in some lobby of the Palace to a late hour of the night, and enjoys unrolling the Christian Scriptures in the company of aged priests.[22]

He also knew when to compromise. He shared with the Monophysite opposition a deep reverence for the theology of Cyril of Alexandria. But, while praising the theology of Cyril, the bishops at Chalcedon had accepted as "orthodox" certain bishops who had attacked Cyril vehemently. It seemed to Justinian as if that part of the proceedings could be disowned in order to appease the Monophysites. Cyril's critics could be declared, retrospectively, to have been "heretics." After a decade of tortuous negotiations, a fifth "world-wide" council (in fact, a mere 156 bishops, drawn from the core of Justinian's empire) decided, in 553, to disown three, long-dead theologians, who were the *bêtes noires* of the Monophysites. This meant the formal condemnation of what became known as *The Three Chapters* – a dossier of the works of Theodore of Mopsuestia, Theodoret of Cyrrhus and Ibas of Edessa.

The pope, Vigilius, was browbeaten into accepting Justinian's drastic re-interpretation of the meaning of Chalcedon. Because of the decisive role played in it by the *Tome* of pope Leo, Chalcedon had been regarded by Latin clergymen as "their" council. Justinian paid little attention to western opinion. Vigilius was bundled on to an imperial ship that sailed up the Tiber to fetch him to court. On one occasion he was dragged from sanctuary in the church of the papal delegation in Constantinople with such violence that the heavy marble altar, whose column he had grasped, almost collapsed upon him. It was not the way that bishops were usually treated in the west. Altogether, it was an ugly incident. It made the "universal" empire of Justinian appear, to many Latins, small and shabby. It was an alien world, "Greek" in its tyrannical ways.

Justinian, however, was quite prepared to sacrifice the good opinion of the Latins to gain Syria. What is remarkable is that the Monophysites, who stood so close to Justinian in their basic assumptions, remained unimpressed even by his attempt to make the Council of Chalcedon inoffensive to them. Driven too fast for too long, the complex mechanisms of imperial persuasion no longer worked. An emperor who wished to command clergymen also had to know how to cajole. In the first decades of his reign, Justinian had done this, with style, through his remarkable consort, Theodora. Known to her Monophysite admirers, quite candidly, as "Theodora, formerly of the brothel," the empress had been a circus performer and, later, the kept woman of a provincial governor.[23] But she was also a devout Monophysite, close to the great theologian, Severus of Antioch (465–538), whose works she read in editions specially prepared for her in large, formal script.[24] One suspects that Justinian was more fascinated by Theodora's intense converted state than by the intricate sexual *savoir faire* ascribed to her by her enemies: she was yet further proof that reform was always possible.

Theodora's patronage kept the Monophysite leaders "in play." Bishops and abbots dispossessed by Justinian were settled, by Theodora, in respectable retirement in Constantinople, temptingly close to the court. By this means they were also kept at a safe distance from their restive flocks. In the early part of his reign, Theodora represented a principle of amnesty, even of caprice, which the forceful Justinian could not allow himself to show. When she died, in 548, Justinian was disconsolate. His subsequent handling of religious opposition did not show the same certainty of touch.

By the 550s, the provinces themselves had changed. Less could be done through the cities. Though backed by force and substantial bribes, Chalcedonian bishops installed in the cities lacked authority. They were frequently discomforted by reminders of the desert, in the form of intransigent Monophysite holy men who came in from the country.

Symeon the hermit suddenly appeared in the main basilica of Amida (Diyarbekir, eastern Turkey):

> a strange and outlandish sight . . . clad in a patchwork of rags made of sackcloth and carrying the Cross on his shoulder.

Symeon urged the congregation not to submit to the "impious" council. He was a reminder that the precious essence of sanctity was not to be found upon a bishop's throne, but out in the hills.[25]

In Syria, the effect of the plague was to accelerate the long-term development by which town and country came to level up with each other. For Monophysite clergy to lose control of the cities was not to be rendered marginal. It was to "relocate," much as a modern business might relocate from a degraded down-town. Bishops took up residence in great monasteries connected with large villages, in which the local aristocracy had built substantial houses and endowed churches as impressive as any that could be found in a city. In Egypt, Syria and elsewhere, informal networks based on great villages had become as important as were the urban structures of the imperial administration and the imperial Church.

Between 542 and 578 Jacob Baradaeus (Burdona'), the Monophysite bishop of Edessa, took the fateful step of ordaining an entire Monophysite counter-hierarchy. The Monophysites would no longer compete for a foothold in the single Church of the empire; they would have a Church of their own. Dressed in the wild ragged cloak of a Syrian holy man, Jacob travelled incessantly all over the eastern provinces, "causing the priesthood to flow like great rivers." He set up twenty-seven metropolitans and was said to have ordained 100,000 clergymen. Not surprisingly, the Monophysites came to be known as "Jacobites," from the numerous ecclesiastical progeny of Jacob Baradaeus.[26]

The Monophysite Church that Jacob created was not like the old Church of the empire. It was not a cellular structure, where separate urban communities were piled one on top of the other, in a pyramid that culminated at Constantinople. It consisted, rather, of a set of region-wide networks. Town and country were equal, because equally covered by the long tentacles of a shared religious identity. Even the frontiers of the empire were ignored. In the course of the sixth century, Monophysite missionaries had created what has been aptly called a "Commonwealth" of Christian kingdoms along the periphery of the empire. The Armenian aristocracy rejected Chalcedon in 551. Far to the south, Axum and Nubia were independent Monophysite kingdoms, and Arab sheiks on the borders of Syria emerged as major patrons of Monophysite monasteries. Monophysite clergymen travelled with ease among their co-religionists from Constantinople deep into Persian Mesopotamia. The heavy collective sense of a single urban community joined around the celebration of the Eucharist, with which we began this chapter, gave way to a world of juxtaposed, extended networks that stretched through town and village alike. Chalcedonians and Monophysites lived side by side, without mingling, throughout the Middle East. Each felt that they had more in common with distant co-religionists than with their "heretical" neighbors in the same city.

The generations after Justinian were marked by disastrous wars with Persia, by increased violence between "Blues" and "Greens," and by the strengthening of the dissident Monophysite churches. But they also coincided with a flowering of hagiography, equivalent to the writings of their contemporary, Gregory of Tours, in their urge to map out all aspects of the sacred. Monophysite and Chalcedonian writers alike needed to uphold the solidarity of their own Christian community. They both did so by exploring the manner in which God's grace penetrated, through miracles and holy persons, into every nook and cranny of society. This is what the Monophysite writer John of Ephesus (507–588) had in common with Chalcedonian writers of the early seventh century, such as John Moschus and Leontius of Neapolis, in Cyprus. While the bishop of Tours had looked mainly to the ancient dead and to the world of nature to find, there, all-redeeming traces of God's Paradise, writers such as John of Ephesus looked, rather, into the great cities and villages, to scan the heaving, faceless mass of the poor. If Christ could be found there, then He could be found everywhere. He had not entirely abandoned a fragmented and disillusioned Christian world.[27]

John of Ephesus' Monophysite theology may have made him peculiarly anxious to look to the poor in this way. For if Christ had taken on human flesh with such absorptive power as to render it divine, the humblest human body, because it bore the same flesh as Christ, was as charged with sanctity as was the Eucharist itself. To flout a beggar was to trample on flesh mysteriously linked to Christ and, so, to God Himself. John wrote of how two ladies, Susanna and Euphemia, emerged as the leaders of the Monophysite opposition in Amida. In a region of cruel winters, they put relentless pressure on the rich to support the poor. Townsmen quaked when they saw Euphemia bearing down upon them, with "her quick and rapid walk . . . with her toes bruised and her nails torn." She would rebuke them for neglecting their fellow-believers:

> While God is knocked down in the streets and swarms with lice and faints from hunger, do you not fear Him?[28]

It was in this manner, with an emphasis on the Christ-like nature of the common man, that sanctity was thought to have flowed back from the desert into the settled land. Each Christian, by partaking in the Eucharist, was joined to every other, by the fragile threads of a shared flesh, common to each other and to Christ:

> An important person took great pleasure in watching wild-beast shows, and hoped for one thing only, to see the fighters wounded by the animals. One day he fell into danger and cried to God: "Lord, come to my help in this misfortune." Then the Lord came to him, His body covered with wounds, and said: "This is how you wish to see me; how then have I the strength to help you?"[29]

Poignant anecdotes such as this mark the end of an age. Large Christian groups, Chalcedonians quite as much as Monophysites, were prepared to forget their ancient loyalties to their cities. Religion provided them with a more certain, more deeply felt basis of communal identity. Even when they lived in villages and cities where their own church predominated – as was often the case in strongly Monophysite regions, such as Egypt – they saw themselves above all else as a religious community. They were fellow-believers. They were no longer fellow-citizens. Although, at the time, the thought remained unthinkable even for extreme Monophysites, within a century from the death of Justinian, the populations of Syria and Egypt, having fallen under Muslim rule, would rapidly forget that they had once lived under a Christian empire.

8

Regimen Animarum:
Gregory the Great

In the late sixth century, of all the major cities of the beleaguered east Roman empire, Rome was the most desolate and
the most neglected. Its population reduced to less than 50,000,
it was the run-down window on the west of an empire drained
by unremitting war with Persia. After 568, Lombard armies
destroyed forever the unity of the reconquered provinces of
Italy. They occupied much of the Po valley, and, at Spoleto
and Beneventum, they came to control the mountainous spine
of Italy. Like the *Sklaviniai* of the Balkans, the Lombard
garrisons represented an unprepossessing alternative to empire,
to which local communities rallied with little difficulty. It was
the inhabitants of the surviving territories of the "Roman"
empire, on whom their war-bands fell with great cruelty, and
not all Italians, who treated the Lombards as "the fiercest of
all nations."

Confronting the Lombards along the estuary of the Po, an
imperial viceroy still resided at Ravenna. In the exquisite
palace church of San Vitale, the altar was ringed by mosaics
placed on the lower walls of the apse. They showed Justinian
and Theodora in their full imperial majesty. Silently part
of every Mass, the image of the imperial couple and their
entourage brought to northern Italy the challenge of a universal

empire. The state represented by the Exarch of Ravenna was not just any state. It was the *sancta respublica*, the "Holy Commonwealth." The surviving "Roman" empire, brought to the western Mediterranean by Justinian, was the only Christian kingdom that enjoyed an immemorial and irrefutable title to world-rule. All others were, in varying degrees, "barbarian" usurpations, whose legitimacy depended, in the last resort, on recognition by the emperor of Constantinople.

Rome was allowed to fall into the hands of its popes. They fed the city. Over 400 estates, the "patrimony of Saint Peter," located, for the most part, in Sicily, provided levies of food and gold coin to maintain the city of Rome, to ransom and relocate refugees from central Italy and to pay the imperial garrisons. The pope and the bishop of Ravenna were the bankers of the east Roman state in Italy: only they were able to advance money to a penniless administration. Yet Rome, also, was an "imperial" city. New mosaics placed in its basilicas made this plain:

> May the enemies of the Roman name be vanquished throughout the entire world by the power of Saint Peter.[1]

The kingdoms of the west, Francia and Visigothic Spain, maintained a healthy respect for the ability of the east Roman empire, even in its weakened state, to destabilize any regime at will. As late as the 660s, a clergyman sent from Rome to Britain was detained, in Francia, as an east Roman agent sent to stir up the Saxon kings against the Franks. The most dramatic religious change to occur in the western Mediterranean – the final adoption of Catholicism as the religion of the Visigothic state, in 589 – took place in almost total independence of the bishop of Rome. It was a conversion brought about, in large part, by the need to beat the east Romans at their own game. By becoming a Catholic kingdom, Visigothic Spain could claim to be the equal of the "Holy Commonwealth" of east Rome.

It is difficult to measure the exact extent of the desolation of Italy. What was clear by 590, when Gregory became pope in Rome, at the age of 50, was that an Italian *ancien régime* had all but vanished, taking with it a distinctive form of upper-class Christianity. From the resignation of Romulus Augustulus, in

476, to the arrival of Justinian's armies, in 534, Italy had been kept recognizably "Roman" through the dominance of a narrow group of landed aristocrats, who were members of the ancient Senate of Rome. With their Italy-wide connections and vast estates, the "Romans of Rome" eclipsed the local churches and the lesser provincial nobility. Unlike the fiercely regionalized magnates of Gaul, they did not need to take over the Church by becoming bishops: bishops remained humble figures, clients of the Roman grandees. There was not much love lost between these great families and the less-refined petty gentry. As a result of their isolation, the "Romans of Rome" lost everything in the wars that accompanied Justinian's reconquest. Their estates were ravaged. They were pushed to one side by a new alliance of "emperor's men" from Constantinople – officials and army officers – and a rough-hewn provincial gentry. By the end of the sixth century, these two groups formed a new Italian society that was as frankly dominated by uncultivated men of war as were the regions held by the "armies" of the Lombards.

What was lost, through this development, was a true leisured class, and the styles of culture and religion that went with such a class. Up to AD 550, money had been available, especially in Rome, to maintain the huge expense of libraries that would house, copy and circulate the ever-growing body of Christian literature. The philosopher and theologian, Boethius (480–524) could work in his Roman library, where light filtered through alabaster windows on to cupboards stocked with Greek and Latin books. He made technical works of Greek philosophy available in Latin. When imprisoned and facing execution for treason, in 524, he wrote a *Consolation of Philosophy* that would dominate the sensibility of the Christian Middle Ages precisely because it bore no sign of Christianity. Its exploration of the relationship between divine providence and human misfortune and its exaltation of the courage of the lonely sage cut deeper into what was truly universal in the human condition than could words taken from any one religious group.

It is a tribute to the undiminished ambitions of learned Italian Christians that they attempted to take advantage of the wider horizons opened up in the first decades of Justinian's reconquest. Cassiodorus (490–583) had served as spokesman for the Ostrogothic kings at Ravenna. He spent frustrating years in Constantinople, as Italian interests were progressively pushed to one side at court. He returned still with high hopes to Italy. He founded a monastery on his estate, called Vivarium from the neighboring fish-pond, outside Squillace (near modern Catanzaro), at the toe of Italy. Looking out on the Ionian sea, backed by a steep mountain range, Vivarium lay among orchards beside a happy stream. It was the center of a well-organized estate, supported by the rents of a dutiful peasantry. Cassiodorus intended it to be a little "city of God."[2]

As he outlined his hopes, in 550, in the *Institutes of Christian Culture*, Cassiodorus regarded his monastery as a place where the classics of Latin Christian literature would be copied and circulated, where translations of Greek works would be undertaken, and where the basic skills of Latin grammar and rhetorical analysis were maintained, as a *sine qua non* for the understanding and the accurate copying of the Scriptures. Small text-books, carefully prepared as "Teach-Yourself" volumes, designed to meet the needs of the average reader, made the culture of a very ancient world available to a less-privileged generation, that could no longer count on having teachers available, in their locality, to explain difficult texts to them by word of mouth. The noisy life of the cities had included the voice of local schoolteachers, beating the intricacies of Latin grammar into their pupils in little cubicles curtained off on one side of the forum. Those voices had fallen silent in much of Italy. Teachers were harder to find. If they survived, it was among the clergy or in monasteries, among men who had less time to devote to explaining, by word of mouth, the intricacies of Latin grammar. Consequently, basic books took on a life of their own. We last hear of Cassiodorus at the age of 81. He had returned "to my old friends, the orthographers:" a text-book on basic Latin spelling was what his monks now needed. They came from a post-war generation, for whom the leisured erudition of the *ancien régime* in Italy was a thing of the past.[3]

What had continued in Italy up to the youth of Gregory was a style of the Christian life that still left room for the devout lay person. In this respect, Gregory remained part of the east Roman Christendom that we have just described. He shared the basic east Roman assumption that lay persons had the same vocation to sanctity as had monks. What held them back were *curae*, the manifold "cares" that accompanied the life of any person constrained by his or her obligations to society. Time free of such cares was the essential preliminary step for those touched by compunction and by a sharp yearning for God – time to create new "habits of the heart," time to pray, to seek advice and comfort from holy persons, time to read the Scriptures on one's own, as carefully as one would read an imperial edict, "so as to learn from God's words to know God's heart." 4

In this style of piety, which assumed literacy and leisure, women were not only the equal of men. They were, if anything, the unspoken model of male behavior. The secluded position of upper-class women provided a centuries-old pattern for a style of life that pious men had to struggle with the greatest difficulty to attain. Men were tied to their public roles. It was harder for them than it was for women to endure a life robbed of public profile, so as to live a semi-reclusive existence, in the world but not of the world. In Gregory's family, the alternation of public eminence and reclusiveness was taken for granted. His grandfather, pope Felix III (526–530), had built the first church – now San Cosma e Damiano – to be set up in the Roman forum. The large inscription in the apse makes plain that the church was Felix's own, fully public largesse to the Roman *plebs*. Yet Gregory's aunts lived a life of sheltered piety in the family palace. It was a life with fluid boundaries. A sense of *noblesse oblige*, and not convent walls, kept the young girls apart from the "world." The youngest aunt rebelled. She married, of all persons, a steward of the family estates – an aspiring member of the petty gentry that had been held at a distance for so long by the great families of Rome.5

When he took up secular office, as Prefect of Rome, in 573, Gregory thought that the life of a devout layman was within his powers to achieve. It was only a little later that he decided that he should become a monk. It was a decision based upon disquiet. He felt that he lacked the moral strength to combine a life of public "cares" with a religious vocation, as so many lay persons still did, in Rome, Constantinople and elsewhere. He turned his father's house on the Clivus Scauri on the Aventine hill into a small monastery placed under the protection of Saint Andrew. His mother, it was said, would bring the daily ration of cooked vegetables, served on the sole remaining piece of family silver.[6]

Gregory knew of the *Rule* of Saint Benedict, but his monastery was not an up-country cottage, as Benedict's monasteries had been. It was a center of fierce asceticism and heavy learning. Gregory ruined his health by austerities: from then onwards his energies were sapped by constant illness. In the manner of a late Roman man of learning, he breathed in the wisdom of the past, especially through prodigious bursts of reading in the works of Saint Augustine. This was the life for which he considered himself best suited – a life without cares.

Hence the bitter disappointment with which Gregory, a man who had fled the pious layman's exposure to worldly cares, fell back, once again, and, this time heavily and forever, into just such a life. To join the Roman clergy was to re-enter public life at its most exacting. Gregory was made deacon of the Roman church and sent to Constantinople in 579. Given the frosty climate of the court, and its lack of interest in Italian affairs, Gregory found time to continue his monastic existence. He later claimed to know no Greek. But he did so when denying authorship of works that circulated in Greek under his name.[7] Though a Latin, the bishop of Rome, and his representative, were expected to have a say in the theological life of the capital. In the Greek world, great churchmen were praised for possessing "elegant fingers, apt for writing on matters divine."[8] Eutychius, who was patriarch of Constantinople when Gregory was present, had introduced himself, at once, by distributing complimentary copies of his theological treatises to leading members of Constantinopolitan society. He sent them

> among the houses of the leading senators, both to men and to women . . . and with his book, he sent the message, "Read and learn."[9]

Gregory pointedly avoided that course of action. Settled in the palace of the papal representatives, Gregory was content to assemble a small group of Latins around himself. He lectured like an abbot among his monks. He expounded to them the "moral" message – that is, the message relevant to progress in spiritual matters – of the book of Job. The *Moralia in Job* showed a man who had decided to place ethics, and not theology, at the center of his thought. In so doing, Gregory showed that he wished to confront a problem that had preoccupied Roman ethical writers since the days of Seneca – the problem of power and of its attendant cares and duties.

In 590, Gregory's fate was sealed: he was made pope. "Under the pretext of becoming a bishop, I have been led back into the world." [10] Until his death, in 604, Gregory's life was summed up in a single phrase from the book of Job: *Behold, the giants groan beneath the waters.*[11] A man who had passed, for a few years, into the contemplative stillness of monastic seclusion, Gregory found himself crushed beneath the oceanic pressures that weighed on every Catholic bishop in the sixth century, and on none more heavily than those who supported the massive structures of the east Roman state.

What makes Gregory unusual and his writings decisive for the entire future of western Europe was the fact that he alone wrote constantly, and with a rare combination of scholastic finesse and deeply personal disquiet, about the exercise of power itself:

> *Ars artium regimen animarum*: The art to end all arts is the governing of souls.[12]

The phrase set the tone for a short work that he published in 593, the *Regula Pastoralis*. He took care to circulate it widely. It was soon known as far away as Francia. It even appeared in Greek. It was Gregory's tract for his times.

One thing was certain in Gregory's world – power was there to stay. Gregory lived in a world where Christianity now touched every level of life. Power, in such a world, meant attention to both the most exalted and to the most humble aspects of existence. Saint Paul was Gregory's ideal. Here was a man whose activities had moved in an unbroken flow from the heights of mystical contemplation to rulings on the legitimacy of marriage, even on the correct times for marital intercourse. Paul the contemplative had entered the "third heaven;" "and yet, with heartfelt empathy, he surveys with care the average person's marriage bed."[13]

Condescensio, a compassionate stepping down to the level of every person in the Christian Church, was the key to Gregory's notion of spiritual power. It was "condescension" in the best meaning of the word: it echoed the vertiginous act by which God Himself had bent to earth, to touch humankind in the person of Jesus Christ. It bridged the fissure between the contemplative life and the world of storm-tossed cares. Such cares were no longer a tragic and debilitating distraction, echoes of the primal fall of the soul from its high station. They were "cares of state." A contemplative's wisdom, nourished by communion with God based upon prolonged meditation on the Scriptures, was placed at the disposal of others: it was intended to inspire a style of rule minutely calibrated to the needs of each subject. And the need of each, for Gregory, was holiness – spiritual progress that would lead, beyond this life, to the luminous joy of the kingdom of God.

Gregory drew deeply on the thought of Augustine. But he was no epigone. On the issue of spiritual power, he thought more urgently and far more consequentially than did Augustine. The *Regula Pastoralis* has the clarity and cutting edge of a diamond. The less consistent thought of Augustine (an intellectual at heart, and a man who wrote in an age where Christianity had not yet gained an outright monopoly of power) was compressed into crystalline hardness by Gregory's reflection on his own experience. He knew that he and his colleagues had to wield real power. *God does not reject the powerful, for He Himself is powerful* (Job 36: 5).[14]

As a result, the ancient tradition of care of the self was transformed. This tradition had favored the lonely self-grooming of the sage. It had lingered with uneasy sensitivity on the passions aroused by the exercise of power. With Gregory, this tradition lost its reserve. Based on *condescensio*, an austere, ascetic care of the self spilled over into the care of others.

Power was redeemed, by becoming power over souls. It was a trust, wielded to advance the common good – the salvation of all believers. It was a trust whose exercise required exceptional finesse. As all men were equals, because equally sin-laden descendants of Adam, rule by the few over the many had to be based upon claims to authentic, personal wisdom. Hence the enduring paradox of Gregory's *Regula Pastoralis*. The book seemed to place the Christian populations of Europe in the hands of a tranquil elite of "physicians of the soul." Rulers of souls were expected to be persons endowed with an ancient doctor's almost uncanny power to "smell out," with a fine nose, the hidden moral fevers and infections that lay deep within the self.[15] It was a searching ideal, that seemed to subject all Christians to the penetrating gaze of spiritual experts. But Gregory upheld his ideal of the Christian *rector*, in all his writings, so as to warn colleagues not to take their position for granted. Judged by such high standards, many a bishop was no better than a lay person: without skill in the rule of souls he was not a true bishop:

> *They have come to reign, but not through Me; princes have arisen, and I know nothing of them.*
>
> (Hosea 8:4)[16]

The medical imagery of the *Regula Pastoralis* was a challenge. The perpetual rhythm of sin and reparation that had bound the Christian communities together for so many centuries was held, by Gregory, to require forms of leadership that could only be provided by persons whom we, nowadays, would call "professionals," even "technocrats." It was not a job for amateurs. Amateurs – magnates turned bishops, in Gaul; emperor's men, in the sees of Italy and the Roman east – were what Gregory feared most. His *Regula Pastoralis* warned them to think twice before undertaking the unique "weight of the pastoral office." Those who ruled in the Church must know how to rule and why they ruled – for rule they must.

Behind Gregory's fierce precision lies the fact that the Christian Church now harbored a number of small but highly significant environments in which power over souls was exercised at its most absolute and its most searching – that is, in the monasteries. Gregory had, himself, been the abbot of a small monastic community. He had shared in the power of an abbot. It was a terrifying power. On one occasion, for instance, he had allowed a man to die alone, without the comfort of his fellows, for a single sin of avarice. He knew the *Regula* of Benedict. Benedict's *Rule* was one of the many monastic "rules" that circulated in Rome. The very anonymity of some of them (such as *The Rule of a Master*) gave them added authority. They were the condensed life's wisdom of recognized masters of the art of souls.

For Gregory, Benedict was a figure of the now-distant past. He had died in around 547. His monastery at Monte Cassino no longer existed. It had been sacked by a Lombard war-band. The story of Benedict's life came to Gregory, like the ghostly bells of a sunken city, from a world before the furious impact of the Lombards. But this did not matter. To read Benedict's *Regula* was to seize the essence of the man. What struck Gregory above all was Benedict's rare *discretio*, the inspired certainty of touch of an abbot who knew how to lead his tiny flock of monks through every spiritual and material emergency. Each monk was bound to his abbot and to his fellows by an awesome code, that was summed up in one phrase: *obedientia sine mora*, "obedience without a moment's hesitation." In the *Rule* of Benedict, absolute power over souls demanded absolute integrity of purpose and absolute clarity as to its final aim.[17]

These were small monasteries. They seldom housed more than thirty monks. The monks lived as close to each other as inmates in a modern prison cell. They knew each other intimately and, alas, at times, they could hate each other with the same, crazed intensity. The monks were never out of each other's sight. At Compludo, in northwestern Spain, the prior would linger for a moment at nightfall in the cottage-like dormitory of the monastery, surveying the beds,

> that, by observing each monk more closely, he may learn how to treat the character and merits of each.[18]

One could have no illusion as to the skill required to govern such small, cramped groups as a true *abbas*, a "father." For the *abbas*, as "father," was the representative, among his monks, of God the Father. So that his words might work, like God's own leaven in the soul of each monk, the abbot

> must vary from one occasion to another, mixing soft words with threats, the sternness of a schoolmaster with the tenderness of a father . . . And let him be aware how difficult, how arduous a thing it is to govern souls and to put himself out to serve so many different temperaments.[19]

Gregory placed the abbot's exercise of his authority, the most intimate and penetrating model of power available to the Christian experience of his time, at the heart of all exercise of power in the Christian community. It was a disturbingly open-ended notion, and potentially universal in its application. Though usually a bishop, a clergyman or an abbot, the *rector*, the ruler of souls, envisaged by Gregory might be any holy lay person, any pious local magnate, any Christian king. Each, in a different but strictly homologous manner, did the same thing: each had been given by God the opportunity to exercise persuasive power in the interests of the one, true goal of a Christian society, the salvation of souls.

Hence the pervasive effect of Gregory's writings throughout the early Middle Ages. Much as a single official language becomes dominant more rapidly in a region characterized by a great diversity of local languages, so, in the seventh and eighth centuries, Gregory's studiously undifferentiated notion of the Christian *rector* achieved a remarkable degree of universality. In a western world that had become a mosaic of contrasting political systems, it provided the lowest common denominator for the description of a Christian use of power. It could be read as validating different aspects of widely differing forms of authority. Gregory's heavy emphasis on the responsibilities of the ruler for the souls of his subjects lent an added note of solemnity and urgency to the impressive, Roman-style legislation of the Visigothic kings of Spain. At the same time, his emphasis on the adaptable, consensus-building qualities required of a Christian *rector* did justice to the more tentative powers of Celtic chieftains in the far, non-Roman North. With a language of power of such coherence, made available in the writings of a pope who enjoyed towering literary authority throughout the Latin world (Gregory's *Moralia in Job*, for instance, had been re-edited in digest form both in Ireland and in Spain by the 660s), it was that much less necessary to look to the actual Christian Roman empire as the model for a Christian state. By speaking of bishops, abbots and kings interchangeably, in terms of a common Christian art of ruling souls, Gregory created what could become, in later centuries, the Europe-wide language of a governing elite. With the *Regula Pastoralis* to inspire them, the literate clergy could feel that they had a mission to rule as clear and as all-embracing as any that had once inspired the governing classes of the Roman empire.

But this is to anticipate. In the ancient world, rulers set the tone, not by books of political theory, but through the manner in which they themselves interacted with their subjects in highly visible situations. Here Gregory played his part to perfection. John the Persian visited Rome from northern Iraq. When he bowed to make the customary reverential prostration, Gregory checked him: the pope was no "lord." Then Gregory bent forward and, with his own fingers, he placed three gold coins in the monk's hand.[20] Gregory's correspondence tells the same tale. It documents a distinctive style of rule. The 866 surviving letters collected in his *Regestum*, his *Register of Correspondence*, were no more than the tip of the iceberg. Quite apart from his correspondence with the court at Constantinople and with other western rulers, Gregory, as pope, was the center of a network of patronage and administration that stretched from Marseille and Sardinia to Sicily and Carthage. Twenty thousand letters, at least, must have been written from Rome in the years of Gregory's pontificate. Sixty-three percent of the letters were rescripts – they were answers to requests for a ruling on administrative and ecclesiastical matters. They would have involved delegations to Rome and the sort of solemn interviews that we know of from the story of John the Persian.

Copies of the letters that were sent out were selected, each year, by Gregory himself. They were transcribed into a large papyrus volume. The letters, as we have them in the *Regestum*, were Gregory's own memoirs of his years as pope. They document a distinctive style of rule. The word "subtle" recurs frequently, in innumerable contexts. Precision, finesse, studied courtesy, mediated in the localities by chosen representatives of an exclusively clerical or monastic background close to Gregory's own views, were the sign of a new broom in the Lateran Palace. So, also, was the occasional letter of rebuke. The bishop of Salona (Solun, near Split), proud ruler of a "Roman" imperial enclave on the Dalmatian coast, justified his lavish banquets by an appeal to the hospitality of Abraham. Gregory was not amused:

> In no way do you give attention to reading the Scriptures, in no way are you vigilant to offer exhortation, rather, you ignore even the common norms of an ecclesiastical way of life.[21]

On his epitaph, Gregory was acclaimed as *consul Dei*: "God's consul." But such reminders of continuity with the Roman past were largely wished upon him. Gregory did not think of himself as a "last Roman." He was a *praedicator*, a man called to give warning at the end of time. The ruins of Rome play such a poignant role in his writings because they were a statement of the obvious. They spoke plainly, and to everyone, of the swift and hidden race of history towards its end. More prosperous societies might delude themselves that God's time stood still for their benefit. The crash of falling masonry around the Forum and, indeed, the entire state of post-Lombard Italy were "an open book" for all to read. The end was close.[22] What mattered, now, was *praedicatio*, the gathering into the Christian Church of what remained of the human race, so as to face the dread Judgement Seat of Christ with the one, sure protection of Christian baptism.

It was a thought calculated to greatly concentrate the mind. The age of *praedicatio* was an age of unexpected excitements. Like soft dawn light creeping beneath a door, Gregory saw, in his own age, a subdued recrudescence of the miraculous powers that had flickered around the first advance of the Apostles. In 594, his *Dialogues* – a collection of miracles discussed in a series of conversations between himself and his friend, Peter – announced to the Christian world that, in recent times, Gregory's native Italy had been filled with vibrant holy men and women, sent by God to warn mankind. The *Dialogues* make plain that, for Gregory, a *praedicator* did not have to be a bishop, or even a "preacher" in the strict sense. Holiness spoke for itself. Old abbot Florentius, perched in the woods above Subiaco, with a pet bear who always knew the correct hours for prayer, had, in his time, drawn a whole countryside to Christ as effectively as did any sermonizer.[23]

Miracles of *praedicatio* had, indeed, begun to happen on a grand scale. In 589, the entire political elite of the last, non-Catholic, Arian kingdom of the west, the Visigoths of Spain, adopted Catholicism. An entire "nation" joined the Church. As we saw, Gregory was studiously excluded from this development. But it confirmed his best suspicions of his age:

> *This is the change which the right hand of the Most High hath wrought.*
> It was [he wrote, to the Visigothic king, Reccared, who had sent a belated, somewhat parsimonious gift of shirts for the poor at Saint Peter's] a new miracle in our time. My feelings are roused against myself, because I have been so sluggish . . . while, to gain the heavenly fatherland, kings are working for the gathering-in of souls.[24]

Gregory had not long to wait. It is a grim comment on the conditions of early medieval Europe that slave-traders were among the most effective, if unwitting, missionaries of the age. They brought about the forcible transfer of whole populations. In 593, Gregory had watched the peasants of the Roman Campagna, "tied by the neck like dogs," driven in droves to the north, by Lombard raiders, to sell to Frankish dealers from across the Alps. In 595, similar dealers brought to the markets of Gaul parties of *Angli*, tribesmen from the Saxon kingdoms of Britain. They were a timely reminder, for Gregory, of pagan nations to whom the Gospel had yet to be preached, before the end of the world could come.[25]

The appearance of these sad figures may have coincided with a delegation from the king of Kent, Ethelbert, who had already married a Frankish wife. Here was a "nation" that might be "gathered in." Gregory was not a man to be outdone by a Visigothic king. He himself would provide the *praedicatio* for this distant kingdom. In 597, an exceptionally large party sent from Rome, headed by a monk from Gregory's own monastery (named, significantly, Augustine) received permission from Ethelbert to settle in the royal center of his kingdom, in the ruins of a Roman town that was later called Canterbury.

The local circumstances that led to Gregory's mission belong to another chapter. There is no doubt as to the high drama of the event as seen by Gregory himself. In July 598, he wrote to his colleague, the patriarch of Alexandria:

> While the people of the English, placed in a corner of the world, remained until now in the false worship of stocks and stones, I resolved . . . to send . . . a monk of my monastery to preach to that people . . . And even now letters have reached us . . . that both he and those who were sent with him shine with such miracles that the miracles of the Apostles seem to live again in the signs that they exhibit.26

Ten thousand *Angli*, he added, had been baptized at Christmas. It was, altogether, an amazing happening, worthy of the end of time.

Gregory died in 604. He had come to expect the unexpected. But he could hardly have foreseen how unusual the future might yet be. Within a century, the first attempt to write his *Life* was made in a monastery perched on the edge of the North Sea, close to Hadrian's wall. Streanaeshalch (modern Whitby, in Yorkshire) was a monastery in which an abbess ruled monks. It had been founded for a lady of royal Anglian blood, who bore the name of a Valkyrie, abbess Hild.27 We have come a long way, within a century, from the Aventine Hill in Rome. In the next chapters we will trace the profound changes of the generations after Gregory I, that made possible the emergence in the far north of strange new Christian regions.

9

Medicamenta Paenitentiae: Columbanus

In 593, the emperor Maurice issued an edict that forbade all persons liable to military service to become monks. Gregory the Great wrote in protest. An entire style of Christian life was at stake. It was never too late to seek holiness. Indeed,

> there are many persons who, unless they abandon all [and enter a monastery] cannot gain salvation in the sight of God.[1]

Gregory appealed to widespread assumptions, in a world where monasteries had been present for centuries. Lay persons were, of course, capable of salvation. But monasteries existed for those called to a sharper, more exacting style of Christian life. Both sensitive souls (such as Gregory himself had been) and great sinners needed "conversion." For sixth-century Christians, "conversion" had come to mean not a change of faith but a change of life. It meant joining a monastery so to "purge" their sins.

The *Rule* composed by Benedict for his monks at Monte Cassino faced this fact with loving precision. It was a *Rule* "for beginners." The monastery was a "school of the Lord's service."[2] It was an elementary school. Upper-class persons, who had attended such schools, knew what this meant. They had struggled at school to internalize the crystalline precision of "correct" Latin under the cane of a schoolmaster. So, in a monastery, grown men were expected to go back to a school of morals. They were to subject their behavior to meticulous supervision, accompanied, when necessary, by instant punishment, blows from the strap included. In an intensely status-conscious society, the most heroic self-mortification of all was to submit oneself, in this way, to the rule of an abbot. In the words of a man who knew his Benedict, Columbanus, the yet sterner Irishman:

For, indeed, this discipline seems hard to hard men, that a man should hang always on the mouth of another.[3]

It was the heavily disciplined life of the monk that guaranteed the prestige of the monasteries. It gave the monks the reputation of possessing an inestimable power of prayer. Indeed, when it came to the power of prayer, women, as nuns, were more than the equals of men. Women were often subjected to peculiarly strict seclusion; for they carried in their own bodies the charged "treasure" of virginity. Their bodies perpetually intact, perpetually hidden behind high walls, observant nuns stood for all that was most awesomely unchanged in a changing world. When Caesarius of Arles set up a convent for his sister, Caesaria, in 512, the *Rule* that he composed for her became a classic. It was marked by meticulous control. He even sketched, in the manuscript, the precise shape of the hair-cuts that the nuns should have. Caesaria's community was worth the care. It had 200 members. Convents were usually larger than most male monasteries, because well-to-do families tended to place in them daughters for whom they did not wish to find a dowry. But, when subjected to fierce discipline, this large group was expected to act as a veritable powerhouse of prayer. The constant intercessions of Caesaria's nuns, in a convent built into a corner of the city's walls, acted as the true supernatural "bulwark" of Arles, at a time when the city needed such protection.[4]

The male monasteries of this period were not the large, self-sufficient communities that they would become. Many were converted villas. The monastic cloister that became so well known in western Europe was an echo of the open peristyle that lay at the center of any Roman country house. Many monasteries were established in marginal lands. A monk sent out to guard the sheep in Galicia was told that he had no option but to shiver on the bleak hillside:

> most monasteries would scarcely have enough food for three months if there was only the daily bread of the region to eat, which requires more work on the soil than in any other part of country.[5]

We are a long way from the great Benedictine houses of the Middle Ages, and a long way, also, from the well-organized estates of the Vivarium of Cassiodorus.

Nonetheless, even the most unprepossessing monastery contained its copy of the Bible and, with it, a minimum residue of literate culture. In central Italy, abbot Equitius would ride a nag with a rope bridle. He looked so like a peasant that no one would turn to greet him. Yet he always carried in his saddle-bag complete *codices* of the Gospels. Visitors to his rural monastery found copyists at work.[6] Religion involved writing. In his *Institutes*, Cassiodorus invested the very act of copying the Holy Scriptures with a mystical aura:

> Oh, sight glorious to those who contemplate it carefully! With gliding fingers the heavenly words are copied, so that the Devil's craft . . . may be destroyed.[7]

In Cassidorus' view, all Latin literature was to be mobilized towards transmitting the Scriptures. All the aids previously used so as to read and copy classical texts were to be used in order to understand the Scriptures and to copy them intelligently. Like a newly formed planetary system, Latin culture as a whole was supposed to spin in orbit around the vast sun of the Word of God.

Most monks were less ambitious than was Cassiodorus in their cultural agenda. For them, the Bible was simply a holy book, sent by God to cast fire into the heart. Every day, in Syria, the learned monk would bow before the Cross and place the Gospel on his forehead, eyes and heart before he began to read:

> God make me worthy [he would pray] that my intellect might enter deep within the external body of this ink.[8]

For simpler monks, even to hold such a book in one's hands was enough. A particularly holy monk at Amida was content with just that:

> he would open his Gospel book and gaze at it, and all at once his tears would gush forth . . . and he would not turn over a leaf, but would keep the book open at the Sermon on the Mount . . . or in places where the subject was threats and the Last Judgement.[9]

Just as, in the *Regula Pastoralis* of Gregory, all authority in the Church culminated, ideally, in a ruler of souls endowed with an abbot's imponderable, barely communicable skill in "searching the hearts" of his charges, so, in monastic circles, all culture culminated in an equally mysterious God-given gift for "searching the Scriptures," by opening one's mind and heart to the inexhaustible, ineffable wisdom that lay beneath the simple surface of the text of the Bible.

Outside the monastery, however, a thoroughly "worldly" Latin culture survived throughout the sixth century. The kingdoms of the west retained Roman-style bureaucracies. The Merovingians, for instance, were both long-haired and literate. They managed to combine an archaic Germanic mystique with control of a government that still needed constant paperwork. At ground level, Latin legal documents, written in the workaday cursive script of local notaries, remained essential for landowners and peasants alike. Wooden estate documents have been recovered from Vandal Africa. Similar legal instruments were scratched on tiles in seventh-century Castile. These two, recent discoveries are evidence of the remarkable continuity of Roman legal norms over many centuries and in many regions.[10]

A simple Latin remained the spoken language of the entire western Mediterranean. Even in North Africa, the "tongue of the Latins" was still spoken in some isolated oases of the Sahara as late as the eleventh century.[11] In Mediterranean Europe, Latin won its final triumph at this time. It replaced all previous local dialects. If Roman rule had vanished in the age of Marcus Aurelius, Gaul and Spain would have become Celtic-speaking countries, like Wales and Ireland. Apart from Brittany, this possibility was out of the question by the year 600.

At the top of society, the late Roman equation of power and high culture was maintained, if in shrunken form. Small cities no longer sent a constant supply of ambitious and well-educated young men, such as Augustine had been, to the centers of power. But those who already wielded power retained much of their culture. In "Roman" families, learned kinsmen would teach their young relatives the precious skills of Latin prose and verse composition. All "barbarian" courts patronized such people. When Venantius Fortunatus came to northern Gaul, in 567, he did not meet illiterate warriors. He met men such as Gogo the *referendarius*, the lord chancellor and tutor of the young kings. Gogo's letters, written in a style that was acclaimed as "succulent and florid," maintained literary friendships with fellow-members of the ruling class in a manner that had changed little since the days of Ausonius and Paulinus of Nola. The "simple," "rustic" Christian style advocated by bishops such as Caesarius of Arles and Gregory of Tours was like *nouvelle cuisine*. It was put forward as a self-conscious alternative, by men who knew that they lived in a world where the old high culture had survived, and that many of their more worldly contemporaries greatly preferred a hearty, old-fashioned "banquet of words" to the chaste simplicity of a Christian preacher's Latin.

In that respect, little had changed in Gaul since the days of Ausonius. Even the new, partly Roman, partly Frankish elite of *potentes* faced the same religious options as had been faced by the contemporaries of Martin of Tours. They, also, were touched by a powerful ascetic message. But Frankish kings and their new aristocracy – mainly military men, subject to harsh codes of honor and instant violence – found it that much harder than did the pensive, alienated and profoundly civilian landowners of the late fourth century to reconcile the demands of their profane life with a sharp sense of the sacred, associated with the new monasticism. For much of the sixth century, barbarian kings had tended to delegate ascetic piety to their womenfolk. Caratene, queen of the Burgundians, was praised for wearing a hair-shirt under her royal robes. She brought a fleck of intense holiness into a hard-living warrior court.[12]

The saintly queen Radegund (520–587) did this on a grander scale. A woman of royal stock from Thuringia, she was brought to Francia, in 532, to become the unwilling wife of king Chlothar. Placed in seclusion in a royal villa, the young girl would lead her companions in solemn processions carrying a home-made Cross. She finally shook herself free from her husband, and forced the bishop of Soissons to accept her as a nun, through shaving off her hair with her own hands. She emerged, in her new status, as a gift-giver in truly royal style. Robes, jewels, great gold-studded belts that were, for a Merovingian queen, the physical condensation on her person of the magical aura of royalty, were piled on the altars of churches or chopped up to be sent to local hermits. Her austerities made her admirers shudder. She bathed the poor, massaging with her own hands the scabby, worm-eaten heads of beggars. She brought a touch of the sacred to the highest society in Gaul. When she retired to Poitiers, in 561, to found a convent of her own, she used her status as a member of the Christian "family of princes" to obtain nothing less than a relic of the Holy Cross itself, direct from the emperor of Constantinople.

The delicate scent of a royal court lingered at Radegund's Convent of the Holy Cross. She received poems and baskets of strawberries from Venantius Fortunatus. A potted laurel stood in her cell. One of her nuns was delighted to recognize the sounds of a love-song that she had composed in her youth, drifting through a window from a festival below. But the monastery had a serious purpose. At a time when local devotion to urban patron-saints was the most intense form of Christian piety in Gaul, Radegund and her nuns prayed, rather, for the kings of the Franks and for their kingdom as a whole.[13]

Radegund, the extraordinary Thuringian, died in 587, only three years before the arrival, in Francia, of the equally extraordinary Irishman, Columbanus. Born in Leinster in around

540, Colum (tastefully rendered into Latin as Columbanus, "the poor little dove") was a product of the new Christian culture of Celtic Wales and Ireland. He had been a monk at the ascetic settlement of Bangor, some 30 kilometers along the shores of the Lough of Belfast. He arrived in Gaul with a retinue of disciples in 590, in the same year that Gregory the Great, a man the same age as himself, became pope in Rome. Columbanus never lacked for books. He knew the *Rule* of Benedict and soon received the *Regula Pastoralis* of Gregory. It was, he said, a book "sweeter than honey to the needy." He recognized, in Gregory, a fellow-master in the art of souls. But Rome remained a distant city to him. He chose to keep to the frontier zones of the north, close to the patronage of non-Roman kings. From 590 to 610 he settled at Luxeuil, in the Vosges. Later, he passed along the Rhine and across the Alps to Bobbio, a site offered to him on the northern edge of the Apennines by the king of the Lombards. He died in 615.

Columbanus did not grow up in a "Christian" country in the same way as Francia could claim to be a Christian kingdom. The solemn sense of a public community, that echoed, if on a smaller scale, the majesty of an "orthodox," Roman empire, was absent in Ireland. In a land of dispersed settlements, vivid enclaves of Christian teaching and Christian endeavor stood out in a land where pre-Christian traditions were ever-present. The son of a Christian mother, Columbanus was destined for the clergy. He was given (as if to a foster-father, according to Irish custom) to a *fer léighinn*, a "reading man" – to a teacher skilled in the exotic new skill of reading Latin. It was possible to achieve high standards of Latinity in Ireland. But communities where such rare skills were taught remained embedded in a pre-literate, still largely pagan society. They were like the *emporia* for foreign goods that had sprung up, at the same time, along the coastlines of Britain and Ireland, from Tintagel in Cornwall to Whithorn in southern Scotland. For a man such as Columbanus, in search of Christian perfection in his middle age, it was easier to take his Latin culture across the sea to Gaul than to remain in a self-confidently profane Ireland.

Columbanus brought with him to Francia an enclave mentality. He throve on being a member of a superior minority.

Fiercely loyal to his teachers and to the precious stock of books that he had already mastered, Columbanus shocked the local Gallic bishops by celebrating Easter on a different date from everyone else. It was the "true" date, the date that he had learned in Ireland. His masters at Bangor had regarded any other system for determining the date of Easter as "laughable." Columbanus instantly wrote to Gregory. It was the pope who was out of step. Had Gregory not read Saint Jerome?

> How then, with all your learning . . . do you favor a dark Easter? An Easter proved to be no Easter?

Perhaps, he opined, Gregory did not know the "most polished letter" sent by Saint Gildas (the zealous author of *On the Ruin of Britain*) to Saint Vinnian, on how to boycott sinful bishops? One suspects that these two luminaries of sixth-century Wales were not household words in the Lateran Palace. No reply from Gregory has survived.[14]

Despite his rough edges and his claim to be a total stranger from the edge of the world, Columbanus acted, in Francia, as a catalyst rather than as a total innovator. He brought a novel solution to problems that had begun to exercise Christians throughout the Latin west. Gaul was, indeed, a Christian country; but in the opinion of Columbanus and his later disciples, it was a country that lacked the *medicamenta paenitentiae*, the strong medicine of penitential discipline.[15] As a result of the ascetic movement sparked off by his activities, and continued by Frankish disciples, drawn largely from the aristocracy, the first half of the seventh century was a watershed in the history of western Christian piety.

Settled in Luxeuil, in northeastern Burgundy, Columbanus and his monks provided the region with the spectacle of stunning asceticism. His sermons to his monks brought back, to a long-Christian region, a thrilling touch of ancient, more heroic days:

> Ever must we cling to God, to the deep, vast, hidden and almighty God.[16]

But Gaul itself had changed. While the admirers of Saint Martin had been land-owning aristocrats, who lived at a distance from the centers of power, Columbanus went straight to the court. He knew, perhaps from his Irish experience, that it was kings, courtiers and warriors who needed the "medicine of penance" more than did most people. It was to them that he addressed his stern message. Luxeuil was, in effect, a royal foundation. Though elk and aurochs roamed the Vosges and Columbanus himself would walk the woods, whistling down from the trees a squirrel which would perch on his neck and run in and out of his cloak, the monastery was placed in a dilapidated Roman spa, surrounded by statues. A large community of 200 monks, it was recruited from among the top aristocracy of Frankish Gaul. Its manuscripts betray the bureaucratic skills that were practiced at the Frankish court, now applied to the copying of holy texts. The moment that Columbanus alienated his royal protector – which he did, predictably and memorably, by refusing to bless the illegitimate sons of Theuderic II in 610 – he was sent into exile.

Luxeuil continued to thrive under Frankish abbots. It became to the nobility of northern Gaul in the seventh century what Lérins had once been to the Romans of the south. It touched a new generation of courtiers. These were the *florentissimi enutriti,* the powerful and cultivated *jeunesse dorée,* brought up in the court of the formidable Dagobert I (623–638). Powerful courtiers in their "worldly" days, such men retired to become, as bishops and founders of monasteries, equally powerful and energetic local figures in the Frankish north: they were Eligius, the controller of the king's mint (Saint Eloi, bishop of Noyon, 641–660), his friend, Audoenus (Saint Ouen, bishop of Rouen, 641–684) and Wandregisil (600–668), who founded Saint Wandrille, in a deserted royal fort on the Seine. Other patrons of the new monasticism were country gentlemen in the rich valley of the Seine around Paris. They established large monasteries, governed by pious relatives, on their own estates. By so doing, they brought an impressive form of Christianity to the new heartlands of the Frankish kingdom.

What concerned such persons was the agonized question that east Romans had long addressed to their holy men: "Can a lay person be saved?" The answer given by Columbanus and his successors was stern in the extreme, in some ways, but merciful in others. Lay persons from the highest ranks of the aristocracy, many of them warriors, could, indeed, hope to be saved. But they would be saved only if they kept close to monasteries. They could either purge their sins through entering monasteries and undergoing the dramatic austerities that such a life entailed. Failing that, they must seek out the prayers of monks and support monasteries by lavish gifts. Ideally, they should expose themselves on a regular basis, even as lay persons, to the austere self-knowledge fostered among monks. Then, and only then, would the "medicine of penance" be sure to work, and the tremulous souls of powerful men and women would pass in safety to God.

By the standards of an earlier age, this was a singularly individualistic solution. In the early Church, reparation for sin had been a dramatic group experience. It was the members of the "people of God" as a whole who excluded notorious sinners from their midst, allowed them to continue on the fringes of the Church, as a separate category of "penitents," and then granted them the "peace" of reconciliation, through a fully public ceremony conducted by the bishop. Penance was a collective drama, that still assumed that the "people of God" were a minority – a pool of light surrounded by the shadows of a pagan world. It was better to endure for a time the humiliation of fully public exclusion from the "people of God," followed by an equally public ritual of reconciliation, than to fall into that outer darkness.

By AD 600, however, a profound change had happened in the Latin west. In most regions, the Church was coextensive with the entire social community. The "people of God" had become too big to be seen. Simply to be a member of the Church gave little reassurance. The average person might remain convinced that all but the most heinous sins were covered, in God's eyes, by participation in the rhythm of a collective Catholicism, such as had grown up in the cities of the fifth century: alms-giving, communal fasting, city-wide acts of penitential self-abasement were sufficient to get one to heaven. But the pious believer, especially if he or she came from an elite background, had always regarded the struggle with sin as a more perilous matter, as involving a deeply personal, seemingly interminable engagement with all layers of the self. Group-rituals, alone, could not file away the "rust of sin." The austere self-formation associated with ancient philosophers was continued in circles of "religious" Christians. The handling of sin was intensely personal. It called for the services of an expert: it demanded, in Christian form, a "doctor of souls," whose skills had to be as refined as those described in Gregory's *Regula Pastoralis*.

As we have seen, east Roman holy men had long offered to their lay clients a "monastery without walls." Lay persons, some of them with truly horrendous sins on their consciences, could expect to receive *plérophoria* from a holy man – quiet assurance that, if they followed his directions, by making amends, the holy man's own prayers on their behalf would secure for them the mercy of God. The way to forgiveness did not pass, by means of public penance, through their fellow-believers in their local church. It passed through an intense relationship with a single holy person.

In that crucial sense, the Christianity of the Celtic World was closer to that of the east than to the strong collective piety of Continental Europe. Lay persons, monks and clergy alike tended to turn to their own "soul friend," to their *anmcharae*, to seek penance at his hands. But they did so in a distinctive environment. In the Celtic world, the "soul friend" had to act not only as a doctor, but as a judge. In Ireland, all law was about making amends. Every wrong was considered to be negotiable. The complicated system of tariffs that characterized Celtic and Germanic laws was driven by an intense and finely calibrated sense of honor. Honor was the mercurial essence of all social status. Honor was constantly being damaged and then refurbished by appropriate satisfaction. Satisfaction was negotiated between individuals and kin-groups, through reparative gestures that took the form of meticulously stipulated gifts and services. In a violent world, it was unwise to leave a man too long with "shit on his face."

An honor tarnished by some injury must be "washed clean" by prompt and concrete satisfaction.[17]

The perpetual striving to reinstate "honor" that characterized Irish law was homologous to the Christian's interminable striving to present to God a self no longer "dishonored" by the stain of sin. Two mentalities converged. In a world where a Roman of Rome, such as Gregory the Great, could enumerate thirty-nine possible types of persons needing advice from a *rector*, suited for each particular temperament and for its opposite, one did not need to come from an archaic society – one of the oldest legal cultures in Europe – to relish infinite precision in the art of souls. But the intricate legal systems of the Celtic world did play a role in the further elaboration of new attitudes to sin and penance. The *Penitentials* produced in the age of Columbanus reveal the ideal of a Christian community where every eventuality could be laid out, as if before the eyes of a judge. Each case had its appropriate penance. In the day-to-day life of a monastery, penance took the form of fasting, recitations of the Psalter, blows of the strap. In the violent world in which lay clients and even clergymen found themselves – a world, that is, of bloodshed – more drastic penances, such as exile, were imposed. Entire narratives, the stuff of any spiritual struggle, were itemized, step by step, for judgement. The *Penitentials* assumed that most sins happened, but that, with due penance, any sin could be forgiven:

> He who [as a monk] loves any woman, but is unaware of evil beyond a few conversations, shall do penance for forty days. But if he has kissed and embraced her, one year . . . He who loves her in mind only, seven days. But if he has spoken [his love] but has not been accepted by her, forty days.[18]

As they survive in their Latin texts, the *Penitentials* are no more than the dry husk of a living process. Penance depended on individual circumstances, which would have been discussed in Welsh or Irish. They bruise a modern sensibility. We are left in little doubt, for instance, as to what young boys got up to in their teens, and the untidy ways that lay people made love. The monastic *Penitentials* were also driven by a strong sense of pollution. The monastery was a holy place and the monk's body was a holy thing. The smallest breaches of a sacral order – a mouse in the beer, body-scabs in the food, biting the Eucharistic chalice with the teeth or receiving the Eucharistic bread with hands still dirtied by the "common" dirt of the fields: these breaches were etched into the consciousness of the monk by appropriate, small penances. The art of the sacred was a high art. No detail of it was to be performed in a slipshod manner. The contribution of the Celtic mental world to the art of the care of souls was, indeed, its precision. Forgiveness was possible for any sin; but that forgiveness would come only if the entire human self were laid bare as the object of another's skillful judgement.

This is what an influential segment of the Frankish aristocracy wished to hear. Penance could be extended to lay persons. Eligius made penance for his adolescent sins at the court of king Dagobert (where temptation must have been rife, in a profane environment, presided over by a monarch who was exuberantly promiscuous, as befitted the long-haired descendant of a sea-monster). The relics that he had hung around his bed notified Eligius, by dripping fragrant oil, that his penance had been accepted by God after months of strictly private austerities, imposed after private confession to a priest.[19] More usually, however, the penitent joined a monastery. A monastery provided the one environment where it was considered possible to reach God, entirely purged by perpetual, meticulous penance that left the soul clean of all "dishonor" at the moment of death. In the monastery founded by Burgundofara (603–645), near Meaux – later known as Faremoutiers, "Burgundofara's monastery" – the nuns made their confession and received penance three times a day. Regular confession was part of a slow but sure unravelling of the past, that enabled the entire person to stand ready, at the end, to face God, cleansed of sin.

Faremoutiers was a place of memorable deathbed scenes. One nun, Sisetrude, was warned in a revelation that she had forty days in which to make her penance. After thirty-seven

days, two angels took her soul to heaven, for a *discussion* –
a tax-audit – of her remaining sins. On the fortieth day, the
angels reappeared. Sisetrude's soul was ready:

> I would go now, my lords, I would go now and delay no
> longer in this life of cares . . . I am now better prepared
> for the road.[20]

Anecdotes such as this reflect a major shift in Christian
sensibility. They brought the otherworld overwhelmingly close.
It is the world beyond death, and not the world around them,
shot through with invisible forces, that writers of the seventh
century, from Gregory the Great onwards, wished most to
explore. Until then, like all other ancient persons, Christians
had felt that they were enveloped in a *mundus*, a physical
universe flecked with hints of the supernatural. The world
surveyed by Gregory of Tours, for instance, had kept much of
its ancient magic. He wrote of a here and now that contained
islands of Paradise and equally chilling touches of Hell –
characterized by the smoking fevers, the screams and the
vengeful fire associated with the instant wrath of the saints.
To Gregory the Great, by contrast, these manifestations of
the otherworld seemed trivial. What truly mattered was the
dread occasion when, at the moment of death, the individual soul confronted the massed ranks of angels, saints and
greedy demons who guarded the thresholds of Heaven and
Hell.

Visions of the otherworld came to circulate widely. They
warned the inmates of the new monasteries that salvation lay
in due penance and in the loving support of their fellow-monks,
massed around them at the moment of death. Many needed
this reassurance. Such was Barontus, a nobleman who, in
later life, had joined the monastery of Logoretum (now Saint
Cyran-en-Brenne) near Bourges. In 679, he fell dangerously ill.
It seemed to him that he was taken on a journey to Heaven
and Hell. The issue was whether Barontus, the late convert,
belonged to the angels who guided him towards a distant
Heaven or to the clawed, toothed demons who jostled his
poor soul as it floated through the air above the countryside
of Bourges. In Barontus' struggle on the edge of death, it

was his entire identity, conscious and unconscious, that was at stake:

> Blessed Peter, addressing the demons, asked politely: "What crime do you have against this monk?" The demons answered, "Major sins! . . . He had three wives . . . He has also committed other adulteries and many other sins . . . " And they went over all the sins that I had committed from infancy onwards, including those which I had totally forgotten.

It was Barontus' almsgiving and, above all, the solidarity of a monastery, none of whose monks, so he was told in Heaven, had ever been lost to Hell, that finally freed him from the claims of the demons and enabled him to return, greatly shaken, to earth.[21]

These stories insist, above all, on the fate of each individual soul. Each soul was thought of as having been registered, in its every act, with the same precision as were the fiscal burdens entered in a late Roman tax-book. At a time when the ability to tax may have weakened considerably in the kingdoms of the north, and among a class of warriors where literacy had become less widespread, the examining angels, at least, maintained, in the imagination of so many anxious penitents, the relentless skills of an imperial bureaucracy. Their precision guaranteed, for good or ill, a sharpened sense of individuality – of an individuality which could even include large areas of the unconscious and forgotten self. For each human person was seen as the sum total of highly specific good or bad actions and intentions.

It was no longer enough to be a member of a massive "people of God." As Gregory the Great insisted, God was the most "subtle," the most exacting, of all judges. He would not be satisfied with unfinished souls. Hence the need for a "purging" fire beyond the grave. This fire, of exquisite sharpness, would sear from those souls who, in any case, would eventually arrive in Heaven, the last half-conscious dross of sins of excess and of neglect. Such sins had previously been dealt with, day by day, through almsgiving, in the bustling churches of an earlier age. Now they were thought of, rather, as being atoned for through a further, silent purgation in the world of the dead.[22]

When it came to the world of the dead, the general solidarity of the community of believers no longer seemed enough to guarantee the safety of the individual soul. The protection afforded by a community did not evaporate. Anxious individuals were not left alone with their souls. Rather, the notion of the "people of God" itself was redefined. Special groups were drawn in around the individual, offering the support that came from tighter, more clearly perceptible bonds. The smaller and more intense group-loyalties that characterized northern society as a whole were given an opportunity to stretch beyond the grave. They linked the living to "their" own dead – to fellow-monks, to fellow-kinsmen, to fellow-followers of a king or a lord. The fervent but somewhat faceless collective sense of the Early Christian community was splintered into a series of more manageable groupings. Small groups, charged with remembering the souls of named individuals, and not the great crowds that had once gathered in the urban basilicas of the south, were the best guarantees of salvation; because it was they who were the most convincing expressions of Christian solidarity.

The idiom by which this solidarity was expressed was the Catholic Mass. As we saw, in the dramatic story of Peter the Iberian, the Eucharist had always been regarded as the high, collective ritual around which an entire community could rally. The souls of the departed were remembered on that occasion. They were even believed to hover around the altar, nourishing their etherial bodies from the sweet smell of Christ, carried in the chalice of the Eucharistic wine.[23] A lady in Gaul, Gregory of Tours tells us, always offered to the priest the best of Gaza wine, renowned for its strong bouquet, to offer in commemoration of her husband. When the priest drank the wine, and substituted *vin ordinaire* at the Mass, the husband appeared in a dream to her: he did not like being fed on vinegar![24]

The symbiosis between the living and the dead, in which the living "fed" the dead through tokens of wine and food, continued, among Christians, the habits of ancient, pre-Christian piety. Now the symbiosis, in which the kin had played so important a part, was held to require more precise and purposive rituals than the mere offering of food. Greater emphasis was placed on the need for a Mass to be said for the "deliverance" of the souls of dead persons. Not only did individual Christian penitents have to "remember" themselves, as they faced their "soul friend" and, eventually, the examining angels and the demons, with the weight of an entire life upon them. They needed to "be remembered" by those closest to them for a long period of time after their death. Furthermore, a crucial part of that act of memory devolved on a religious expert. Only a priest could celebrate the Mass. Not even the prayers of cloistered women, once so highly valued, could do what the Mass of a male priest did – wrench the soul from the power of the demons. Hence the unusually rapid spread of a "grass-roots" Christianity, associated with the memory of the dead. By AD 700, even the smallest tribe in Ireland had its own Mass-priest. They took care to maintain him. They held him to strict accountancy. They watched his chastity carefully. For they needed to have a man among them who could celebrate a valid Mass on behalf of their dead kin. He performed for them the one ritual which was basic to a Christian group, by "singing of what is not seen." [25]

As a result of this change of mentality, the landscape itself took on firmer Christian features. This can be seen most clearly in the entire area between the Rhineland and the English Channel. The prestigeful burials of an earlier period, pagan and Christian alike, had assumed that the most memorable moment in the ritual of death was the laying to rest of a body swathed in visible, impressive tokens of its status – robes, jewelry, swords. Now Christian memory demanded longer-term arrangements. Aristocrats would allocate whole estates in perpetuity, or would dedicate freedmen to local shrines for the memory of themselves and their kin. Having made such expensive provision, in solid stone, in land and in dependent persons, they could afford the luxury of humble "Christian burial" in nothing but a shroud. Some even took care of their pre-Christian ancestors. At Flonheim, in the Rhineland, one family built a chapel over the graves of pagan relatives, to ensure that they, also, lay close to the saving Mass. The humbler dead crept in, from cemeteries on high deserted ridges to the solid comfort of small stone churches, each surrounded by its own graveyard. It was often around such cemeteries that the villages of medieval northern Europe came to be formed.

The growth of a new preoccupation with salvation through prayers for the dead was accompanied by a striking growth of monasteries, founded on royal lands and on the estates of magnates, in northern Gaul. Two hundred and twenty monasteries and convents had been founded in Gaul by the year AD 600. A further 320 were added in the subsequent century, largely in the north. They represented a relocation of Christianity into the countryside that was as crucial as that which had happened, in the previous century, in Syria. It was a countryside dominated by the Frankish kings and by their courtiers. Heavy soil, tilled by a disciplined peasantry, made the valleys of the Seine and the Marne richer and more populous than ever before. Monasteries and convents founded on family land, and dedicated to the intense cultivation of the memory of the dead, acted as permanent landmarks. Touched with eternity, they staked out the claims of the kings and of a powerful aristocracy upon the landscape of Neustria, the "New Western Lands" of the Franks.

Monasteries such as Faremoutiers and Chelles were unprecedented departures. They were "double monasteries" – convents of nuns served by monks. In such "double monasteries," the sense of status of the Frankish *potentes* won out over old-world Southern scruples on the mixing of the sexes. Formidable ladies of high class ruled both men and women, in monasteries that would have been like miniature "holy cities," set in a countryside of waving wheatfields served by a well-developed technology of watermills. These monasteries were not the small, self-consciously marginal ventures of an earlier age. Many were endowed with up to 20,000 hectares of land apiece. The abbey of Corbie, for instance, received, in the form of gifts from the royal warehouse near Marseilles, regular supplies of olive oil, of Cordova leather, of quires of papyrus, imported from Egypt through Marseilles, even of dates and pistachios. Every year, 3,650 kilograms of precious goods were carried north to Corbie, in fifteen wagons provided by the king. Relics, carefully labelled and wrapped in exquisite silk from Constantinople and Iran, were placed in shrines and monasteries, to make of them microcosms of a world-wide Christian order now brought to rest, with appropriate grandeur, in the new lands of northern Francia.

The world had begun to tilt away from the Mediterranean. The wealth of northern Gaul was markedly increased, after 600, by Frankish access to the Rhine estuary and to the new commerce of the North Sea. Northwestern Europe had begun to find its own voice. When Gertrude, abbess of Nivelles (south of modern Brussels) died, in 658, it mattered that it was on Saint Patrick's Day. It is our first reference, in a Continental source, to Patricius. After two centuries, the eccentric Romano-British bishop had become one of the great saints of the north. Gertrude's family (from which, eventually, Charlemagne would be descended) was spoken of as famous "to all the inhabitants of Europe."[26] It was a self-conscious use of an old geographical term to speak of a new reality – a western world seen now, not from Rome or Constantinople, but from Ireland and Francia. As "Europe," the northwestern frontiers of the old empire had come to be aware that they possessed an identity of their own, different from the less-familiar lands to their south and east. Just how different the ancient, eastern heartlands of Christianity would become, in the decades when Gertrude ruled at Nivelles, will be the subject of the next two chapters.

10
Christianity in Asia

In 591, a party of eastern Turks arrived at Constantinople. They bore the sign of the Cross on their foreheads:

They declared that they had been assigned this by their mothers; for when a fierce plague was endemic among them, some Christians advised them that the foreheads of their young be tattooed with that sign.[1]

A tribe from Inner Asia had adopted an apotropaic device from Christians established along the chain of oases that led from Persia to China.

Christians of the east Roman empire knew that they lived in a wide world. Nisibis (Nusaybin, eastern Turkey), the frontier city of the Persian empire, lay thirteen days of travel to the east of Antioch. But it was known that a further eighty days took the traveller beyond Persia into Central Asia, and another 150 days to Hsian-fu, the western capital of China. Yet it was a manageable world. An idiosyncratic merchant from Antioch (known to us by the colorful but misleading name of Cosmas "Indicopleustes" – Cosmas the India-Sailor) had traded down the Red Sea to Axum and Socotra. He knew of communities of Christians from Persia settled along the Coromandel Coast, the originators of the modern "Saint Thomas' Christians" of Kerala. His *Christian Topography* (written in around AD 540) surveyed, with optimism, a clearly delineated territory. Heaven stretched as a vast dome above a reassuringly flat earth. No unknown races lurked in an Antipodes vainly imagined by pagan philosophers. Already the religion of one world-empire, the empire of the Romans, and widespread in the Persian empire, it appeared to "Cosmas" as if Christianity had only the distant fringes of Asia left to conquer.[2]

In the generations that followed the death of Justinian, it did, indeed, seem as if Asia had become a smaller place. The Chinese empire made its presence felt deep into Inner Asia, as far as the Tarim Depression and the great oasis of Turfan. After 550, embassies from Po-tzu, from Persia, were a regular occurrence at the court of Hsian-fu. Even Antioch and Syria were described, for the first time, in Chinese gazetteers of the "Western Lands." Small Christian communities, adapting differently to different environments along the way, were part of a steady trickle of information, merchandise and displaced persons that took place along the entire length of the Silk Route, from Antioch to China.[3]

In the Near East itself, the Christian populations lived in the shadow of two world-empires, the Christian empire of east Rome and the Zoroastrian, Sasanian empire of Persia. For them, the two empires were "the two shoulders of the world." Their frontiers cut across a largely undivided culture, with the result that Christians who lived in Roman and Sasanian Syria and Mesopotamia remained in close contact with each other, and yet were part of empires that spread the cultural achievements of their peculiarly vibrant region far to the west and to the east. Thus, Cassiodorus, in Italy, modelled his cultural program, in part, on what he had heard of the great Christian Academy founded at Nisibis; while translations made from Greek into Syriac in Roman territory passed, within the year, to bishops in Merv, and from thence to the oasis cities of eastern Turkestan. "Cosmas" was greatly impressed by the visit of one such figure, the Persian Mar Aba, who had travelled with ease from Iran to Antioch. Mar Aba was a representative of the cosmopolitan world of the Fertile Crescent. The future *Katholikos*, the patriarch, of the Nestorian Church in Persia, from 540 to 552, Mar Aba was an Iranian convert to Christianity. He learned his Syriac in Persian Mesopotamia and his Greek in Roman Edessa. He returned home to Ctesiphon, the capital of the Persian empire, bringing memories of how the Great Liturgy was celebrated in the Hagia Sophia at Constantinople. Political and, even, linguistic barriers meant little to him, as he wandered "like a New Abraham" from Mesopotamia to the Mediterranean and back again.[4]

As in the days of Bardaisan, the Fertile Crescent remained a world open at both ends, whose inhabitants, on either side of the Roman–Persian frontier, had more in common with each other than they did with the distant rulers who controlled their destinies. The same was true further north. The ambivalence of a frontier area was made particularly plain in Armenia. The high mountain valleys that stretched between Mesopotamia and the Caucasus were a reservoir of military manpower. Like the Swiss *Landesknechten* or the Scottish Highlanders of later times, Armenians were prominent in the armies of both empires. They came from a culture that relished heroes. A seventh-century arithmetic exercise for Armenian schoolboys went as follows:

I heard from my father that, in the times when Armenians were fighting the Persians, Zarwen Kamsarakan performed memorable feats of prowess. Attacking the Persian army, he killed half on the first attack . . . a quarter on the second . . . and an eleventh on the third. Only 280 Persians survived. How large was the Persian force before he laid them low?[5]

Armenia looked both east and west. In its social structure and lay culture it was a westward extension of the feudal society of Iran. Yet it was not Zoroastrian. Christianity had entered the mountains of Armenia both from the Syriac-speaking plains around Edessa and from the river-valleys that led up from Caesarea in Cappadocia to Erzerum. Under king Trdat III (298–330), and his adviser, Grigor, "Gregory the Illuminator," Armenia became a nominally Christian kingdom, in around 314, at the same time, that is, as the fateful conversion of Constantine in the Roman empire. The independent kingdom of Armenia did not survive. It was divided, in

387, between Rome and Persia. But what did survive was a common Christianity. Armenians on both sides of the frontier belonged to the same Armenian Church, under a single Armenian *Katholikos.*

The creation of an Armenian alphabet, around 400, by Mesrop Mashtots (who died in 439) led to a flowering of Christian Armenian literature. While Coptic and Syriac had been the final adaptation, to Christian purposes, of millennial literate cultures, the clerical elites of Armenia moved, within fifty years, into literacy. As a result, Armenian historiography echoed, directly, the pre-literate world of the epic minstrels. Indeed, despite the triumphal narratives that looked back to the heroic age of Trdat and Saint Grigor, the conversion of the warrior-aristocracy of Armenia was a slow process. In the disabused words of P'awstos Buzand (Faustus the Bard, who wrote around 470):

> [The Armenians] did not receive Christianity with understanding . . . but as some purely human fashion, and under duress . . . Only those who were to some degree acquainted with [book]learning were able to obtain some partial inkling of it. As for the rest . . . they cherished their songs, their legends and epics, believed deeply in them and persevered in their old ways, in their blood-feuds and enmities.[6]

If these proud warriors related to the Church at all, it was in the manner of the kings of the barbarian west – as princely donors, careful to make offerings "for the forgiveness of their sins," but with little intention of amending their own pre-Christian ways. One *Katholikos* (described disapprovingly by P'awstos) saw this only too clearly:

> [The *Katholikos* Yohan would] go down on all fours, braying with the voice of a camel . . . "I am a camel, I am a camel, I bear the sins of the king; put the sins of the king upon me" . . . And the kings wrote and sealed deeds for villages and estates and put them on Yohan's back in exchange for their sins.[7]

P'awstos' realistic estimate of his fellow-countrymen was

not popular with his ecclesiastical colleagues. Armenian Christianity required heroic foundation-myths if it was to survive. This heroic element was provided by an epic encounter between Christian Armenians and their Persian overlord, at the battle of Avarair, in 451. A faction of the nobility of eastern Armenia, led by Vardan Mamikonian, died fighting the king of kings, Yazdkart II (439–457). Yazdkart had attempted to impose Zoroastrianism on their country. But they fought Yazdkart, not so as to become independent of the King of Kings of Iran, but so as to remain his faithful vassals. They simply demanded that their Christianity should not be counted against them. They wished to retain their honor and their standard of living as the marcher-lords of the Persian empire, whose secular *mores* (religion apart) were so like their own.

The brilliant narratives of Lazar of Pharp, in around 500, and Elishe Vardapet, Elishe the Teacher, ensured that the 1,036 Armenian warriors who fell at Avarair would be remembered, forever after, as Christian martyrs. Vardan and his companions were presented as the heirs of the Maccabees. Faced, as the Maccabees had been, by a formidable empire, their ranks thinned by apostasy, Vardan and his army had died to preserve the "traditions of their fathers." Their loyalty to Christianity took the form of a solemn "Covenant," sworn upon a copy of the Gospels. It was a Covenant that embraced nobleman and peasant alike. On both sides of the frontier between Rome and Persia, all Armenians were henceforth expected to be loyal to a single "patrimonial faith." They resembled the militant Israel of the Maccabees. It was a more precise and aggressively embattled use of the Old Testament and of the history of the People of Israel than any invoked by clerical writers in the warrior-kingdoms of the west.[8]

To the south of the warlike highlands of Armenia, it was not a heroic battle, but an ecclesiastical event, the fateful Council of Chalcedon, which also happened in 451, that determined the future identity of Syriac-speaking Christianity. The condemnation of the teachings of Nestorius, first at Ephesus and then at Chalcedon, placed a theological barrier across northern Mesopotamia that parallelled the political frontier between Roman Edessa and Persian Nisibis. Until then, the Christian communities in the Persian empire had been an eastward extension of the religious culture of the church of Antioch. The great Antiochene exegete, Theodore of Mopsuestia (350–428), had created the intellectual climate that produced Nestorius. He was revered by his admirers as "the Universal [that is, the World Class] Exegete." For those who still looked to Antioch, to condemn Nestorius was to disown the seemingly bottomless wisdom of Theodore, a past-master of Scriptural exegesis. The churches in Persia were unwilling to do that. By contrast, hard-line Monophysites, bitter enemies of Nestorius, came to predominate in Roman Edessa. Boundaries hardened. For the first time in the history of Syriac-speaking Christianity, it became increasingly impossible to come to study at Edessa from Nisibis, Edessa's sister city, only a few days' travel across what had been a largely dormant frontier. In 489, the school for students from Persia in Edessa was closed. At the same time, the churches in Persia rallied, explicitly, to the doctrines of Nestorius, thereby founding what has been known, ever since, to western scholars, as the "Nestorian" Church.

Barsauma, the high-handed bishop of Nisibis, from 470 to 496, was accused by later Monophysite writers of having deliberately pushed his Church into accepting the heresy of Nestorius so as to seal the frontier between Rome and Persia: each empire would now have a different, and mutually hostile, form of Christianity within its frontiers. But the split, in fact, was the result of a far longer development. The Christians within the Persian empire had begun to feel at home. In the fourth century, many had been foreigners, descended from the thousands of Syrians brought back as captives by Shapur I in the 260s. Times had changed. Christians now came from the Iranian population itself, through intermarriage and, occasionally, through conversion. Pehlevi (middle Persian) joined Syriac as the other language of the Nestorian Church. A sixth-century Nestorian Cross – a distinctive, quasi-cosmic symbol, half a Cross and half an ancient Mesopotamian Tree of Life – has been discovered as far east as Travancore, with a Pehlevi inscription. Pehlevi, also, would have been the language of the successful Christian entrepreneurs who controlled the pearl-fisheries of the Persian Gulf. Their bishops needed to warn them to allow their divers to rest on Sundays. Christian Rogation ceremonies took place, along the shore, to clear the waters of giant sharks. Such persons did not think of themselves as "Romans" *manqués*, but as Persians who happened to be Christians.⁹

The emergence of a silent majority of Persian Christians in the hinterland coincided with a dramatic transfer of Syriac high culture from anti-Nestorian Edessa to the Persian side of the frontier. Nisibis became one of the great university-centers of the Near East. Westerners were greatly impressed by what they heard of the schools of Nisibis. Here was a phenomenon that did not exist in the Mediterranean world – a city committed to teaching nothing but the Christian Scriptures.¹⁰

Thousands of students from all over Mesopotamia flocked to Nisibis, the new "Mother of Wisdom." The result was a spurt of translations from Greek into Syriac. Eventually, all of the writings of Theodore of Mopsuestia became available in Syriac translation, and, with Theodore, came also Aristotle and Galen. Elementary logic, whose rules had been laid down by Aristotle, was essential for understanding the exact meaning of crucial passages in the Scriptures. It was also necessary for religious controversy. It was a sternly impartial, "technocratic" tool, wielded by an elite prepared to enter with zest into religious controversy with its many Christian and non-Christian rivals. In the Greek and Latin worlds, culture had been dominated by literary works – Virgil and Cicero in the west, Homer and Demosthenes in the east – that retained an undeniable pagan flavor. The literary masterpieces of a frankly non-Christian past, filled with references to pagan myths and to pagan ritual, lurked disquietingly at the corner of the mind of any Greek or Latin student of the Bible. This was not so in the Syriac world, as it spread to the east: here the austerely neutral skills of logic and medicine provided the "secular" knowledge necessary for controversy and exegesis.

The school at Nisibis itself resembled the contemporary rabbinic academies that produced the Babylonian Talmud in the large Jewish villages of Mesopotamia. Unmarried young men, distinguished by a semi-monastic style of life and dress, settled in the cell-like rooms of a former caravansary. They would memorize the Psalms, the New Testament, select readings from the Old Testament, and the intricate chants and specially composed hymns that were the glory of the Nestorian, as of every other Syriac, liturgy. Headed by a teacher such as Narsai, who wrote over 300 religious *Odes*, the school of Nisibis was to be a training-ground for religious poets. For in the culture of the Syriac-speaking world as a whole, holy books were supposed to saturate the heart. They did so by being translated into melodious sound, carried by the magical sweetness of the human voice.[11]

Hence the *qeryana*, the "Reading" of the Scriptures, was essential for the culture of the Syrian Churches. In the *qeryana*, the Syriac vernacular that spanned the Fertile Crescent was raised to a new pitch. It became a tongue rendered sacred by the repeated, exquisite recitation of the Word of God. So beautifully did Mar Jacob read the Psalms in church that a visiting bishop quite forgot what he himself had intended to say in his sermon.[12] Even exegesis itself was not a purely intellectual probing of the Scriptures. It was a re-recitation of the Scriptures, a reverential "robing" of the Word of God by reading aloud, interspersed with explanations, in a manner that closely resembled the Midrashic techniques of the rabbis.

Carried, in this way, on the voices of young men, such a culture was particularly well-suited to the vast "internal mission" that maintained a remarkable degree of cultural and religious unity among Nestorian communities that, eventually, came to stretch from Mesopotamia to China. A large Nestorian cemetery discovered at Semirechye, in eastern Kazakhstan, shows that Nestorian communities survived up to the time of the Mongol empire in the thirteenth century. It also shows how this could be so. Eight hundred years after the founding of the school of Nisibis, and over three months of travel from Mesopotamia, Nestorians had maintained a quite distinctive style of transmission for their religious culture. The tombs were still inscribed in a bold Syriac script that had changed little over the centuries:

The year 1627 [that is, from the foundation of Antioch

by king Seleucus! – AD 1316] . . . in the Year of the
Dragon, according to the Turks. This is the grave of
Sliha, the famous Exegete and Preacher . . . son of the
Exegete Petros. Praised for his wisdom, his voice was
raised like a trumpet.13

The expansion of the Nestorian church was due to the sheer
size and strategic position of the Persian empire. Northern
Mesopotamia was the western fringe of a political system
that stood at the crossroads of Asia. Nestorian missions
were a paradoxical result of the achievements of aggressive
Zoroastrian rulers. The Sasanians tamed the fragile flood-
plains of the Tigris and the Euphrates. They doubled the area
of settlement and maintained levels of irrigation unequalled
before modern times. As a result, their empire was hungry for
manpower. Khusro I (530–579) and Khusro II Aparwez, "the
Victorious," (591–628) renewed the policy of Shapur I. Their
wars against east Rome were slave-raids on a colossal scale.
These largely Christian captives were settled in new towns
and villages both in Mesopotamia and along the fertile but
precarious oases that edged Central Asia.

For these communities, the King of Kings was a formidable,
but studiously distant presence. The pressures towards religious
conformity that were so heavy in east Rome and in the Christian
kingdoms of the west did not weigh as heavily upon the
subjects of the Sasanian empire. The occasional aristocrat who
converted to Christianity was subjected to gruesome public
execution, as a renegade from Zoroastrianism, the *beh den*,
"the Good Religion." But Zoroastrianism was considered to
be too good a religion to be wasted on non-Persians. It was,
indeed, a compliment to the Armenians on the part of Yazdkart
II that he thought them capable of sharing the religion of true
Iranians. Usually, as long as subject religious groups were loyal
and paid their tribute, they were not greatly troubled.

As a result, Christians emerged at the court of Khusro II
as privileged royal servants, somewhat like the "King's Jews"
of medieval Europe. Shirin, his principal wife, was a devout
Nestorian. Yazdin of Kerkuk was his all-powerful financial
minister. Yazdin was acclaimed as "the Constantine and the

Theodosius" of the Nestorian church. When the armies of Khusro II broke the defenses of Syria, after 610, and reached as far as Egypt, in 619, these high-ranking Christians joined with gusto in the spoliation of their "heretical," east Roman neighbors. When Jerusalem fell to the Persians, in 618, a relic of the True Cross itself made its way across the Fertile Crescent, to the royal palace at Dastkart (set, appropriately, within sight of the ruins of ancient Nineveh, from which the Assyrians had struck at Jerusalem twelve centuries previously). But it ended up as the treasured property, not of the pagan King of Kings, but of the Nestorian Christian community of Yazdin's Kerkuk.[14]

Moving with little difficulty in a pluralistic society, groups of Nestorian Christians fitted with ease into the vast horizons that opened up from Persian Central Asia. Nestorian communities joined other groups in the cosmopolitan oasis-cities of Merv and Samarkand, and soon settled, also, among the Turkish nomadic tribes who acted as the overlords of the trading-cities of eastern Central Asia. Even Monophysites writing near Antioch were forced to admire the success of their rivals along the very edges of the known world. For "simple-minded" Turks, they admitted, even Nestorianism was better than nothing!

> Their feasts they celebrate with great pomp, and they love more than any other people the commemorations of the saints and martyrs. They do not accept any other holy books than our own, in Syriac. In their gatherings, they translate the Holy Books into their own, Turkish language, but they do not venture to change into the Turkish language the admirable name of Jesus Christ . . . nor of Mary, the Mother of God . . . but they preserve them exactly as they are in the Syriac tongue.[15]

Nestorians established themselves, also, further to the east, along the foothills of the Hindu Kush and the Tien Shan mountains, in the autonomous trading cities of Soghdia. The Soghdians were wide-ranging merchants. Known to the Chinese as men "with mouths full of honey, and gum [to catch every penny] on their fingers," their journeys knit Asia together. Many became Christian. A Nestorian cross with a Soghdian inscription has been found as far away as Ladakh, on the route to Tibet. Syriac formed the basis of the script of the Uighur kingdom of southern Mongolia. In the Turfan oasis of western Chinese Sinkiang, manuscripts of the Manichees were found: the perpetual *Doppelgänger* of Syriac Christianity had reached Inner Asia, and would survive in China until the fourteenth century. There was a Nestorian church in the nearby village of Bulayiq. Its library included a Soghdian translation of the *Antirrheticus* of Evagrius of Pontos (346–399). This was a work on the spiritual struggle of the monk, written in Egypt by a friend and adviser of none other than Melania the Elder, the heroine of Paulinus of Nola. The book of Evagrius, a Christian master of the art of contemplation, was read, in this unimaginably distant setting, close to Buddhist monasteries that housed its equivalent, *The Sutra of the Causes and Effects of Actions*, also in Soghdian translation. Most surprising of all, the Mongolian word for "religious law," used of Buddhism – *nom* – may be a distant echo, through Soghdian, of the Greek *nomos*, "law," carried as a loan word, in the Syriac *namousa*, to the heart of Asia. It was a long way for Bardaisan's "Law of the Messiah" to have come![16]

In 635, Nestorians submitted a "Defence of Monotheism" to the Chinese emperor at Hsian-fu. Three years later, in the same year, indeed, as Jerusalem was lost forever to Muslim invaders, works of Syriac theology, derived, ultimately, from the fourth-century Antiochene culture of Theodore, the "Universal Exegete," were formally placed, in Chinese translation, in the imperial library, among the many *exotica* of the distant Western Lands.[17]

These events were the distant outcome, in part, of an escalating conflict between east Rome and Persia. Each of the two super-powers of western Asia had reached out, far into Inner Asia, to seek allies and commercial advantages in an effort to tip the balance in a struggle for total control of the Middle East. After 603, it was as if the keystone of an ancient arch had collapsed. The days of Xerxes or, alternately, of Alexander the Great, had come again. Between 610 and 620, Antioch, Jerusalem and Alexandria fell to Persian armies. The watch-fires of the Persians could be seen across the water from Constantinople, at Chalcedon. Then the emperor Heraclius

(610–641) struck back into the heart of the over-extended empire of Khusro II. He invaded northern Mesopotamia with nomadic cavalry drawn from beyond the Caucasus. He celebrated Christmas Day 627 in the great Nestorian church at Kerkuk. Khusro II was murdered. The True Cross was returned in triumph to Jerusalem, accompanied by Heraclius himself – the first and last time that an east Roman Christian emperor set foot in the Holy Places.

Heraclius' triumph took place against the background of a war-weary Middle East. The cities of the Fertile Crescent had been emptied by massive deportations. The olive groves around Antioch had been hacked to the ground in vindictive raids. Southern and central Syria, long drained by the plague, was an impoverished region, that had already begun to look south, towards the Arabian peninsula rather than towards the Mediterranean. Large areas of Mesopotamia were awash again, through neglect of the royal dams. More dangerous still, for the continued existence of the two existing empires, local leaders throughout Syria and Mesopotamia had learned, again and again, for over a generation, the necessary art of surrendering, with good grace, to foreign conquerors. These conquerors would soon come, and from a familiar direction – from the restless tribes of the south. But they came in a totally unexpected form – as the bearers of yet another, Arabic version of the monotheistic faith shared by Jews and Christians.

The Arabian peninsula had been drawn into the religious and political confrontations that swept the settled land. Far from being inhabited by ignorant starvelings, as the inhabitants of the settled land believed, the peninsula was a gigantic echo-chamber, in which the conflicting religious options of the Near East had already been translated into Arab terms. Opposing religions were yet another element in the perpetual confrontation of tribe against tribe, of oasis against oasis, that had created a pattern of conflict which linked the northern Euphrates to the Yemen, thereby ensuring that ideas spread with remarkable speed from one end of the Arabian peninsula to the other.

To the north, an extensive frontier zone had developed along the borders of Syria and Persian Mesopotamia. The shayks of the Banu Ghassan could point to "their desert," as a place of refuge and a reservoir of tribal fighting men, feared for their swift raiding. But the same shayks were also major landowners in Syria and patrons of the local Monophysite church. The most renowned poets in the Arab world frequented the courts of the Banu Lakhm, at Hira, on the Persian frontier. But the "camp" of Hira was also a Christian holy city – the burial place of *Katholikoi* of the Nestorian Church and the scene of heated disputes between Nestorians and Monophysites.[18]

Altogether, religious confrontation was in the air. On the edge of the mountains of Yemen, the oasis city of Najran was ruled by an oligarchy of Christian merchants who were as rich as any in Edessa or Alexandria. In 523, they had been brutally crushed by an Arab king, Dhu Nuwas, who had opted for Judaism, in order to create, in the rich lands of southern Arabia, a "Davidic" kingship that was independent of the Christian powers. As we saw, Dhu Nuwas was defeated by the Axumite Christian, Ella Atsbeha, but not before the fate of the Najranis and the pros and cons of Christianity and Judaism had been hotly debated throughout the Arab world. Far from the inhibitions imposed by the dominant orthodoxies current in a Christian empire, the central issues of both faiths were open to fierce contention: was Christ divine or was He a mere human being? was He greater than Moses or simply a crucified sorcerer?[19] For the historian, what is remarkable about the Arabian peninsula around the year AD 610, was not that Christianity and Judaism were well known. It is, rather, that, in the person of Muhammad of Mecca (570–632) it produced a prophet who, in the opinion of his followers, as of all later Muslims, had received from God authority to transmit, to his fellow-Arabs, God's own, definitive judgement on both faiths.

The Mecca and the Hijaz in which Muhammad grew up (in the same years as Columbanus was settled in Luxeuil and Gregory the Great lamented the state of Rome) was a self-consciously old-fashioned region. The local sanctuary, the Ka'aba, housed idols of different tribes, joined, apparently, with characteristic adaptability, by an icon of the Virgin and Child brought from Ethiopia. It was the center of a pilgrimage, whose month of holy truce had encouraged caravans to pass, with safety, through the oasis, thereby enriching the city. The dominant family, the Quraysh, were quite content with their "non-aligned" status. They were happy to be frank idolaters, in a world where Jews and Christians were only too close.

Not so Muhammad. In 610, at the age of forty, the visions began to come. They came from the One God (in Arabic: Allah), "the Lord of the Worlds." They came irregularly, in sudden, shattering moments, up to his death in 632. In them, the same God Who had spoken to Moses and to Jesus, and to many thousands of humbler prophets, now spoke again, once and for all, to Muhammad. Vivid sequences, carefully memorized by Muhammad's followers and passed on by skilled reciters throughout the Arabic-speaking world, these messages from God – nothing less, indeed, than snatches of the voice of God Himself speaking to the Arabs through Muhammad – were not written down until after 660. When written out, they formed the single book known to us as the *Qur'an.*

Qur'an and the Syriac *qeryana* come from the same root *qr'*, to read, to cry aloud. Both accorded the fullest measure of authority to a religious message when it was carried, directly, by the human voice:

> I thought that it would be a good thing if I could listen to Muhammad [a once-skeptical Meccan was believed to have said] . . . When I heard the *Qur'an* [that he was reciting] my heart was softened and Islam entered into me.
> By God [said another], his speech is sweet.[20]

But for Muhammad's followers, this was no Syriac religious ode, a human composition offered by man to God. It was an echo of the voice of God Himself, of a God Who had never ceased, throughout the ages, to "call out" to mankind. Now this voice repeated itself, in a final, majestically definitive summation.

It was this aspect of the *Qur'an* that instantly offended Jews and Christians. For the messages relayed by God through Muhammad claimed to undo the past. Neglect and partisan strife had caused Jews and, particularly, Christians, to slip away from, even to distort, the messages that they had once received from their prophets, Moses and Jesus. Christians were told, in no uncertain terms, that they had littered the Near East with strictly unnecessary institutions, such as monasticism. They were also warned by God that the Christological controversies which had absorbed their energies for so many centuries were based on a gigantic misunderstanding:

> And behold [at the Last Judgement] God will say: "O Jesus, son of Mary! Didst thou say unto men: worship me and my mother as gods in derogation of God?" He will say: "Glory to Thee. Never could I have said what I had no right to say." (*Qur'an* v: 119)

Criticisms of Judaism and Christianity were less central to the overall course of Muhammad's revelations than was his message to the Arabs themselves. He was acutely conscious of having been sent by God to his fellow-countrymen to warn them, in clear Arabic, to change their pagan ways. He was to tell them that the Ka'aba of Mecca had been the spot where Abraham, the ancestor of the entire Arab race, through his son Ishmael, had once sacrificed to the true God alone. The Quraysh had filled it with idols. In reclaiming the Ka'aba for His worship alone, Muhammad and his followers would regain for the Arabs as a whole the powerful blessing of God. They should surrender themselves to the will of God, as all truly religious persons had done since the beginning of time.

The name adopted by the new religion, "Islam," and the word used to describe its adherents, "Muslims," came from the same Arabic root, *slm* – to surrender, to trust in one God. It summed up an entire view of history. Islam and Muslims had always existed. Wholehearted trust in God and the rejection of all other worship had invariably distinguished true monotheists from ignorant polytheists. God had fostered this monotheism by sending His prophets to the Jews and to the Christians. Now the Arabs were summoned to partake in the same, perennial faith. Otherwise, they would be lost. The gaunt ruins of so many dead cities, that lay along the caravan routes of the Arabian peninsula, spoke to Muhammad quite as clearly of the swift approach of the Last Judgement, as did the ruins of Rome to his older contemporary, pope Gregory. Both men, the Arabian prophet and the Roman pope, thought of themselves as sent by God to warn a world in its last days:

> Do they not reflect in their own minds? Have they not
> travelled the land and seen what was the end of those
> before them? They were superior to them in strength:
> they tilled the soil and populated it in greater number
> than these have done.   (*Qur'an* xxx: 19)

> But how many countless generations before them have We
> destroyed? Canst thou find a single one of them now, or
> hear so much as a whisper?   (*Qur'an* xix: 98)

If the Arabs listened to God's warning, however, they might
face a very different prospect:

> Before, We wrote in the *Psalms*: . . . *My servants, the
> righteous, shall inherit the earth*.   (*Qur'an* xxi: 105)

A remarkable group of young men, caravan merchants and
warriors, had been the Companions of Muhammad throughout
his career. They had defended his cause with arms, in the
authentic Arab manner. They had "striven hard," risking their
wealth, even their lives, to maintain his honor and safety:
the word *jihad*, usually translated as "holy war," originally
meant little more than that. In 622, they emigrated with him
to the oasis of Medina. By this *hijra*, this emigration of a
leader and his armed band, they had recreated themselves
as a new tribe, a small and determined nation in arms,
like any other Arab tribe. Muslims, in all later centuries,
would count the years from that date. In 630, Muhammad
and his Companions returned in triumph to Mecca. They
purged the Ka'aba of its idols. It was the same year as the
emperor Heraclius had brought the Holy Cross in triumph
to Jerusalem. But, in the course of the long war between east
Rome and Persia, the frontier between Palestine, Syria and the
nomads had collapsed. Syria and Palestine were there for the
taking.

Muhammad died in 632. Having established their authority
throughout Arabia, his Companions were ready to offer their
Arab allies conquests of which they had not dared to dream.
They were blunt men of war. They were quite as convinced
as the emperors Justinian and Heraclius had ever been, that

God blessed the armies of those who believed truly in Him. They intended to use these armies to *inherit the earth*. As an Armenian writer reported it:

They sent an embassy to [Heraclius] the emperor of the Greeks saying: "God has given this land as an inheritance to our father Abraham and to his posterity after him. We are the children of Abraham. You have held our country long enough. Give it up peacefully, and we will not invade your country. If not, we will retake with interest what you have withheld from us." [21]

The imagined reaction of Heraclius, in a Nestorian source, was equally revealing. A military challenge from the "tents" of the south, at a time when the frontiers of both empires had been fatally weakened by decades of warfare, was only to be expected. But this would be different:

This people [the emperor said] is like an evening, between daylight and nightfall, neither sunlit nor dark . . . so is this people neither illumined by the light of Christ nor is it plunged into the darkness of idolatry. [22]

Let us see how the Christian populations of the Near East adjusted to the gigantic Arab empire that had brought with it such a troubling anomaly: a new "twilight religion," Islam – that is, yet another monotheistic faith, convinced that it alone represented the culmination of God's purposes on earth.

11

"The Changing of the Kingdoms:"
Christians under Islam

The greatest political revolution ever to occur in the history of the ancient world took place in the two generations that followed the death of the prophet Muhammad in AD 632. Arab armies, led by believing Muslims, drove the east Romans from Syria and Egypt, and soon conquered the entire Sasanian empire. Carthage fell in 698, and the Visigothic kingdom collapsed in 711. Only in 717 were the Muslim warfleets halted outside Constantinople; and, in 733, Charles Martel (who was the nephew of Gertrude, abbess of Nivelles) punished a Muslim raiding party on its way to loot the shrine of Saint Martin at Tours, in a major battle near Poitiers. Apart from these two checks, the Muslim achievement was unparalleled. For the first time in human history, the populations of that archipelago of settled regions that stretched from Morocco and Andalusia to Central Asia and the Punjab found themselves part of a single political system.

Christian contemporaries could only do justice to so immense a change by invoking the vision of the succession of great empires in the Book of Daniel. In this succession, Rome had been treated as the last empire. Now the new "kingdom of the Arabs" replaced Rome. It was the final, gigantic flare-up of human grandeur before the return of

Christ to earth. Those who witnessed the events of the seventh century knew, without a doubt, that they were participating in the last, and most dramatic, "changing of the kingdoms." [1]

Altogether, a significant change took place in the attitude of many Christians to the passing of time. Gregory the Great, even Gregory of Tours and John of Ephesus, had been both oppressed and heartened by a sense of the rapid end of the world and of the imminent approach of the Last Days. By this belief, they expressed their hopes and fears for the state of Christianity itself, as the Church entered its last, most testing days, threatened from within by bitter divisions and by the spread of false beliefs, but challenged, at the same time, to gather in all peoples. Now a more urgent sense of Apocalyptic changes, which involved the rise and fall of entire empires as a prelude to the return of Christ to rule the earth, replaced the more inward-looking anxieties of churchmen of a previous generation. It was a shift that did justice to the headlong changes that occurred throughout the Middle East in the course of the seventh century.

The creation of a stable Islamic empire is not the subject of this book. It was the most unexpected outcome of those breathtaking years. In itself, nomad pressure on the weakened frontiers of the settled land might have done little more than produce large areas in Mesopotamia and Syria that resembled the *Sklaviniai* of the Balkans. They would have become lawless frontier zones, withdrawn, if only for a short time, from the immemorial grip of empire. The Muslim leaders themselves were far from certain that their conquests would be irreversible. As long as Constantinople and the heartlands of the east Roman empire remained unconquered, the Christian empire might yet strike back. Legends circulated that Muhammad had warned his followers:

> Persia is [only a matter of] one or two thrusts and no Persia will be after that. But the *Rum* [the east Romans] . . . are people of sea and rock . . . Alas, they are your enemies to the end of time.

Up to AD 700, nothing as yet was certain:

Islam has started as a foreigner [to all lands] and may again become a foreigner, folding back [on Mecca and Medina] like a snake folding back into its hole.

To stand watch for one night on the coast of Syria, scanning the horizon for the dread return of the east Roman navy, was deemed a more pious action than to spend all night in prayer in the Ka'aba of Mecca.[2]

Despite these forebodings, a permanent Islamic state emerged. It was created by forceful Muslim rulers who enlisted the active collaboration of the surviving members of the provincial elites, both Zoroastrian Persians and Christian east Romans. Coming after generations of breakdown, where anything could have happened, this vast new state was the result of a firm vote on the part of the settled populations of the Near East for the stability of empire – any empire – over potential anarchy. The Islamic empire linked the former subjects of east Rome and Persia in a single political system, whose local administrative underpinning was recognizably continuous with all that had gone before.

This was not so at the top. The state set in order by the Califs Abd al-Malik (685–705) and al-Walid (705–715) was a defiantly Islamic state. The past was severely censored. Administrative practice continued as before – east Roman in Syria and Egypt, Persian in Mesopotamia; but after 699 Arabic became the sole official language of the empire. A new gold and silver coinage was issued to replace the coins of east Rome. The coins were cleared of all representations of human figures. Only passages from the *Qur'an*, in a firm Arabic script, could be seen on every coin. In 692, Abd al-Malik began to build the Dome of the Rock on top of the deserted site of the former Jewish Temple at Jerusalem. It was a frankly competitive statement. The new dome towered above the dome of Constantine's Church of the Holy Sepulcher. Inside, Arabic inscriptions from the *Qur'an* made plain to visiting Muslim pilgrims God's definitive judgement on the entire past of Christianity:

Oh People of the Book [that is, Christians, defined by their possession of Holy Scriptures] do not go beyond the bounds of your religion . . . Jesus, the son of Mary, was [only] God's Messenger . . . It is not for God to take a son . . . The true religion with God is Islam. (*Qur'an* iv: 171 and iii: 19)

The founders of the Islamic empire believed, as unthinkingly as did their Christian contemporaries, that there was a direct relationship between the favor of God and the foundation of great empires. As one Arab Muslim told a local Christian hermit:

It is a sign of God's love for us and His pleasure with our faith, that He has given us dominion over all peoples and faiths.[3]

Like the Romans of the fifth-century west, Christians of the settled land (and especially the subjects of the surviving east Roman empire) preferred to treat their conquerors as wild men from nowhere, with whom they had nothing in common. Greek and Latin sources never spoke of "Muslims." They spoke of Islam in purely ethnic terms. Muslims were "Saracens" or "Hagarenes" – that is, descendants of Ishmael, Abraham's bastard son by his servant Hagar. Islam, for them, was no more than "a new, deceptive heresy." It was not even a very interesting heresy. It was an incompetently plagiarized form of Christianity, thought up by Muhammad so as to give a cloak of religious respectability to the ravages of his blood-thirsty nation.[4]

Such long-lasting stereotypes of Islam buoyed the morale of the east Romans as they faced the most formidable military challenge that they had ever encountered. But within the territories embraced by the Islamic empire, the reality was less clear-cut. The Christians of the Near East settled down to live with their new masters in a state of perpetual ambivalence. Their position within the Islamic state was far better than any enjoyed by Jews and pagans in the Christian empire. Jews and Christians were treated as "Peoples of the Book." Even if they had not proved worthy of His calling, they had at least received their Scriptures from God. They paid a special poll-tax – the *jizya* – in return for the "benefaction" of not having been faced, as were outright pagans (in theory at least), by the stark alternative of submission to Islam or war to the death. It was a tax that was intended to make plain their subordination. Those who offered the *jizya* were to be careful to present the money on their upraised palms, in such a way that their hands should never be seen to be above those of the Muslim recipient! In return for this mark of inferiority, Christians and Jews were positively encouraged to survive in large numbers within the Islamic empire. Individual converts were, of course, welcome. But forced conversion was out of the question in most cases. The "Peoples of the Book" could continue their religious practices, under their traditional leaders, as long as they supported the Muslim armies with their wealth, through taxes. For Muslims, the massive presence of two superannuated religious dispensations merely highlighted the triumphant novelty of Islam, "the best community ever brought forth to mankind." [5]

In the seventh and eighth centuries, the Middle East was utterly unlike the predominantly Muslim, totally Arabic-speaking world that it is today. Islam remained the religion of armed camps, linked to new or to greatly expanded cities. Damascus in Syria, Fustat (near Cairo) in Egypt – appropriately named from the *fossatum*, the earthwork, of a former Roman legionary camp – and the boom cities of Basra and Kufa in southern Iraq: these were the great "ports of entry," that assembled the populations of the Arabian desert for future deployment throughout the settled land. The mosques that stood in the midst of these cities were not interior spaces, enclosed glimpses of Heaven on earth, as were the Christian basilicas. They were vast open courtyards, both the forum and the parade-ground of a religious "nation in arms." Resplendent with marbles and columns taken from conquered royal palaces, sheathed with mosaic work provided by a humbled east Roman emperor – as was the courtyard of the Great Mosque at Damascus – these mosques were, indeed, like great pleasure-gardens, as full of light and color as was the Paradise promised in the *Qur'an* to true believers. Their shimmering majesty spoke directly of the superabundant blessings lavished by God, in this world also, on His chosen community.

Like the great Spanish cities established in the New World in the sixteenth century, the new Muslim cities of the Near East were vivid, but encapsulated, centers where the culture and religion of the conquerors soon came to prevail. But outside these remarkable gathering-points of self-confident Muslims, Islam rested as lightly as a mist along the contours of what had remained a largely Christian landscape. In upper Egypt and in northern Iraq, local Christian elites remained firmly in control. They administered the taxes and proudly maintained the churches and great monasteries of their region. A Christian holy man in the foothills of the Zagros gained privileges for his convent through curing the favorite horse of the local Muslim emir. Muslims often consulted Christian hermits.[6] The image of Jesus, in Islamic legend, was modelled on vivid memories of the great monks of Egypt and Syria.

Nearer the centers of power, in Palestine and Jordan, the Muslim armies had passed swiftly northwards, leaving behind them villages where churches were still being built in the very year that Roman rule collapsed in Syria. Jerash was a city that was still dominated by its ancient pagan temple. One small mosque only appeared, alongside fifteen fully functioning Christian churches. The local manufacturers of terracotta lamps at Jerash solved the problem of the emergence of yet another world-religion by inscribing them, on one side, in Greek, with "The Light of the Christians is the Resurrection," and, on the other, in Arabic, with "In the Name of Allah, the Merciful, the Compassionate."[7]

At the court of Damascus, Christian civil servants continued to play a crucial role. Thus, a settled Christian Arab of Damascus, Mansur, had been responsible for the taxes of the region for the emperor Heraclius. Mansur's son, Sarjun (Sergius), as a servant of the Califs, taxed the entire Middle East. Only in AD 700 did Sergius' son – Mansur b. Sarjun – leave court. A typical member of a pious east Roman family devoted to public service who had turned to religion, Mansur, like Gregory the Great in Rome, abandoned the "cares" of office to become a learned monk. He is known under his monastic name, John: John of Damascus – John Damascene – a prolific writer in Greek and a founding father of the medieval orthodox tradition.[8]

Different Christian groups reacted very differently to the new situation in which they found themselves. The Chalcedonians came to be known, quite simply, as "Melkites" – as "the Emperor's People." The collapse of the east Roman empire, in which they had been the established Church, was a cruel blow to their morale. Yet all was not lost. Prolonged controversy with Monophysites, and, more recently, under Heraclius, with Jews, had taught local Chalcedonians how to look after themselves. A characteristic genre developed at this time. It consisted of *Questions and Answers* and included imaginary debates with religious enemies. In the undergoverned empire of Heraclius orthodoxy could no longer be imposed by force from on top. Hostile groups lived cheek by jowl. The "orthodox" Chalcedonian believer was enabled, by such texts, to meet any challenge, delivered anywhere and on any topic, with a brisk return of fire. By treating Jews and all Christian groups with even-handed indifference, the Islamic empire merely declared a permanent "open season" for religious disputes between Jews and Christians, Chalcedonians and Monophysites.

Anastasius of Sinai, a learned Chalcedonian, who had worked among "Roman" captives from Cyprus, set by their Arab masters to work in the lethal asphalt deposits of the Dead Sea, wrote for such persons an encyclopedic catalogue of answers for every kind of religious doubt and a series of *Stories to Strengthen the Faith*. Anastasius knew his Muslims. He knew that they believed that a man predestined to die fighting in the holy war would bear on his face unmistakable signs of his impending "martyrdom." He also knew that some Christians had become Muslims and that many others treated Islam as no more than an innocuous variant of their own religion. He wrote to warn such people. Pious Christians in Jerusalem, he told them, had actually heard at night the cries of the demons, as they worked to clear the debris from the Temple Mount: they were helping, "their allies, the Saracens," to make the site ready for the supreme blasphemy of Abd al-Malik's

Dome of the Rock. Two Christian sailors had even visited Mecca. At night they saw a hideous form arise from the earth to devour the meat of the camels and goats offered, in sacrifice, around the Ka'aba. This proved, Anastasius insisted, that the sacrifice at the Ka'aba was no "true sacrifice," instituted by Abraham. Muslim sacrifices were ghoulish rites, that would never ascend to Heaven as pleasing to God.[9]

Syrians and Egyptians of the "Jacobite" Monophysite Church were no great lovers of the Arab nomads. But they arrived at less dramatic conclusions than did the humiliated Chalcedonians. God had "nodded His assent" to the Arab conquests. They were a punishment on the east Roman emperors for having persecuted the true – Monophysite – Church:

> When He saw that the measure of the sins of the Romans was full to overflowing . . . He stirred up the sons of Ishmael and enticed them hither from their southern land . . . Yet it was by striking a bargain with them that we secured our deliverance. This was no small gain, to be delivered from the tyrannical kingdom of the Romans.[10]

In order to justify their claim to be the true Church, the Monophysites became the remembrancers of the Near East. Monophysite historians of the Church constantly turned back to the fateful decisions of the Council of Chalcedon, the "Great Prevarication," and to the persecutions that the upholders of the true faith had suffered from successive east Roman emperors in the fifth and sixth centuries. In the 760s, Chalcedonians and Monophysites presented the Muslim governor of Alexandria with rival petitions:

> The Chalcedonians sent him a letter [only] a few spans long . . . and when he read it he laughed and shook his head.

The Monophysites, however, knew their late Roman history. They recounted in detail, from contemporary sources, the disastrous consequences in Alexandria of the Council of Chalcedon – persecutions, lynchings, punitive massacres:

> When the judge heard that, he clapped his hands together and said to those around him: "Oh, what a tyrannical deed was that!"[11]

For Middle Eastern contemporaries of the young Charlemagne, events of the 450s, that took place in the now-distant east Roman empire, were still contemporary history.

Hence the tenacity of the grip upon the past exercised, especially, by the Syriac-speaking Jacobites of northern Syria. From Antioch to China, Syriac remained one of the great languages of culture throughout medieval Asia. And, with Syriac, time stood still. In the west and in Constantinople, drastic changes in book-production led to the adoption of a new, more compact script, known as "minuscule." As a result, the flowing script of earlier Greek and Latin manuscripts became almost illegible to the average clergyman after the ninth century. Books that were not recopied into "minuscule" script at that time were as good as lost to future ages. A crevasse of this nature, between the present and the past, did not open up in the well-stocked monastic libraries of Syria and northern Iraq. Up to this century, any learned Syriac-speaker could take up and read a manuscript written in the age of Justinian.

The great *Histories* of the Monophysite Church, compiled from earlier writers by Michael the Syrian (1166–1199) and by Gregory Abu al-Faraj, known as Barhebraeus (died 1286) look back without a break to the fifth century AD. To read them is to catch an unmistakable echo of the world of late antiquity in contemporaries of Richard Coeur de Lion, Saint Louis and Marco Polo. The Mongol Laws of Chingiz Khan, wrote Barhebraeus, have gnomic elements: they reminded him of the *Gnomai* of Gregory Nazianzen. As for their shamanist belief in the journey of the soul, this, of course, says the learned Syrian, with over a thousand years of unbroken culture behind him, can be found in the writings of Aflatun – of Plato – when he discusses the doctrine of the transmigration of souls![12]

For the Nestorians of the former Persian territories, Muslim rulers were, if anything, a marked improvement on the erratic patronage of a pagan King of Kings. The Nestorians of Iraq positively welcomed the establishment of a strong, frankly monotheist empire:

> Before calling them, [God] had prepared them beforehand to hold Christians in honor . . . How otherwise could naked men, riding without armor and shield, have . . . brought down the proud spirit of the Persians?[13]

The Nestorian hierarchy benefitted from an empire whose horizons were even larger than those of the Sasanians. In the 780s, at a time when Harun al-Rashid was launching his last great expeditions into east Roman Anatolia and when the armies of Charlemagne fought their last, bitter campaigns in the woods of pagan Saxony, Nestorian bishops were at work on the edge of the world, in regions

> destitute even of Arabs and Jews, who confess One God, the Creator of Heaven and Earth.[14]

They hacked down the holy trees of the pagan mountain tribes of the Caspian highlands. They revived the Christian mission in Hsian-fu. Timothy I (780–823), the Nestorian *Katholikos* of the "Church of the East," took full advantage of the new situation. He reminded a bishop, who had asked for a pension with which to spend a comfortable retirement in Baghdad, that Nestorian monks who possessed nothing but their staff and satchel, were walking the roads that led to India and China. He even planned a new bishopric "for the peoples of Tibet."[15]

What these conflicting Christian groups soon had in common was a shared enthusiasm for the new language of the Arabs. Arabic, the language of the "clear-spoken ones," was a Semitic tongue akin to Syriac, but of overwhelming richness and precision, as sharp and flexible "as the blade of a rapier." It became the one Near Eastern language in which it was believed that every human thought and every human feeling – from love, war and the desert hunt to the most elevated of metaphysical abstractions – could be expressed. By AD 800, it was the allure of an entire profane culture, expressed in Arabic, and not Islam itself, that threatened to alienate the Christians of the Islamic empire from their own past. As a Christian bishop wrote in Cordoba:

> Many of my fellow-Christians read verses and fairy-tales of the Arabs, not in order to refute them, but to express themselves in Arabic ever more correctly and elegantly . . . Alas! All talented Christians know only the language and the literature of the Arabs . . . They express themselves . . . with more beauty and more art than do the Arabs themselves.[16]

If they were to remain in control of their own laity, the clergy had to do the same. To take one example: the Chalcedonian, Theodore abu Qurra (*ca.*740–*ca.*825) wrote most of his works in Arabic. He kept pace with Muslim theological debates. When he defended the worship of icons, passages from the *Qur'an* and sayings ascribed to Muhammad were what engaged his attention. The debates on the same issue that raged at Constantinople at the same time meant nothing to him. An Arabic-speaking Christianity looked, increasingly, to Islam for its vocabulary and theological agenda, and not to the Christian centers of the west.

The transfer of the center of the Islamic empire from Damascus to Baghdad, which was founded in 762, completed the triumph of Arabic in eastern Christianity. Baghdad lay close to the imposing ruins of Sasanian Ctesiphon. Nestorian administrators and doctors were as much in evidence in the court of Harun al-Rashid (788–809) and his successors as they had been, two centuries before, in the reign of Khusro II Aparwez. The legal restrictions imposed on the "Peoples of the Book" weighed lightly on this extensive class of non-Muslim technocrats:

> The Christians now have costly mounts and thoroughbred horses. They have packs of hounds and play polo, wrap themselves in costly fabrics and affect [pure Arab] patronymics.[17]

Such persons were essential to the new Muslim ruling class as doctors, as astrologers, indeed, as human artesian wells. Only learned Christians who had retained knowledge of Syriac and who enjoyed intermittent contacts with Greek-speaking fellow-Christians, could tap the vast subterranean reservoir of medical, scientific and philosophical knowledge that had slowly seeped into the Syriac churches that were now subject to the Islamic empire. Men whose culture reached back to the days of the foundation of the School of Nisibis now became transmitters of Greek learning to the elites of Baghdad.

The Nestorian court-doctor, Hunayn ibn Ishaq (died 873) worked carefully as a translator. He would compare old Syriac translations (made in the days of Justinian) with Greek texts that had become available in Baghdad through diplomatic missions to Constantinople. As a result, more works of Galen came to circulate in Arabic than were ever available in the Greek-speaking world of east Rome – not to mention translations of Euclid, Ptolemy and much of the logical and metaphysical tradition of late classical philosophy.

For Christian translators and their Muslim readers alike there was something reassuringly neutral about such subjects. As far back as the fifth century, Syrian Christians had tended to privilege a philosophical and technological culture that was soundproof to confessional differences. Now, at the Muslim court of Baghdad, a perennial "Greek" wisdom was patiently put together, in Arabic, part by part, like the reconstruction of a great dinosaur – an awesome antediluvian creature, untouched by the bitter religious confrontations of modern times. It was as fellow-philosophers, as *falasifa*, bound by the value-free rules of *kalam*, of logical argument, and not as fellow-monotheists, that Jews, Christians and Muslims could meet with greatest ease, "to bargain . . . as brothers who share in the goods that they inherit from a single father."[18]

Events such as these took place at the fulcrum of a very ancient world, at Damascus, Edessa and Baghdad. They happened far away from the northwestern tip of Eurasia that had begun to call itself, a little self-consciously, "Europe." To Muslim observers, east Rome, *Rum*, was the Christian region that really mattered. Constantinople was the capital of the last, proud empire to resist the call of the Prophet. It was for the heart of that empire that Muslim armies reached, throughout succeeding centuries, until it finally fell, to the Ottoman Turks, in 1453. By contrast, the west was a distant place. It was viewed by Muslims much as it had been viewed by previous civilized Near Easterners, Greeks and Syrians. It was a vast, indeterminate land, inhabited by unkempt and warlike peoples. It was marginal to the great "changing of the kingdoms" that had taken place in the ancient heartlands of civilization.[19]

The east Roman empire, whose territories ringed the eastern and southern shores of the Mediterranean, from Damascus to Carthage and the straits of Gibraltar, was the only Christian state to feel the first, shattering impact of the Arab advance. To Christian countries further north, these great events were still distant matters, that apparently caused little anxiety. In around 680, Arculf, a Frankish bishop, made his way to the Holy Land. He travelled, without apparent molestation, in a land very different from his native Gaul. No wagons were to be seen; for camels, and camels only, carried all loads. The Holy Places were as they had always been. The great church of the Ascension on the Mount of Olives still glowed like a beacon above Jerusalem:

> under the terrible and wondrous gleaming of these [lights], pouring out copiously through the glass shutters of the windows, all mount Olivet seems on fire, and the whole city, situated on the lower ground nearby, seems to be lit up.

Arculf did note that "the unbelieving Saracens" had built themselves "a church" in Damascus. But that is all. He returned peacefully to Constantinople to see "the Emperor of the World" – appropriately called Constantine IV – bending to kiss the fragment of the relic of the Holy Cross, which Heraclius had saved from Jerusalem as Syria collapsed before the Arabs.[20]

Even after the Arab conquest of Spain, in 711, no one in the north was certain that the invaders who had reached the western Mediterranean had come to stay. A Saxon lady from southern Britain was warned not to travel south to the Mediterranean. She should wait until the attacks and threats of the Saracens, which have lately manifested themselves in the lands of the Romans, should have quieted down.[21]

In 724, a party of Saxons actually reached Syria as Christian pilgrims. Their strange clothes caused a stir. A local Muslim dignitary declared that they meant no harm. He had seen such men: "they wish only to fulfill their religious law." They came from

the western shores, where the sun sets . . . and we know of no land beyond their islands, but only water.

Their leader, Willibald, returned to Europe – but not before being arrested by the authorities for attempting to smuggle precious balsam out of Palestine in the hollow of his pilgrim's staff! – to become, eventually, a bishop in southern Germany.[22]

It was a Europe that had changed since the 630s. The pious Saxon pilgrims came from a region that had been Christian for barely a century. Arculf's account of the Holy Places was written down, complete with careful illustrations, not in Gaul, but at Iona, a great Celtic monastery perched off the western coast of Scotland. Far away from the "changing of the kingdoms" that would prove decisive for the future history of Asia and of Africa, a new dimension had come to be added to the Christianity of the west. It is to the "Western shores" – to the Irish and to the Saxons in Britain – that we must now return.

12

Christianities of the North: Ireland and Saxon Britain

In the same decades of the seventh century as saw the last triumphs and, then, the collapse of the east Roman empire in the Middle East, the northern peripheries of the Mediterranean world took on a new profile. As far apart as Malaia Pereščepina, in Ukraine, and Sutton Hoo, perched on the North Sea coast of Suffolk, spectacular burials show the wealth and the range of international contacts enjoyed by a new style of northern ruler. The grave of Malaia Pereščepina may be associated with a Bulgar prince, who had played a role in the diplomacy of the emperor Heraclius. It contained, in all, 20 kilograms of golden objects, gathered from Constantinople, the Balkans, Iran and Central Asia. Sutton Hoo, though less rich, is equally impressive in the variety of its objects, and in the mobilization of labor they implied. The excavated mound contained a ship 26 meters long, weapons and ornaments that showed contact with Denmark and southern Sweden, jewelry made from 4,000 garnet chips (such as would have required the full year's labor of seventeen skilled craftsmen to set), gold coins from Francia, spoons and a great silver dish from Constantinople, Romano-British enamels, and yellow silk from Syria.[1]

So magnificent a setting-aside of wealth echoed, over a

century later, the sumptuous burial of Childeric, the father of Clovis, at Tournai: but with one disturbing difference – recently discovered human skeletons arranged around another mound at Sutton Hoo imply, perhaps, that not only horses were sacrificed on such occasions. Across the North Sea, in Denmark, distant echoes of Roman triumphal imagery, conveyed on coins, surfaced in a sudden proliferation of golden amulets. Constantius II, the conscientiously Christian son of Constantine, lived on, transformed into the image of a war-god. For Christians and pagans alike, successful warrior-kingship and a demonstrative relationship with victory-bringing deities went hand in hand.

The northern world was changing. From Ireland to southern Sweden, aggressive dynasties, with more effective military retinues, more control of local resources and considerable contact with the rich world to their south had begun to turn societies that had known little or no state-system into "kingdoms." Though fragile as spiders' webs compared with the post-imperial solidity of the Frankish and Visigothic kingdoms, these new political units represented a decisive change. After 560, the O'Neill dynasty, in northern Ireland, came to cast a more grandiose, harsher shadow of "empire" over the land: hard-dealing warrior-kings, they fought to create ever-larger pyramids of client kings, who would provide them with goods and services. In the areas of Britain controlled by the Saxons, similar hegemonies emerged. As in Ireland, the locus of such power shifted frequently. Ethelbert of Kent (560–616) ruled from the south. Later, power shifted to the north. Under Oswald (634–642), Oswy (642–671) and Egfrith (671–685), the kings of Northumbria ruled the frontier zone traversed by Hadrian's wall, from the edge of the Highlands of Scotland to the Humber.

Prestige and links with the ancient past, of whatever kind, counted for such rulers. Established within the walls of Roman forts along the North Sea, the kings of East Anglia claimed to be descended both from the war-god, Woden, and from "Caesar." In Britain, the Saxons had long held the eastern coastline. The estuary of the Rhine, the Channel coast of Neustria and a Seine valley increasingly dominated by great monasteries, were as close to the Saxons of Britain, by ship, as was the heavily wooded hinterland of their own country. Appropriately described as "entrepreneurial kings," they had learned how to play Clovis to their less-fortunate relatives and rivals. They appreciated, though from a safe distance, the solid success represented, throughout northern Europe, by the Frankish Christian court of a great overlord, such as Dagobert I. They exchanged slaves gained in their wars for the wealth of the Frankish Rhineland.

In Ireland, Christianity changed, from being the religion of a minority, to become the exclusive faith of powerful royal clans. In 558, the *feis Temro*, the solemn sacral act by which the high-king of Tara (Temair) slept with the guardian goddess of the land, was celebrated, for the last time, by Dermot mac Cerball. Dermot was pushed aside in 561, at the bloody battle of Cúl Drebene. A member of the O'Neill royal line, Columba (another Colum, like Columbanus, soon to be known, in Irish, as Columcille, "the dove of the Church") had played a role in this victory. Already a clergyman, he was accused of shedding blood in the battle and excommunicated. He left Ireland as a penitential exile, around the age of forty. He settled in Iona, off the coast of Mull, in 565, the year that Justinian died in Constantinople. By the time of his death in 597 – the same year that the mission of Gregory the Great landed in Kent – Columba had created a spiritual empire in the north, that resembled the new, far-reaching kingship of his O'Neill kinsmen. Iona was the center of a pyramid of loyal monasteries, that stretched from the south of Ireland to the Hebrides. After 635, the monks of Iona re-established Christianity in Northumbria. Lindisfarne, called to this day "Holy Island," became the Iona of the northern Saxons. Closely connected with two of the most extensive hegemonies in the British Isles, the O'Neills of Ireland and the kings of Northumbria, Iona came to dominate the Celtic world from its most northerly tip. It was the beginning of a new age of Irish Christianity.

In retrospect, Irish writers had little difficulty in understanding the towering success of a man such as Columba. Iona was cut off from the mainland by a stretch of "glass green" sea.

It was the classic "desert" of the Early Christian imagination recreated, in a Celtic idiom, in the remoteness of an offshore island in the wild Atlantic. Yet it was situated at the center of the political world of the north, where Ireland and northern Britain met.

Columba was believed to have chosen Iona because it was the first island from which the coast of his beloved Ireland was no longer visible. He once picked up with tenderness an exhausted crane from Donegal that had landed at his feet: like himself, the noble bird was an exile. In the monastic community of Iona the hard laws of nature in a warrior society were miraculously held in suspense: a knife blessed by Columba would no longer draw blood. But, for all this, he remained the saint of a warrior class:

> And in the terrible clashings of battles, by virtue of prayers, he obtained from God that some kings were conquered and other rulers were conquerors.

Men of war, even "bloodstained sinners," had escaped certain death in battle through chanting Irish hymns in his honor. In a quiet landscape, ringed by the hills of Scotland, the battle-fields of Ireland remained always present to Columba and his monks:

> He heard his companions . . . talking on the way about two kings . . . "My children [he said], why do you thus idly converse about these men, seeing that both the kings of whom you are now talking have recently perished, beheaded by their enemies? On this day . . . sailors arriving from Ireland will tell you the same."[2]

The stories were recalled by Adomnán (628–704), a descendent of Columba's kinsmen and abbot of Iona. In his day, Adomnán was the greatest ecclesiastical politician of the northern world. He was one of the few early medieval churchmen who enjoyed sufficient authority to control warfare. In 697, he persuaded fifty-one kings and forty churchmen to agree to the *Cáin Adomnáin*, Adomnán's Law, an Ireland-wide *Law of Innocents*, that protected women and clerics from the effects of intertribal violence. It was one of the many ways in which

Columba's spiritual empire had come to work its way into the political life of an entire society.[3]

In a world without Roman towns, whose solid walls and long-established populations guaranteed the status of their bishops, monasteries, such as Iona, were the few fixed points in an ever-changing landscape. Bishops and clergy existed in Ireland. But they lacked glamor. They belonged to the humble world of the small tribes. Their status rose and fell as each tribe passed from one powerful overlord to another. This was not the case with monasteries such as Iona in the far north, Kildare in Leinster and the vocal "metropolitan" see of Saint Patrick, at Armagh. These religious centers recreated, in Christian form, the great high places that acted as intertribal joining points. At the end of the seventh century massive earthworks – many of them the result of 100,000 man hours of labor – came to ring the sacred enclosures of Christian monasteries. In a major Christian monastery, monks, students and their dependents could be numbered in hundreds. In a land without large conglomerations of population, great monasteries were the nearest things to cities. Paradoxically, it was Christian poetry in Irish that celebrated the pagan high-places of Ireland. Their glories were now evoked, so as to provide an epic backdrop for the thriving, pan-tribal sanctuaries of Christian times:

> Tara's great fort withered with the death of her rulers:
> Great Armagh remains with a host of venerable heroes.
> It has been quenched – great the downfall – the
>   pride of valiant Loegaire:
> the name of Patrick, splendid, famous,
>   this is the one which grows.[4]

In a sudden flowering of Irish hagiography, at the end of the seventh century, each major monastic center strove to bring its long-dead founders into the present. Cogitosus' *Life* of Saint Brigid of Kildare (who died in 520) was written around 650. It culminated with a description of the saint's present shrine – a tomb of shimmering gold and jewels, surrounded by chandeliers and royal treasures, worthy of a Merovingian bishop, housed in an exquisitely carved wooden church on the rich plain of the Curragh.[5] Muirchú soon followed, around

680–700, with a *Life* of Patricius, written for the see of Armagh.

In the case of Muirchú's *Life* of Patricius, we can measure the extent to which an imaginative chasm had opened, in the course of two centuries, between the hesitant Christianity of the late Roman frontier and the triumphant new Christendom of seventh-century Ireland. Muirchú had Patricius' *Confessio* before him as he wrote. But he gave his readers what they wanted – a religious leader larger than life, cut to the measure of the modern "heirs" of Patricius, the great bishops of Armagh. In Muirchú's *Life*, Saint Patrick (as we can now call him, having abandoned the humble Patricius of history) is made to confront Loegaire (Leary), the high king at Tara,

> where was the greatest kingdom of these peoples, the capital of all paganism.

In a triumphant confrontation with the king and his druids, Patrick

> drove an invincible wedge into the head of all idolatry . . . For the faith of idols [so Muirchú asserted] was wiped out on Patrick's arrival and the Catholic faith filled every corner of the land.

Even the proud Coroticus was duly punished by being turned into a wild fox![6]

In these euphoric legends, we are faced with nothing less than the *ex post facto* Christianization of an entire society, through the appropriation of its culture by a new class of religious experts. Irish society had long been accustomed to being divided into carefully designated groups, each with its appropriate degree of honor. The monks and clergy now came to form yet another such separate caste. They replaced the druids, the ritual experts of the old religion. They divided with the *filid*, the "seeing men" – the poets – the supreme status enjoyed, in Irish society, by groups of persons traditionally associated with numinously intricate verbal skills.

The Christian clergy entered with gusto into this role. In a society that had evolved a script such as Ogham largely as a means of esoteric communication, the clergy were literate, and, better than that, literate in a mysterious, totally alien tongue. In legendary accounts of his progress, Patrick was said to have brought, with every baptism, the further magic of a "written A.B.C." His clergy advanced through a land without writing, holding open texts "like drawn white swords."[7] A monastery was a place of numinous, unknown sounds:

a lasting, low-voiced congregation . . . high knowledge feeds me, the melodious [Latin] song of believers.[8]

To copy Latin words was, in itself, a miraculous task. Columba could perceive, by divine prescience, when there was one letter "i" misplaced in an entire, near-perfect copy of the Psalms.[9] In a Christian region where books of any kind were rare objects, Cassiodorus' mystique of copying the Scriptures was yet further tinged with the magical awe that surrounded the *áes dána*, the "men of skill," the master-craftsmen whose legendary cunning provided secular rulers with the ornaments and jewelry appropriate to their status. Covering the great vellum pages of Gospel-books with exquisite illuminations, the monks became *áes dána* to the "High King of Heaven." They were not simply copying a text. They were turning it into the equivalent of jewelry. The Book of Kells (so called from its place of discovery) had probably been prepared at Iona by a successor of Adomnán. It came to rest in the shrine of Saint Brigid at Kildare, where it was known as "the High Relic of the Western World." A twelfth-century traveller, Gerald of Wales, recorded his impression of its pages:

If you look at them carelessly . . . you may judge them to be mere daubs . . . You would see nothing subtle where everything is subtle. But if you take the trouble to look very closely and to penetrate with your eyes to the secrets of the artistry, you will notice such intricacies, so delicate, so subtle . . . so involved and bound together, so fresh still in their colorings, that you will not hesitate to declare that all those things must have been the work not of men but of angels.[10]

With their distinctive dress and shaven heads, the clergy – and especially the monks – placed themselves to one side of the warrior society in which their kinfolk were still inextricably involved. The sound of their bells formed a pointed contrast to the spine-chilling yell of the warband.[11] Irish clergymen fastened, with enthusiasm, on the purity-laws of the Old Testament: such laws guaranteed their own status as a "pure" priestly caste.

Cut off from society in this way, the monks became a sacralized, positive version of the small groups that had always formed the violent antithesis to settled life. Bands of landless, unmarried young men – "kings' sons," exiles and outlaws – lived a wild existence in the woods and boglands. Eating horse-flesh, marked by sinister tokens of their vows of vengeance, frequently employed by the powerful as "enforcers," these groups shadowed Irish society like the grey shapes of the *cú glas*, the ever-present wolves – "grey dogs" that had broken loose from human control.[12]

For monks, however, and especially for converts of royal background, exile was an honorable state. But it was always an awesome one, in that it involved separation from the comfort and protection of one's kingroup. It was as an "exile of God" that Columba had been established at Iona. As we shall see, the notion of "exile" determined the movements of many Irishmen and Saxons in Continental Europe. Though the spread of Christianity might have been a result of such movements, it was only part of the phenomenon of *peregrinatio*, of endless pilgrimage for God undertaken in foreign lands. For a man without kin, all places were equally strange, equally "heathen" lands. All Europe lay at the feet of such persons, for the simple reason that, away from one's own home country, all places were equally empty of human meaning and, so, could be filled with the vast, invisible presence of God.

Though technically "outsiders" to Irish society, the new caste of monks and clergy were, in fact, deeply implicated in it. The laws of clientage and reciprocity kept the lay world close to them. In the retinue of a great abbot, laymen and clerics mingled: his extended household was an extension of his monastery to such an extent that the Old Irish word for "family," *muinter*, is taken from it. Tenants of monasteries were called *manaig*, "monks." Although married, they were indeed monks in their fierce loyalty to "their" lord, the abbot.

In return for this support, the monks and clergy gave their lay clients the priceless, if imponderable, countergift of "the Reading" – regular recitation of the Psalms and the Gospels.[13] They would say Mass for their souls and would bury them in "holy" ground, close to a Christian shrine. The *Penitentials* tell us so much about the sexual practices of the laity because married persons, as the clients of monasteries, demanded the same careful services of penance and forgiveness as did the monks themselves. They felt entitled to help and blessing in their day-to-day life. Even the austere Columba was remembered as having worked a miracle that turned the heart of a woman married to an ugly husband into frank sexual enjoyment.[14]

Patterns of dependence radiated from every monastery, bringing segments of the laity into closer contact with the new ascetic caste than we might, at first sight, expect. Only human wolves, untamed warriors who occupied the ungoverned edges of society, were deemed to lie entirely outside the reach of the holy. *Laicus*, "layman," *láech*, was the term applied in Old Irish to such persons: they were the ultimate "laymen," men incapable of penance, whose feral life highlighted, by contrast, even the most intermittent piety of the average Irish Christian.[15]

It was on these terms that Ireland could be declared, by AD 700, to be a Christian country. As a result, the pre-Christian past continued in the present with a self-confidence that was inconceivable in Continental Europe. For the Irish language itself was now controlled by the new masters of words. It was the clergy, as writers, who saved the exclusively oral literature of their land. By becoming written texts, pre-Christian Irish law and Irish poetry became part of the new Christian order.[16]

The great collection of Irish law, the *Senchas Már*, appeared in the 720s. It was a remarkable tribute to the creativity and to the new sense of unity of a Christian region. It applied to lawyers in the entire Irish-speaking world. In size and comprehensiveness no single legal compilation had appeared to equal it in western Europe since the *Theodosian Code* of 438. In it, the ancient laws of Ireland were brought into the Christian present, by being treated as if they were an adjunct to the Old Testament. Its Christian compilers maintained that the "law of nature" had inspired the poets and judges of pre-Christian Ireland. The "law of nature" was a divinely ordained prelude to the "law of the letter," to the "blessed white language" of the Christian commandments, in the same way as the Old Testament had been a prelude to the New. Thus, ancient Irish laws gained weight and majesty through being charged with the same sense of a venerable past forever active in the Christian present as were the laws of the Old Testament. The Old Testament, indeed, spoke of a past that seemed reassuringly familiar to members of a tribal, warrior society. On the basis of Old Testament practice, even polygamy, one legal tract argued, might have its place in a Christian Ireland:

For the Chosen People of God were in a plurality of marriages, so it is no easier to censure than to praise it.[17]

In marked contrast to seventh-century Ireland, Christianity came to the Saxon kingdoms established in Britain (in the territories soon, but not yet, known as "England") from the outside, as part of a wider process characterized by memorable gift-exchanges. Between 597 and 700, an ambitious class of new rulers, accustomed to reaching out for exotic goods, made their own the prestigeful religion of their Continental and Irish neighbors.

In parts of western Britain, Saxons may well have received their Christianity from neighboring British princes, even from their own Romano-British peasantry, for whom Christianity had remained a folk-religion. But no glory was attached to receiving gifts from the "Welsh," the *wealh*, the despised and hostile "foreigners" *par excellence*. What was remembered, rather, was the arrival in each Saxon kingdom of parties of impressive strangers (usually bishops from across the sea, with their monastic retinues) whose movements and success depended, for well over a generation, on the unpredictable calculations of prestige of Saxon kings and their warrior-aristocracies.

It was a situation calculated to generate misunderstandings and false hopes. Thus, when Gregory I sent his imposing "mission" to Ethelbert, king of Kent, in 597, he may have hoped for nothing less than the rapid revival of the former Christian order of Christian Britain, as it had been in the last century of the empire: metropolitan bishops, each with twelve colleagues settled in lesser cities, would return to the Roman governmental centers of London and York. What Augustine and his party of forty monks found, on arriving at Kent, was a very different Britain. They met a Saxon king determined to use every asset – including a new religion – to maintain his own distinctive, local style of hegemonial overlordship.[18]

Ethelbert knew how to control foreigners, lest the world they represented should undermine his own prestige. He had been married for fifteen years to a Christian Frankish princess, Bertha. Bertha had been free to practice her own religion, with a Frankish chaplain-bishop, in a Romano-British church in Canterbury. But the Franks were not eager to insist on Ethelbert's conversion. They did not want a Christian equal, and Ethelbert, for his part, had no intention of becoming the spiritual "subking" of rulers with hegemonial ambitions quite as marked as were his own. To receive baptism from Rome was a different matter. Ethelbert could make contact with the safely distant, imagined center of the Latin Christian world, and, beyond Rome, could gain recognition from the Roman emperor himself. Gregory's letters to Ethelbert were welcome in Kent. They were accompanied "by numerous gifts of every kind." These showed that the pope intended "to glorify the king with temporal honors." Bertha was told that her piety was well-spoken of in the imperial palace of Constantinople. Ethelbert was told that he could imitate Constantine, a ruler who had

> converted the Roman State from the false worship of idols . . . together with the nations under his rule [so that he] surpassed his predecessors in fame.[19]

Yet, when they arrived, Augustine and his party found themselves confined to an offshore island. Ethelbert would only meet them in the open air. He would not enter a building to speak with them, lest, as sorcerers, they swayed his judgement. It was a gesture to his more conservative followers. Ethelbert showed that he would not allow himself to be "bewitched" by the religion of these foreigners, in such a way as to forsake traditional rites, without due consultation with his own nobility. Even when Ethelbert was baptized, and Augustine found himself free to preach in Kent, the monastic community at Canterbury resembled a cordoned-off residence of privileged foreigners – valuable but potentially disruptive persons, best kept under surveillance close to the royal court – than it did the extensive network of re-established "Roman" bishoprics that Gregory had planned.[20]

Nor could they move fast. No dramatic burst of temple-breaking (such as had characterized the heroic days of Saint Martin of Tours and Theodosius I) accompanied the arrival of the new religion. Gregory wrote that pagan shrines were to be re-consecrated with holy water. The solemn sacrificial feasts that had challenged the gods, through the reckless gift of so much food, to grant the counter-gift of fertility to the crops and livestock, were to be replaced by Christian banquets on the feasts of martyrs. They would take place in wooden booths set up outside the new churches, but would continue to carry the same associations of divine good cheer. We should not mistake this famous letter for a gesture of tolerance. Gregory wrote it as a good subject of the supremely self-confident eastern empire. From Italy to Upper Egypt, it was now accepted that no former pagan space should go unclaimed: crosses carved on the doors, even the creation of a church within them, must make plain that all temples had been superseded by a triumphant Christian dispensation. Yet he justified the practice in terms that left room for considerable flexibility:

> It is doubtless impossible to cut out everything at once from their stubborn minds: just as the man who is attempting to climb to the highest place rises by steps and slow stages, not by leaps.[21]

Language itself eventually betrayed a process of enforced adaptation to local conditions. *Pascha*, the Latin version of the Jewish feast of Passover, the *Pesah*, still current in all Romance languages and adopted, unchanged, at this time, in Old Irish, became in England, as in all other Germanic-speaking lands, "Easter," a name frankly derived from *Eostre*, the pagan goddess from whom the month was named.

Of greater long-range importance even than the fate of temples was the fact that Augustine provided Ethelbert with a skill, with which he could shine as a new Clovis to his people. Ethelbert issued "with the advice of his counsellors a code of law after the Roman manner." But, unlike Clovis' *Salic Law*, Ethelbert's *Laws* were not issued in Latin, but in Anglo-Saxon. It is a remarkable indication of firm purpose and adaptability. Within a decade, unknown Roman or Frankish scribes had turned a Germanic dialect into a written language. They did so in order to create documents which would protect their Church. The *Laws* made plain that the new foreigners enjoyed the personal protection of the king. They begin by stating that theft of "the property of God and the Church" required twelve-fold compensation. Even the honor of a Christian priest was proclaimed – and in the vernacular – to be as sensitive as that of the king himself, and to be worth nine-fold compensation.[22]

But Ethelred remained a hegemonial ruler in the intensely personal style of his Saxon peers. Christianity followed the footsteps of a politics of prestige, conducted by the exchange of gifts and of women. Paulinus, the Italian disciple of Augustine, did, indeed, reach York in 619. But he did so in the retinue of Ethelbert's daughter, Ethelburga, given as a wife to the formidable overlord of northern Britain, Edwin. Yet, despite that marriage, Edwin took nine years to decide to become a Christian. When he finally did so, in 628, he ensured that it was a thoroughly royal occasion.

At a public debate of his followers, memorable sayings were exchanged: old retainers waxed wise:

This is how the present life of man on earth, King, appears to me [said one] in comparison with the time which is unknown to us. You are sitting feasting with your earldormen and thegns in winter time; the fire is burning on the hearth . . . and all inside is warm; while outside the wintry storms of rain and snow are raging; and a sparrow flies swiftly through the hall . . . it flits from your sight, out of the winter storm and back into it again. So this life of man appears but for a moment: what follows, or, indeed, what went before we know not at all. If this new doctrine brings us more certain information, it seems right that we should accept it.[23]

This was how Saxons liked to think that they had changed their minds in matters of religion.

More forcibly, the pagan high priest, who had until then been debarred by taboo from joining the king in war, received a warhorse and a spear, with which to desecrate his own shrine. The gesture made plain that ancient ideas of the sacred, that were based upon sharp ritual distinctions between male and female, war and peace, and that involved all classes in wooing the earth for her fertility, could be brushed aside: wealth and prosperity now lay with the warhorse and the spear, in the king's warband alone. Mass baptisms and preaching took place, on one occasion for thirty-six days on end, at the royal center and former Celtic temple-site at Yeavering, where large wooden halls had been built for prolonged feasting, supplied by livestock from the neighboring hills. Such moments were long-remembered in Northumbria. An elderly priest told the historian Bede, in around 730, that he had been told by an old man, of how

> he had been baptized at noon by bishop Paulinus in the presence of king Edwin with a great crowd of people . . . [Paulinus, he remembered] was tall, with a slight stoop, black hair, a thin face, a slender and aquiline nose . . . at once impressive and terrifying.[24]

Yet Edwin had only another five years to live. His death in battle, in 633, was followed by the collapse of Christianity in his kingdom. Paulinus and Ethelburga fled by sea to Kent, with little to show for their stay in the north other than a great golden Cross and chalice, Christianized remnants of the once-famous "treasure" of Edwin.

Forced into prominence by their royal hosts, the tiny groups of foreigners fell one after the other as their patrons died. Ethelbert went first, in 616. Determined to maintain his position by marrying Ethelbert's second wife, his son showed what he thought of the clergy (who disapproved of such a marriage) by returning, for a time, to pagan sacrifices. In Essex, the pagan sons of a king who had been a client of Ethelbert reminded their bishop that Christianity, also, was subject to Saxon codes of gift exchange:

When they saw the bishop, who was celebrating solemn mass in church, give the Eucharist to the people, they said to him . . . "Why do you not offer us the white bread which you used to give to our father . . . If you will not oblige us in so trifling a matter as this, you cannot remain in our kingdom."[25]

For Redwald, king of East Anglia, Christ might be a distinguished guest; but He had to learn to live with other, local gods:

in the same temple he had one altar for the Christian sacrifice and another small altar on which to offer victims to devils.[26]

A descendant of Redwald, a good Christian who died in 713, remembered being shown this temple as a little boy.

These anecdotes provide a unique glimpse of indigenous value-systems at work along the northern frontiers of Europe. Christianity reached the Saxon kingdoms on sufferance and, for well over a generation, its representatives were carefully "screened" by kings and noblemen who knew exactly what they wanted from a foreign religion. Yet the stories themselves are taken from an account of the coming of Christianity to Britain that was written, over a century later, to assert that such erratic responses were a thing of the past. The historian in question, Bede (later known as the Venerable Bede), came from a Northumbrian family. Born in 672/3, he grew up among monks. At the age of seven (that is, at an age when warrior-sons, also, were entrusted to a foster-father) he had been given by his parents to the abbot of Wearmouth. He became a monk in the sister-monastery of Jarrow. The two monasteries formed a pair. They had been set up and equipped at great cost, from 674 onwards, by a succession of noble and royal patrons. Built in stone, "in the Roman manner," they dominated the estuaries of the Tyne and the Wear, looking out to sea, as the royal barrows at Sutton Hoo had done. Like Sutton Hoo, they spoke of the power of a ruler who could afford to cast so much wealth, beyond recall, into an institution closely connected with the remembrance of the dead.

Bede wrote his *Ecclesiastical History of the English Nation* in his old age, in 731. It came half a century after the great flowering of Irish hagiography and a decade after the appearance of the *Senchas Már*. It, also, was an *ex post facto* declaration of triumph. Saxon Britain, like Ireland, could be declared to have become a Christian land.

But while the Irish took the unity of their law and language for granted, Bede went out of his way to view Britain as a whole, much as Gildas, whom he had read, had done. He endowed the Saxon kingdoms with a providential role in the island. They were not merely the scourge of the sinful Britons, as they had been for Gildas. They were a new people, united, if in nothing else, in common adherence to Catholic Christianity. Bede was the first author to treat the disparate groups of settlers as a single *gens Anglorum*, a "nation of the English." He did this in part because Gregory the Great, who knew no better, had used the same undifferentiated term. But he used the term, particularly, so that the *gens Anglorum* could be described as a single people, newly established in their own Promised Land, the island of Britain. They were responsible to God, as a group, for their sins, exactly as the People of Israel had been.

As in ancient Israel, so with the *Angli*, it was the behavior of the kings that invariably tipped the balance of God's favor towards the people as a whole. In the greatest sins of all, frank syncretism and recurrent apostasy, it was simpler, as in Israel, to blame the kings than to linger over the complex hesitations of an entire population. By the same token, the momentary flashes of peace and grandeur enjoyed by the *Angli* under major hegemonial rulers could be ascribed to their willingness to listen to Christian bishops, many of whom Bede presented as worthy heirs of the Hebrew prophets – vivid figures, whose interventions were as drastic, and as mercifully intermittent in the day-to-day life of a warrior society, as had been those of a Samuel or an Elijah.

Bede dedicated his *Ecclesiastical History* to a king – a literate man, whose piety soon forced him into exile. He made sure that good kings would be remembered even in their most spectacular reverses. Unlike the accepting but disabused account of Clovis by Gregory of Tours, a raw sacrality – the

product of fiercely maintained local memories – flickers around
a figure such as king Oswald of Northumbria. Oswald was
Edwin's successor. He had been baptized at Iona. Even the
moss from the wooden Cross around which Oswald fought
his first decisive battle, in 634, continued to heal the faithful
up to Bede's own days. The product of an Ionan Christianity,
where royal kin, as abbots, knew how to reverse the values
of a warrior-society in their own behavior, Oswald, as a king,
knew how to invert the codes of the war-band at moments of
high Christian festival. He showed that "hack silver" could be
used in unexpected ways:

> the story is told that on a certain occasion, one Easter
> Day, when he sat down to dinner with bishop Aidan, a
> silver dish was placed on the table before him . . . They
> had just raised their hands to ask a blessing on the bread
> when there came in an officer of the king . . . telling him
> that a great multitude of poor people from every district
> were sitting in the precincts and asking alms of the king.
> He at once ordered . . . the dish to be broken up and the
> pieces divided among them. The bishop, who was sitting
> by . . . grasped him by the right hand, and said, "May this
> hand never decay."[27]

Sure enough, the blessed hand of Oswald was cut off when
he died in battle in 642. It was preserved undecayed in a chapel
in the royal fort of Bamburgh, overlooking the North Sea, close
to Lindisfarne. The earth on which Oswald had fallen, even
wood from the stake on which his head had been fixed by
his enemies, worked miracles. His last battle-cry, a prayer
for the souls of his doomed retinue, became proverbial. In
the same decade as Muslim armies, also staffed by warriors
who regarded themselves as potential martyrs, swept into Syria
and Iraq, Oswald became the first warrior-king in Europe who,
simply by the fact of having died a violent death in battle, was
believed to have gained supernatural powers usually associated
with a Christian martyr or ascetic.[28]

Oswald, however, belonged to a distant, heroic age, which
Bede tended to idealize, in order to castigate his more comfortable times. Oswald made a good story. But what had mattered

in the period between 640 and 700 was not so easily recounted. In this period, a substantial and irrevocable change set in. Once they had tested the new religion to their satisfaction, the kings of Saxon Britain and their aristocracy emerged as givers to the Church on a heroic scale. Their kingdoms were marked by the ruthless affluence of a frontier society. A relatively small warrior-aristocracy and their royal leaders gained constant access to new wealth, through conquest and tribute at the expense of the British, through more drastic organization of the considerable resources of a sub-Roman agrarian economy, and through the grim concomitant of early medieval warfare, a lively slave trade. This new wealth was "redeemed" and rendered permanent by making lavish provision for a predominantly monastic form of Christianity, of which Bede's Jarrow and Wearmouth were only one spectacular example among many.

Slowly but surely Saxon Britain came to resemble northern Francia, as we have described it in the decades that followed the impact of Columbanus. It was a rich world, where kings and their courtiers sought to atone for their sins and to secure the future fame of their families. Altogether, Britain, Francia and parts of Ireland moved to the same rhythm at this time. Each region boasted a local aristocracy determined, whether as monks or, simply, as patrons, to transfer to their own homeland vivid microcosms of a once-distant Christian order. It is to this remarkable process of relocation that we must now turn, in order to understand what the new Christianities of the north shared with other regions and how they differed significantly from the very ancient, Mediterranean Christendom on which they drew with such enthusiasm at this time.

13

Micro-Christendoms

In the pre-literate world of the North, the presence of books unleashed, in the privileged few who handled them, a sense of breathless hurry. At Melrose, in southern Scotland, the old prior, Boisil, summoned the young saint Cuthbert:

> "I warn you not to lose the chance of learning from me, for death is upon me. By next week my body and voice will have lost its strength."
> "Then tell me what is the best book to study. One that can be got through in a week."
> "Saint John's Gospel . . . I have a commentary in seven parts. With the help of God we can read one a day and perhaps discuss it if we want."[1]

When Bede faced death, in 735, he was gripped by the same sense of urgency. Some texts still lay unfinished:

> "I cannot have my children learning what is not true [he said] . . . Take your pen and mend it, and then write fast." Then Wilberht [his pupil] said: "There is still one sentence . . ."
> And he said: "Write it! There now, it is written. Good."
> And then [in Christ's words]: "It is finished."[2]

Only then did Bede sit back in his chair to await death. A man who died with Anglo-Saxon Christian poems on his lips, Bede had written over forty books in a flawless Latin.

Behind Bede's achievement lay two generations characterized by the massive transfer of goods from Gaul and Rome to Northumbria. Benedict Biscop (628–690), a Northumbrian nobleman turned monk, had founded Wearmouth and Jarrow. On six occasions, beginning in 653, Biscop travelled to Rome. Even his name, "Benedict," came from abroad. It signalled his enthusiasm for Saint Benedict, the author of the *Rule*. An entire library, collected by this northern magnate as he made his Grand Tour of Christian Italy, arrived at Tyneside – along with a singing-master to teach the style of chanting practiced at Saint Peter's in Rome, relics, icons, embroidered silks (worth, in themselves, three large estates), experts in glassware from Gaul and

masons who could build a church for him according to the Roman manner which he always loved.[3]

Supported, also, by lavish royal gifts, the twin monasteries housed 600 monks. They were maintained by the services of many thousands of tenants. Bede had access to over 300 books, some of which had once been connected with Cassiodorus' Vivarium. It was the largest library to be assembled north of the Alps at this time.

Exotic "Roman" skills could place almost as heavy a burden on local resources as Roman frontier garrisons had once done. To possess the entire works of Gregory the Great was to create, by patient copying, an eleven-volume set of 2,100 parchment folios, that weighed almost 50 kilograms (the modern standard edition weighs only 3!). The skins of over 500 calves were required to make one major Bible. Yet the gift exchange that knit together the widely separated Christian regions of Europe demanded the production of such portable treasures. The *Codex Amiatinus* (now on show in the Biblioteca Laurenziana in Florence, and named from Monte Amiata, where it had come to rest) was produced at Wearmouth. It was one of three large copies of the entire Bible made from an Italian original. In 716, Ceolfrith, abbot of Wearmouth, set out to Rome with a retinue of no fewer than eighty monks. He intended to place the great *codex* on the tomb of Saint Peter.

A perfect copy of the Bible in the "correct" Latin edition of Saint Jerome, and weighing over 35 kilograms, it was intended to be a stunning and appropriate counter-gift to Saint Peter, protector of Wearmouth, from an "Abbot of the Ultimate Land." Ceolfrith died on the way. The *Codex Amiatinus* finally came to rest in Italy. So perfect a copy was it, that it was long taken to be, not the product of a late seventh-century Northumbrian monastery, but a Bible produced in Italy at an earlier age.

The transfer of so many Mediterranean books to the British Isles was the symptom of a more widespread process. By the seventh century, the decline of trading networks in the Mediterranean and the hardening of political and confessional boundaries in the Middle East ensured that, despite the enthusiastic movements of a few distinguished travellers, the Christian Churches had become profoundly regionalized. Christianity was a patchwork of adjacent, but separate, "micro-Christendoms." No longer bathed, unconsciously, in an "ecumenical" atmosphere based upon regular inter-regional contacts, each Christian region fell back on itself. Each needed to feel that it possessed, if in diminished form, the essence of an entire Christian culture. Often singularly ill-informed about their neighbors, or deeply distrustful of them, the leaders of each "micro-Christendom" fastened with fierce loyalty on those features that seemed to reflect in microcosm, in their own land, the imagined, all-embracing macrocosm of a world-wide Christianity.

In such a mood, "encyclopedic" works, which organized all previous knowledge, were not seen by contemporaries as the bloodless digests of a once-rich past (as modern scholars tend to view them). Far from it. They were greatly valued. Like high-energy vitamin capsules, they reassured contemporaries that the total nourishment of Christian truth, once distributed with insouciant abundance through so many books, was now available in their own times, to be "activated" in the urgent, deeply existential task of building up a local Christendom.

The phenomenon can be seen to happen from Ireland to Persia. Already, around 600, the writings of Theodore of Mopsuestia were presented, by the Nestorian teachers of Nisibis, as containing the sum total of human knowledge. Theodore had assembled the "scattered limbs" of wisdom, and made of them "a single, perfect statue."[4] The omniscience ascribed to one great teacher guaranteed the cultural integrity of the Nestorian Church in Persia. Theodore had long been acclaimed by his followers – and with good reason – as the "World Class Exegete." But in distant Bangor, also, the proud autonomy of the teachers of Columbanus rested on similar claims: one of them, Mo-Chuoróc maccu Neth Sémon (hardly a widely known figure!), was also styled, by his admirers, "doctor of the whole world."[5]

In 636, the *Etymologies* of bishop Isidore of Seville (*ca.*560–636) were published by his disciples. A twenty-book summation of all knowledge, in the form of separate entries on the "origin," and, hence, the meaning, of significant terms used in the pagan and Christian books available to Isidore, the *Etymologies* promised to introduce the reader to every aspect of useful knowledge available to past generations of wise Latins. Isidore's *tour de force* confirmed the hopes of an entire local elite. He gave them all they would ever need to know. He enabled them

to view, in his own person, the full *tableau* of ancient wisdom . . . After Spain had suffered so many blows, God raised him up to restore the monumental fabric of the Ancients, lest, through senile loss of memory, we slip back into rustic ways.[6]

In 665, the Armenian savant, Ananias of Shirak, in his *K'nnikon*, claimed to have brought back to

this country, the heritage of Saint Grigor, the land that loves Christ,

a complete summary of cosmology and of chronological computation. Henceforth Armenians could do without the Greeks.[7]

There was a competitive edge to all such ventures. In the western Mediterranean, the Visigothic kings of Spain and their episcopal advisers, of whom Isidore was among the most enthusiastic, put forward their own version of a "true" Christian commonwealth in thinly disguised competition with the "kingdom of the Greeks." They had reason to be edgy. The Visigothic monarchy was elective and prone to civil war. Justinian had taken advantage of this weakness to invade southern Spain. Even after "imperial" garrisons had been dislodged from the southern coast of Spain, in the 620s, the eastern empire remained a threatening presence in Carthage, Sicily and Rome. East Roman ships might yet return.

Having established a firm alliance with the Catholic bishops through their conversion from Arianism in 589, the Visigothic kings of Spain succeeded in holding together for over a century the largest undivided political unit in seventh-century Europe. It was a remarkable achievement, maintained, in part, by intermittent bursts of solemn words. Like the imperial codes of east Rome, the royal laws covered all subjects and claimed to solve all problems. They ranged from occasional, grandiose mandates for the forcible baptism of Jews throughout the kingdom to lists of compensations for injuries caused to villagers by local bulls.

The entire Catholic episcopate of the Visigothic kingdom was summoned, on seventeen occasions between 589 and 694, to councils held at the new royal capital of Toledo. Perched on a defensible spur above a bend of the river Tajo, Toledo lay on the edge of the plateau of Castile in such a way as to command, without being absorbed by, the rich but vulnerable provinces of the Mediterranean south. Toledo was a "new Jerusalem," a solemn urban theater where bishops and kings together acted out the great hope of a self-sufficient "micro-Christendom."

The councils insisted, above all, on the uniform observance of "correct" Catholic rituals. The Nicene Creed was to be correctly recited at Mass in every church. Major festivals were not to be celebrated on dates determined solely by local custom. Each must be observed on the same day throughout the kingdom, "as it is celebrated throughout the entire world." The "entire world," in fact, amounted to the territories controlled by the Visigothic kings:

Let one norm of praying and singing the Psalms be preserved throughout all Spain and [the Visigothic parts of] Gaul . . . nor should there be any further variation among us in ecclesiastical custom, seeing that we are held within the same faith and within a single kingdom.[8]

Like fissures opening in a heavy building, cultic anomalies were troubling symptoms of wider potential disorder. Incorrect tonsures on monks and clergymen; incorrect chants in the liturgy; residues of pagan practice in the countryside; the permanent anomaly of Jews celebrating non-Christian festivals in major cities: these brought the wrath of God down upon His people. They were as much cause for alarm as were desertion from the royal army, rebellion or the constant hemorrhage of the labor force caused by the escape of slaves and by the movement of vagrants across the threatening vastness of the Iberian peninsula:

for it is in such a way that divine wrath has caused many kingdoms of the earth to pass away.[9]

In 711 the worst happened, precisely from the direction that the kings had always feared and, predictably, at a time of civil war. It was not, however, the east Romans who entered Spain from their small outposts in the Maghreb, but the more determined Arabs and their numerous Berber allies. The Visigothic kingdom, though "established with ancient solidity," was the only western Christian state to fall, with ominous speed, to the armies of the "unspeakable Saracens."[10]

One characteristic product of the Spanish "micro-Christendom," the encyclopedic work of Isidore of Seville, had already been enthusiastically received all over northern Europe. Irish clerical scholars fastened on the *Etymologies*. They called it the *Culmen*, "the summit of all learning." Such a book gave members of the Christian clergy, a caste defined by their arcane learning, the means to master the entire exotic world associated with their strange, new Latin tongue. Through Isidore, all Latin wisdom might come to their native land. It could be believed that the learned men of Ulster had given away their knowledge of the epic cycle of their tribe – the *Táin*, the story of Cattle Raid of Cooley – in exchange for a single copy of the *Culmen*![11]

In Britain, the need to relocate an entire Christendom was not confined to books. Once they decided to patronize the new religion, Saxon kings needed to be told what was the correct form of Christianity to set up in their land. Such a need explains the meteoric career of a man such as Wilfrid (634–709), the first native Saxon to become bishop of York. Like Benedict Biscop, Wilfrid travelled frequently to Gaul and Rome. He claimed all over Britain to have brought back the Roman customs that he had observed there. Unlike Benedict, the self-effacing monk, Wilfrid was notorious for

> the number of his monastic foundations, the vastness of his buildings, his countless followers arrayed and armed like a king's retinue.[12]

For all his unpopularity at certain times of his career, Wilfrid brought to the kingdom of Northumbria a touch of "style," such as had long been admired in the episcopal magnates of Gaul.

This was because Wilfrid radiated knowledge of the correct, "Roman" forms of Christendom. An impressive figure, capable of remaining sober at royal banquets and "endowed with a wonderful memory for texts," Wilfrid had a Saxon aristocrat's gift for establishing intense friendships.[13] In Britain, Gaul, Frisia and Italy, Wilfrid moved as a distinguished foreigner from court to court, bearing with him intricate, arcane knowledge. Magnetically omniscient, Wilfrid was sought out as foster-father for their sons by members of the Northumbrian nobility.

Wilfrid knew the correct form of tonsure for monks and clergymen. It was the round tonsure on the crown of the head, once worn by Saint Peter and plainly visible on ancient images of the saint. It was not the vertical mutilation of one's long-flowing hair – a mark like a scalping – that signalled the Celtic monk's abandonment of his warrior-status. Wilfrid knew the correct, Roman way of discovering the date of Easter every year. He moved with the confidence of an expert retailing universal truths in a highly localized world, where, from Ireland to the Armenia of Ananias of Shirak, "false Easters," Easters celebrated on divergent dates due to conflicting systems of computation, divided Greeks from Armenians, Saxons from Britons, and Irish, and the Irish, predictably, among themselves.

Wilfrid engaged in a competitive universalism. He did not act as the authorized representative of the popes of Rome, nor, indeed, was he an altogether faithful interpreter of Roman customs. He was concerned to use his claims to knowledge of the "true" Roman traditions so as to establish his own "micro-Christendom." In order to bring the skills of an imagined, admired center to a former periphery, other groups had to be declared to be truly peripheral. At a council summoned by the king of Northumbria at the royal monastery of Streanaeshalch/Whitby, in 664, Wilfrid told bishops and abbots, who were loyal members of the great monastic confederacy of Iona, that their founder, Saint Columba, may have been holy; but that he was out of touch with the rest of the world: on the date of Easter, he had been misled "by a rustic lack of sophistication." Only the despised Britons and the monks of Iona, now identified with the rude nations of the distant North, were isolated. They should join the larger unity which Wilfrid represented.[14] (The proud "sons of Columba" had heard such language before, and from fellow-Irishmen. In 630, Cummian, a learned man of southern Ireland, who had rallied his region to the "Roman" system of calculating Easter, after a year spent in seclusion studying this deliciously arcane matter, had informed the great abbot of Iona that he and his community were no more than a "pimple on the chin of the earth.")[15]

The bitterness of controversy on the date of Easter along the edges of the Christian world was not due entirely to the competitiveness of leading clergymen. It was maintained by the need to reconcile two different needs. The learned wished to ensure that Easter, the highest feast of the Christian year, was grounded in a system of time that was as majestic as the *cosmos* itself. The succession of Good Friday, the day of the Crucifixion, and Easter, the day of Christ's resurrection, had to echo the events of the Creation itself – it was on Friday that Adam had fallen, at the very dawn of human time. Yet every individual Easter, in the Christian Church, was calculated on a lunar calendar so complex that no church could maintain it correctly, unless they remained in constant contact with "state of the art" computational systems, that linked churches in faraway regions to former centers of Christian culture in the Mediterranean, such as Alexandria and Rome. It was never enough, in Ireland or in Armenia, to trust to local custom and to the turning of the seasons. To know the correct date of Easter, one had to communicate with other Christians in other regions. To his admirers, Wilfrid was nothing less than the bearer of knowledge necessary to root local celebrations of Easter in "true" time, in a time where the rhythms of the *cosmos* and those of an imagined world-wide Christendom coincided, thereby creating, every year, a perfect local reflection of the vast macrocosm in which Church and universe alike were united.

Suitably endowed by a succession of kings and noblemen, Wilfrid built up his own "micro-Christendom" in the North. At Hexham, for instance, he cannibalized the stones of Hadrian's Wall to erect a basilica church of Continental proportions, with room for a congregation of over 2,000. As his biographer wrote: "We have never heard of its like north of the Alps." At Hexham, "the crypts of beautifully dressed stone [on which it is still possible to read Roman military inscriptions!] . . . the many winding passages and spiral staircases" were designed to echo exactly, in miniature, the haunting catacombs of Rome and, especially, the galleries that led down beneath the floor of Saint Peter's at Rome to the tomb of the Apostle. Just as the pilgrimage-site and cemetery of Giendalough, in Ireland, set at the joining point of upland valleys in the Wicklow Mountains, could be spoken of as "the Rome of the Western World," so Wilfrid's Hexham was to be a "Rome" placed within reach of the northern Saxons.[16]

Such ambitious schemes were possible in seventh-century Britain. Christianity became part of the fabric of new kingdoms at precisely the time when royal power, within each kingdom, became more determined, more prepared to reach down to tap the wealth and to control the behavior of all segments of the population. By 700, Britain was no longer a land of fragile chieftainships and "stateless" warbands. And, as in Spain, bishops were expected to be conspicuous at court. In both Spain and Britain, the clergy had been touched by the thoughts on power of Gregory the Great. Gregory's studiously open-ended definition of the Christian *rector* meant, in effect, that kings did not represent profane force alone: they also could be "shepherds." They were responsible for the souls of the entire "people," much as bishops were responsible for their own congregations and abbots for their monks.

Now that Anglo-Saxon was a written language, the clergy, who controlled the writing of the laws, tinged royal law with a mystical sense of responsibility for the good fortune of an entire "people." The *Laws* of Ine (688–693), king of Wessex, were issued "out of consideration for the health of our souls," because, just as in distant Toledo, the "health of souls" was considered to be an integral part of the "stability of the kingdom." [17]

Ine, for instance, commanded that all his subjects should baptize their children within thirty days of their birth. It was a significant gesture in a society where infanticide remained a normal means of controlling population. Rituals had always existed to decide when a child was "human," and so entitled to human care. In neighboring Frisia, the mother of a future bishop was saved from being disposed of by drowning, as a new-born baby, because a nurse gave her "human" food, by smearing her mouth with honey. Christian baptism was now urged, by royal law, as the one rite through which new-born children were to be definitively accepted into human society.[18]

And to be part of society was to pay taxes. On Saint Martin's Day (November 11) all householders were to deliver "church-*sceattas*," a compulsory contribution to the Church. Royal taxation, appropriated in part by the Church, made Christianity a presence throughout Britain. As Bede complained:

> there are very small towns and villages . . . in inaccessible mountains and wooded valleys, where for many years no bishop has been seen. However, no one of these places is immune from paying tribute to the bishop.[19]

It was a problem which both Bede and a subsequent generation of Saxon clergymen had to face, both in Britain and, as we shall see, in northern and central Europe.

The Christian presence in Britain had been set in place, largely, from on top. It had taken the form of a remarkable growth of monasteries. As in northern Gaul, so in Britain, it was through monasteries that kings and their families strove to leave a permanent mark on the land. Local aristocracies followed their lead. Many local figures were the descendants of demoted chieftains. They were anxious not to be entirely forgotten. Over large areas, family-foundations, in which upper-class women, as abbesses, played an unusually prominent role by continental standards, brought Christianity home, in a characteristically northern manner, by passing it on to an extended "family" of retainers, tenants and neighbors.

The manner in which pastoral care would be organized in Britain revealed differing attitudes as to what constituted a Christian community, and as to how this community should relate to the sacred. To a greater degree than on the Continent, Christianity in Britain and Ireland was a "religion of monks," centered on great monasteries. It was not unlike Buddhism, a religion characterized by the *sangha*, by a core of world-renouncing monks, that spread from southern Asia into a very different world, among the warriors, traders and nomads of Inner Asia and Tibet, at just the same time, in fact, as Christianity came to spread far beyond its Mediterranean heartlands into the strange world of northern Europe.

Gregory the Great, by contrast, had not envisioned such a "religion of monks." He had wanted to set up a tight and active network of bishoprics. Bishops were to be the rulers of and the "fathers" to their congregations, much as they had been in the small towns of Gregory's Italy. Bede, also, wished for such a system, and deplored the extensive, under-staffed dioceses of his native Northumbria. An episcopal structure that partially realized the ideals of Gregory was eventually set up. But even then, the grandiose Wilfrid, with his sprawling diocese and costly buildings, may have understood his native land better than did the distant pope. Saxon Britain was more like Ireland than it was like Italy. Imposing pilgrimage-shrines and monasteries inhabited by monks and nuns, with their numerous lay dependents, stood out as vivid oases of the holy in a largely untamed spiritual landscape. This was not a landscape that could be neatly parcelled out and Christianized, as Bede would have wished, by the regular ministrations of bishops and their clergy. Christianity spread, if at all, on ground level. It radiated outwards from scattered centers, through intermittent, highly charged contact with the sacred: through high moments of festival, through pilgrimage to high places, through memorable supernatural duels between Christian holy persons and their visible and invisible enemies – sorcerers, demons, fire and the bleak hostility of the northern weather.

The model for such expansion was not the ministration of a *rector* to his "subjects," as Gregory had proposed in his *Cura Pastoralis*. It was, rather, the gift-exchange. Local warriors gave support to the Church in exchange for the impressive counter-gift of blessing in this world and salvation in the next. But, as befitted the givers of gifts, they left the exchange as equals. Their profane identity was largely untouched by the new religion, much as, in the great Pictish stones of southern Scotland, impressive Christian stone crosses bear, on the other side, or even flitting in and out of the carvings of the Cross itself, scenes of the nobility engaged in their favorite pursuits, hunting and the slaughter of their enemies.

Not all regions would, necessarily, be brought into this gift-exchange. When a party of Northumbrian monks was swept out to sea on their rafts in a sudden storm, the locals stood by and jeered:

> Let God not raise a finger to help them! They have done away with the old ways of worship and now nobody knows what to do.[20]

Plague was followed by massive apostasy in the upland valleys around Melrose.[21] Nor were those who gave to the churches permanently loyal to them. Pagan sacrifice by individuals remained so widespread that a late seventh-century *Penitential* was content to distinguish between sacrifices made for small gains and more culpable rites, performed for larger matters.[22] Saxons resorted, in emergencies, to divination by the casting of lots. All that had changed was that they were now able to justify the divinatory techniques of their ancestors by appeals to examples of the casting of lots mentioned in the Bible. Altogether, the "people of the English" were all too like the "people of Israel," as Bede read of them in the Old Testament:

> Even in the Land of Promise, they continued always to limp along with the rites of idols together with those of the Lord.[23]

Bede did not have an Irish lawyer's wry appreciation of the Old Testament as the implicit charter, for his own generation, of an entire profane way of life. If the "conversion" of the Saxons was to take place, this meant that they must move from a position where Christianity was one cult among many, as it had been in the fragile Israel of old, to the world of the New Testament, so that "the old trace should be gradually removed from them."

Whatever he may have wished, Bede knew that it was not only bishops and clergymen who would bring that about. The narratives in his own *Ecclesiastical History* make this plain. Christianization often took place through somewhat anomalous persons, connected with the tentacular network of lay clients and local patrons who gathered around every Saxon monastery, as they had done in Ireland. A wide penumbra of half-participants mediated Christianity to their region. We should not be misled by the inward-looking and other-worldly self-image of an early medieval monastery. Each monastery was a microcosm of local society. It owed its success, in large part, to this fact. It shared the values, the limitations and the skills of its milieu. Studious masters of Latin, such as Bede, were a small minority even among their fellow monks.

Bede did not expect otherwise. Converted warriors came to monasteries to do something more urgent than master the Latin language. As in northern Gaul, they came to save their souls, through prolonged penance under a strict rule. In Britain they needed it. Barontus, near Bourges, had only a checkered marital career to answer for. At Much Wenlock, in the warlike border country between the Welsh and the Saxons, a monk was haunted by the sight

of a man upon whom he had inflicted a heavy wound . . . The bloody and open wound and even the blood itself cried out against him.[24]

Sebbi, king of Essex, was typical of many who must have retired to monasteries all over Britain. They practiced a penitential asceticism in the hope of a "good death:"

Being of kingly temperament, [Sebbi] feared that, if he felt great pain in the hour of death, he might, by his words and gestures, act in a way unworthy of his character.[25]

An angel granted the old warrior a peaceful passing. Such men were no Latinists. It was for his fellow-monks and for the clergy that Bede urged the writing down and the memorizing in Anglo-Saxon of basic Christian prayers and formulae. He died engaged on an unfinished, projected translation into Anglo-Saxon of the Gospel of Saint John.

Marginal figures, largely untouched by Latin, played a crucial role in interpreting the new religion to the majority of their fellows. Visions came to such persons. Drythelm, a married layman, had a vision of "awful flaming fire and freezing cold," followed by the view of "a very broad and pleasant plain, full of the fragrance of growing flowers." The angel who accompanied him explained that these were not Hell and Heaven, "as he had often heard of them." They were two intermediate stages of the Christian soul after death, a near-Hell and a near-Heaven, to which believers would go, dependent on the degree to which they had done penance in this life. On the strength of the vision, Drythelm set up as a hermit. He was able to reassure a wide clientele that, as a result of what he had seen, they should believe that the conventional ecclesiastical remedies for sin – penance, almsgiving and the prayers of friends – if undertaken seriously, could modify the fate of Christian laymen and monks, caught between the seemingly inflexible alternative of Heaven or Hell.[26]

Such mediators of Christianity posed a problem. Saint Guthlac (675–714) was converted from the life of a warrior at the age of twenty-four. He dedicated only two years to becoming literate and then retired, for the rest of his life, to the "eerie shadows" of the Fenland, at Crowland. Some thought that this was not enough. The book-producer of a bishop who visited Guthlac was uncertain:

> he had lived among the Irish and had seen false hermits, posing as engaged in various religious exercises, whom he found could really predict the future and work other miracles, but by what power he knew not.[27]

Guthlac passed the test. There must have been many who did not. A vernacular visionary culture, stirred by Christianity but unamenable to ecclesiastical control, lay dangerously close to the sacred precincts of every great monastery.

Hence the enthusiasm that Bede showed for the controlled visionary experience of Caedmon, a lay brother at the great royal monastery of Streanaeshalch/Whitby. Whitby, in itself, stood for all that was self-confidently unusual in the Christianity of Northumbria. It was a "Double Monastery" in northern Frankish style. An abbess of royal blood ruled both nuns and monks. Abbess Hild (614-680) was a reminder of a heroic, transitional world. She had been the first princess in Northumbria to be baptized by bishop Paulinus. By no means the sheltered product of a cloister, as Bede himself was, her life fell into two halves. She had lived in the world and been a married woman for thirty-three years, then she was a nun and abbess for a further thirty-three:

> So great was her knowledge of affairs that not only ordinary people but kings and princes sought and received her advice. She compelled all those under her to devote much time to the study of the Scriptures [so that five bishops and many clergy emerged from her training at Whitby]. All who knew Hild . . . used to call her "Mother."[28]

It was on the edge of this aristocratic culture, with its Latinate inner circle, that Caedmon claimed to have received a vision urging him to compose Biblical poetry in Anglo-Saxon verse. His claim was accepted by the monks, who set him to work on the story of the Creation.[29]

There was nothing "popular" or "folkloristic," in a modern sense, about such verse. Versification was a noble's skill, an intricate instrument of social memory, usually deployed in warrior epics and in the praise of royal lineages. A visionary and royal quality clung to the religious poetry of the age. The powerful *Dream of the Rood* – a vision of the Holy Cross – spoke of the Crucifixion of Christ as if it were the bloodsoaked death of a warrior king. Lines from the poem were later carved, in runic script, over the edge of a tall stone Cross set up at Ruthwell (in Dumfriesshire, Scotland), that may have marked a boundary of the Northumbrian kingdom. The Cross itself was majestically "Roman" in its monumental carving. It emphasized both the Lordship of Christ and, in the heavy gesture of Mary Magdalen as she bent to wipe His feet with her hair, the all-important monastic call to penance. It was the product of an ostentatiously non-local style. It brought a wider world to Northumbria, that pointed to Gaul and Rome, just as the vinescrolls and the twining border of exquisitely stylized flowers on a similar Cross, at Bewcastle (a little north of Hadrian's Wall), reached beyond Rome to Egypt and Iran.[30]

In the same way, the *Dream of the Rood*, though written in Anglo-Saxon and transcribed in runes, was by no means the reflection of a purely local culture. The *Dream* spoke of the Cross, at times, as a gold-sheathed treasure, hung with jewelled banners. This was a clear reflection, in a distant, local microcosm, of images taken from the macrocosm of the world-wide Christian cult of the Holy Cross, which flourished in the seventh century. It was in this way that the Holy Cross was set up, in the Hagia Sophia, to be adored by the "emperor of the world" and his court. Bishop Arculf had witnessed the ceremony in 680 and described the scene to abbot Adomnán at Iona. Similar crosses were placed, as tokens of victory, by the warrior-aristocracy of Armenia, in 640 (six years, that is, after Oswald had set up his own wooden Cross to do battle with pagan rivals for the kingdom of Northumbria) on the walls of the votive church at Mren, now perched in no-man's-land on the frontier between Turkey and the former Soviet Union.

Seen against this wide panorama, the "micro-Christendom"

of Bede's Britain was still part of a Christian "global village." It shared with the many, equally regionalized "micro-Christendoms" that stretched, like so many beads on a string, from Iona across Europe and the Middle East, a common pool of inherited images and attitudes. Yet the position of this particular "micro-Christendom" and of its neighbors, in Gaul and Italy, would change dramatically in the course of the eighth century. The balance of power in Europe shifted. Saxons who had grown up in the years that Bede completed his *Ecclesiastical History* came to be swept up in the greatest political revolution to occur in western Europe since the passing of the Roman empire. The unprecedented coagulation of military power in the hands of the eastern Frankish aristocracy who supported Charles Martel; the replacement of the Merovingian kings of Francia by a new, "Carolingian" royal dynasty; the conquests of Charlemagne: within half a century of Bede's death, these developments brought the unaccustomed weight and novel sense of purpose of a kingdom of truly "imperial" dimensions to bear on the Christian populations of a large part of continental Europe. Regional "micro-Christendoms" fused to form, for the very first time, the only "Christendom" that mattered in Europe.

This happened, in part, because the ancient Christianity of the east Roman empire itself had changed deeply in its aims and texture as a result of prolonged internal crisis brought about by the Islamic invasions. No longer a distant, sometimes threatening, but ever-present representative of an older world-order, that had not yet been declared entirely out of date, the "empire of the Greeks" came to be seen as a smaller, alien society. It could be regarded, by many clergy in the West, as a failed Christendom, against which they could measure their own achievements and their own distinctive style in ruling Christian souls. It is to this set of changes that we must turn in the four remaining chapters of this book. For good or ill, many features of the Western Europe that is still with us emerged, with unmistakable sharpness, for the very first time, in the course of the later half of the eighth and in the ninth century. The changes of this period, in East and West alike, marked the true end of a very ancient world.

Part III

The End of an Ancient World
AD 750–1000

14

The Crisis of the Image: the
Byzantine Iconoclast Controversy

In the days of old [wrote a Muslim geographer in AD 982]
cities were numerous in *Rum* [the east Roman empire],
but now they have become few. Most of the districts are
prosperous and pleasant, and have each an exceedingly
strong fortress, on account of the raids of the [Muslim]
fighters of the faith. To each village appertains a castle,
where they take shelter.[1]

By AD 700, the former world-empire of east Rome, called
Rum by the Muslims, had become a sadly diminished state. It
had lost its eastern provinces and three-quarters of its former
revenues. For two centuries on end, until around 840, it faced
near-annual attack from the Islamic empire – a state ten times
larger than itself, with a budget fifteen times greater, capable
of mustering armies that outnumbered those of the *Rumi* by
five to one. The most hotly contested frontier of the Christian
world lay, not in the woods of Germany, but a little to the
west of modern Ankara, in what had been ancient Phrygia. A
chain of fortified garrison-towns, their walls rapidly piled up
from the spoils of ancient classical monuments, blocked the
way that led from eastern Anatolia, where the Muslim armies
would gather, to the valleys that led down to the Aegean coast
and from there to Constantinople. Every November, a thick

blanket of snow gripped the highlands, blocking the passes and turning the fortresses of Phrygia into "cities of Hell" for the Arab invaders. Winter, and the vast distances of an Anatolian plateau skillfully defended by east Roman generals, stood between the densely populated villages of the Aegean, the heart of what remained of the empire, and ever-present Muslim armies.

It was this embattled heartland that survived. Between 717 and 843, western Asia Minor, the coastlines of Greece and the Balkans and, at the furthest edge of the Ionian sea, Sicily and Calabria (the *Magna Graecia* of the early Middle Ages) were firmly incorporated into a new political system. The modern term "Byzantine" (which we have avoided until now) is apposite for the compact, Greek empire that replaced the old-world grandeur of the "Roman" empire of the east. The emperors continued to call themselves "Roman" and treated the Muslims as no more than temporary occupants of the "Roman" provinces of Egypt and Syria. But they now ruled a more cohesive state, made up of a largely Greek population. Westerners called it, increasingly and with justice, "the empire of the Greeks."

Though reeling from the attacks of outsiders, the new "Byzantine" emperors were very much lords of their own territories. Few barriers stood between them and direct control of their subjects. The old city-councils and the civilian provincial elites associated with the cities were swept aside. Four great *Themata* – Themes, stationed armies – massive regional commands of up to 15,000 troops each, dominated the countryside of Asia Minor. Their generals came from the highlands of the eastern frontier. Many were Armenians. Some were even fluent in Arabic. Altogether, the new elites of the empire were hard men, soldiers and ranchers, who did not pretend to possess urban graces. But they were pious Christians, loyal servants of Christian emperors in a time of constant emergency. The populations they defended were made up, overwhelmingly, of villagers. No urban elites stood between the villages and the central power, as they had done in previous ages. The inhabitants of such a rural society, if they looked outside their village at all, looked up directly to their emperor. They identified themselves through loyalty to a Christian emperor, who shared the same embattled faith as themselves. Their empire was defined by their religion quite as sharply as was the empire of the Muslims. Theirs was the empire of "the baptized people."

At the center of a drastically simplified society, Constantinople stood alone. Other cities had become mere fortresses and market-towns. But Constantinople was a depleted city. Its population had shrunk to around 60,000. Spacious gardens crept into its center, sheltering monasteries and great pleasure palaces, often built in a new, non-classical Near Eastern style, associated with Persia and with the luxurious life of Arab princes. The inhabitants of Constantinople were largely immigrants from the Balkans. They had lost their past. The ancient public decor of Constantinople spoke to them of a fairy-tale world, which they understood only dimly. The classical statues that Constantine had lavished on his city now struck them as alien, vaguely threatening presences, out of place in a Christian present.[2]

Yet, in this greatly reduced city, the Imperial Palace, the gigantic Hippodrome with its imperial box, and the Golden Gate, through which victorious armies still occasionally made their entry, remained in place. So did Justinian's Hagia Sophia. In the nearby library of the Patriarch of Constantinople, it was still possible to find and even, with some difficulty, to understand the "orthodox" meaning of the writings of the great Greek Fathers of the Church. In what had become no more than one "micro-Christendom" among others, the emperor and clergy of Byzantium were convinced that in those writings lay the essence of a total "orthodox" system of belief. Texts of the Fathers were excerpted and arranged in encyclopedic anthologies. The organization of the overwhelming richness of the past into trenchant collections of citations and the resolution of theological problems through manuals of *Questions and Answers* was as necessary a pursuit in Byzantium as it was in the Spain of Isidore of Seville. The Byzantine clergy were also as concerned as were the bishops of Spain, that "orthodox" belief should be reflected in uniform traditions of worship observed throughout the empire.

It is not surprising, given this situation, that the religious life of the period was characterized, not by renewed theological controversy, but by heated debates on a concrete Christian religious practice – the veneration of painted images of Christ, of His Mother and of the saints.

What was at stake in what is known to modern scholars as the "Iconoclast Controversy," was how to find, in a society thrown into a state of perpetual mobilization, fully visible rallying-points for a battered "baptized people." The worship of the Christians of East Rome must please God if God was to help them. For those who revered icons (the self-styled "Iconodules"), icons brought Christ, His Mother and the saints down among their people. They were made accessible through portraits (either faces or full length), painted on boards or made in mosaic panels that usually hung separately in public places, on the walls of churches and in private houses. By contrast, the great narrative cycles of scenes from the Old and New Testaments, that could be found in many ancient basilicas, were less likely to function in this way. They were too crowded to become the focus of intense devotion. In times of need, images were carried in processions: the solemn movement of an image guaranteed the presence of the supernatural protector whom it represented. They received gestures of veneration. The deep bowing, the kisses, the lights and the incense which Byzantines bestowed on other unambiguously sacred objects, such as the Eucharist, the Gospel-books and the tombs of the saints, were also directed towards "holy" images.

For those called (by their enemies) the Iconoclasts, the "icon-smashers," it was far from certain that such images were "pleasing to God." In His Ten Commandments, God had expressly forbidden the worship of images made by human hands. He might, indeed, turn His face away from His people because of their idolatry. In their hour of need, the "baptized people" should not turn to

> inanimate and speechless images, made of material colors, which bring no benefit.[3]

What was never at stake, in this controversy, was whether art should continue in Byzantium. What was at stake was a more urgent issue: which of the many physical objects currently venerated by Christians were truly acceptable to God, so that worship directed to them might ensure His continued protection rather than provoke His anger.

In the first century of the controversy, the Iconoclasts enjoyed the advantage of offering to the "baptized people" a symbol of unquestioned visual power, untouched by the ambiguities that afflicted painted images. They upheld the sign of the Cross. The Cross was a symbol which every Byzantine Christian shared, and which every Muslim was known to despise. It had the weight of the past behind it. It had been the "victory-bringing sign" under whose auspices Constantine had won his battles and had founded the Christian empire. Nor was the Cross the product of some artist's imagination. Its prototype existed in the form of the relic of the True Cross, which was adored, every year, at Constantinople. To force the Cross to the foreground, so that it should replace all other images, was the sign of a Christian empire stripped for battle and re-united to its triumphant past.

The emperor who initiated the controversy, Leo III (717–741), began his reign with a spectacular sign of God's blessing. In 717, he used the devastating "Greek Fire" (a new invention, brought to Constantinople by refugee Syrians who had gained from the petroleum-rich regions of northern Iraq knowledge of the chemistry of substances that would burn on the surface of water) to sweep the last and greatest Muslim naval expedition from the sea of Marmara. His decision to act against images coincided with a terrifying volcanic eruption in the Aegean, in 726. As ashes darkened the sky above Constantinople, a new sign of the Cross, its power acclaimed by an inscription, was set up over the entrance to the Palace. Apparently, it replaced an icon of the face of Christ. The icon was declared to be a "voiceless thing" of no known efficacy. Bishops on the frontier received tacit permission to destroy images in the churches as they would destroy pagan idols. The Byzantines were the "people of God." They were now a beleaguered people, as the People of Israel had been. It was an anxious image, as it was for their distant contemporary, the venerable Bede, in Britain. No longer subjects of a world-empire, unproblematically identified with God's purposes on earth, the Byzantines feared that they might be altogether deserted by God, as the People of Israel had been deserted by Him, because they had lapsed into idolatry.

A prolonged state of public emergency determined the tone and set the pace of the Iconoclastic controversy. This ensured that the controversy itself was a mercifully desultory affair. Byzantines could not afford the luxury of a prolonged and divisive theological controversy, such as had once raged around the Council of Chalcedon. Apart from the occasional vicious act of violence by Iconoclast officials, treasured in retrospect by later Iconodule writers, a life-boat mentality prevailed at Constantinople. A small governmental class and an upper clergy, largely recruited from that class, were anxious to maintain what little remained of the Christian empire. They tended to follow a firm, imperial lead.

Leo and his son, appropriately named Constantine V (741–775), knew what they wanted – that their Christian subjects should pin their hopes on trustworthy objects of devotion. As the armies of Iconoclast emperors slowly turned the tide of the Muslim advance, they could count on the loyalty of the populations they had defended and on the active enthusiasm of troops who proved increasingly victorious, and who had won their battles without the help of icons. There was no need to hurry. Only in 754 did Constantine V assemble a council of the Church, in his suburban palace at Hieria, to secure a definitive declaration, on theological grounds, of the illegitimacy of image-worship. Only ten years later, after 765, were leading Iconodule monks lynched and humiliated. Not until then did the Patriarch alter the mosaics in a private audience hall adjacent to the Hagia Sophia, by placing abstract crosses in roundels that had once contained sixth-century portrait-heads of Christ and the saints: forty years after Leo's first initiative, the head of the Byzantine Church decided that it was time to declare, in a discreet manner, that he, also, meant business!

A temporary ending of Iconoclasm, at a council summoned in 787 by the empress-regent Irene in the name of her son, Constantine VI, was a clamorous victory. The council met at Nicaea, deliberately chosen so as to make of it a triumphal re-enactment of Constantine's first "world-wide" council. But the restoration of images did not last. By 815, what is known as "the second Iconoclasm" was back in power. This is not surprising. Strong, successful rule had come to be associated with the absence of images. All that was needed was a renewed public emergency for Iconoclasm to be re-instituted as the policy of the emperors. This happened as a result of a major crisis in the Balkans.

Constantinople was overshadowed by the Bulgarian Khanate, that had been established on both sides of the Danube since the 680s. "Children of the Huns," the last of the great nomadic overlordships of southern Russia, the Bulgars threatened the rich, disciplined plains of Thrace, on which Constantinople depended for its food supply. Based on a homeland in the Dobrudja, the Bulgars upheld a style of monarchy opaque to Christianity, and bid successfully against the empire for the loyalty of Slav settlers in the Balkans. In 811, Khan Krum (802–814) defeated and killed the emperor Nicephorus. Nothing like it had happened since the death of the emperor Valens at Adrianople in 378. Krum turned the emperor's skull into a drinking cup with which to share the wine of triumph with his Slav allies.

Fortunately, Krum died in 814, but not before his armies had reached the walls of Constantinople. Nicephorus' successor, Leo V, knew what he should do:

Why is it that the Christians all experience defeat at the hands of the [pagan] nations? I think it is due to the worship of images and nothing else . . . Only those who have not venerated them have died natural deaths, and have been escorted with honor to the Imperial Tombs . . . It is they whom I intend to imitate in rejecting images, so that, having lived a long life, I and my son should keep the empire to the fourth and fifth generations.[4]

With all eyes upon him, at the Epiphany ceremony at the Hagia Sophia, Leo deliberately passed by the representation of Christ and His Mother woven on the altar cloth. He was seen not to bow towards it. Only six years later, Leo was assassinated in church. But under his successors, Michael II (820–829) and Theophilus (829– 842), images remained out of favor. Holy pictures were deliberately hung high up on the walls of Constantinopolitan churches. They were allowed to speak only from a safe distance, "as if they were written texts." Plainly, for both sides, after a century of inconclusive maneuvering, the gesture of bowing to images of holy persons, and of kissing them reverently, had become a highly charged, "politicized" issue.[5]

In the end, Iconoclasm was undermined by the success of its imperial sponsors. The threatened "baptized people" of the 730s clambered back, painfully, into the position of a world-power. Baghdad proved too distant a capital from which to secure the total conquest of Asia Minor. After 840, a degree of wealth and leisure returned to the elites of Constantinople. Greek diplomatic missions to Baghdad capitalized on the notion of their cultural superiority. Byzantium, and not the upstart Islamic empire, was the crown of civilization. It was the fountainhead of the "Greek" wisdom so greatly prized at the court of the Califs. In a similar mood, Iconodules looked back on Iconoclasm as an un-Byzantine aberration. Only "half-barbarous" rulers, devoid of Greek culture, so they claimed, could so mistake the rich traditions of their Church.

In fact, a firm iconodule position emerged only at the very end of the controversy. This was largely due to the zealous partisanship of the great abbot Theodore of Studios (759–826), whose fighting spirit and hatred of compromise touched the elites of Constantinople; to the careful refutation of the theological ideas of the emperor Constantine V by the patriarch Nicephorus (750–828), in his *Antirrhetikos* (written in 818–820); and to the adoption of the views of the distant and hitherto little-known Syrian, John of Damascus. Between them, these three figures created an attitude to icons which, though it claimed to represent the perennial wisdom of the Church, was as novel a departure as was the radicalism of the Iconoclasts.[6]

The Iconoclast controversy marked a crucial moment of transition. In the course of the eighth and early ninth centuries, a very ancient Christianity was subjected, by both parties, to thorough-going reassessment and reorganization. Like a succession of restless thunderstorms, the controversy cleared the skies for the long, late summer of Byzantine orthodoxy. In order to understand how this was so, we have to go back, in time, to the sixth and seventh centuries, to the reigns of the emperor Justinian and Heraclius and to the first century of Islam.

Ever since the middle of the sixth century, eastern Christians had faced, if in a very different manner, the same problem that had come to weigh, silently, on their western fellows: Christianity had come to embrace their entire social world. The collective comfort of Christian worship slackened insensibly. The great basilicas, the high drama of the Eucharist and the chanted hymns (such as the *Kontakia* created in the 540s by the Syrian, Romanos Melodes) were not enough. In a more fragmented world, where the collective sense of the east Roman cities had been weakened by schism and impoverishment, it was a time for more private loyalties to develop, within what could be assumed to be a wholly Christian world: *philoponoi*, for instance, "zealous persons," small groups of devout laymen, each formed around a small shrine, became a prominent feature of many late sixth-century cities. What Latin Christians sought through their more personalized penitential practices, eastern Christians had found in holy persons. Now it came to be believed that portraits of such holy persons made them present even at a distance. These portraits were usually made on small portable tablets, following a long tradition of memorializing heroes, personal benefactors and beloved parents. Having been healed by Symeon the Younger, outside Antioch, in the 550s, a woman set up his portrait in the inner quarters of her house. "Being overshadowed by the Holy Spirit which also dwelled in the saint," the image began to work miracles. It did so in the privacy of the woman's quarters, many miles away from the mountaintop where Symeon lived. A woman came to the house to be healed of a fifteen-year-long illness:

For she had said to herself: "If only I see his likeness, I shall be saved."[7]

For such scenes to take place, a change had to happen in eastern Christian piety. A new style of relations to the supernatural world developed. The image, as it were, "broke ranks." It became a privileged artefact, singled out for particular devotion. Angels, saints, Christ and the Mother of God had long looked down from the walls of churches. But they were part of a collective monumental decor: except for a few cases, their very majesty, and their association with the high, collective drama of the liturgy, made them inaccessible. They lacked the "personal touch" of the new-style icons. Representations of holy figures were also to be seen everywhere, from the fourth century onwards. They were placed on the cutlery, on the ornaments and on the clothing of every Christian house. The door-posts of stables in northern Syria bore figures of Symeon Stylites: his presence protected the livestock housed within them. Scenes from the Gospels were embroidered on the kaftan-like robes of well-to-do believers in Egypt. But these also spoke with a muted voice. Their very presence acted as talismans. They were not meant to catch the eye of the believer, but to warn away the ever-present demons who lurked in the lower reaches of the material world.[8]

The new images, by contrast, were separated from all others. Lights burned before them. Drawn veils hinted at a sacred privacy. The air around them carried a whiff of incense, as befitted a sacred place. They demanded "worship" – that is, a reverential bow and the intimate gesture of a kiss. They were "presences" in their own right. They tugged at the heart of the believer as a grandiose mosaic or a talisman did not do. They created new "habits of the heart." Images demanded active imaginative engagement. In 692, for instance, a council that met under the dome of the Imperial Palace in Constantinople, the Council *in Trullo*, insisted that the sign of the Cross, also, should receive similar passionate attention. The sign of the Cross was not to be placed on the thresholds of houses, as it had often been placed, as a talisman, a "victory-bringing sign," that offered mute protection to the owner. The Cross must be placed at eye level, so that the believer should offer to it conscious veneration, "in mind, in word, in feelings."[9] Furthermore, if the Cross were to bear an image, this must not be an abstract symbol, such as the Paschal Lamb. It must bear the full, human image of Christ, so that the believer might never be allowed to forget the fact that Christ, as God, had, indeed, come down to earth in a human body.[10] The ruling was later claimed by the Iconodules as a charter for their own cause: in the words of John of Damascus, by means of such an image,

> the mercy of him who became visible in the flesh is burned into my soul.[11]

In the seventh century, however, it was far from certain whether this streak of piety would come to predominate. While veneration of images occurred in this period, it remained a practice that was hard to justify in the light of the Old Testament prohibition on idolatry. The issue was brought to the fore by an unexpected crisis in Christian–Jewish relations. In 638, the emperor Heraclius imposed Christian baptism on all the Jews of the empire. It was a characteristically hubristic measure. As in Visigothic Spain, it showed that the "baptized people" thought that every member of their empire not only ought to be a Christian, but, more importantly, that they could become a Christian, if needs be, without any great difficulty. Over-confident that the Christian religion was that of the overwhelming majority of his subjects, Heraclius, to the dismay of many clergymen, simply assumed that the Jews, once baptized, would become good Byzantine Christians. This did not happen. If anything, the situation put Christians on the defensive. It became all the more urgent to take Jewish criticisms of Christianity seriously, if Jews were to be absorbed into the Christian communities. Jewish criticisms of Christian image-worship as a form of idolatry play a significant role in the literature of the 630s and 640s. Because of Heraclius' high-handed action, the issue of idolatry was placed on the intellectual agenda of the eastern churches.[12]

By AD 700, Muslims had assembled their own, formidable battery of criticisms of Christian practice. As Arabic spread, these criticisms came to trouble Christians. A man such as Theodore abu Qurra, as we have seen, wrote his defence of images in Arabic and addressed Muslim arguments. He wanted to ensure that Christians were not made to "feel ashamed" by their Muslim neighbors, when they venerated and kissed icons.

Whatever the early Muslims thought of art in general – and the splendid palaces of Arab rulers show that many had little objection to profane frescoes – Muslims universally considered that the bowings and kissings that Christians practiced before images were similar to those once offered to their idols by the unenlightened kinsfolk of Abraham/Ibrahim: they were actions unworthy of true monotheists.[13]

In certain Muslim circles, at a slightly later date, it was asserted that artists who attempted to make living creatures seem real were blasphemous. It was a form of rebellion against God for a human being to claim that he could endow with signs of life, creatures who received the "spirit of life" from God alone. At the Last Judgement, artists, and makers of statuary in particular – one thinks of classical statues, such as the statue of Venus that had stood in the public baths of Alexandria untouched, throughout the Christian dispensation, only to be removed by a Muslim ruler – would be challenged by God to "blow life" into their productions. God was an artist Who tolerated no rivals. His supreme masterpiece, among the Muslims, was His book. It was on the flowing lines of their unique "Arabic *Qur'an*" that pious Muslims were encouraged to feast their eyes. The rapid rise of calligraphy and of public inscriptions as a privileged art-form in the Islamic world shows growing Muslim contempt for the Christian alternative.[14] The days were past, when the mosaic floor of a Muslim house at Ramlah, near the coast of Palestine, built around 680, could contain both the image of an arch – the *mihrab* that showed the direction of Mecca, towards which all Muslims prayed – and, close to it, a large, bouncing panther.[15] Even Christians appear to have taken this new mood seriously. In Palestine and Jordan, the floor mosaics of churches erected in previous centuries show signs of half-hearted attempts to remove not only human figures, but also any living creatures, by excising them or by turning them into bunches of flowers.[16]

Muslim ideas did not necessarily cross the Byzantine frontier. If they had, they would not have been welcome. The Iconoclast emperors were fiercely Christian. They were devoted to the public symbol of the Cross at a time when it was known that Muslim rulers had removed that sign from all public spaces in their empire.[17] In his theological treatise, Constantine V objected to the practice of painting portraits of Christ precisely because he believed passionately what Muslims denied: Christ was not just another man, as the *Qur'an* said; He was both man and God, and a mere human painter could not hope to capture the mysterious immensity of such a joining. Art trivialized a Christian message maintained, in all its fervor, by the Iconoclasts.[18]

But when a pious member of the powerful administrative family of Mansur, the Christian Arab, John of Damascus (675–753/4), wrote his *Defence of Holy Images* and other treatises in defence of orthodoxy, in the late 720s, both Muslim and early Iconoclast arguments were known to him. It was typical of the embattled and authoritarian mood of the Byzantine empire, that only a Christian living under Muslim rule was free to write in defense of images, and that he had the leisure and the library-resources to do so. It is also characteristic of the regionalism that had fallen across the entire Christian world, that John's writings were scarcely known in Byzantium until after 800. They only later came to play an essential role in the formation of a theology of images, associated with the definitive "Triumph of Orthodoxy" after 843.

The consensus arrived at after the "Triumph of Orthodoxy" would dominate Byzantine Christendom and its neighbors until modern times. In many ways, it marked a new departure. Compared with the sensibility that emerged in the course of the eighth and ninth centuries, previous attitudes to the sacred had been massive and somewhat faceless. As we have seen, the turning to images revealed a sharp hunger for a precise human face. But images were delicate things. They maintained the illusion of a precise human presence. The sharply contoured, classical features of real persons were refined down, as it were, to rest on the two-dimensional surface of a board. Icons were "presences;" but they were presences in which the one feature that had made a "presence" truly alive for ancient persons was pointedly absent. They were not statues. They had discarded the bulbous, menacing physicality associated with classical statues, which Christian Byzantines now tended to identify with pagan idols. The eye had to work upon the icon, reverently, to summon up the fullness of a living presence from their flat, bright surface.

For the Iconoclasts, even such painting was a treacherous, pagan skill. In any case, images, by definition, could not "make present" what mattered most in Christ and the saints – the "unlocalizable" fullness of Christ as God and the unearthly glory in which the saints now shone in heaven. The gaudy colors and the uncertain lines of a painted image only served to heighten the gap between the "dead matter" of a painting and the vibrant spiritual reality that it claimed to represent. It was better to rally to what was known to have been offered by God to all Christians, rather than to trust to the arbitrary brush-strokes of mere artists. The sign of the Cross had blazed from the heavens to guide the emperor Constantine. At the liturgy, all baptized Christians could glimpse God among them, in physical form, in the white bread of the Eucharist. No solemn consecration had ever raised a work of art, "out of the profane into the holy," as did the priest's words of consecration, spoken over the sacraments. Far from rejecting all visual elements in worship, the Iconoclasts directed Christians to objects of which they could be certain. They defined, clearly, the areas into which the Christian visual imagination should not stray.[19]

John of Damascus, and his successors, by contrast, included painted images among the objects on which a Christian could, and should, rely. John's most decisive intellectual maneuver was to claim for images the same secure ability to represent the unseen that earlier authors had claimed only for the liturgy and for the sacraments of the Church. He did this largely under the influence of a remarkable work, the *Celestial Hierarchies* of Dionysius the Areopagite (known to us, alas, as Pseudo-Dionysius, a Christian Platonist of the sixth century, but to John and his contemporaries as none other than an Athenian philosopher who had become the disciple of Saint Paul).

The Platonic arguments which, over four centuries previously, had been used by pagan philosophers to justify the statues of the gods, as adequate reflections of their hidden majesty, now returned, in this remarkable treatise, to invest the entire material world with a deep sense of sacrality. The visible worship of the Christian Church was only one part of an entire visible universe which functioned, as a whole, as God's own, immense icon. God was so far above human imagination that only a proliferation of visible symbols, granted by God to His creatures, could "lead them by the hand" towards His essence. Images were essential. They bridged the vertiginous chasm between the seen and the unseen. Saints and angels, for instance, could only appear to human beings by making "icons" of themselves. If angels appeared in serried ranks, like an emperor's bodyguard, this was not because they were really like that. They appeared, in this way, "as a concession to the nature of our mind." But nor was such an appearance an illusion. It was how angels themselves had wished to bring human worshippers nearer to God, by encouraging them to visualize His unseeable ministers in this particular way and in no other. In making an icon, the artist, as it were, was only "playing back" a process of making the invisible visible that had first flowed, on God's merciful initiative, from the invisible angels to human beings.[20]

John's use of this argument addressed a widespread anxiety. It was not so much art as the visual imagination itself that was suspect in Christian circles. The ancient images of the gods had remained charged with sinister power. They still could enter the dreams of believers, as when a Constantinopolitan woman saw herself making love to the beautiful statues that Constantine had placed – evidently with no such anxiety – in the Hippodrome. The spiritual teachings of the Desert Fathers had increased this suspicion. They stressed the protean and potentially demonic quality of the unguided visual imagination. Barsanuphius of Gaza told a worried layman that not all dreams of holy persons were reliable. Only a dream of the sign of the Cross was entirely safe – for this was the one feature of the Christian imagination that the demons could not bring themselves to imitate.[21]

The price for absence of anxiety about images, however, was the acceptance of guidance from a single source. The unbroken tradition of the Church was held to be the sole source of all Christian imagery. John of Damascus and his successors insisted not only that images had always been venerated, in some form or other: they claimed that every image that was venerated in their own days had been venerated, in the same form, since the days of Christ and the Apostles. The Gospel written by Saint Luke was said to have included illustrations, that were the prototype of all future Christian representations of the life of Christ.[22]

Tradition was further validated by visions. For visions merely added up-to-date confirmation of the belief that the Church already possessed a complete and totally reliable set of "Identikit" representations of every holy figure. The Christian imagination did not need to fear that it wasted itself in vain on arbitrary creations. When, in 867, a mosaic of the Virgin with Christ on her lap was set up for the first time in the apse of the Hagia Sophia, it was an awkward presence. It was still swamped by the faceless glory of the golden mosaic dome and by the shimmering, multicolored marbles that Justinian – very much a Christian of the sixth century – had considered quite sufficient, in themselves, to bring heaven down to earth in his great new church. But to look at the new mosaic was to look past it, into a scene that had always been available to believers, and always exactly as they now saw it:

> Before our eyes stands motionless the Virgin carrying the Creator in her arms as an infant, depicted in painting as she is in writings and as she has appeared in visions.[23]

After 843, the churches eventually came to be filled with such visions, frozen in mosaic and fresco. They notably lacked the random quality of earlier centuries. In the fifth and sixth centuries, lay persons and clergymen, as donors and as the founders of great new churches, had filled the basilicas of the eastern empire with every form of visual magnificence. They strove to bring Paradise down to earth; and it was still a very ancient Paradise. On the mosaic floors of churches all over the eastern Mediterranean, Paradise lay all around the believer in exuberant floral decorations, in frank hunting scenes, in classical personifications of the virtues and of the elements. Majestic figures were present on the walls; but, as in the church of San Vitale in Ravenna, they were set in a bright green jungle of fernlike ornament, that spoke of the Garden of Paradise with a frank joy in vegetable abundance.

Now, it is as if the heavy atmosphere of Paradise had cleared a little. What drew the imagination was no longer, to such an extent, the idea of a place of abundance that lay tantalizingly close to the material world – as Gregory of Tours and many of his eastern contemporaries had believed. What the orthodox believer now saw, on entering a Byzantine church from the ninth century onwards, were human faces, arranged on the walls as if they were standing in solemn order in the court of heaven. The non-human exuberance of Paradise vanished. The saints were brought into the present in orderly ranks, as the faces and figures of saints and Apostles, of the Virgin and of Christ Himself rose up the walls, from ground-level, each one occupying its accustomed, carefully allotted space. Every church was a "spiritual hospital." Sick souls could enter any church and find in it the same comforting vision of a heaven whose saintly inhabitants pressed in around them, on the walls, with quiet, clearly recognizable faces.[24]

But this could happen only because, after the 840s, the visual imagination of the believer was allowed to wander as little as it had done under the iron ferule of the Iconoclasts. Images were there to "lead by the hand." And they now did so firmly and in a single, authorized direction. In Byzantium, icons met a long-established need to touch the invisible world and to make its figures "present." But these icons could be neither arbitrary nor idiosyncratic. They were expected to change as little through the ages and from one place to the other as did the changeless persons whom they represented. The uniformity and the remarkable predictability of the decoration of orthodox churches and of the icons later produced for individual use betray the confidence with which, after 843, a newly established religious elite engaged in a novel exercise in religious pedagogy. They had caught even the visual imagination of the "baptized people" in the fine web of ecclesiastical control. The only images that could be venerated were those which the leaders of the church declared to have been passed down to the faithful by the tradition of the Church, in a precise and, theoretically, invariable form. Believers must

> accept with simple heart everything that has been handed down to the Church . . . when they see [images] they understand nothing in them except what is [legitimately] signified in them.[25]

Icons, themselves, of course, continued to "break ranks." They did not always do what their clerical defenders claimed that they should do. They still spoke to the heart, and, so, to fiercely private needs. Up to this day, a part of the marble paving of the narthex of the Hagia Sophia is visibly lower than the rest. A pilgrim from Novgorod in the fourteenth century was told why this was so. It was worn by the feet of innumerable believers who came to kiss the icon of the "Confessor Savior," that hung to the left of the doors of the main church: it was the image

> before which people confess their sins when they cannot confess them before a father confessor because of the shame.[26]

The Iconoclast controversy took place in an empire forced to turn in upon itself. Throughout the eighth century, the imperial armies had been pinned down by a seemingly endless defensive war on the eastern frontier. To retain Sicily as the westernmost bulwark of a naval empire based on the Aegean, all Italy to the north of Calabria was neglected. In 751, Ravenna fell to the Lombards. King Aistulf held court in the former palace of the Exarch, and doubtless offered his gifts, as a good western Catholic, on the altar of San Vitale, under the silent gaze of Justinian and Theodora. If Rome was to maintain its autonomy, the pope had to look for new protectors. He soon found them. After 751, the northern Franks, and not the emperors of Constantinople, were the arbiters of Italian politics and the privileged protectors of Rome. At the Council of Nicaea, in 787, Pope Hadrian's envoys spoke with enthusiasm of the pope's model "spiritual son," Charles, king of the Franks. Charles had already taken over Italy. He had "conquered all the west" and had even "subjected barbarous tribes to the Christian faith." It was unwelcome news: that part of the pope's letter was not translated into Greek.

When the *Acta* of the Council of Nicaea were sent to Rome and forwarded to the Frankish court in a Latin translation, the clerics around Charles were pleasantly disappointed. It struck them as a slipshod and incorrect document. Their own Church had done better by treating images as essentially neutral: they were not to be "adored," as the Council of Nicaea seemed to suggest that they should be; but neither were they so important that they had to be smashed. The Greeks had wasted their energies on a trivial matter. The memorandum prepared by an expert, Theodulph, was read to Charles and carefully explained to the Frankish monarch. Notes in the margin of the manuscript record Charles' reactions. The Greek Church should not have acted on its own:

> [it] should have sent to the churches of all the regions around it to enquire of them whether images should or should not be adored.

"*Probe*": "That's it!" was Charles' comment. Bishops should teach the "people beloved of Christ:" *recte*, "of course!"[27]

While the eastern empire had fought its way back from the brink of annihilation, a new political order had emerged in the west. It was connected with a new dynasty, the "Carolingian" descendants of Charles Martel. Both its rulers and its clerical elite knew how to absorb and to educate whole new Christian peoples. They made clear, in a decisive half-century, that they would do so in a manner very different from that of the Greeks. They were unusually confident that they lived in a Christendom, and that they were even entitled to an "empire," that was independent of east Rome.

15
Closing the Frontier: Frisia and Germany

The middle of the eighth century saw the emergence, in Europe and the Middle East, of political systems that had lost contact with their roots in the ancient world. With the foundation of Baghdad, in 762, the Islamic empire took on its definitive, oriental face. East Rome became "Byzantium." It lost its civilian elites and its world-wide horizons. It became a beleaguered, but more cohesive, state. The Iconoclast controversy showed the extent to which its new rulers were prepared to seek the much-needed favor of God by calling to account customs inherited from a richer, more easy-going past. New men from new territories (from eastern Iran, in the Caliphate of Baghdad, and, in the Byzantine empire, from eastern Anatolia) were forced to build fast, in a world that had lost many of its ancient landmarks.

In northwestern Europe, the Frankish state passed through a similar period of urgent turmoil. The newly formed nobility of Austrasia, that had grown up in the frontier-territories of northeastern Gaul and east of the Rhine, rallied increasingly to a family connected with the Maas and the Ardennes, led by Pippin of Herstal (d.714), the nephew of abbess Gertrude of Nivelles. As "mayor of the palace," in effect, as the strong "sub-king" of a symbolic Merovingian ruler, Pippin's son,

Charles (d.741) – later named, all too appositely, Charles Martel, "the Hammer" – revived the ancient "terror of the Franks." Charles showed his supporters what success in war could do, in acquiring new wealth to be distributed among themselves. In 733, he stopped a Muslim army on its way to loot Tours, and, from then onwards, looted the Christian regions of the south as efficiently as the Muslims, had they succeeded, would have looted his native Francia.

A group of *bellatores*, men of war, enthusiastic hunters and spasmodically pious givers to new, northern-style monasteries, the nobles of Austrasia owed little to a south still cluttered with ancient memories. Unlike the "Romans" of Aquitaine, they could not understand Latin, even if it was read slowly to them. Frankish was their language. Writing was not their business. The things that counted for most in their world – oaths of loyalty and tales of heroic deeds – were best expressed by the power of the spoken word alone.

This aristocracy and its would-be leaders, the family of Pippin and Charles Martel, found that they could strike anywhere, from Aquitaine to the Rhine estuary, Thuringia and the Danube, to extract wealth and to tighten up previous ties of submission. Ranging, now, far outside their homeland, Austrasian Franks became the dominant partners in a confederation of widely differing regions that had always been associated, in a looser fashion, with the hegemonial rule of the Merovingian kings. Even their horses, apparently, shared their confidence. In the next century, the great theologian Gottschalk, when dealing with the problem of divination, wrote that warhorses possessed a sixth sense: they became more frisky when they knew that their army would win. Accompanying a Frankish campaign, now 1,500 kilometers east of Francia, along the Dalmatian coast, he had asked his godchild to observe the horses. He was proved right. The horses of the Frankish cavalry cavorted merrily, before yet another victorious charge.[1]

Such fighters needed a "real" king. The symbolic monarchy of the later Merovingians had been based on an archaic, pre-Christian mystique, combined with the profane, bureaucratic styles of a post-Roman court. It was not so much ineffective as out of date. Royal power could not be allowed to remain merely symbolic nor largely profane. As in Byzantium and in Bede's Britain, so in Francia, dominant elites wanted to leap the centuries by identifying themselves with the ancient "People of Israel." The "People of Israel" had chosen their kings so as to be effective. They were there "to lead the people out to war." The "people of the Franks" should do the same.[2]

The popes of Rome, also, needed new protectors. Forceful Lombard kings, no longer held in check by east Roman garrisons, threatened to turn Rome, the precarious but still impressively cosmopolitan outpost of a venerable world-empire, into a southern provincial town within their own Italian kingdom. To gain, at least, a breathing space, pope Zacharias followed centuries-old maxims of imperial diplomacy, by fostering a new power across the Alps, whose rise might distract the Lombards. Duly consulted by Charles Martel's son, Pippin, in 751, the pope declared that the "people of the Franks" could dispense with the Merovingians. It was a dangerous world. Rome itself had changed from being a city placed at the center of the western Mediterranean, a safely Christian lake, to become a city that was uncomfortably close to the North African and Spanish frontier between Christianity and Islam. The Christian "order", now reduced to the northern shores of the Mediterranean, was threatened by weak kings. The Franks, at least, could have a strong king with full papal approval – and a safely distant one at that.

Pippin was made king, and in an up-to-date manner. He was anointed with oil, as the Kings of Israel were known to have been. The Lombards reacted to this potential threat by occupying Ravenna. Early in January 754, Zacharias' successor, pope Stephen II, arrived in Francia, exhausted by a hurried journey across the Alps in the middle of winter, to beg, in the name of Saint Peter, for Frankish help in Italy. It was an unheard-of journey. The pope repeated the ceremony of anointing in such a way as to designate Pippin's own family as the sole royal stock entitled to rule the Franks: king Pippin initiated the "Carolingian" dynasty named from Charles Martel. Pippin's eldest son, a solemn ten-year-old, escorted the battered pontiff to his father's villa. He would be known to future generations, in the late, late Latin of Gaul, as Charles *le magne*, Charlemagne, Charles the Elder (to distinguish him from his own, shortlived son of the same name). Stephen got protection for Rome. Pippin returned to Francia in 756, after two campaigns across the Alps, with a "heap of treasures and gifts." He had forced the Lombard kings to give him one-third of the royal treasure stored behind the high walls of Pavia.

Massive infusions of wealth, in the form of tribute and plunder from the south, and frequent access to Rome, due to the accelerated pace of Frankish diplomacy, placed, in the hands of bishops and abbots close to the new king, the means of building up a triumphantly "correct" micro-Christendom in Francia. Their opportunities made the efforts of a previous century – of "Romans" such as Benedict Biscop and Wilfrid, even of the episcopate of Spain, with its solemn emphasis on cultic uniformity – seem, in comparison, frail and parochial.

The will to extend this particular micro-Christendom throughout much of western Europe can first be seen at work most clearly along the periphery of Francia, in the process of Christianization in Frisia and Germany. That process amounted to a closing of the frontier. What had once been a more open world, characterized by looser social and political structures and by far greater fluidity in its religious allegiances, found itself drawn into an ever-tighter system of religious control, fostered by men inspired by a new sense of order, and who enjoyed the protection of increasingly resourceful and self-confident Frankish kings.

The Frankish kingdom had retained its Janus-like quality. Formed in a Roman frontier zone, the ancient *limes* still traced an unmistakable line, that marked the joining of two worlds. The weight of a long Roman and Christian past could be felt along the Moselle, the Rhine and the Danube. Metz boasted forty churches, some of which were already 400 years old. At Mainz, solid Roman walls enclosed venerable basilicas, in which a "Roman" liturgy was celebrated with Mediterranean opulence – so much so that, two centuries later, a Muslim visitor declared that the city smelled of fragrant incense as much as did Damascus.[3] South of the Danube, also, the palimpsest of a former Roman order was not yet totally expunged. Pockets

of Christianity survived as the "folk-religion" of "Romans."
A Christian slave escaping from the woods of Saxony was
heartened by the sight of Regensburg, with its ancient Roman
walls and stone church.[4]

Weightier even than these ancient presences was the new
development, in northern Gaul and in parts of the Rhine valley,
of a manorial system. The demesnes of great landowners were
exploited through the forced labor of peasants grouped in
stable settlements. The system showed that a local nobility,
with strong royal rule behind them, could tame a recalcitrant
landscape and control a once-evasive peasantry in such a way
as to extract a surplus of wealth comparable, at last, to
that which had once been gathered, with such unremitting
persistence, by the tax-collectors of the Roman empire.

It was against these solid structures that the lands to the
north and east of the old *limes*, many of which had long been
overshadowed by Frankish dominance, came to appear truly
peripheral. They seemed part of an older Europe. Frisia and
Saxony, from the North Sea coast to the Teutoburger Wald,
were staunchly pagan. Elsewhere, Christianity was present, but
(much as in sixth-century Ireland) as one cult among many. An
Alemannic lady might be buried at Wittislingen with a brooch
that bore a perfect Christian epitaph, with classical echoes.
But she lay among her family's prestige-graves. Apparently,
no church was near. Brooches dedicated to Woden were found
in the same region. Christianity might be the religion of her
family; but it was not, as it was in Francia, expected to
be the sole religion of the entire community. In Bavaria,
a pagan sorceress would bring animals to the local church,
as a thank-offering for the success of her incantations. The
panels around the tomb of Saint Corbinian (d.725), at Freising,
included an image of a stallion with a gigantic extended penis.
A reminder of an earlier, less-discriminating age of *ex votos*, it
was later removed by Corbinian's more fastidious successors.[5]

In comparison with Francia, the power of local chieftains
was weak. The Old Saxons functioned without a king. A caste
of nobles were content to choose, by lot, a leader whom they
would follow in wartime alone.[6] Great holy trees were vital
to them, as the sacral gathering points of their confederacies.

The mercurial fluidity of such arrangements confirmed the worst suspicions of Christians. In Francia, Britain and Ireland, kingship – and an increasingly strong kingship at that – was identified with civilization. An eighth-century Christian author wrote of the outermost edge of the world as ringed by ominously stateless societies, "by brutish peoples, without religion and without kings."[7] The spectacular flowering of Christianity among the ambitious kings of Britain stood in disquieting contrast to the near-total opacity to the new faith of the kingless Old Saxons and, further to the east, of the Slavs – despite the proximity of many Slav tribes in the Balkans and along the Dalmatian coast to large centers of Christian population. The proper Old Testament "order" of strong, believing kings was cut down to size by the immense, muted presence, in so much of central and northern Europe, of ancient, less-forceful styles of rule, associated with tribal chieftaincies, where individual clans and their clients competed for prestige among each other, without the expectation that any one family or group would win out, irrevocably, at the expense of their fellows.

In Merovingian times, the old Roman *limes* had remained a firm, notional barrier in the back of the minds of kings and bishops. Dagobert (623–638) encouraged the occasional bishop who wished to "preach to all nations." But this was part of a policy of regaining areas where the Roman frontier had receded, as around Utrecht and the Channel coast. There was to be no room in Gaul for lawless zones, inhabited by unbaptized communities, "without belief in God or reverence for men." Later, Saint Amandus (d. *ca.*684) was allowed to preach to the Basques of the Pyrenees. A Basque epic poet mocked the bishop and his Gospel.[8] Sure enough, a century later, in 778, the same Basques descended from their mountains, to cut to pieces one of the few armies that Charlemagne ever lost – the contingent of Count Roland in the pass of Roncevalles. But across the *limes*, in central Europe, where law and order were not at stake, Dagobert had been happy to be a hegemonial overlord in the more relaxed, old style. As long as the Old Saxons paid their annual tribute of 500 cattle, the paganism of their oath to him – on their swords – mattered little. The frontier was an open world. Samo, a

Frankish slave dealer from Sens, set up his own chieftainship among the Slavs of Bohemia, from 623 to 658. As a Frank, he may still have thought of himself as a Christian. But it did not worry him to settle down, with twelve wives, among non-Christian "dogs."[9]

In Ireland and Saxon Britain, by contrast, the imaginative barrier of the *limes* never existed. What mattered was *peregrinatio*, the act of becoming a stranger to one's country for the sake of God. Compared with the elemental wrench of self-imposed exile, by which a man abandoned his own kin, the ancient frontiers of Europe meant nothing. Furthermore, seen with the sad eyes of Christian strangers, it was plain that Christianity had not come to many of the regions of northwestern Europe with which they were most familiar.

While the idea of "exile of God" had developed in Ireland, the structures of the new Saxon churches in Britain were calculated to produce a supply of impressive wanderers. Given to a local monastery at an early age, between five and seven, able men found themselves entering middle age only to confront a dangerous emotional and social situation. At the age of forty, they faced the prospect of becoming abbots or bishops, figures of authority among their own kin and region, and, so, inextricably implicated in the compromises that had produced, in Britain as earlier in Ireland, an established Christianity shot through with deeply profane, barely post-pagan elements.

It was better to leave home, to seek elsewhere the clarity of a true Christian order. Among such persons, religious exile and a profound sense of a Christian world as it should be went hand in hand.

The first of this new generation of strangers, Willibrord (658–739), was a product both of Wilfrid's micro-Christendom in Northumbria and of Ireland, where he received his vocation when studying, already as an exile, at Cluain Melsige (Clonmelsh, County Carlow). In 690, he arrived, with a small party of monks, to offer his services to Pippin of Herstal, the father of Charles Martel. Unlike an earlier stranger from Ireland, Columbanus, Willibrord did not offer "medicine" for the souls of Pippin and his entourage. His burning wish was to save the souls of pagans – of the Frisians of the Rhine estuary, who had recently fallen under Frankish domination, but also, if needs be, of other pagan peoples, the Danes and the Old Saxons.[10]

We have Willibrord's own *Calendar*, written in a clear Irish script, with entries in his own hand. It is a glimpse of the new Europe of an exile, a wide world held together by the ritual commemoration of distant saints and dead persons: Patrick, Brigid and Columba, the three great saints of Ireland, appear together with three kings of Northumbria. Furthermore, when writing the date of his seventieth birthday, Willibrord adopted a new dating-system: he wrote of it, much as we do, as "AD 728" – "in the 728th year from the Lord's Incarnation." The system had been elaborated earlier; but it suddenly became important for a small group of men whose sense of time was as majestically universal as was their sense of space. (In this, of course, they had been preceded by the Muslims, who regularly dated the year, throughout their vast empire, from the *Hijra*, the fateful journey from Mecca to Medina of the Prophet and his Companions, in 622). Up to then, and, in many circles, long afterwards, time in Europe had been regional time, and, often, time that still looked straight back to Rome – the "era" of a province often being counted from the year that it had been incorporated in the Roman empire. The regnal years of local rulers and, for the popes, the regnal years, even the honorary consulships and the tax-cycles (the *Indictions*), of the east Roman emperors, were regarded as the measure of time. In Willibrord's world (as in the dating system used by Bede in his *Ecclesiastical History*) there was only one time because there was only one world-ruler – the Lord Christ, whose reign over all humankind had begun with the year of His birth, and would continue until the end of time.

Seen across the sea from Willibrord's Northumbria, Frisia was the gateway to Europe. Frisian merchants linked the fast-spending Saxon kings of Britain to the goods of the Rhineland. Precious glasswork, minted silver, even heavy mortars of German stone were exchanged for slaves. Throughout northwestern Europe, Frisian commercial activity brought about the end of a very ancient world. After 670, Merovingian gold coins, greatly reduced but still recognizable echoes of Roman imperial coinage, gave way to silver *sceattas*. These were minted for the use of merchants in a thriving economy now tilted towards the North Sea. Rather than bearing the sign of the Cross, many showed Woden, with triumphantly sprouting hair. Franks and Frisians fought for the control of Dorestad (Duurstede, Holland), an emporium on the Rhine. Dorestad became one of the great ports of Europe. In 800, its wooden wharves and merchants' houses covered 250 hectares, while a Roman Rhineland city such as Mainz covered no more than 100. Further north, among the *terpen* – the artificially raised mounds – of modern Groningen and Vriesland, a society of free farmers and merchants enjoyed rare affluence. Well fed, they had livestock to spare. They produced large quantities of valuable, tweedlike cloth. Frisia was a standing rebuttal of the growing Christian conviction that paganism was synonymous with underdevelopment.

Pagan Frisia represented a still undecided "might have been" for the entire North Sea. King Radbod (685–719) established a sub-Frankish state on the borders of Francia. He was a strong king with the power to command his chieftains and to hurt his enemies. And it was a pagan kingdom. Radbod was careful to maintain the pagan rites that gave so much prosperity to his people – even, it seems, the grim practice of the sacrifice of victims chosen by lot, and left to drown in the tide, as the great North Sea rose to take them to itself. It was later said of Radbod that, when once persuaded to accept baptism by a Frankish bishop, he asked whether he would meet his ancestors in Heaven. The Frank's answer was an unambiguous "no." Wherewith the old king stepped back out of the font. He would rather be in Hell with the great men of his lineage than share Heaven with lower-class persons such as the bishop.[11]

Willibrord was not expected to win over kings such as Radbod. Rather, he was a consolidator. When the tide turned in favor of the Franks, after Radbod's death and, especially, after a spectacular naval expedition by Charles Martel, in 734, against the northern shores of Frisia, Willibrord and his monks set to work, in the re-established city of Utrecht, to "weed out" paganism in zones that had fallen under Frankish rule. "Consolidation," however, meant many things on such a frontier. In 698, Willibrord received, from Pippin of Herstal, a former Roman villa at Echternach, near Trier, in which to found a monastery. An ancient Roman road, that ran through the lands of Pippin's family, connected Echternach to Utrecht, some 400 kilometers away.

Echternach throve. It was, in its way, as much a center of Christianization as was the frontier bishopric. In a manner characteristic of northern men of war, the local nobility chose to define themselves through public acts of giving to Willibrord, recorded in charters witnessed by their peers. Willibrord was a holy person, a *vir strenuus*, "an active, Apostle-like worshipper of God." He was the favored dependent of Pippin, their own lord. To give to Willibrord was to touch a source of salvation and, at the same time, to join a group of fellow-givers who stood out in their own region.

These men were landowners whose families had, comparatively recently, established themselves in what had once been an inhospitable frontier zone between the Waal and the Maas. Their ancestors had been quite content to be buried, as chieftains, among their own dependents, in isolated settlements on the land that they themselves had won. Those who gave land to Willibrord were a new generation. They formed a tight, distinctive group. They were "nobles" in the up-to-date Frankish manner. They were no longer buried with their retainers, but elsewhere, near Christian churches. They had broken with the pre-Christian code that had linked them, as chieftains, to their followers, in death as in life. They were great landowners, and their followers had become their peasants. They had been greatly enriched by their own lord, Pippin, and, so, they were ostentatiously faithful to Pippin's invisible Lord, the God whom Willibrord served with such Apostolic zeal. It is in these small ways that, region by region, an open frontier came to be closed along the edges of the Frankish kingdom.[12]

In 716, Willibrord was joined by an impressive but troubled

compatriot, from a monastery in southern Britain – a six-foot-tall man of forty, the author of an up-to-date Latin grammar, called Wynfrith, later known as Saint Boniface (675–754), the "Apostle of Germany." Wynfrith came to the Continent as a man already gripped by passionate loyalty to principles of order. In grammar, as in all else, "the customs of past ages" must be measured by "the correct taste of modern times." His grammar was utterly modern. It rejected the pagan past. Its examples of good style were taken from the writings of the Christian Fathers alone. Wynfrith drew on its opening pages a square enclosing a Cross with the name of Jesus Christ.[13] His heart remained filled with a sense of four-square, arcane solidity. He could shed the past. On his first visit to Rome, for instance, in 719, he followed Northumbrian custom by taking a Roman name, Boniface. But, unlike Benedict Biscop, he abandoned forever his Saxon name. From henceforth, Wynfrith was Boniface and Boniface only.

Yet the churches of southern Britain remained close to him, bound "through the golden chains of friendship made for heaven."[14] Boniface summed up the hopes of an entire generation, frustrated by the very success of their own, less-heroic Christianity. For Saxon bishops, monks and nuns, it was good to think of Boniface. He was out there, on the dangerous edge of the world. He reminded the Saxons of Britain, on one occasion, that the Old Saxons claimed to be kin to them: "we are of the same blood and bone."[15] The Old Saxons had only put forward this claim, however, after Charles Martel had led a punishing Frankish expedition against them, in 738. If they had to give way to Christians, they would give way to those with whom they shared a fictive kinship rather than to the overbearing Franks. It was not a claim which the Saxons of Britain themselves had previously felt very strongly. But it was agreed, in Britain, that Boniface lived in a heroic environment. Even a king of Kent wrote to him for a gift of falcons: he had heard that falcons were "much swifter and more aggressive" in Saxony.[16] In a poignant manner, noble nuns, less free to follow a man's stern road to exile, looked to him as a distant, comforting *abbas*, even as a surrogate brother. His lifelong friend, bishop Daniel of Winchester, soon plied him with advice as to how to argue with pagans. He must not do so

in an offensive and irritating manner, but calmly and with great moderation.

Among other arguments, he should point out that

whilst the Christians are allowed to possess the countries that are rich in oil and wine and other commodities [the gods] have left to the heathens only the frozen lands of the North . . . [They were] frequently to be reminded of the supremacy of the Christian world.[17]

Supported by Charles Martel and then by Pippin, the future king, Boniface received from the popes (between 722 and 739) a series of ever-widening commissions to act as a missionary bishop and supervisor of new churches throughout "Germany." After 742, the pope designated Boniface as the privileged counsellor of Pippin and of other "rulers of the Franks," in summoning councils of the Frankish Church. Boniface's position was unprecedented. His powers were ambiguous. Frankish bishops had their own, firm views on how best to set up a Christian order. In Francia, Boniface was by no means the hero of his generation. Some Frankish bishops, indeed, struck him as standing for all that he had left Britain to escape. They were aristocrats. They believed that a man must hunt; and that a man of honor, even a bishop, must, of course, kill with his own hands the killer of his father (the father being, also, of course, a bishop!). It hurt Boniface to mix with such people at court, and to share Frankish good cheer with them at Pippin's great feasts. He had no option. He wrote to his friend Daniel:

Without the patronage of the Frankish prince I can neither govern the faithful . . . nor protect the priests . . . nor can I forbid the practice of heathen rites and the worship of idols in Germany without his orders and the fear he inspires.[18]

Altogether, correct order was hard to find in Francia. Even books were written in a crabbed hand, that strained his failing eyesight. He remembered a copy of the Old Testament prophets that had been used by his teacher:

> I am asking for this particular book because all the letters in it are written out clearly and separately.[19]

By now a blind old man, Daniel replied by ordering the transcription of long passages from Saint Augustine on the need for patience when living with evil men. Written in North Africa, almost four centuries before, now copied by a Saxon in Winchester for a Saxon at Fulda, in central Germany, these were what a friend could offer:

> culled from the works of ancient scholars, things useful to bear in mind in the midst of so much barbaric lack of order.[20]

Only the new-won lands gave Boniface the opportunities for which he craved. In the same year as the pope appeared, so unexpectedly, in Francia, Boniface was back in the far north. He toured a Frisia barely pacified by Frankish armies. On June 5, 754, his entourage reached Boorne, on the edge of the North Sea. It was an impressive sight. Almost by accident, the great man became a martyr. A band of pirates – hard sea rovers, not, it appears, indignant pagans – fell on his party. In the great, iron-bound treasure chests, which every nobleman carried with him when travelling, they found, not, as they had hoped, loot, but the heart of Boniface's sense of order: texts.

> Disappointed in their hope of gold and silver, they littered the fields with books . . . throwing some into the reedy marshes . . . By the grace of God, the manuscripts were discovered a long time afterwards, unharmed and intact.[21]

We can still see some in the *Landesbibliothek* at Fulda. One is a thoroughly ordinary book: an anthology of Patristic texts, partly concerned with the Arian controversy – the unpretentious building-blocks of a micro-Christendom. It has violent cuts across the margins. It may well be the book which Boniface raised, instinctively, above his head, as the pirate's sword descended.

In the course of thirty years, Boniface had left his mark throughout western Germany, from Bavaria to the watershed of the Lahn and the Weser, beyond which stretched the territories of the unconverted Old Saxons. His mission-churches remained vulnerable. As late as 752, thirty of them were destroyed by Saxon raids. The lands that had begun to receive Frankish settlers along the Main and the Neckar – the future Franconia – provided him with a stable core, from which to organize Christianity in Hesse and Thuringia. He founded Fulda in 751, and described it to the pope as being "in a wooded place, in the midst of a vast wilderness." That was what Romans expected to hear. Fulda, in fact, lay on the main prehistoric trackway that crossed Germany from east to west, and had been a Merovingian fort.[22]

Germany was not quite what it seemed. Boniface had been sent, in the words of the pope,

for the enlightenment of the German people who live in the shadow of death, steeped in error.[23]

What he found, instead, was much Christianity, and almost all of the wrong sort. Cultic practitioners exchanged rituals. Pagans baptized Christians. Christian priests sacrificed to Thunor, ate sacrificial meats and presided at the sacral funerary banquets of their Christian parishioners. Theirs was an oral Christianity, that mangled essential Latin formulae. A Bavarian priest performed his baptisms *In nomine Patria et Filia*. He had confused both case and gender. Boniface doubted that such a baptism was valid.[24]

In Hesse and Thuringia, local chieftains were anxious to please the Franks; but they knew the limits of their powers. Near Amöneburg, Dettic and Dervulf practiced "sacrilegious worship of idols . . . under the cloak of Christianity."[25] In Thuringia, Heden was both a pious donor to Saint Willibrord and, later, it appears, responsible for a pro-Saxon policy that led to apostasy. It was not to convert a pagan population but, rather, to end an age of coexistence that Boniface decided, in the 730s, to cut down the mighty Oak of Thunor at Geismar, which had stood at a joining point between half-Christian Hesse and the pagan Saxons. He was careful to use its holy timbers to build an oratory of Saint Peter in the same place.[26]

More disturbing yet, for Boniface, were Christian rivals – clerical entrepreneurs who had moved into the new territories from Ireland and Francia. Despite Boniface's coldness towards them, many such clergymen were far from being mere adventurers. In Bavaria, they represented a previous missionary establishment, set up largely by Irish "exiles of God," whose methods had proved quite as effective, in southern Germany, as they had been in northern Britain at an earlier time. Vergil, abbot and, later, bishop of Salzburg (745–784) had once been Ferghil, abbot of Aghaboe. He was as much a zealous "Roman" stranger as was Boniface. A man of combative esoteric learning, Vergil shocked Boniface by preaching that "there is below the earth another world and other men." The bishop's opinion blended classical speculation on the Antipodes with Irish belief in the world of "The Other Side," a fairy counter-kingdom that flanked the human race. It was a notion calculated to dwarf the efforts of a man such as Boniface, who had striven hard enough to bring Christianity to nations already known to him. It was dispiriting to be told that yet more existed beneath the earth. Yet Vergil was able to intervene successfully with the pope to protect the poor priest who had muddled the Latin of his baptismal formula. The pope told Boniface, sharply, that mere lack of grammatical precision did not invalidate a Christian sacrament.[27]

Far more dangerous were those who, in Francia and Germany, threatened to create their own idiosyncratic version of a Christian mission. They did so from elements long associated with a dramatic style of "frontier" Christianity. To Boniface and to the Roman synod that condemned them, in 745, Clement, an Irishman, and Aldebert, a Frank, were troubling figures. They seemed to caricature the vivid holy persons who had, in fact, represented Christianity in much of Gaul, Britain and Ireland.

Clement and Aldebert stood for very different Christian options, that addressed contemporary problems in a very different manner from that upheld by Boniface. In Francia and Germany, Boniface, along with other representatives of a "correct" Christian order, had come face to face with local communities on the issue of marriage. They strove to apply canonical rules in the choice of marriage-partners derived, nominally, from Old Testament prohibitions on incest. These norms reflected, in reality, the marital strategies to which the inhabitants of the more populous, urbanized centers of the Mediterranean had long been accustomed. Boniface and the Frankish bishops refused to recognize marriages within a wide range of prohibited degrees. In the small communities of northern Europe, however, it was hard to find a neighbor who was not also a cousin. In noble and royal families, close kin-marriage and the marriage of widows to the brothers of the deceased had been a means of keeping power in a few hands. A strict application of canonical marriage law, as it had evolved in distant Rome, amounted to inserting a lever that forced open the closed networks of northern kin-groups. It was a form of pressure from outside the local community that echoed the new demands that the Church had also begun to make, both in Francia and in Saxon England, for a part of the local community's local produce, in the form of tithes. The local distribution of marriage partners and, to a novel extent, the local distribution of wealth were now made to depend on the judgement of others, who represented the wider norms and demands of an increasingly well-organized Christian Church. Local groups did not take kindly to such meddling.

Clement, by contrast, supported the marriage of the widow to the dead man's brother precisely because it was a practice found in the Old Testament. An Irishman, he did so in the same spirit as that shown by the lawyers of the *Senchas Már*. He closed the chasm that threatened to open between the non-Christian past and the Christian present. He reassured his flock that, when He descended into Hell, Christ had taken out the souls of all humanity, of all past ages:

> believers and unbelievers, those who praised god and those who worshipped idols.[28]

This was not what king Radbod had been told!

Aldebert was an even greater challenge to a man such as Boniface. Born of simple parents, he wrote of himself as a bishop "by the grace of God" – much as the eccentric Patricius had done. His mother had dreamed of a calf emerging from her side: the mother of Columbanus had "seen the sun rise from her bosom."[29] Aldebert, like Boniface, claimed that he had received authority direct from Rome. He knew the contents of a letter dropped by Jesus Christ Himself from Heaven, that now lay on the tomb of Saint Peter.[30] Thus authorized, he created his own Christian mission far from the towns. He was said to have considered pilgrimage to Rome unnecessary. He, himself, was a living relic. Any place where he preached was as much a self-sufficient Christian "microcosm" as was any other. He set up chapels and Crosses in the fields and at springs. In the absence of country churches, Saxon landowners in Britain had been content with just such Crosses on their estates.[31] Above all, Aldebert offered instant penance. There was no need to tell him one's sins through confession. He already knew them all. Preaching in the hills around Melrose, Saint Cuthbert had inspired almost the same awe: the villagers confessed to him because they were convinced, by his mere appearance, that he already knew what they had done.[32] Boniface made himself unpopular by securing Aldebert's condemnation. He had taken away from the people of Francia

a most holy Apostle, a patron-saint, a man of prayer, a worker of miracles.[33]

We do not know how widespread Aldebert's preaching had been. But the terms of his condemnation, taken together with the manner in which Boniface had set about his own mission and the way in which his example was remembered by successors, hints at a watershed in attitudes to the process of Christianization as a whole. We have moved imperceptibly – but, we must remember, not irrevocably and only in one articulate current of opinion – into a new world, no longer entirely dominated by ancient models. The erratic Aldebert represented one, vivid strand in a very ancient Christianity. He stood closer to Saint Martin of Tours and to Saint Cuthbert than to the new elite gathered around a man such as Boniface.

Boniface radiated order. He cleared up anomalies and put an end to long habits of compromise. From his point of view,

Gaul and Italy were no less prone to "barbaric lack of order" than were the supposedly wild woods of Germany. In 743, he wrote to pope Zacharias. He had been told by pilgrims who had visited Rome from Germany that the Kalends of January were still celebrated there:

> in the neighborhood of Saint Peter's church by day and by night, they have seen bands of singers parade the streets in pagan fashion . . . They say that they have also seen there women with amulets and bracelets of heathen fashion on their arms and legs, offering these for sale to willing purchasers.[34]

If "ignorant common people" from the north saw such unabashed, ancient profanity in the very center of Christendom, they could hardly be expected to pay heed to the strictures of their priests at home.[35]

Boniface and those around him linked up, across two centuries, with the tradition represented by Caesarius of Arles. After a long period of neglect, Caesarius' works came to be copied again in Germany. When an *Index of Superstitions and Pagan Practices* was drawn up in 743, in connection with Frankish councils, the details of the list show that northern Francia was not late Roman Provence. The *nodfyr*, the "fire of need" created anew by rubbing wood, with all other fires extinguished, to fortify the powers of the land against cattle-plague (practiced in Marburg in the seventeenth century and in the once-Scandinavian Western Isles of Scotland as late as 1767); women who could devour the moon and eat out the hearts of men; sacred spots deep in the woods still known by their ancient, Celtic name – *nimidae*, from *nemed*, "holy:" these hint at a sacred landscape of which Caesarius had never dreamed. So, also, did the new practice of making sacrifices in honor of Christian saints. But the attitude which brought such a list together was significantly similar to that of Caesarius. It was that paganism, as such, had ceased to exist. All that the bishops had to deal with, now, were "survivals," "superstitions," *paganiae*, "pagan leftovers." The continued existence of such practices merely showed the ignorance and the stubborn attachment to old habits of an unenlightened

Christian people – "rustic" in the true sense of under-educated. They did not betray the continued, uncanny presence of old gods.[36]

In a sense, Boniface and his successors were the heirs of the previous century of Christian expansion. In much of northern Europe, Christianity had come from the top downwards. It had been adopted as the religion of enterprising and adaptable leaders, of kings and aristocrats. The old beliefs had barely been confronted – as they had been, for centuries, in the memory of Christians around the Mediterranean. They had simply been pushed to one side, in a society whose leaders had declared themselves Christian and left the rest to time. They were rarely perceived as a consistent and resilient religious system. Old beliefs were no more than one set of anomalies among many others. They were often associated with the lower classes of society, or with marginal figures who had always been both feared and despised, even in pagan times, such as witches and sorcerers. Men such as Boniface, with their fierce sense of order, were confident that they could root out such misplaced practices, many of which already contained Christian elements, through a combination of severity and education. As a result, Christianization was no longer perceived, by many influential leaders of the Christian people, as taking the form of an outright clash of supernatural powers. It became, rather, a *mission civilisatrice.* Much energy would be devoted, in the Carolingian empire, to the eradication of ill-formed habits – of "popular illusions" we would say – through *praedicatio* in the strict sense, by preaching and by regular attendance at ceremonies whose meaning was to be carefully spelled out, by the priest, to those who partook in them. Communicated by the quiet authority of the preacher's voice, and far less often, even among the heroes of Christian mission, by the raw flicker of spiritual acts of power, a Christian message, contained in unambiguous and venerable texts that only learned persons could read in their original Latin, would work its way, slowly downwards, into the "fleshly" hearts of the rest of the population. For the first time, Gregory the Great's notion of the Christian *rector*, as preacher and guide of souls, came to rest on a clearly defined sociological and cultural niche, occupied by one group of persons alone. Only members of the clergy had access to Latin knowledge or (as was more usually the case) could claim special closeness to those who did, indeed, enjoy that knowledge. They were expected to stand out as privileged interpreters and educators of their flock. Their cultural advantage was, in itself, a standing miracle.

The ideal of the "Apostolic Man" reached back, in a Latin tradition known to all eighth-century clergymen, to the *Life of Saint Martin*, a text heavy with stories of charismatic power. Such an ideal still drove genuinely courageous men, such as Willibrord and Boniface. It comforted those who admired and supported them. But the "Apostolic Man" no longer stood alone. He was slowly overshadowed by a more subdued, but resolute, figure – the *populi paedagogus*, the Educator of vast new lands.[37]

But this is to anticipate. In the half-century after the death of Boniface, it was the novel power of the Frankish kings that predominated in Germany. Charles Martel and Pippin had made the "people of the Franks" frightening, once again, in Europe. From 768 to 814, Charlemagne, in the course of a reign as long as that of Augustus and of Constantine, made them overpowering. In 772, he led his Franks into Saxony. They desecrated the great intertribal sanctuary of the Irminsul, the giant tree that upheld the world, and returned in time, with much plunder, for the hunting season in the Ardennes. Next spring the Franks were in northern Italy. In 774, Charles became king, also, of the Lombards. For the first time since AD 400, the entire area from Ravenna to Utrecht found itself under a single ruler.

But it was in Germany, and not in Italy, that Charles showed himself to be a ruler as determined to be obeyed in all matters as any Roman emperor had been. The Old Saxons were not merely to be bullied into ceremonial submission to a distant overlord, as in the days of King Dagobert. They were potential "subjects." As subjects, they had to be Christians. It was an unusually vehement war, characterized by the storming, one after another, of well-defended hill-forts. The very flexibility of a kingless society prolonged the misery. Total surrender of the Saxons as a whole was impossible. Fifteen treaties were made and broken in thirteen years. One Saxon nobleman, Widukind, was able to avoid submission for decades on end. He fled to the Danes and involved even the pagans of Frisia in his resistance. An entire Frankish order was challenged in the north. Charles found himself forced to take over more territory than he had, at first, intended to occupy, pressing on from central Germany into the northern heathland, as far as the Danes. In 782, 4,500 prisoners were beheaded at Verden. Only Romans had been so self-confidently barbaric in their treatment of unreliable neighbors. In 785, Widukind finally submitted and accepted Christian baptism. Charles issued his *Capitulary on the Region of Saxony.* A *Capitulary* was a set of administrative rulings "from the word of mouth of the king," grouped under *capita,* short headings. These were very different in their brusque clarity from the rhetoric of Roman imperial edicts. They registered, in writing, the invisible, purely oral shockwave of the royal will. The royal will was unambiguous. The frontier was, now, definitively closed. No other rituals but those of the Christian Church could be practiced in a Frankish province:

> If anyone follows pagan rites and causes the body of a dead man to be consumed by fire . . . let him pay with his life.
> If there is anyone of the Saxon people lurking among them unbaptized, and if he scorns to come to baptism and wishes to absent himself and stay a pagan, let him die.
> If anyone is shown to be unfaithful to our lord the king, let him suffer the penalty of death.[38]

A small body of clergymen (notably Alcuin, a Saxon from Boniface's Britain, himself connected with the family of Willibrord) were challenged by such brusqueness to restate, more forcibly than ever before, a view of Christian missions that emphasized preaching and persuasion. The activities of Willibrord and Boniface, indeed, were made to appear more "educational" in retrospect, by their disciples, than they were at the time.[39]

When it came to the Saxons, however, most later writers took little notice of Alcuin's reservations. They accepted the fact that, as befitted a strong king, Charlemagne was entitled to preach to the Saxons "with a tongue of iron." Education began, rather, at home. The emergence of a distinctive Christianity in the west, was characterized, in the reigns of Charlemagne and his successors, by the alliance of a substantially new Church with a new political system, both of which were unusually committed to exhortation and persuasion, as they came to rest, with unprecedented weight, upon the populations of a large part of western Europe.

16
"To Rule the Christian People:" Charlemagne

After 785, Charles controlled the former European core of the Western Roman empire – northern Italy and all Gaul – and had absorbed its German and North Sea periphery. He showed what a warrior-king could do when backed by unprecedented resources. In 792, he turned against the Avars of western Hungary. In order to ensure supplies for future campaigns, he planned to join the Main to the Danube by digging a canal between the Regnitz and the Altmühl. He was defeated by the geology of the region. The preparatory diggings for the *Fossa Carolina*, "Charles' Ditch," can still be seen. In 1800, Napoleon's engineers considered resuming the project. In twenty weeks Charles had been able to spend two and a half million man-hours, the labor of 8,000 men: in a previous century, a great Irish abbot could hope to mobilize only 100,000 man-hours, over many years, to build the sacral earthwork of his monastery. Times had changed. Charles was not a warrior-chieftain in a fragile, epic mode. He trod with the heavy tread of a *dominus*, of a lord of Roman determination, capable of deploying resources on an almost Roman scale. For the Franks, however, the Avar war itself retained an epic quality. Wagon-loads of plunder made their way back to the Ardennes:

the site of the Khan's palace is now so deserted that no

evidence remains that anyone has ever lived there. All the Avar nobility died in the war, all their glory departed. All their wealth and their treasure assembled over so many years were dispersed. The memory of man cannot remember any war of the Franks by which they were so enriched and their material possessions so increased.[1]

In 796, work began on a *palatium*, a palace-complex appropriate for an emperor, at a thermal spa on the edge of the Ardennes, Aachen – Aix-la-Chapelle, "The Waters of the [Imperial] Chapel." The palace was no larger than the residence of a provincial governor of the age of Justinian. But it was a satisfying microcosm. It had all the components necessary for an imperial center: an audience hall, porticoes that led to a large courtyard at the entrance to a round, domed chapel. Aachen was a stage-set, in which the ceremonies that surrounded a ruler of "imperial" pretensions could be played out. Only the chapel has survived. It echoed the palace-church of San Vitale at Ravenna. A great mosaic of Christ, flanked by the four creatures of the Apocalypse – Christ, that is, as Judge and Ruler of the world Who would come at the end of time – filled the dome. Charles sat on his throne on a high gallery, halfway between Christ, his Lord and the model of his own kingship, and the "Christian people" gathered below him. In the eyes of contemporary admirers, he had been raised up by God

to rule and protect the Christian people at this last dangerous period of history.[2]

On Christmas Day, AD 800, Charles was in Saint Peter's at Rome, having come south to investigate a conspiracy against the pope, Leo III. Bareheaded and without insignia, as was normal for a royal pilgrim, he prayed at the shrine of Saint Peter. When he arose, Leo – apparently unexpectedly – placed a crown on his head; the Roman congregation acclaimed him as an "Augustus;" and Leo "adored" him – that is, the pope threw himself at Charles' feet, as he would have done to his former lord, the east Roman emperor. It was a one-sided attempt, on the part of the pope, to have a say in recognizing, on his own terms, the formidable "imperial" power that had developed, far from his control, at Aachen. It probably says more of Charles' own sense of the sweep of history that he had gone out of his way to be at Saint Peter's on that particular day. The new AD dating meant much to him. He wished to worship at the tomb of the Apostle on the eighth centenary of Christ's birth.[3]

He returned north after the ceremony. It was from Aachen that he intended to "steer" his "Roman empire." For the last years of his life, from 807 to 814, he resided permanently at Aachen, making it a fixed capital – a marked departure from the mobile kingship of earlier times. It was there that he was observed by Einhard, who wrote the classic *Life of Charlemagne* shortly after 817. A tiny little man from the petty nobility of the Maingau, too small to be a warrior and far too clever to languish as a cloistered monk in distant Fulda, Einhard had supervised the near-perfect copies of Roman bronzework that can still be seen in Aachen. He knew a solid ruler when he saw one. He also knew how to surprise his contemporaries by carefully chosen references to the ancient world. A Cross that he dedicated to the monastery of Saint Servatius in neighboring Maastricht rose from a perfect miniature of a Roman triumphal arch, set now with figures of Christ and the Apostles. His portrait of Charles is equally, unexpectedly Roman. He modelled it on Suetonius' *Life of Augustus*, a rare text, to which this ingenious little man had gained access.

Einhard's Charles was not a sainted king, as Bede had portrayed king Oswald. He was a man of flesh and blood, a Frank among Franks, just as Suetonius had gone out of his way to make Augustus, the first emperor, appear, for all his universal power, to be still a Roman among Romans. The realism of the portrait linked Charles to his principal supporters and the beneficiaries of his success, the victorious "people of the Franks:"

His nose was slightly longer than normal . . . His neck was short and rather thick, and his stomach a trifle too heavy . . . He spoke distinctly, but his voice was thin for a man of his bulk . . . He spent much of his time on horseback and out hunting . . . for it is difficult to find another race on earth who could equal the Franks in this activity. He took delight in steam baths and thermal springs . . . [and] would invite not only his sons, but his nobles and friends as well . . . so that sometimes a hundred men or more would be in the water together.[4]

When the great man finally fell ill, the scholarly would have liked to believe that he had spent his last days "correcting books." Einhard, however, says that Charles went out, for the last time, to hunt. When he died, on January 28, 814, it is Einhard who recorded the simple epitaph:

Charles the Great, the Christian Emperor, who greatly expanded the kingdom of the Franks.[5]

The consolidation of the "greatly expanded kingdom of the Franks" required a continuous effort at "monarchy-making," such as had not been seen in western Europe since the reformed empire of Diocletian and Constantine. Compared with the powers that the Roman state had wielded at that time, Charles could only touch the distant regions of his empire with the tips of his fingers. But he touched them relentlessly. Loyalty could never be taken for granted. In 785, for instance, in the monastery of San Vicenzo, at Volturno, in southern Italy, the monks began the regular prayers for Charles as king. No sooner had they reached the Psalm, *O God, in Thy name make me safe*, than abbot Potho, a member of the old Lombard nobility, got up and refused to sing.

If it were not for my monastery [he said] I would kick the man like a dog.[6]

Faced by much resentment and by widespread non-cooperation, the best that Charles and his circle could do was to communicate that, in a shaken world, the new imperial order found at Aachen represented the only effective guarantee of social and religious stability; and that those who joined in would be allowed to thrive at the expense of those who did not. Charles controlled a spoils-system that ramified throughout Europe. He manipulated with great skill a reserve of inducements that no ruler had possessed since Roman times.

For those who could be persuaded to be loyal, Charles, in his middle age, seemed a reassuringly old-world figure. Lack of loyalty to one's lord, at any level of society, was known to shock him. Associations of equals that seemed to undermine loyalty to superior lords – such as local sworn leagues and, even, the raucous toasting-feasts of Frisian farmers – were savagely punished. They were a "blasphemy" that the emperor would not tolerate.[7] The ceremonial life of Aachen did not cut Charles off from his *fideles*, his loyal dependents. With its combination of hierarchy, prompt obedience and studiously relaxed good cheer, the royal court was an image of a lordly, stable society, which any powerful person might hope to recreate, around himself, in his own region, provided that he retained Charles' favor.

It was Charles' business to uphold this order and to make it work, through energetic bursts of consultation with the leading figures of each region. Each group was given its own "law," was urged to live by it and faced the heavy consequences of imperial disfavor should they fail to do so:

> In this year [AD 802] the lord Caesar Charles stayed quietly at the palace at Aachen: for there was no campaign that year . . . In October, he convoked a universal synod [at Aachen] and there had read out to the bishops, priests and deacons all the canons [the laws of the Church] . . . and he ordered these to be fully expounded before them all. In the same assembly likewise gathered together all the abbots and monks . . . and they formed an assembly of their own; and the *Rule* of the holy father Benedict was read out and learned men expounded it before the abbots and monks . . . And while this synod was being held, the emperor also assembled the dukes, the counts and the rest of the Christian people . . . and all had the laws of his people read out, each man's law was expounded to each, emended . . . and the emended law was written down . . . And an elephant [a gift from none other than Harun al-Rashid of Baghdad] arrived in Francia that year.[8]

Charles was at his most "imperial" on such occasions. This

was because he was seen to be acting in a manner that revived, in Christian times, the action of the godly king Josiah, when he had promulgated the rediscovered Law to the people of Israel:

And the king went up into the house of the Lord ... and the priests and the prophets, and all the people, both small and great: and he read in their ears all the words of the book.[9]

Although local laws prevailed, each in its own region, in secular matters, in matters of religion the "Christian Law" was the true, universal law of Charles' empire. It was what every baptized Christian had in common with every other subject of a Christian emperor. The confident insistence on this one, overarching "Christian Law" reflected the rapid development, in Francia, since the days of Charles Martel, king Pippin and Boniface, of a new clerical elite. This elite possessed a substantially new means of communication – a clear new writing script, that could be used to diffuse texts in a grammatically "correct," truly international Latin. While the leading lay persons of Charles' empire rallied, in their own way, through oral interchanges that have almost entirely escaped us, in the case of the monks and clergy we can see the rapid creation of a "nobility of the pen" dependent on the court. Just as the true political map of Gaul had once been the map of its episcopal sees, so Carolingian Europe was criss-crossed by a network of great cathedral-churches and monasteries. The monasteries of Germany, in particular, such as Fulda, Reichenau and Saint Gall, have been likened to Roman legionary camps, settled on the new *limes*. Charles and his successor, Louis the Pious (814–840), controlled 180 episcopal sees and 700 great monasteries (in some 300 of which they had a direct interest). It was from members of the clergy and from among the more gifted monks (such as Einhard) that Charles drew a continuous supply of personnel, zealously committed to maintaining a cohesive Christian order.

At the court, the regional "micro-Christendoms" of an earlier age began to flow together. What Carolingian Europe lacked, by way of a centralized bureaucracy radiating from a single capital city, as at Constantinople, it began to make up for, after 780, in a manner better suited to a highly regionalized society. Skilled and enthusiastic scribes and educators were drawn to Charles' court, were formed there and then sent out to churches and monasteries that were the nodal points of an extensive lateral network of religious centers. The provinces of the east Roman empire always lived under the shadow of Constantinople. They were never covered in the same way by an empire-wide network of centers of culture, each with roughly similar resources in every region, as was Charlemagne's Europe.

Alcuin of York (735–804) is usually held to be representative of what was, in fact, a highly diverse group of persons. He had been lured to Charles' court in 782. He stood for the high "Roman" traditions of Bede's Northumbria. He was very much a career-scholar. He shared Boniface's dislike for local churches ruled by stylish and unlettered noblemen.[10] To belong to a great monastery was to feel a sense of *noblesse oblige* all of its own:

> Look at the treasures of your library, the beauty of your churches . . . Think how happy the man is who goes from these fine buildings to the joys of the Kingdom of Heaven . . . Think of what love of learning Bede had as a boy and how honored he is among men . . . Sit with your teacher, open your books, study the text . . . [11]

> Look at your fellow-student [he urged a recalcitrant disciple] who has always kept close to God and now holds an eminent bishopric, loved, praised and sought after by all.[12]

Alcuin came to a Francia that had begun to develop the *sine qua non* for a collaborative venture, based on the proliferation of uniform, correct texts – a new script. What later became known as "Caroline minuscule" was a smaller script, more regular and altogether more legible than its predecessors. Italian Humanists of the fifteenth century, when they discovered Carolingian manuscripts, were so struck by their elegance and solidity, that they were convinced that they were reading manuscripts written by Romans of the classical period!

"Caroline minuscule" was the end-product of one of those silent continuities that are usually ignored in historical narratives of the early Middle Ages. It was not a script that had been developed by the *literati*, but by unassuming "technicians of the written word." These persons had maintained the routines of writing legal documents at the local level and in the courts of barbarian kings, in a manner that linked the later Roman empire directly to the age of Charlemagne. They needed to write fast, to save writing materials and, above all, to produce documents that could speak for themselves – that looked distinctive and that could be read, at any time, by total strangers. Now this no-nonsense style was further developed and applied to the essential texts of the "Christian Law."

Not all ancient books spoke for themselves. Roman literary manuscripts, for instance, had lacked anything approaching a modern system of punctuation. Words, even entire sentences and paragraphs, merged into each other. Only those who already knew what a text said, or who had mastered the grammar and syntax of Latin so instinctively as to know what it could not say, could read such a text with ease. This was not the sort of book that Alcuin intended to produce at his *scriptorium* at Tours, where he had been placed, as abbot of the monastery of Saint Martin, in 797:

> May those who copy the pronouncements of the holy law and the hallowed sayings of the fathers sit here. Here let them take care not to insert vain words . . . May they divide the proper meaning into phrases and sentences . . . so that the reader reads nothing false or suddenly falls silent [because faced by an unfamiliar text] when reading aloud to the brethren at Church.[13]

The development of "Caroline minuscule," and the new standards of legibility that went with it, mark a significant breach with the past. Books in Europe were no longer what they had been in the ancient world: they became considerably more like books as we know them. But it could not in itself bring about a dramatic increase in the speed of book-production. A *scriptorium* might be staffed by fifteen scribes at one time. A copyist worked at the rate of thirty pages a day. What made the difference, rather, was the greater degree of collaboration and continuity in book-production that became possible in a Carolingian *scriptorium*.

The development of a common "house style" meant that large manuscripts could be produced by piecework, with each scribe copying a given section. The corporate structures of monasteries in the west, and their unusually rich endowments, when compared with Byzantium, placed time on the side of the slow but sure build up of resources. The library of Reichenau had 415 volumes, 138 of which were connected with the liturgy (mass-books, lectionaries and psalters) along with a characteristic collection of books of local and royal law. It was a small and grimly functional collection when compared with the 280 books, 147 of which were secular, many of them being pagan Greek novels, that were "drawn in from all sides" and annotated by the wealthy public servant and future patriarch Photius (810–893) at Constantinople, or the 600 heavy bookshelves of the Muslim historian, al-Waqidi. But, unlike the collections of Photius and al-Waqidi, Reichenau's library was not a fragile, private venture. It was a permanent collection, carefully catalogued. Books circulated from it. An increasingly uniform script and the frequent transfer of personnel broke down the cultural "subsistence economy" that had previously tied even the greatest monastery to its region. It is possible that 50,000 books were copied in ninth-century Europe. This amounted to a stock of texts sufficient to guarantee the cultural autonomy of Latin Christendom, in matters of theology and canon law, for the remainder of the Middle Ages.

Such progress, however, created its own anxieties. If "the pronouncements of the holy law" were to be made universally applicable, in written form, they had to be entirely "legible" in the deepest sense of the word. If God's law was rendered opaque and ambiguous, through lack of understanding and, indeed, through elementary faults of transmission, caused by slipshod copying or by incorrect reading aloud, then that law would be misunderstood. Heresy was sure to follow. God would not heed the prayers of those who prayed to Him in a garbled manner:

for often, while people want to pray to God in the proper fashion, they yet pray incorrectly because of uncorrected books.[14]

Only grown men, trained scholars, and not young boys, should copy Gospel-books, Mass-books and the Psalms. For Latin, even the Latin of these basic Christian texts, had become opaque to most of the inhabitants of Charles' empire.

Charles and his advisers made their concern for the situation plain in the *Admonitio Generalis*, the *General Warning*, that was issued in 789. The *General Warning* appeared in the same year of Charles's reign as that in which King Josiah had rediscovered and read aloud to the people the original text of God's Law to Moses. Like Josiah, Charles also strove

by visitation, correction and admonition to recall the kingdom which God had given him to the worship of God.[15]

We are dealing with a clerical elite slowly forced, by circumstances, to close the frontier of Latin culture. The Latinate world of Alcuin and his peers was fragile in the extreme. It was like a submarine cruising at a dangerous depth: its shell might collapse, at any moment, beneath the oceanic pressure of an overwhelmingly non-literate Christianity. This showed itself at every level. There was, for instance, a real danger that a non-literate Christianity, or a Christianity nourished on texts of suspect origin, might circulate uncontrolled over wide areas, avoiding, as it were, the check-points set up by the literate. The *Admonitio Generalis* condemned, once again, the notorious *Letter from Heaven*, said to have been written by Jesus. A little over a generation after Boniface's condemnation of Aldebert, it was again making its rounds. A generation later still, the same letter was invoked by an Irish visionary of dubious reputation. What was peculiarly annoying about such a document was that it was entirely orthodox in its contents. It insisted on the observance of Sunday as a day of rest as strictly as did Charles himself and his bishops in their legislation. But it did so by invoking so exalted a source as to dwarf the authority of the powers that be. It was considered, by all too many, better to observe Sunday on the strength of an edict seen by a visionary to have been written by Jesus in His own hand, "in the third heaven, with letters of gold," than to do so through obeying the laws of the empire.[16] As in the days of Gregory of Tours, the greatest danger that many bishops faced was not paganism: it was a Christianity of the non-literate that was convinced of its own essential orthodoxy. When, for instance, at a later time, a holy woman began to preach near Fulda in the vernacular, she was savagely punished, for having dared to do what bishops should have done.[17]

Even the nominally literate were at risk. In Gaul, Italy and Spain, Latin was written incorrectly because those who transcribed it were convinced that they still knew Latin, although they already thought and spoke in languages closer to their modern Romance equivalents. They had ceased to be "Romans" without realizing it. The result was "rusticity," a Latin so careless, so idiosyncratic and, hence, so unpredictable, as to be almost incapable of being understood by outsiders, much less copied by them.

But this was not a linguistic problem alone. What was at stake was the slow erosion of an ancient style of participation in Christianity. As we have seen, in the case of Britain and Ireland, high moments of contact with the sacred, through pilgrimage and festivals – and not, despite the wishes of many conscientious clergymen, regular preaching and regular participation in the sacraments – had been central to the Christian life of most regions of Europe, and especially of those that did not have large urban communities. In a Romance-speaking area such as Gaul no great saint's festival was complete without its banquet of high Latin words, read aloud from Latin texts. This situation had continued up to the time of Alcuin. At Ponthieu, for instance, a long and unpolished *Life of Saint Richiarius* (Saint Riquier) had been read out at the saint's festival since the days of king Dagobert. Every year, its Latin phrases bathed uneducated speakers in a half-translucent, sacral version of their own "rustic" tongue. Its reading led them into a world of barely verbalized, but intimate contact with great men and holy things. Little had changed since the days of Gregory of

Tours, when a great basilica, such as that of Saint Martin at Tours, rang with Latin readings. These readings were the signal for miracles of healing; they were met by cries from the possessed; they would be picked up by listeners as heavy with omens for their own future.

Now the clergy themselves wanted more polished texts, of which they could be proud. They lived in a wider world. *Lives* for local consumption alone were not enough. If Latin texts were to pass, without misunderstanding, from region to region, they had to be written in a predictable, "corrected" grammar. They also had to be read aloud "correctly," with a uniform pronunciation. In the case of Alcuin, this meant the new, "classical" pronunciation of Latin that had evolved in the British Isles in almost total isolation from Latin as a living spoken language. It was a stable Latin, pure and predictable, because it was a dead Latin. Its grammar was fixed, its pronunciation bore little relation to what would be heard spoken by the "rustics" of Gaul. In the new "correct" Latin, every unit of spelling had its own unit of sound: in a world where *directum* was usually pronounced as *dreit* (modern *droit*) and *monasterium* as *moustier*, such a rule of pronunciation rendered correctly pronounced Latin virtually incomprehensible.

For the inhabitants of many Romance-speaking parts of the Frankish empire, public readings in a "corrected" pronunciation placed the Latin of Church services as far above their heads as it had always been to the inhabitants of Ireland, Britain and the Germanic lands. It was alien to them. Their language was alien to it. For the first time, in 813, a council of bishops in Tours declared that homilies – the selected sermons of former preachers such as Caesarius of Arles – were to be read out in Latin, but that they should also be translated, by the preacher *in rusticam Romanam linguam aut Thiotiscam*: "into the language of rustic Romans or into German (Deutsch)."[18] Statements in Latin needed to be self-consciously translated: it was not enough that they should be simplified. The "Christian Law" became universal, in Charlemagne's empire, at the moment when its Latin core was about to become universally inaccessible to all but a tiny minority of trained readers. In the gap that had opened, now in all parts of Europe, between Latin and the bulk of the "Christian people," the voice of the "preacher" was expected to be heard more frequently than ever before. For only a "preacher," as translator and pedagogue, could pass on the correct meaning of a Christian law that had become opaque in its Latin form.

This situation did not come about all at once. It was constantly modified, throughout the period, by local variations and by the very different fate of different classes. Among the powerful, many lay men and lay women maintained the late Roman equivalence of power with high culture. Frankish gentlemen, also, liked to be seen engaged copying and emending texts. Seneca's letters, for instance, were copied by Ragambertus, a *laicus barbatus*, "although unworthy, a lay man, beard and all." The lady Dhuoda wrote instructions to her son on his way to court. For Dhuoda, God was still "to be found in books." What was most characteristic of the period was not the drift of Latin beyond the reach of all members of the "Christian people." It was the urge, on the part of a reformed upper clergy, to communicate in whatever language lay to hand. Latin was energetically supplemented by an elite determined to bring the law of God home to every baptized Christian.

In this, they were supported by the practice of the great new empire in which they found themselves. Throughout his reign, Charles reached out to impose oaths of loyalty on ever-widening sections of the population. It was an aggressive policy. It rendered all those who took such oaths fully liable, in case of default, to the harsh penalties of "infidelity." The oaths were administered in such a way that those who took them could never claim that they had not understood what was spoken on that occasion: each person was henceforth engaged by his oath,

> with all my will and with what understanding God has given me.[19]

The clergy were urged to adopt the same approach to their parishioners. We can see this most clearly in the case of a bishop who lived close to Aachen, Ghaerbald of Liège

(785–809). Ghaerbald presided over what had already become a "medieval" Christian landscape. It was no longer character-ized by a loose-knit scatter of sacred joining-points, to which a dispersed population resorted on high festival days. In Liège and in many parts of Francia, village, church and cemetery had come together. Even church-bells could be heard. The sound of bells no longer marked out an oasis of the sacred in the midst of violent, profane noise, as they had done in Ireland. Rung at regular hours determined by the liturgy, bells were supposed to impose a Christian rhythm on the day for an entire population.

Royal law had increasingly made the payment of tithes compulsory. Tithes were one aspect, among others, of a rein-vigorated system for extracting rent, services and taxes from the peasantry. Ghaerbald urged his clergy both to instruct their congregations and to keep lists of tithe-payers. It was important that they should understand more fully, if they were to embrace with the well-schooled loyalty of good subjects, a faith that offered services for which they were expected to pay on a regular basis. All Christians must be made fully aware of the exact nature of their baptismal vows, and, so, of the extent to which these vows bound them to God and His Church. In effect, this meant that the god-parents of each child vouched for their god-child. They memorized and repeated the Creed and the Lord's Prayer on the child's behalf. The god-parents would stand around the priest or bishop, each carrying a god-child on the right arm or, in the case of older children, with each child standing on the right foot of his or her god-parent.[20]

To enforce baptism without so much as a minimal degree of indoctrination – as had happened in the case of the Saxons and the Avars – shocked men such as Alcuin. Avars were not like those early converts described in the Acts of the Apostles, such as the centurion Cornelius. A Roman centurion, Alcuin pointed out, had received a liberal education. As a result, he understood the preaching of the Apostle Peter and could be instantly baptized. This was not to be expected of the Avars around Vienna – "a brutish and unreasonable race, certainly not given to literacy."[21] They should be allowed at least a token forty days of Christian preparation. Bishops in Saxony, he complained, had been forced to become "collectors of tithes" before they were able to act as "preachers of the Gospel."[22]

For Charles, baptism and the payment of tithes meant loyalty. On the frontier, the quicker they were imposed the better. In Francia itself, however, he took such matters seriously. In 802/806, Ghaerbald received a letter from Aachen:

> At Epiphany, there were many persons with us who wished [as sponsors] to lift up infants from the holy font at baptism. We commanded that each of these be carefully examined and asked if they knew and had memorized the Lord's Prayer and the Creed. There were many who had neither of the formulae memorized. We commanded them to hold back . . . They were quite mortified.[23]

As well they might have been. With characteristic resourcefulness, Charles and his advisers had fastened on the widespread informal practice by which a sponsor "lifted" the child from the baptismal font. This had been a largely profane practice, by means of which families sought out alternative patrons and allies, through involving them in the baptism of their children as "co-parents." It was an ingenious arrangement, that showed the ability of generations of post-Roman persons to impose their own "vernacular" meaning upon Christian rituals, and to make them serve new social needs. Charles and the clergy captured the practice, by making of the sponsors, for the first time, "god-parents" in the sense to which we have become accustomed. God-parents were incorporated in the baptismal liturgy. They acted as the fully cognizant guarantors of the child's oath of loyalty to God.

In the newly incorporated territories of Germany there was need for loyalty. The old gods were ever-present as alternative lords. Baptismal vows copied out in variants of Old High German included a specific list of renunciations:

> and I forsake all the Devil's works and words: Thunor, Woden and Saxnote and all the uncanny beings who are their companions.[24]

Like the *lingua Romana rustica*, "French," the *lingua Thiotisca*, "German," was a studiously general term. It did not imply the clear perception of specific "national" languages. Nor were these languages valued for their own sake. German remained, in the words of one scholar, "a monkey" compared to the splendid "peacock" of the Latin tongue. But the Queen of Sheba, he hastened to add, had offered to king Solomon both "peacocks" and "monkeys:" when necessary, the Christian Law could be transmitted in both languages. "French" and "German" entered public consciousness because of the work of a generation of unusually zealous communicators, led by a man obsessed, as any early medieval politician had to be, with loyalty. The vernacular languages were the last link of a vast chain of command, that passed the same message, from God, through Charles, to the clergy and, so, to all Christians within the empire.[25]

We are dealing with a singularly purposeful body of men. In their writings, many of them appear as the first technocrats of Europe. They knew the Christian Law in its majestic entirety. They knew how to guide the Christian people to fulfill its goals. Faced by opposition, they tended to dismiss it, quite bluntly, as unenlightened.

To take one extreme, and slightly later, example. Agobard became archbishop of Lyons in 816, where he acted, also, as imperial commissioner. Born in Spain and trained at Aachen, Agobard had little patience with local customs. He was told that certain persons in Burgundy were universally believed to have the power to bring down hail on the fields of their neighbors, and that they were allied to a race of persons from "Magonia," who sailed through the clouds in boats, to take the harvests back to their distant country. It was, perhaps, an aerial version of the Irish belief in "The Land of the Other Side," that had survived since Celtic times in Gaul.[26]

Agobard was not impressed. He intervened to save four poor wretches who had been brought before him. They risked being stoned to death as inhabitants of Magonia who had fallen to earth. Of all the bitter grievances that came his way, in Burgundy, this was not one that he had to take seriously. Agobard justified his dismissal of the case in unambiguous terms. In so doing, he betrayed a slight but significant shift in attitudes to the supernatural. Previously, it had been taken for granted that demons did, indeed, have control of the lower air, and that ill-intentioned persons frequently allied themselves with the demons to cause harm. Good Christians, by contrast, refused to make contact with the shadowy counter-empire, whose power, in the material world, was rendered all too palpable by the crash of thunder and by the hailstorms that fell like a scythe upon the vineyards. Holy men, indeed, were raised up by God to hold an all-too-real counter-empire at bay in their region. They challenged it in the name of the yet greater power of Christ. But it remained, nonetheless, a massive presence.

Agobard, by contrast, drained the counter-empire of much of its solidity. The "Christian Law," as Agobard presented it in a series of citations from the Old Testament, proved that all power in the supernatural world belonged to God alone. No human being could influence the weather. Without God's permission, not even the demons had the power to hurt mankind. Demons, of course, existed. But reports of their activities in Burgundy could be safely discounted. They were merely believed to have been active, and such belief was, in his opinion, a popular illusion. It proved that the uneducated were no more than "half-believers." For "stupidity [was] an essential element in misbelief." Faced by religious practices of which he disapproved Agobard was content to declare that the Devil found it easy to delude

> those over whom he thinks he has the best chance of prevailing, because they have barely any faith and lack the ballast of reason, girls, young boys and persons of low intelligence.[27]

For Agobard, the application of the universal "Christian Law" in backward Burgundy assumed not only that Christianity was true and endowed with greater supernatural power than its rivals: in its authorized exponents, Christianity and cultural superiority went hand in hand.

Agobard was not alone in his sharp dismissal of popular practices. In their concern to reassess a Christian inheritance that had been shaken in the previous century and to root out abuses in worship that had crept into the Church, an earlier generation of clergy around Charlemagne had already shown that they had much in common with the Iconoclasts of Byzantium. Theodulph, the future bishop of Orleans (798–818), was a characteristic representative of this new mood. In 793, as we have seen, he was commissioned to prepare a memorandum on the cult of images, in the form of a detailed rebuttal of the *Acts* of the Iconodule Council of Nicaea of 787. It was read out before Charles. The manuscript still contains a precious record of the emperor's approval. The text has been called the *Libri Carolini*. It was not well known at the time: Charles came to consider it too radical a statement to be circulated widely. Nevertheless, partly because it was a semi-secret memorandum, it summed up with unusual harshness attitudes which Theodulph held in common with his colleagues. A wilful caricature of the Byzantine position, Theodulph's treatment of the religious assumptions of east Roman Christians reveals, with the clarity of a self-parody, the hard edges of a distinctive Latin Christendom.[28]

For Theodulph, God was a distant ruler, sharply separated from His creatures. God was to His creation "as a lord to his servants." ("*Optime*," "Excellent idea!" was Charles' comment at that point.)[29] It was His will alone that bridged the chasm between Himself and human beings. He did not offer to the human race a gentle flow of visual symbols, which linked the invisible to the visible world in a seemingly unbroken continuum, as Greek thinkers such as Dionysius the Areopagite and John of Damascus liked to believe. He preferred to make Himself known by His commands. Law was God's greatest gift to mankind. When it came to the visual tokens of His will, He had used a stern economy of means. He had granted to His people a few, dependable visible signs through which He had approached them and they could approach Him. To the people of Israel He had given the Law and the Ark of the Covenant. "Shimmering with so many awe-inspiring and incomparable mysteries," the Ark was a unique artefact. In creating it, the skilled Bezaleel, "filled with the Spirit of God," had not followed his own visual imagination but the command of God alone. It was a work of art untouched by the arbitrary quality that characterized all other forms of artistic creation.

Icons, turned out from artists' workshops in Constantinople, could not claim to be like the mighty Ark.[30]

For human beings, in normal conditions, to create artefacts was to risk fantasy. It was to wander into a self-created world of purely human visual images. Nothing, in itself, guaranteed the "sanctity" of an icon. Icons partook in the frightening indeterminacy of all profane activity. Without its written label, an icon of the Virgin could be the portrait of any majestic and beautiful woman – even, perhaps, an image of Venus.[31] Painted images, therefore, could not have a place among the *res sacratae*, the few consecrated, holy things whose creation had been explicitly enjoined by God. The consecratory prayers of the Mass; the text of the Scriptures; in ancient Israel, the Ark of the Covenant: these were truly holy things. They were held at a safe distance from mere human will, sheathed in the mighty will of God. When he built his own exquisite little chapel at Saint Germigny-des-Prés, near Orleans, Theodulph placed the Ark of the Covenant in the mosaic apse above the altar. In a place reserved for "consecrated things," only visual objects known to have been given by God to his people, by His express command, should meet the eye.

Not that holy places could not be sumptuous. Frankish ambassadors travelling to Constantinople said that they had found there many dilapidated basilicas, their roofs open to the sky and their lights untended. They came from a world of imposing shrines. They professed to be shocked to find that a society which devoted so much energy to painting pictures paid so little attention to the fabric of their holy buildings. But the splendor of a basilica, such as that of Saint Martin at Tours, was carefully disassociated, in their minds, from its frail human creators. The majesty of a shrine was the projection into the visible world of a world beyond the human will. This was most evident in the case of the Mass. A ritual ordained by God, it was celebrated, in the Frankish realms, with stunning glory. It was equally evident in the tombs of the saints. For here the authentic "presences" of holy persons could be found. Tombs associated with real human bodies were shown by miracles to be the favored dwelling place on earth of the saints who lived in Paradise.

The shrines and relic-cases of Theodulph's world spoke with blunt magnificence. Their unearthly shimmer showed that "the lords," the saints, were "in" them. Before such objects, the faithful should, indeed, bow with reverential awe – as Gregory of Tours had done, a full two centuries earlier. With such tombs available, there was no need for the human imagination to play its dangerous games. In Byzantium, the eyes of believers strained towards an icon, often placed in the profane setting of their private houses, in a vain attempt – so Theodulph thought – to conjure up from an arbitrary likeness painted on flimsy wood the vast fullness of the "presence" of the saints. It was better to go to a church and to kneel before a well-known tomb.

The artistic traditions that Theodulph associated with the sacred had tended, in the north at least, to turn away from the human face. Stately human figures could still be seen on the walls of basilicas all over the west, from Rome to Wearmouth and the shrine of Saint Brigid in Kildare. They served as "books for the uncultivated." They played a crucial role in communication. For they reminded the bulk of the population of Biblical narratives which only the learned could read for themselves in the original text. They were humble *aide-mémoire*. They were necessary, but they were not "holy things."

In any case, realistic representation was peripheral to the principal endeavor of northern artists. The highest art, in the north, was not concerned with catching the "living" likeness of a human being, as was the case in a classical tradition of human representation that had survived unbroken in Byzantium. The work of the jeweller and not that of the portrait painter was the most prized. For the magical cunning of a craftsman consisted in taking raw wealth – precious stones, precious fragments of gold and silver (often unceremoniously hacked from ancient pieces, or in the form of coins extorted as tribute) – and transforming it into condensed signs of power. Hence the skill devoted to the great brooches, the belts, the ornamented armor and similar regalia by means of which the kings and nobles of Ireland, Britain and Francia sheathed their own persons with stunning tokens of their status.

The religious artist took this process of transformation one step further. The scribes of the Book of Kells and the craftsmen who produced the great votive crowns, the Crosses and the relic-cases of Gaul and Spain were not concerned to catch a "likeness." Their task was to take "dead" matter, associated with the profane wealth and power of great donors – precious pigments, the skins of vast herds, gold and jewels – and make them come alive, by creating from them objects whose refulgent, intricate surfaces declared that they had moved, beyond their human source, into the realm of the sacred. The creation of images played only a small part in this solemn reworking of raw wealth.

Most important of all, Theodulph's religious world was dominated by a written text. Carefully copied and passed down through the centuries, the Holy Scriptures stood out as the unique manifestation of the will of God. Like the Ark of the Covenant in ancient Israel, the Scriptures were a charged presence. Here was the entirety of God's commands to His people, congealed in Latin words. To transmit the Scriptures by careful copying; to ponder their meaning; to explain them to the "Christian people," at whatever level was necessary: this was the highest art of all, because it was essential to the government of souls. It was a perennial art. When Moses had taught the people of Israel, he had done so

> not by painting but by the written word . . . nor was it written of him that "He took paintings," but *Moses took the Book . . . and read in the ears of the people the words of the Book.*[32]

Theodulph and his colleagues placed at the summit of their religious culture the figure of the attentive reader. At the still center of Latin clerical culture lay a holy book – in the words of a contemporary Irish poem on an ideal monastery, the monk would be sure to find there:

> bright candles
> over the holy white scriptures.[33]

A tradition of the meditative absorption of the Bible, tinged with an indefinable edge of mystic joy, reached back from

Theodulph, over four centuries, through Bede and Gregory the Great, to the Vivarium of Cassiodorus and beyond, to the leisured and literate intellectuals of the age of Augustine. What had changed was that the Latin book had become a world of its own. It stood out in majestic isolation from what was now an alien babble of vernacular tongues. To understand the Scriptures and to explain their contents to the "people beloved of Christ" was all the more urgent. It shocked Theodulph that his Christian colleagues in the east seemed unaware of the perils and the opportunities of this situation. An entire "Christian people" needed the sharp *words of the Law*, and the Greeks, with proud insouciance, took the "soft" option: they offered their charges the trivial medium of "little pictures:"

> You, who claim to have preserved the purity of the faith by means of images, go and stand before them with your incense. We will search out the commands of our Lord by eager scrutiny, in the bound books – the *codices* – of God's own Law.[34]

Behind the contemptuous tone affected by Theodulph lay a great fear. Incorrect Christian worship might erode a boundary between the sacred and the profane which had been put in place, recently and with considerable effort, in the Latin West. The stark contrast between a world of profane objects and the small cluster of "sacred things," around which the clergy grouped itself as privileged mediators and interpreters, was basic to Theodulph's arguments. It underlay his studiously shocked view of Byzantium. Here was a society where far too many things were treated as holy. What a Byzantine in the tradition of John of Damascus would have seen as the sign that God's mercy had suffused the entire created order with a generalized sacrality, struck Theodulph as a dangerous blurring of the sacred and the profane. Byzantine Christians elevated mere paintings to the same level as the vibrant tombs of the saints. In speaking of their rulers, also, Byzantines appeared to blur the difference between the human and the divine. Byzantine emperors claimed to be "colleagues," "co-rulers" with Christ. Petitions by holy men to the emperor dared to speak of "the divine ears." Theodulph considered this to be the hallmark of a Christendom that had not succeeded in sloughing off the heavy burden of its grandiose pagan past.[35]

In Charles' empire, by contrast, the profane and the sacred were kept apart. Nor was the pre-Christian past allowed to mingle dangerously with the Christian present. Each had its proper place. Each, indeed, as we shall see, enjoyed a certain merciful freedom from the other. Condemned by Theodulph to a humble profanity, Latin artists did not have to strain, as did the later painters of icons, to catch the exact likenesses of holy figures, to freeze in paint an unchanging vision preserved for them, since time immemorial, by the orthodox tradition. They were free to change their minds. In an analogous manner, French, Italian and Spanish were free to evolve as they slipped rapidly out of the control of a Latin now deemed to be a perfect, but safely dead, language. The pre-Christian past, also, might come to flank the Christian present, provided that it remained resolutely profane. If divorced equally from the high, true, sacrality of the "Christian Law" and from the sinister, negative sacrality of pagan practice, the ancestral cultures of western Europe were free to continue, as the resilient vernacular culture of a Christian "laity." It is to this development that we must turn in our last chapter.

17

In Geār Dagum:
"In Days of Yore" – Northern
Christendom and its Past

In the 820s and 830s Dorestad was the greatest port in western
Europe. During the reign of Charles' successor, Louis the Pious
(814–840), four and a half million silver coins were struck at its
mint. They showed a Cross placed in the middle of the façade of
a classical temple, and bore the inscription *Religio Christiana.*
An ostentatiously Christian empire lay at the southern end of
the trade routes that led across the North Sea into the North
Atlantic. Beyond Dorestad and Frisia stretched non-Christian
lands, characterized by fragile chiefdoms. In Denmark, along
the fjords of Norway and in the lowlands of southern Sweden,
small kings rose and fell according to their ability to gain access
to wealth, through trade and plunder on the waters of the North
Atlantic and the Baltic.

Hedeby in Denmark and Birka (Björkö) in southern Sweden
were the Dorestads of the north. They were *emporia*, ringed by
fortified ditches. Christian and even, at a later time, Muslim
merchants were encouraged to visit them, and to bring the
prestigeful gifts of the south to an intensely competitive and
adaptable society, made up of small groups of farmers turned
warriors and seamen.

The "Northmen," as the Franks called the varied inhabitants of Scandinavia, had remained fiercely loyal to their gods. Only gods could impart to their worshippers the supra-human vigor and good luck that gave to individuals and to groups a competitive edge over their many rivals. The imperial solidity of the "Christian Religion" coinage of Dorestad was matched, in Denmark, by thousands of golden amulets, dedicated to shrines or worn on their persons, so as to increase the numinous good fortune of successful chieftains. The goods appreciated in Scandinavia included, as one would expect, high-quality Frankish swords. But less-visible goods, seen as an exotic source of spiritual power, might follow. Christ, the Frankish god, could find acceptance; but provided that He lived up to the expectations of brittle warriors. There was a chance that He would. The hilt of a Frankish sword, found in Sweden, bears a verse from the Psalms:

Blessed be the Lord my strength, which teacheth my hands to war and my fingers to fight.   (Psalm 144: 1)[1]

When it came to war, a matter of truly religious seriousness, Franks and Northmen thought alike: sacred words – Latin Psalms or arcane runes – showed that the gods were close to hand, to enhance the efficacy of a warrior's weapons.

Scandinavia itself consisted of a band of coastal settlements, caught between a North Sea, ringed by Christian kingdoms, and a vast hinterland that stretched to the Arctic Circle and eastward to the edge of the Siberian forest zone. This was a world of hunters and pastoralists, of Lapps and Finns, whose shamanistic rites, performed in animal costumes, implied an open frontier between the human and the animal and between the spirit and the human world.

Shamanistic practices were partly adopted by the Northmen, thereby ensuring that observers from the distant Christian south were brought into contact with belief systems and rituals associated, originally, with Siberia. It was to missionaries who had come to Birka, and who knew of such animal transformations through masking, that Carolingian scholars turned for information that would bring the *Etymologies* of Isidore of Seville up to date on the topic of the dog-headed races of men who lived at the far edge of the earth.[2]

In the ninth and tenth centuries, the North Atlantic became what Germany and the southern end of the North Sea had been in earlier centuries. It was a new, immense "Middle Ground," where Christian and pagan met. Its distances dwarfed the Christian lands of western Europe. It extended far to the southeast, along the Baltic and down the river systems of what is now Russia to Kiev on the Dnieper, and far to the northwest, through Iceland and Greenland to "Vinland" and Anse-les-Meadows on the coast of Newfoundland.

By AD 1000 this "Middle Ground" had closed, and Christianity had come to predominate in the North Atlantic also. Put very briefly, the Viking raids of the later ninth century inflicted great damage on Ireland and England and effectively destroyed the unity of the proud Christian empire of Charlemagne and Louis. But a "Viking" was an "entre-preneurial" king on the war-path, on the *vik*, in search of tribute and prestige, much as the kings of Saxon Britain and even Clovis and Charles Martel had once been. Scandinavia was soon filled with Christian wealth, with Christian slaves and with Christian ideas. A world once isolated from western Europe by the sea was sucked inexorably into the political and social structures of the Christian south by the very success with which the Viking fleets came to bridge the North Atlantic, linking Dublin to Iceland and the Baltic to Kiev.

When they came to accept Christianity, the Northmen preferred to remember having done so on their own terms. In 987, the Scandinavian settlers at Kiev, known to outsiders (and eventually to themselves) as *Rus'*, decided to accept Christianity from Byzantium, but not before sending observers to report on western Catholicism and Islam. In 1000, the farmers of Iceland voted, at their annual Assembly at Thingvellir, to adopt a single "Christian law" rather than face the disruptive consequences of prolonged division between pagan and Christian families.

Eventually Christianity spread to the furthest corners of the North Atlantic. Christian Crosses marked the headland burial of a Scandinavian adventurer from Greenland, shot by Eskimo on the coast of Labrador:

"Call it Krossanes for ever more" [he said]. For Greenland was at that time Christian.[3]

The runic grave-inscription of the chieftain Ulvljot, set up west of Trondheim in 1008, dated his death by the coming of the new religion:

Twelve winters had Christendom been in Norway.[4]

Even in the distant north, *Kristintumr*, "Christendom," a word coined in Saxon England and now adopted in Norway, had come to stay.

AD 1000 takes us a long way from the ancient world. It is as close in time to the 1520s, when the Spanish conquistadors first encountered the great temple-cities of Mexico and Peru, as it is to the resignation of Romulus Augustulus. Yet this last closing of the "Middle Ground" in North Atlantic Europe throws into sharp relief processes and attitudes that had made non-Mediterranean western Christendom as a whole distinctive for many centuries before.

To begin with, vast physical distances and equally tenacious differences in outlook separated the various corners of the North Atlantic. In 826, Harald Klak, an exiled Danish king, came south to be baptized. He hoped to return with Frankish support to assert hegemonial power over his fellow-chieftains. The emperor Louis himself acted as his god-father. He was brought to the palace at Ingelheim, where the frescoes in the main hall conjured up the huge confidence of the Franks that their empire represented the culmination of Christian history. Founders of pagan empires – Alexander the Great and the ancient Romans – were placed at the back of the hall. Near the apse, where Louis stood with his newly-baptized Danish sub-king, were the emperors of a more advanced and greater age – "true" emperors, because Christian emperors, Roman and Frankish alike. Constantine and Theodosius I faced their equals, Charles Martel, shown conquering the Frisians, and Charles, as he "drew the Saxons under his [Christian] laws." Harald Klak, now dressed in a purple cloak, was to join such kings. He was to establish in Denmark a more forceful style of kingship, linked to Frankish wealth and to Frankish Christianity.[5]

What seemed possible at Ingelheim, however, was by no means practicable in Denmark and southern Sweden. Harald Klak proved an immediate failure: overmighty kings were not welcome in Denmark. Anskar, a monk of Corbie, who first attached himself to Harald's retinue, was later made bishop of Hamburg and Bremen. He visited Birka in 830 and 852. Until his death in 865, he enjoyed a commission to evangelize the north that was as wide as that once held by Boniface in Germany. Far from the Frankish armies, Anskar was not the confident consolidator of previous, looser allegiances to Christianity that Boniface had been. He remained a peripheral figure to the chieftains he visited. The certainties of the imperial heartlands did not apply on the edge of the Baltic. At a time when Agobard of Lyon could assert the undivided sovereignty of God so as to brush aside popular illusions in Burgundy, Anskar faced a society that was quite prepared to accept Christ – but only as one god among many, and provided that His usefulness was indicated by traditional forms of divination. To take one example. A raiding party of Swedes stranded in Kurland discussed their dilemma:

> "The God of the Christians frequently helps those who cry to Him [they said] . . . Let us enquire whether He will be on our side." Accordingly, . . . lots were cast and it was found that Christ was willing to help them.

They later learned from Christian merchants that a forty-day fast from meat would count as an acceptable return to Christ for His help:

> After this, many . . . began to lay stress upon the fasts observed by Christians and upon almsgiving . . . because they had learned that this was pleasing to Christ.[6]

In the vivid *Life of Anskar* by Rimbert, his disciple, a man of Danish origin, every successful contact between Christianity and the local population was framed by such a scene. We have come a long way from the triumphal narratives of supernatural confrontation and dramatic conversions of rulers, such as had fed the Christian imagination of the Mediterranean and, to a lesser extent, of northwestern Europe. In retrospect at least, Scandinavian societies chose to associate their adoption of "Christendom" with solemn moments of decision-making, in which the new religion was subjected to long-established divinatory techniques before it gained public approval.

Such narratives effectively cut down to size not only the efforts of missionaries from the Christian south, but also the role of local kings. Kings, especially when they now enjoyed the plundered wealth of England and Francia and acted in alliance with Christian rulers, could be overbearing. Harald Bluetooth of Denmark (950–986) monopolized responsibility for the change of religion. He built a large church at Jelling, flanked by a great inscribed rock that showed a fiercely bearded Christ whose outstretched arms were lost in a tangle of snake-like ornament. The runic inscription declared that Harald had "won all Denmark to himself and made the Danes Christian." He even made his father, Gorm, a Christian in retrospect. Gorm, the old pagan, was taken from the neighboring royal burial mound and was placed in the church close to the altar.

The settlers of Iceland, by contrast, had come to the island, after 870, so as to escape the rising power of the kings of Norway. Despite – indeed, one suspects, because of – the forceful Christian rule of Olaf Tryggvason (995–1000), across the sea from Iceland at Trondheim, they were determined that, if they were to become Christians, it should be entirely on their own terms, and not through pressure from a neighboring Christian king. In the Assembly of 1000, they authorized their "Law Speaker," Thorgeir of Ljósvatn, to decide for them whether they should accept Christianity as the sole "law" of the island. A resolutely kingless society, made up of isolated farmsteads set in an immense landscape divided by steep fjords, lava-flows and lowering glaciers, their "law" was the only thing that Icelanders had in common. A division between pagans and Christians would have destroyed what little consensus existed in these fragile settlements:

Let us all have one law and one faith. For it will prove that, if we sunder the law, we will also sunder the peace.

An old-fashioned pagan, Thorgeir could only "speak the law" with authority after he had "gone under the cloak:"

He lay down and spread his cloak over himself, and lay all that day and the next night, nor did he speak a word.

It was a shamanistic séance, that employed a form of divination, through sensory deprivation, that was common to Gaelic Scotland, Scandinavia and Finland. It was by the summoning of spirit powers, in a pan-North Atlantic ritual, that Christ was declared, next morning, at the Law Rock, to be the new god of the Icelanders:

all people should be Christian and those be baptized who were still unbaptized in this land: but as for infanticide, the old law [which allowed it] should stand, as also the eating of horseflesh.

Even sacrifice was allowed for a time, provided that it was not seen by outside witnesses.[7]

What is, perhaps, the most significant feature of this account is that it was written down over a century later, in the *Book of the Icelanders* of Ari Thorgilsson the Wise, in 1122/33, at the behest of the bishop of Skálholt. To Icelandic clergymen of the age of Saint Bernard the fateful decision of Thorgeir "under the cloak" constituted the only narrative of Christianization worth remembering. If the Icelanders had become Christian, they could only have done so by following the wise procedures laid down by their ancestral law.

The story of the conversion of the Icelanders was only one example among many of a problem which non-Mediterranean Christian societies had faced from the seventh century onwards. In every area, the Christian Church had depended for its establishment and eventual success on the wealth and protection of the powerful. From Columba to abbess Hild, Wilfrid and the great Frankish bishops of the Rhineland, whose aristocratic reflexes so shocked Boniface, men and women of royal or noble descent had acted as the leaders of the Church and the builders of its cultural resources. Whether deployed by the "entrepreneurial" kings of Saxon Britain or, with self-confident majesty, by Charlemagne, Christianity had become part of the language of power throughout northwestern Europe. But at the root of that power there lay a past tantalizingly beyond the reach of the Christian present.

To take one small but revealing example. In the late eighth century, a priest in Northumbria edited the genealogies of the kings of the *Angli*. These kings were men whose vigor and good fortune were ascribed to their royal lineage. The Northumbrian kings, in particular, had made the power implied in their blood-line manifest by patronizing splendid monasteries. The priest did not hesitate to impose his own, up-to-date Christian views upon the genealogies. He was careful to exclude all sons born out of Christian wedlock to concubines. But he did not exclude the gods. The genealogies would not provide a title to power if they did not reach back to their root. At that root, heading the priest's list of the ancestors of every Anglian kingdom, stood the god Woden. They had all come from a god.[8]

As long as power based upon genealogies was taken seriously, the gods were taken seriously. They were not regarded, even by the clergy, as the trivial creatures of classical mythology, on whose love-affairs and inconstant emotions Christian apologists of the Mediterranean had lingered with scorn in earlier centuries. Nor were they the creatures of sinister demonic illusion. Solemn figures even in their decline, they were like an ancient dynasty that had once ruled the earth until forced to abdicate in favor of the Christ of modern times. As Christian kings, their human descendants still bore traces of their distinctive, towering stature. Indeed, the more they did so, the more effective they would be as defenders of the Church.

Not only power, but the skills of the settled world came from the gods. Those skills belonged to the deep past. Knowledge of "the white Scriptures" was a phenomenon of recent times. But mere books could not contain the arts of life. These had come from an age when gods and men had lived side by side. In Ireland, indeed, they had been taught to men by the neighboring "tribe of the gods:"

And though the faith came, these arts were not put away, for they are good and no demons ever did good.[9]

The fact that we know anything of the past of pre-Christian Europe depended on a process which is extraordinary in itself. As the only literate class in northern Europe, it was the clergy which consigned to writing – and so made available to the future – the epics and the pre-Christian laws of Ireland, Saxon Britain and Germany. They did this because knowledge of such things was essential to law and order and to their own status in society. Precisely because the central institutions of the Church were microcosms of local society, many monks, nuns, royal chaplains, bishops and their clerical dependents were noblemen and noblewomen, and continued to think as such in their new roles as religious leaders.

To be noble was to live well, to be seen to live well and to foster the memory of a past that lay always on the edge of the Christian present – a past where human glory, human tragedy, the working out of human obligations was so much more vivid and clear-cut, so much more brimming over with magnificent lack of measure, than was the gray, Christian present. Toasting with great drinking horns that carried as much liquor as a present-day bottle of Moselle, high talk and loud laughter, to the ancient sound of the harpist, were an essential part of such a life – as were horses with tails bobbed in the new, "pagan" Scandinavian fashion, a retinue complete with hawks, performing bears and minstrels, and (particularly shocking if worn by well-born clergy) elegant trousers.

All these were associated, at one time or other, with the clergy and monasteries of Saxon England and Francia. They were regularly condemned, throughout the eighth and ninth centuries, in episcopal councils in both regions. Yet clerics close to the lay elites were never altogether disapproving. In an overwhelmingly oral society, epic memories were far more than entertainment, more even than titles to rule. They were the unwritten law-codes of an entire warrior-class. Charles himself, for all his "Roman" title, knew that the cultivation of such memories was an essential strand in his power. Not only did he cause

the unwritten laws of all the tribes that came under his rule to be compiled and reduced to writing. He also [Einhard added] directed that the age-old, non-Latin poems in which were celebrated the warlike deeds of the kings of ancient times should be written out and preserved.[10]

Frankish epics have not survived. Louis the Pious, brought up in Aquitaine and surrounded by "Romans" of the south, did not favor the project. Huge power, based on the solid, post-Roman structures of Gaul and Italy and touched by memories of Rome itself, did not need that extra magical charge from an epic tribal past beyond the Christian present. In neighboring Britain, by contrast, king Offa of Mercia (757–796) was as capable as Charles would be, of organizing the labor of his subjects to create titanic earthworks. Offa's Dyke stretches for 150 miles (longer than all the Roman walls of Britain put together) between the Saxon Midlands and Wales. But Offa's power still deployed an epic, Saxon style, tenacious of the past. The royal mausoleum-church of his father, at Repton, flanked ancient burial mounds. Offa's pedigree ascended into a galaxy of figures known from legend. It may well be that the Anglo-Saxon epic of *Beowulf* was committed to writing at his court.[11]

Beowulf was a record of events larger than life that took place *in geār dagum*, "in days of yore." It was a mere fragment, preserved for us by the accident of writing, from a vast reservoir of memories. The text, as it now stands, assumed a reader's knowledge of at least twenty similar legends. Made up of gripping vignettes of loyalty and courage, of tragic conflict and ceremonious good cheer in a well-ordered royal hall, acted out in ancient times in a distant homeland, such a tale constituted the moral "gene-pool" of a warrior-aristocracy, constantly spliced and respliced to meet the needs of every occasion.

In ninth-century Germany, similar attempts were made to add to present Christian power the numinous third dimension

of an epic past. With characteristic *de haut en bas* thorough-
ness, the Carolingian patrons of this venture brought together
the epics of various groups, who had not previously shown
any interest in what they had in common with each other,
under the single rubric of "Germanic" tales. Franks, Goths
and Saxons had flaunted parallel pedigrees. They did not
think of themselves as related. Franks, indeed, preferred to
imagine that they were Trojans, not Germans. Now, whatever
was recited in the *lingua Theotisca*, in German, was treated
as the common "usable past" of an imperial aristocracy that
had come to dominate central Europe from the Rhine estuary
to Hungary.[12]

The Carolingian "discovery of Germany" was not limited to
the vernacular. It took place, also, in Latin, through decisions
made in the *scriptoria* of monasteries founded by Boniface
and later set up in Saxony, after Charles' slow and murderous
absorption of the region. To take one example. The *Histories*
of Ammianus Marcellinus, written around 395, contain a
uniquely vivid and circumstantial record of fourth-century
frontier warfare along the Rhine and the Danube. They describe
the sudden appearance of the Huns and the catastrophic defeat
of the emperor Valens at Adrianople in 378. They survive in
one manuscript only, copied in the ninth century at Boniface's
Fulda. Without the decision made in a German monastery to
divert efforts usually spent on copying the "Christian Law" to
copying the work of a fourth-century military man and evident
pagan, simply because he had so much to say about the German
world of his time, we would know next to nothing about the
early stages of what we have come to know as the "barbarian
invasions." Whole chapters of this book could not have been
written.

In the same way, Tacitus' famous work *On Germany* was
used again, for the first time in 300 years, in a preface to a
book recording the miracles associated with the transfer of
the relics of a saint all the way from Rome to Wildeshausen
in Saxony. The founder of Wildeshausen, Waldbert, was
none other than the grandson of the great Widukind, the
stubborn leader of pagan resistance to Charlemagne. Now
ensconced in his home territory as abbot of the monastery

he himself had founded – with the further provision that only members of his kin should succeed him – Waldbert was no more prepared than the Irish had been, at an earlier time, to believe that Christianity had created a break with the noble past of his own tribe. It had merely added further luster to a pre-existing natural excellence. In the words of the Preface:

> The Saxons of old went out of their way to maintain many effective customs and high moral standards, as far as the law of nature was concerned. Such a way of life would have gained them the true blessedness of Heaven if only they had not suffered from lack of knowledge of the Creator.[13]

Faced by a past that had by no means lost its solemnity, the solution favored by the clergy was to treat it, simply, for the first time, as the past. By ceasing to be a god, Woden was condemned to history. He was a towering creature, but a creature subject to human time, held at a distance from the present. The world of the gods no longer existed, as it were, beside the present, as an instantly accessible reservoir of supra-human energy, easily tapped through sacrifice, through spells and through the heavy workings of strong liquor – the poet's honey drink of memory. The gods were deemed, by the clergy, to be long-dead, imposing figures of an *ancien régime*.

It was not easy to keep the gods safely in the past in this manner. Up to the age of Saint Francis and Chartres cathedral, Odin (the Northmen's Woden) remained far more present than any long-dead king could ever hope to be in Iceland and Norway. A "culture hero" and a powerful ego-ideal, Odin would manifest himself with uncanny ease to people and even in people. A small but vivid detail shows this. The father of the great recorder of the *Sagas*, Snorri Sturluson (1179–1241), was Sturla, the wily Christian priest of Hvamm on the Breidafjord in western Iceland. At the height of a dispute, where Sturla had shown his trickery to full advantage in legal argument, the wife of his opponent attempted with a knife to blind him in one eye:

"Why should I not make you look like him [the one-eyed Odin] whom you most want to resemble?"[14]

When Snorri himself came to write down the *Saga* of Olaf Tryggvason's violent imposition of Christianity in the fjords around Trondheim, he was careful to record that Odin had appeared to the king as the ever-present guardian of the past of Norway. One night, as Olaf rested at Ogvaldsness,

> an old and very wise-spoken man came in. He wore a hood coming down over his face and he was one-eyed. He had things to tell of every land . . . The king found much pleasure in his talk. [The stranger knew, for instance, all about Ogvald, the king whose ancient burial mound gave its name to the headland.] He told the king those tales and many others about the ancient kings and other stories of olden times.

It was all that Olaf's bishop could do to persuade the fascinated king to go to bed. Only next morning, when the stranger had vanished, did Olaf realize that his moment of spell-bound access to the past had come from Odin, "the god heathen men had long worshipped."[15]

In an overwhelmingly non-literate culture, words carried from the past were quite as dangerous as was sacrifice. Saxon converts were expected to renounce not only the "works" but the "words" of Woden, Thunor and Saxnote. Words that were not tamed by Christian models could bring back into the present certain powers that were not believed to be non-existent but to have been placed, by Christians, in the past. We can only glimpse how powerful such words could be. When famine struck the settlements in Greenland, the prophetess Thorbjorg called for an assistant to recite, at the appropriate moment, the "Spirit Locking" spell. Gudrid had been taught the spell in Iceland by her foster-mother:

> "But this is a kind of lore and proceeding I feel I cannot assist in . . . For I am a Christian woman."
> "Yet it might happen [Thorbjorg reminded her] that you could prove helpful to people in this affair."
> [So] Gudrid recited the chant so beautifully that no one

present could say that he had heard the chant recited in a lovelier voice.[16]

Not surprisingly, given so many beguiling alternatives, Christian authors of the *Penitentials* commended those who set about the serious things of life – such as the gathering of healing herbs – with Christian words.[17] If the past was to be drawn into the present, then it must be a past linked to the beginning of Christian time, where Christian figures, and not Woden and Baldur, had trod the woods of Germany. It was such spells that clergymen were quite prepared to write out in High German, for themselves and for their clients:

Christ was born before wolf and thief were, and Saint Martin was Christ's shepherd. May Christ and Saint Martin take care of these dogs so that no wolf nor she-wolf should cause them harm, wherever they may run in wood or way or heath.[18]

The priest on an estate in Anglo-Saxon England would heal an infertile field by saying Mass over four sods taken from its four corners. He revived the tired soil by a Christian ritual heavy with echoes of God's first creation of the garden of Eden:

Then let the plough be driven forwards and the first furrow opened up, then say:
"Hale may thou be, earth, mother of mortals! Grow pregnant in the embrace of God, filled with food for mortals' use."[19]

Just as the past, if it was not Christian, had to be kept beyond arm's reach, in the past, so the beings of the past were expected to ring a Christian present, provided that they also were held at bay. The Mediterranean model of the demonic, current in the early Church, had filled the air with subtle spirits. They were the last, the least reliable, chill and blustering representatives of a chain of beings that stretched upwards, from earthbound man, through the moon, to the ethereal splendor of the stars. It was a vertical model, rooted in a distinctive notion of the cosmos. What we meet in the north, by contrast, was a more horizontal model – a patterning of human society surrounded, on every side, by the encroaching wild. A "middle world" was forever brushed by the grim or alluring denizens of an "outer world."

In Ireland, for instance, the human and the non-human were placed in concentric rings. There was room, in such a map of the world, for innumerable categories of beings. Settled human life lay at the center, domesticated animals in the middle, and, along the edges, there flitted the gray shapes of wolves. In the same way, monks were ringed by tame, penitent lay persons, who, in turn, were hemmed in by the dread bands of outlaws and brigands; and Coroticus, cursed by Saint Patrick, had suddenly fled as a fox into the wild to which his hard heart belonged.[20] An entire, alternative population of "The Other Side," the fairy kingdom of later times, also ringed the settled land, as did the ancestors. In the great barrows that studded the landscape, the ancient heroes of Ireland were locked forever in a past that knew neither the saving hope nor the penitential sadness of modern times. They could be visited. It was at the grave-rock of Fergus mac Roich in Connacht that the scholar in search of the full version of the *Táin*, the Tale of the Cattle Raid of Cooley, was taken into the mist for three days and three nights, to be told, by Fergus himself,

> in fierce majesty, with a head of brown hair, in a green cloak . . . with gold hilted sword,

the full, authentic version of the story.[21]

We know this, of course, because an Irish cleric wrote it down. He was in two minds about it – or felt he should present himself as such. In his Old Irish colophon to this Old Irish text, he was the proud transmitter of the past:

> A blessing on everyone who shall faithfully memorize the *Táin* as it is written here and shall not add any other form to it.

In Latin he adopted a more distanced tone:

> But I who have written out this history, or rather this fable, give no credence to the various incidents related in

it. For some things in it are the deceptions of demons, others are flights of poetic fancy; some are probable, others are improbable; while others are intended for the amusement of foolish people.[22]

But there was nothing fictional or illusory about the creatures of the wild who flanked the human race in Saxon England, Germany and Scandinavia. Their being drew substance from the inhuman landscapes that were their appropriate haunts – monsters of the eery coastal marshlands of Britain, entire riding-parties of dethroned gods deep in the woods of Saxony, trolls on the lava-fields and glacier snouts of Iceland. Grendel, the monster slain by Beowulf, was real, as was his mother. They had been seen:

> huge prowlers of the marshes, patrolling the moors, alien intruders . . . an ill-formed creature stalking the paths where outcasts go.[23]

They were the primal outlaws, the all-too-concrete, menacing counterparts of heroic human figures, deemed capable of having held them at bay in the distant past. Hygelac, a sea-king mentioned in *Beowulf*, was so large that from the age of twelve no horse could carry him:

> His bones are preserved in an island in the Rhine, where it flows into the ocean, and are shown to those who come from afar as a miracle.[24]

Included in a Latin *Book of Monsters* that drew, also, on the description of the marvels of India said to have been presented to Alexander the Great by his tutor, the wise philosopher Aristotle, the larger-than-life Hygelac – and, by implication, the baleful Grendel – were not misty beings. For the clergy who set their pens to work to record them in writing, they were an unquestioned part of the topography of Europe.

This was a moral topography, that could be fitted with relative ease on to a sharp, Christian patterning of the world. Grendel's pedigree reached back, not to respectable, old-world gods, as did the pedigrees of Saxon Christian kings, but to the primal outcast of the Old Testament – to Cain, the slayer of his own kin.[25] Monsters such as he continued, into the present, a past whose basic pattern, read by clergymen in the Old Testament, always pitted human beings, subject to human restraints on pride and violence, against the perennial race of the giants – menacing outsiders, the tyrannical embodiments of power and ambition unrestrained by human law.

We should see the coming of Christianity to much of western Europe against this distinctive imaginative landscape. It was not a patterning unique to that region. Ananias of Shirak, viewing the storms that whipped across the surface of Lake Van, noted that many believed that they were caused by the struggle of a primal hero to remove from the lake the dragons that lurked in its depths.[26] Throughout Armenia, blacksmiths would begin the week by striking their anvils so as to strengthen the chains which bound the giant Artavazd in his mountain prison.[27] But it was a pattern that implied a sharp distinction between center and periphery, between settled life and a murmurous population of outcasts who existed but did not belong. It gave weight to the Christian claim to possess the center, to stand now for settled life.

Seen in that light, the establishment of the Church merely completed a process that may well have characterized religious change in Europe since neolithic times, as diverse groups and rituals came to cluster, ring after ring, around increasingly complex societies, with ever-sharper boundaries between those who belonged and those who did not. The world of order; the world of human settlement defined in sharp contrast to the wild; the world identified in aristocratic epic with the bright halls of the chieftains and, on a humbler level, with the tilled fields, the tamed livestock and even – the most astonishing example of the furthest reach of human control – the predictability of the swarming bees as they returned to their owner's hive: all this could be seen as now lying under the protection of Christ.[28] Christian rituals upheld that world. Christian kings ruled it.

After almost a millennium, "Christendom" and permanence had come to coalesce, even around the uncertain shores of the North Atlantic. Christendom was a notion that now carried the charge of perpetuity. Times had changed. In AD 95,

Titus Praxias, in Phrygia, in western Asia Minor, made a testamentary bequest which ensured that his memory would survive in his home town: every year roses would be placed on his tomb, and the town-councillors would gather for a memorial banquet. These arrangements were to remain in force

> for as long an age as the rule of the Romans shall be maintained.[29]

Around 871/889, a Kentish nobleman, the earldorman Alfred, granted 200 pence in alms to the church at Canterbury, to be rendered for Masses for his soul,

> as long as baptism should last and money can be raised from the land.[30]

We have come a long way, in time and in space, from the Edessa of Bardaisan. Yet, in many regions, we are still looking at a world that had remained continuous with its past. Thanks to the campaigns of the Iconoclast emperors of the eighth century, the Phrygia of Titus Praxias, though greatly changed, had remained under "the rule of the Romans." In Byzantium, Christianity and empire had coexisted for well over half a millennium.

This fact was made abundantly plain in the second half of the ninth century. No longer pinned down by Muslim raids and more secure in its control of the coastal plains of the Balkans, the Byzantine empire was prepared to reach out, once again, to make its presence felt as far as the steppes of southern Russia and on the middle Danube, where the new Slav principality of Moravia had developed in the vacuum left by Charlemagne's defeat of the Avars. The Byzantine elites who had celebrated the Triumph of Orthodoxy, and their successors, were well aware that they enjoyed new prosperity and were conscious of having regained the cultural superiority to which they, as orthodox Christians and the direct heirs of Greek wisdom, felt entitled. Such an elite produced a remarkable pair of missionary brothers, Constantine (826/7–869) and Methodius (815–885). Born in Thessalonica, they came from a governmental family that already knew the Slavonic world of the Vardar valley. In Byzantine fashion, the brothers retained all the skills and the duties of top civil servants and diplomats, even when they had adopted the life of a clergyman and a monk. They had no doubts as to the superiority of the empire that they served. They were prepared to cover vast distances, at the behest of the emperor, to represent its faith to barbarian nations. In 860/1 Constantine was on the eastern edge of the southern steppes of Russia, expounding the Christian faith to the Khan of the Khazars, in a three-cornered debate with Jews and Muslims:

> Our empire is that of Christ, as the prophet said, *the God of Heaven shall set up a kingdom, which shall never be destroyed.*[31]

The Khan was unimpressed. The Khazars eventually opted for Judaism, which kept them at a safe distance from the two over-confident empires to their south, Christian Byzantium and the Islamic Califate.

Others needed contact with the glory of such an empire. In 863, prince Rastislav of Moravia wrote to the emperor of Byzantium for Christian teachers. What was at stake, at Byzantium, was whether the reopened Danubian route, that passed from Passau and Salzburg, across modern Hungary and the extended empire of the Bulgars to Constantinople, would fall under imperial dominance, through a chain of Christian kingdoms provided with Byzantine clergy. What Rastislav wished to ensure was that, if Christianity was to be consolidated in Moravia, his principality should not be considered yet another "open frontier," to be closed by Frankish bishops, from Salzburg and Passau, in the interests of the Frankish Christian empire, as Boniface had once done, in central Germany, a century and a half before. A church organized from distant Byzantium would give him the independence that he needed.

Skilled diplomats, in an age of accelerated cultural contacts between Byzantium and its neighbors, which had included the translation of so many Greek texts into Arabic, Constantine and Methodius had no hesitation in working out an alphabet so as to provide Rastislav with what the Frankish clergy were unwilling to provide him: a complete Slavonic liturgy and set of Gospel readings translated from the Greek. The

318 *The End of an Ancient World:* AD *750–1000*

script they first used, Glagolithic, was somewhat arcane, as suited men used to diplomatic missions. Only later did a simpler Slavonic script emerge, directly modelled on Greek and named "Cyrillic," after the name which Constantine took, on becoming a monk, in good Byzantine fashion, on the eve of his death. The two brothers brought to the edge of the Carolingian empire a microcosm of all that was most sacred in Byzantium, transposed into the language of yet another "barbarian" people. In translating a code of Byzantine imperial law, they also provided Rastislav with the possibility of holding court as a distant mirror-image of the emperor himself.[32]

The Moravian mission of Constantine and Methodius was, even in its origins, a quixotic venture. It did not last long. The Byzantine brothers were duly hated by their Frankish rivals as religious interlopers. But they were a momentary reminder, at a time when it was far from certain which power would predominate in the Danubian regions, of a very different style of Christian empire, and so of Christian missionary practice, from that to which the Carolingian clergy were accustomed. It was a style that would continue to remain effective in all those areas where the roads still led to New Rome. When, a century later, the representatives of the *Rus'* came south from Kiev, in 987, to seek out an appropriate form of Christianity, they found it in Constantinople:

> the Greeks led us into the edifices where they worship their God, and we knew not whether we were in heaven or on earth. For on earth there is no such splendor or such beauty, and we are at a loss as to how to describe it. We only know that God dwells there among men, and their service is fairer than the ceremonies of other nations. For we cannot forget that beauty.[33]

Byzantium, indeed, thought of itself as an island of order preserved by God in the midst of so much barbarous disharmony. Byzantines believed that Heaven was reflected on earth in the still surface of their orderly liturgies. These liturgies were shared by all orthodox believers. Liturgy formed a golden bridge that raised to Heaven the tongues common to laity and clergy alike – Greek, Syriac, Armenian and, since the

time of Constantine and Methodius, Church Slavonic. The
common painted wood of images, also, was raised to Heaven
in the same way, by a diffused sense of the sacred. Icons were
endowed with the ability to bring holy persons from the court
of Heaven down to earth, in a manner which Latin Christians,
such as Theodulph of Orleans, condemned as a denial of the
essential otherness of truly sacred things.

The harmony expected of those brought close to Heaven
in church was shown in the orderly conduct of orthodox worshippers. Bulgarians who sought Christianity from
Constantinople, in the same years as Constantine and Methodius were active in Moravia, were told, in no uncertain terms,
in 864, by the Byzantines whom they consulted, that they would
have to sacrifice their trousers and their Central Asian turbans
if they wished to take part in the liturgy.

Humble though they might be, the Bulgars, like all other
orthodox believers, were privileged to stand in the court of
Heaven. They should dress accordingly. The court of Heaven
remained a "Roman" court. To become an orthodox kingdom
was to become a microcosm of Byzantium – to such an extent
that, in the narthex of the cathedral of Saint Sofia in Kiev, the
Hippodrome of Constantinople appears on an eleventh-century
fresco, echoing the imperial majesty still to be found close to
the heart of eastern Christendom.

Consulted by the Bulgars, in 866, on the delicate issue of
their trousers, the Latin pope, Nicholas I (858–867), and his
advisers, by contrast, considered such anxieties misplaced. In
the pope's opinion, local ethnic custom was irrelevant to
matters of worship. In this ruling, Nicholas showed shrewd
tolerance and, at the same time, a certain nonchalance based
upon contempt. Ethnic styles of dress, such as proliferated in
western Europe, where trousers were a matter of honor in the
north but not in Rome, were part of the profane world. They
could never be expected to mirror Heaven. It was better not to
weigh too heavily upon them. For they lay outside the clearly
delimited area of the sacred.[34]

In the west, the laity were left to their profane customs.
They were, indeed, allowed to become a caste of their own.
An ancient Christian past had retained much of its weight

in Byzantium, and with it a sense of the unity of an undifferentiated "baptized people," bathed in the mercy of God, where no one group could claim an outright monopoly of the sacred, and every group might be touched, if only spasmodically, by its high demands. Such a sense had not dissolved entirely in the west. But it had weakened. Particularly in northern Europe, the laity had come to resemble the warrior caste that flanked the Brahmins in India. They had their own, honored but separate place in a social hierarchy ordered in relation to the sacred. They had their own traditions, often written down in their own language. These traditions were tolerated, even fostered, by members of the clergy. They were a part of the resolute profanity that was a necessary complement to the sacred. A profane culture, deeply rooted in the non-Christian past, upheld law, power and the cultivation of the earth.

Such a culture was essential to the wealth and security of the clergy, but it was held, in no uncertain terms, to be subordinate to them.

The clergy alone controlled the sacred. They administered the sacraments. The learned among them had unique access to substantial libraries and to a training in the Latin tongue. They saw themselves as "rulers" of the profane world. They drew on the tradition of Gregory the Great's *Regula Pastoralis*, which had stressed, with unique urgency, the responsible and finely calibrated use of spiritual power.

Men such as Boniface, Theodulph and Agobard, reared on Gregory and set in place to govern the first empire in the west since Roman times, were the representatives of a new managerial elite. They were increasingly confident that they could embrace and guide the profane world. They no longer simply encountered it, in dramatic moments of confrontation, cursing and blessing.

From the Archimedean leverage point of their superior knowledge of the Christian Law, they claimed the right to move the opaque mass of a world that was no longer pagan but that had remained deeply profane – the world, that is, of the Christian "laity" – in the direction most conducive to their salvation. Whether they would succeed, for how long and on what terms is a theme that can be safely left to another volume of this series.

Notes

CHAPTER 1

1. Bardaisan, *Book of the Laws and Countries*, 583–9 and 607: translation H.J.W. Drijvers, Assen, 1965, pp. 41–53 and 59–61.
2. A.V. Paykova, "The Syrian Ostracon from Panjikent", *Le Mouséon* 92 (1979): 159–69; E.C.R. Armstrong and R.A.S. Macalister, Wooden book found near Springmount Bog, Co. Antrim, *Journal of the Royal Society of Antiquaries of Ireland* 50 (1920): 160–6.
3. Saint Boniface, *Letter 26 [35]*: translation E. Emerton, New York, 1976, p. 65.
4. Thomas of Marga, *The Book of Governors*, 5. 4: translation E.A. Wallis Budge, London, 1893, p. 480.
5. G. Schlegel, *Die chinesische Inschrift auf dem uigurischen Denkmal in Kara Balgassun*, Helsinki, 1896, pp. 57–61.
6. Bardaisan, *Book of Laws*, 595, p. 51.
7. Theophylact Simocatta, *Histories* 4. 11. 2–3: translation M. and M. Whitby, Oxford, 1986, p. 117.
8. *The Epic Histories Attributed to P'awstos Buzand* 3. 7: translation N. Garsoian, Cambridge, Mass., 1989, p. 73.
9. Galen of Ephesus, *de sanitate tuenda* 1. 10, C.G. Kühn (ed.), *Galeni Opera* 6, Leipzig, 1825, p. 51.
10. *Sanhedrin* 98b: translation I. Epstein, *Babylonian Talmud*, London, 1935, p. 666.

CHAPTER 2

1. *Pap. Oxy.* 2782, *Oxyrhynchus Papyri* 26, London, 1970, p. 79.
2. *Collatio Legum Romanarum et Mosaicarum* 15. 3: translation M. Dodgeon and S.N.C. Lieu, *The Roman Eastern Frontier and the Persian Wars (AD 226–362)*, London, 1991, p. 135.
3. Eusebius, *Life of Constantine* 4. 10: translation E.C. Robinson, *Nicene and Post-Nicene Fathers* 1, repr. Grand Rapids, 1979, p. 443.
4. *Didascalia Apostolorum* 12 [2.57]: translation R.H. Connolly, Oxford, 1929, p. 119.
5. *Didascalia Apostolorum* 19 [5.1], p. 161.
6. Eusebius, *Ecclesiastical History* 8. 7. 4: translation A.C. McGiffert, *Nicene and Post-Nicene Fathers* 1, p. 329 and G.A. Williamson, Penguin, Harmondsworth, 1965, p. 336.
7. Lactantius, *Divine Institutes* 3. 26: translation M.F. McDonald, *Fathers of the Church* 49, Washington, D.C., 1964, p. 234.
8. Tertullian, *On Purity* 13: translation W. Le Saint, *Ancient Christian Writers* 28, London, 1959, pp. 86–7.
9. *Didascalia Apostolorum* 2 [2.16], pp. 52–3.
10. *Didache* 1: translation J.B. Lightfoot, *The Apostolic Fathers*, London, 1891, p. 123.
11. *Baba Bathra* 9a: translation I. Epstein, *Babylonian Talmud* 11, p. 42.
12. Lactantius, *Divine Institutes* 6. 11, p. 423.

CHAPTER 3

1. Isidore of Pelusium, *Letter* 1. 270: *Patrologia Graeca* 78: 344A.
2. See the newly-discovered *Sermon Mayence* 61. 25, F. Dolbeau (ed.), "Nouveaux sermons de saint Augustine pour la conversion des païens et des donatistes", *Revue des études augustiniennes* 37 (1991): 37–78, at p. 76.
3. *Codex Theodosianus* 9. 16. 2: translation C. Pharr, Princeton, New Jersey, 1952, p. 237.
4. Orosius, *History against the Pagans*, preface: translation I.W. Raymond, New York, 1936, p. 30.
5. *Codex Theodosianus* 15. 5. 5, p. 433.
6. R.S.O. Tomlin, "The Curse Tablets", *The Temple of Sulis*

Minerva at Bath 2, B. Cunliffe (ed.), Oxford, 1988, pp. 232–4.

7. Saint Augustine of Hippo, *Ennaratio 1 in Psalm 34*, 7: translation S. Hebgin and F. Corrigan, *Ancient Christian Writers* 30, London, 1961, pp. 193–4.

8. Egeria, *Travels* 25. 8: translation J. Wilkinson, London, 1971, p. 127.

9. K.S. Painter, *The Water Newton Early Christian Silver*, London, 1977.

10. Athanasius, *Apology to Constantius* 30. 41, *A Library of Fathers*, Oxford, 1873, p. 180.

11. M. Tardieu, *Studia Iranica* 17 (1988): 153–82.

12. *The Cologne Mani-Codex*: translation R. Cameron and A.J. Dewey, Missoula, Montana, 1979.

13. Saint Augustine of Hippo, *Confessions*, 8. 6. 15 and 8. 19.

14. Sulpicius Severus' *Life of Martin*, *Letters* and *Dialogues* are translated in F.R. Hoare, *The Western Fathers*, New York, 1954, pp. 3–144 and A. Roberts, *Nicene and Post-Nicene Fathers* 13, repr. Grand Rapids, Michigan 1975, pp. 3–122.

15. Paulinus, *Letter* 29. 12: translation P.G. Walsh, *Ancient Christian Writers* 36, New York, 1966, p. 115.

16. M.M. Mundell and A. Bennett, *The Sevso Treasure*, Journal of Roman Archaeology: Supplementary Volume 12, Ann Arbor, Michigan, 1994, pp. 55–97.

17. M. Meslin, *La fête des Kalendes de Janvier dans l'empire romain*, Brussels, 1970.

18. Saint Augustine of Hippo, *Sermon Mayence 62*, F. Dolbeau (ed.), Nouveaux sermons IV, *Recherches augustiniennes* 26 (1992): 69–141.

19. H.R. Idris, Fêtes chrétiennes en Ifriqiya à l'époque ziride, *Revue africaine* 98 (1954): 261–76.

20. Paulinus in Ausonius, *Letter* 31. 63: translation H.G. Evelyn-White, *Ausonius* 2, Loeb Classical Library, London, 1949, p. 128.

21. Saint Augustine of Hippo, *Letter* 231. 6. The best translations of the *Confessions* are those of H. Chadwick, Oxford, 1991 and F.J. Sheed, repr. Indianapolis, Indiana, 1992.

22. Prosper of Aquitaine, *The Call of All Nations* 2. 35: translation P. De Letter, *Ancient Christian Writers* 14, Westminster, Maryland, 1963, pp. 149–51.

23. Saint Augustine of Hippo, *On Rebuke and Grace* 12. 35: translation P. Holmes and R.E. Wallis, *Nicene and Post-Nicene Fathers* 5, p. 486.

24. Saint Augustine of Hippo, *On Virginity* 44. 45: translation C.I. Cornish, *Nicene and Post-Nicene Fathers* 3, p. 434.
25. Saint Augustine of Hippo, *Against the Two Letters of the Pelagians* 3. 5. 14: translation P. Holmes and R.E. Wallis, p. 408.
26. Saint Augustine of Hippo, *Sermon Mayence* 60, F. Dolbeau (ed.), *Revue des études augustiniennes* 37 (1991): 42–52.
27. Saint Augustine of Hippo, [newly-discovered] *Letter* 2*. 3: translation R. Eno, *Fathers of the Church* 81, Washington, D.C., 1989, p. 20.
28. Saint Augustine of Hippo, *City of God* 14. 1: translation H. Bettenson, Penguin, Harmondsworth, 1976, p. 547.

CHAPTER 4

1. Saint Augustine of Hippo, *Letter* 199. 35 and 47: translation W. Parsons, *Fathers of the Church* 30, New York, 1955, pp. 384 and 394.
2. Hydatius, *Chronicle* 1. 4 and 6 and 2. 2: translation R.W. Burgess, Oxford, 1993, pp. 73, 75 and 107.
3. Sidonius Apollinaris, *Letter* 4. 20. 2–3: translation W.B. Anderson, *Sidonius Apollinaris* 2, Loeb Classical Library, London, 1965, pp. 137–9.
4. Vegetius, *Epitome of Military Sciences* 2. 5. translation N.P. Milner, Liverpool, 1993, p. 35.
5. *Book of Constitutions* 97: translation K.F. Drew, *The Burgundian Code*, Philadelphia, 1949, p. 84.
6. *Anonymus Valesianus* 12. 61: translation J.C. Rolfe, *Ammianus Marcellinus* 3, Loeb Classical Library, London, 1952, p. 547.
7. Gregory of Tours, *History* 2, preface: translation L. Thorpe, Penguin, Harmondsworth, 1974, p. 103.
8. Gregory of Tours, *History* 2. 7, p. 116.
9. Gregory of Tours, *History* 2. 32, p. 147.
10. *Life of Caesarius of Arles* 1. 32: translation W.E. Klingshirn, Liverpool, 1994, p. 25.
11. Gregory of Tours, *History* 2. 16, p. 131.
12. Sidonius Apollinaris, *Letters* 5. 14 and 7. 1, pp. 217–19 and 287–93.
13. *Life of Genovefa* 3. 11: translation J.A. McNamara and J. Halborg, *Sainted Women of the Dark Ages*, Durham, North Carolina, 1992, pp. 23–4.

14. Paulinus of Perigueux, *Life of Martin* 6. 93, *Corpus Scriptorum Ecclesiasticorum Latinorum* 16, Vienna, 1888, p. 142.
15. Sidonius Apollinaris, *Letter* 7. 9, pp. 335–59.
16. P'awstos Buzand, *Epic Histories* 6. 2: translation N.G. Garsoian, p. 234.
17. Translated by E.C.S. Gibson, *Library of the Nicene and Post-Nicene Fathers* 13, pp. 201–545.
18. Constantius, *Life of Germanus* 1: translation F.C. Hoare, *Western Fathers*, p. 286.
19. Ennodius, *Life of Epiphanius* 1. 14: translation G.M. Cook, Washington, D.C., 1942, p. 37.
20. Leo, *Letter* 10. 2: translation C.L. Feltoe, *Nicene and Post-Nicene Fathers* 12, p. 9.
21. Caelestine, *Letter* 21. 2, *Patrologia Latina* 50: 529A.
22. Saint Augustine of Hippo, [New] *Letter* 20*. 31: translation R.B. Eno, p. 148.
23. Leo, *Sermon* 24.2: translation Feltoe, p. 135.
24. Eusebius, *In Praise of Constantine* 3. 6: translation H.A. Drake, Berkeley, California, 1978, p. 87.
25. *Synod of Alexandria of 362*, M. Tetz (ed.), *Zeitschrift der neutestamentlichen Wissenschaft* 79 (1988): 272.
26. Shenoute, *Against the Origenists* 821, T. Orlandi (ed.), Rome, 1985, pp. 62–3.
27. Nestorius, *The Bazar of Heraclides* 2. 495–521: translation G.R. Driver and L. Hodgson, Oxford, 1925, pp. 363–79.
28. Isaac of Antioch, *Memra 8: On the Bird that Sung at Antioch* 149–450, G. Bickell (ed.), Giessen, 1873, pp. 91–105.

CHAPTER 5

1. Eugippius, *Life of Severinus* 20. 1: translation L. Bieler, *Fathers of the Church* 55, Washington, D.C., 1965, p. 78.
2. Eugippius, *Life of Severinus* 19. 2, p. 77.
3. Eugippius, *Life of Severinus* 7. 1, pp. 64–5.
4. Eugippius, *Life of Severinus* 8. 3, pp. 65–6.
5. F. Glaser, "Eine weitere Doppelkirchenanlage auf dem Hemma-berg", *Carinthia I* 183 (1993): 163–86.
6. R. Bland and C. Johns, *The Hoxne Treasure*, London, 1993.
7. Gildas, *On the Ruin of Britain* 3. 2: translation M. Winter-bottom, London, 1978, p. 16.
8. *The Exeter Book: The Ruin* 21: translation S.A.J. Bradley,

Anglo-Saxon Poetry, London, 1982, p. 402.
9. Aneurin, *Y Goddodin* 85: translation A.O.H. Jarman, Llandysal, 1990, p. 56.
10. Patricius, *Confession* 16: translation A.B.E. Hood, London, 1978, p. 44.
11. Patricius, *Letter to Coroticus* 2–3, p. 55.
12. Patricius, *Confession* 12, 34 and 38, pp. 43, 48 and 49.
13. *The First Synod of Saint Patrick* canon 6: translation L. Bieler, *The Irish Penitentials*, Dublin, 1975, p. 55.
14. See C. Donahue, *"Beowulf*, Ireland and the Natural Good", *Traditio* 7 (1949/1951): 263–77 and M. McNeill, *The Lughnasa*.
15. Gregory of Tours, *History* 2. 27: translation L. Thorpe, pp. 139–40.
16. Translation K.F. Drew, *The Laws of the Salian Franks*, Philadelphia, 1991.
17. Gregory of Tours, *History* 2. 42, pp. 157–8.
18. *Council of Agde*, *Concilia Galliae*, C. Munier (ed.), *Corpus Christianorum* 148, Turnhout, 1963, p. 192.
19. Gregory of Tours, *History* 2. 31, p. 144.
20. Gregory of Tours, *History* 2. 37, p. 152.
21. Gregory of Tours, *History* 2. 38, p. 154.
22. G. Camps, "Rex Gentium Maurorum et Romanorum. Recherches sur les royaumes de Mauretanie des vie et viie siècles", *Antiquités africaines* 20 (1984): 183–218.
23. *Kaleb Inscription*: translation S.C. Munro-Hay, *Aksum*, p. 230.
24. I. Shahid, "The *Kebra Nagast* in the Light of Recent Research", *Le Mouséon* 89 (1976): 133–78.
25. Gildas, *On the Ruin of Britain* 15 and 18, pp. 21 and 22–3.

CHAPTER 6

1. G. Pomarès, *Gélase 1er: Lettre contre les Lupercales*, Sources chrétiennes 65, Paris, 1959.
2. Leo, *Sermon* 27. 4: translation C.L. Feltoe, p. 140.
3. Gildas, *On the Ruin of Britain* 4. 2, p. 17.
4. *Sixteenth Council of Toledo (693)*, canon 2, J. Vives (ed.), Madrid, 1963, pp. 498–500.
5. Besa, *Life of Shenoute* 151–2: translation D.N. Bell, Kalamazoo, Michigan, 1983, p. 84.
6. Shenoute, *Letter* 24, *Corpus Scriptorum Christianorum Orient-*

alium 96: *Scriptores coptici* 8, Louvain, 1953, p. 45.

7. *Corpus Inscriptionum Graecarum* 4, no. 8627, Berlin, 1877, p. 295.

8. *Life of Caesarius* 1. 27: translation W.E. Klingshirn, p. 22.

9. Caesarius, *Sermons* 13. 4 and 54. 6: translation M. Mueller, *Fathers of the Church* 31, New York, 1956, pp. 78 and 270. See D. Harmening, *Superstitio*, Munich, 1979.

10. Caesarius, *Sermon* 44. 7, p. 225.

11. Caesarius, *Sermon* 193. 4: translation M. Mueller, *Fathers of the Church* 66, Washington, D.C., 1972, p. 34.

12. Caesarius, *Sermon* 52. 3, *Fathers of the Church* 31, p. 260.

13. Caesarius, *Sermon* 33. 4, p. 167; *Fourth Council of Toledo (633)* canon 11, Vives, p. 195.

14. As well as the *History*, the following works of Gregory of Tours have been translated: *Glory of the Martyrs* and *Glory of the Confessors*: translation R. Van Dam, Liverpool, 1988; *Life of the Fathers*: translation E. James, Liverpool, 1985; *Miracles of Saint Martin* and *Miracles of Saint Julian*, in Van Dam, *Saints and their Miracles*.

15. See *Venantius Fortunatus: Personal and Political Poems*: translation J. George, Liverpool, 1995.

16. *Historical Memoirs of the Duc de Saint-Simon* 2: translation L. Norton, London, 1967, p. 155.

17. Gregory of Tours, *Glory of the Martyrs* 83, p. 108.

18. Gregory of Tours, *Glory of the Confessors* 39, p. 51; *Miracles of Saint Julian* 45, p. 192.

19. Gregory of Tours, *Miracles of Saint Martin* 3. 1, p. 260.

20. Gregory of Tours, *History* 9. 10: translation L. Thorpe, p. 493.

21. Gregory of Tours, *History* 2. 24, p. 218.

22. Gregory of Tours, *Life of the Fathers* 9. 2, p. 80.

23. Gregory of Tours, *History* 9. 6 and 10. 25, pp. 485–7 and 584–6.

24. *Life of Desiderius of Cahors* 16, B. Krusch (ed.), *Corpus Christianorum* 117, Turnhout, 1957, p. 362.

25. Gregory of Tours, *Miracles of Saint Julian* 46b, p. 193.

26. Gregory of Tours, *Miracles of Saint Martin* 2. 43 and 55, pp. 251 and 255.

27. Gregory of Tours, *Glory of the Confessors* 23 and 50, pp. 39 and 60; *Glory of the Martyrs* 67, 73 and 77, pp. 91, 96 and 100.

CHAPTER 7

1. *Life of Peter the Iberian*: translated R. Raabe, Leipzig, 1895, p. 57.
2. G. Khoury-Sarkis, "Réception d'un évêque syrien au vie siècle, *L'Orient syrien* 2 (1957): 137–84.
3. Leontius, *Life of John the Almsgiver* 9 and 45: translation N. Baynes and E. Dawes, Oxford, 1948, pp. 217–18 and 256; see V. Déroche, *Études sur Léontios de Néapolis*, Uppsala, 1995, pp. 146–53.
4. Severus of Antioch, *Letter* 1. 8: translation E.W. Brooks, *Select Letters of Severus*, London, 1903, p. 43.
5. Severus of Antioch, *Letter* 1. 9, p. 46.
6. *Life of Peter the Iberian*, p. 72.
7. Jacob of Sarug, *On the Spectacles of the Theater* 5: translation C. Moss, *Le Mouséon* 48 (1935), p. 108.
8. *The Chronicle of Joshua the Stylite* 30: translation W. Wright, Cambridge, 1882, pp. 20–1.
9. See R. Doran, *The Lives of Symeon Stylites*, Kalamazoo, Michigan, 1992.
10. Rufinus, *History of the Monks of Egypt* 11, *Patrologia Latina* 21: 431 D.
11. See P. Van den Ven, *La vie ancienne de S. Syméon Stylite le Jeune*, Brussels, 1970.
12. Ps.-Ephraim, *On Hermits and Desert-Dwellers* 497–505: translation J.P. Amar, *Ascetic Behavior in Greco-Roman Antiquity*, V.L. Wimbush (ed.), Minneapolis, 1990, p. 79.
13. W.E. Crum and H.G. Evelyn-White, *The Monastery of Epiphanius* 2, New York, 1926, pp. 194–5.
14. *Barsanuphe et Jean de Gaza: Correspondance*, no. 686: translation L. Regnault, Solesmes, 1972, p. 441.
15. John Lydus, *On the Magistracies of the Roman State* 1. 12: translation A.C. Bandy, Philadelphia, 1983, p. 25.
16. *Codex Justinianus* 1. 11. 10. 2: translation P.R. Coleman-Norton, *Roman State and Christian Church* 3, London, 1966, p. 1049.
17. *Constitution "Deo Auctore"* 2 (530): translation A. Watson, *The Digest of Justinian*, Philadelphia, 1985, p. xlv.
18. Procopius, *On the Buildings* 1. 1. 23: translation C. Mango, *The Art of the Byzantine Empire*, Englewood Cliffs, New Jersey, 1972, pp. 72–8.
19. Justinian, *Novella* 30. 11.2 (536). See the vivid contempo-

rary account of the wars by Procopius, *The Wars*: translation H.B. Dewing, *Procopius*, Loeb Classical Library 1–5, London, 1954.

20. Procopius, *Wars* 2. 22–3, Dewing 1, pp. 451–73. See an equally vivid account, extracted from the *Ecclesiastical History* of John of Ephesus by a later chronicler, in *Chronicon anonymum pseudo-Dionysianum*: translation R. Hespel, *Corpus Scriptorum Christianorum Orientalium* 507, Louvain, 1989, pp. 62–82.

21. See L. Conrad, Epidemic Disease in central Syria in the late sixth century, *Modern Greek and Byzantine Studies* 18 (1994): 12–58.

22. Procopius, *Wars* 7. 32.9, Dewing 4, p. 423.

23. Procopius, *The Secret History* 9–10, Dewing, Loeb Classical Library 6, pp. 103–29, and G.A. Williamson, Penguin, Harmondsworth, 1966, pp. 82–93; John of Ephesus, *Lives of the Eastern Saints* 13: translation E.W. Brooks, *Patrologia Orientalis* 17, p. 189.

24. Severus of Antioch, *Letter* 1. 63, p. 198.

25. John of Ephesus, *Lives of the Eastern Saints* 5, pp. 102–3.

26. John of Ephesus, *Lives of the Eastern Saints* 59, *Patrologia Orientalis* 18, p. 696.

27. See John Moschus, *The Spiritual Meadow*: translation J. Wortley, Kalamazoo, Michigan, 1992.

28. John of Ephesus, *Lives of the Eastern Saints* 12, p. 179.

29. *Les Sentences des Pères du Désert. Nouveau Recueil* 442: translation L. Regnault, Solesmes, 1970, p. 64.

CHAPTER 8

1. G.B. de Rossi, *Inscriptiones christianae urbis Romae* 2:1, Rome, 1888, p. 146.

2. Cassiodorus, *Institutes* 29. 1: translation L.W. Jones, *An Introduction to Divine and Human Readings*, New York, 1946, p. 131.

3. Cassiodorus, *de orthographia*, preface.

4. Gregory I, *Letter* 5. 46. A selection of the *Letters* of Gregory have been translated by J. Barmby, *Library of Nicene and Post-Nicene Fathers* 13.

5. Gregory I, *Homilies on the Gospels* 38. 12: translation D. Hurst, Kalamazoo, Michigan, 1990, p. 352.

6. John the Deacon, *Life of Gregory* 1. 10.

7. Gregory I, *Letter* 10. 14.
8. Eustratius, *Life of Euthychius* 80, *Patrologia Graeca* 86: 2365B.
9. John of Ephesus, *Ecclesiastical History* 2. 42: translation J. Payne-Smith, Oxford, 1860, p. 148.
10. Gregory I, *Letter* 1. 5: translation J. Barmby, p. 75.
11. Gregory I, *Moralia in Job* 17. 31: translation *A Library of Fathers* 21, Oxford, 1845, p. 299, citing *Job* 26. 25.
12. Gregory I, *Pastoral Care* 1. 1: translation H. Davis, *Ancient Christian Writers* 11, Westminster, Maryland, 1950, p. 21; also translation in *Nicene and Post-Nicene Fathers* 13, pp. 1–72.
13. Gregory I, *Letter* 1. 24.
14. Gregory I, *Moralia in Job* 9. 25, *A Library of Fathers* 18, Oxford, 1844, p. 515, citing *Job* 36. 5.
15. Gregory I, *Pastoral Care* 1. 11, p. 41.
16. Gregory I, *Pastoral Care* 1. 1, p. 22.
17. *The Rule of Saint Benedict* 5: translation T. Fry, Collegeville, Minnesota, 1980, p. 187.
18. Fructuosus of Braga, *Rule for the Monastery of Compludo* 3: translation C.W. Barlow, *Fathers of the Church* 63, Washington, D.C., 1969, p. 157.
19. *Rule of Benedict* 2, pp. 171–9.
20. John Moschus, *Spiritual Meadow* 151: translation J. Wortley, p. 124.
21. Gregory I, *Letter* 2. 17.
22. Gregory I, *Letter* 3. 29: translation J. Barmby, p. 129; *Homilies on the Gospels* 28. 3, p. 224.
23. Gregory I, *Dialogues* 3. 15: translation O.J. Zimmerman, *Fathers of the Church* 39, New York, 1959, p. 136.
24. Gregory I, *Letter* 9. 122: translation J. Barmby, *Nicene and Post-Nicene Fathers* 13:2, p. 34.
25. Gregory I, *Letter* 5. 36.
26. Gregory I, *Letter* 8. 30: translation J. Barmby, p. 240.
27. *The Earliest Life of Gregory the Great*, B. Colgrave (ed.), Cambridge, 1985.

CHAPTER 9

1. Gregory I, *Letter* 3. 61.
2. *Rule of Benedict* 73. 8, T. Fry (ed.), p. 297.
3. Columbanus, *Rules* 9: translation G.S.M. Walker, Dublin, 1970, p. 139.

4. Caesarius of Arles, *The Rule for Nuns* 56: translation M.C. McCarthy, Washington, D.C., 1960, p. 189.

5. Fortunatus of Braga, *General Rule* 9: translation C.W. Barlow, p. 190.

6. Gregory I, *Dialogues* 1. 4: translation O. J. Zimmerman, pp. 20–1.

7. Cassiodorus, *Institutes* 30: translation L.W. Jones, p. 133.

8. Philoxenus of Mabbug, *Letter to a Friend*: translation G. Olinder, *Acta Universitatis Gothoburgensis* 56:1, 1950, pp. 14*–15*.

9. John of Ephesus, *Lives of the Eastern Saints* 14, *Patrologia Orientalis* 17: 215.

10. C. Courtois and L. Leschi, *Tablettes Albertini*, Paris, 1952; Isabel Velázquez Soriano, *Las Pizarras visigódas*, Murcia, 1989.

11. S. Lancel, "La fin et la survie de la latinité en Afrique du Nord", *Revue des études latines* 59 (1981): 269–97.

12. E. Diehl, *Inscriptiones latinae christianae veteres* 1, no. 46, Zurich, 1970, p. 13.

13. A *Life* of Radegund was written both by Venantius Fortunatus and by the nun Baudovinia: translation J.A. McNamara and J. Halborg, *Sainted Women of the Dark Ages*, pp. 60–105, with Gregory of Tours, *Glory of the Confessors* 104, pp. 105–8.

14. Columbanus, *Letter* 1. 2 and 7, G.S.M. Walker, pp. 3 and 9.

15. Jonas of Bobbio, *Life of Columbanus* 1. 11: translation E. Peters, *Monks, Bishops and Pagans*, Philadelphia, 1981, p. 80.

16. Columbanus, *Sermon* 1. 5, p. 67.

17. F. Kelly, *A Guide to Irish Law*, Dublin, 1988, pp. 129–33 and P. O'Leary, Jeers and Judgements, *Cambridge Medieval Celtic Studies* 22 (1991): 15–29.

18. *Penitential of Cummean* 2. 18: translation L. Bieler, *Irish Penitentials*, p. 117.

19. *Life of Eligius* 1. 8, *Monumenta Germaniae Historica: Scriptores rerum merovingicarum* 4, Hanover, 1902, p. 675.

20. Jonas of Bobbio, *Life of Columbanus* 2. 11: translation J.A. McNamara and J.E. Halborg, *Sainted Women*, p. 162.

21. *Vision of Barontus*: translation J.N. Hillgarth, *Christianity and Paganism*, pp. 195–204.

22. Gregory I, *Dialogues* 4. 41, pp. 247–9.

23. Jacob of Sarug, *On the Offering for the Dead* 90: translation S. Landersdorfer, Munich, 1913, p. 305.

24. Gregory of Tours, *Glory of the Confessors* 64, pp. 70–1.

25. *The Rule of Patrick*: translation *Ériu* 1 (1904): 216–24.

26. *Life of Gertrude* preface, J.A. McNamara and J.E. Halborg, p. 223.

CHAPTER 10

1. Theophylact Simocatta, *Histories* 5. 10. 15: translation M. and J. Whitby, pp. 146–7.
2. Cosmas Indicopleustes, *Christian Topography* 2. 137–8 and 147–8, translation J.W. McCrindle, Hakluyt Society 98, London, 1897, pp. 47–51 and 71–3.
3. M. Mikawaya and A. Kollautz, "Ein Dokument zum Fernhandel zwischen Byzanz und China", *Byzantinische Zeitschrift* 77 (1984): 6–19 and P. Schreiner, "Eine chinesische Beschreibung Konstantinopels", *Istanbuler Mitteilungen* 39 (1989): 493–505.
4. Cosmas Indicopleustes, *Christian Topography* 2. 125, p. 24.
5. J.-P. Mahé, "Quadrivium et cursus d'études au viie siècle en Arménie", *Travaux et Mémoires* 10 (1987): 159–206, p. 196.
6. P'awstos Buzand, *Epic Histories* 3. 3: translation N.G. Garsoian, p. 84.
7. P'awstos Buzand, *Epic Histories* 6. 10, pp. 237–8.
8. Elishe, *History of Vardan and the Armenian War* 3: translation R.W. Thomson, Cambridge, Mass., 1982, pp. 105–9.
9. J.M. Fiey, *Communautés syriaques en Irak et Iran*, London, 1979.
10. Cassiodorus, *Institutes*, preface 1: translation L.W. Jones, p. 67.
11. A. Vööbus, *Statutes of the Schools of Nisibis*, Stockholm, 1962.
12. Thomas of Marga, *Book of the Governors* 2. 3: translation E.A. Wallis Budge, p. 120.
13. D. Chwolson, Syrische Grabschriften aus Semirjetschie, *Mémoires de l'Académie impériale de Saint Pétersbourg*, vii sér., 34 (1886), no. 4, pp. 14–15.
14. B. Flusin, *Saint Anastase le Perse* 2, Paris, 1992, pp. 95–127 and 170–2.
15. A. Mingana, "The Early Spread of Christianity in Central Asia and the Far East", *Bulletin of the John Rylands Library* 9 (1925): 363.
16. O. Hansen, *Berliner soghdische Texte* 2, Mainz: Akademie der Wissenschaften, 1954, no. 15, pp. 830–1; *Mongolian–English Dictionary*, F.D. Lessing (ed.), Bloomington, Indiana 1973, p. 59, s.v. *nom*.

17. F.S. Drake, "Nestorian Monasteries of the T'ang Dynasty", *Monumenta Serica* 2 (1936/7): 293–340; P.Y. Saeki, *The Nestorian Monument in China*, London, 1916.
18. I. Shahid, *Byzantium and the Arabs in the Sixth Century*, 2 vols., Washington, D.C., 1995.
19. I. Shahid, *The Martyrs of Najran*, Brussels, 1971.
20. Ibn Ishaq, *Sirat Rasul Allah: The Life of Muhammad* 171 and 228: translation A. Guillaume, Oxford/Lahore, 1955, pp. 121 and 158.
21. Sebéos, *Histoire d'Héraclius* 30: translation F. Macler, Paris, 1904, pp. 95–7.
22. *Chronicle of Séert* 106, *Patrologia Orientalis* 13, p. 626.

CHAPTER 11

1. Sebéos, *Histoire d'Héraclius* 32, pp. 104–5.
2. S. Bashear, "Apocalyptic and other materials on early Muslim-Byzantine wars", *Journal of the Royal Asiatic Society*, ser. 3, 1 (1991): 173–207.
3. Cited in A. Palmer, *The Seventh Century in West Syrian Chronicles*, Liverpool, 1993, p. xxi.
4. Theophanes, *Chronicle* AD 622: translation H. Turtledove, Philadelphia, 1982, pp. 34–5.
5. *Qur'an* 3. 110.
6. *History of Rabban Hormizd* 23: translation E.A. Wallis Budge, London, 1902, p. 150; *History of the Patriarchs of Alexandria*: translation B. Evetts, *Patrologia Orientalis* 5, p. 156.
7. F.E. Day, "Early Islamic and Christian Lamps", *Berytus* 7 (1942): 62–79, p. 78.
8. M.-F. Auzépy, "De la Palestine à Constantinople (viie–ixe siècles): Étienne le Sabaite et Jean Damascène", *Travaux et Mémoires* 12 (1994): 183–218, pp. 193–204.
9. B. Flusin, "Démons et sarrasins", *Travaux et Mémoires* 11 (1991): 381–409, pp. 404 and 407.
10. Dionysius of Tel-Mahre, *Chronicle* 42: translation A. Palmer, p. 141.
11. *History of the Patriarchs*, *Patrologia Orientalis* 5, pp. 122–5.
12. Bar-Hebraeus, *Chronography* [413]: translation E.A. Wallis Budge, Oxford, 1932, p. 356.
13. John bar Penkaye, *Riš Melle* 14 [141]: translation S. Brock, *Jerusalem Studies in Arabic and Islam* 9 (1987): 58.

14. Thomas of Marga, *Book of Governors* 5. 11: translation E.A. Wallis Budge, p. 508.
15. Timothy, *Letter* 13: translation O. Braun, *Corpus Scriptorum Christianorum Orientalium* 75: *Scriptores Syri* 31, Rome, 1915, p. 70.
16. Alvarus, *Indiculus luminosus* 35, J. Gil (ed.), *Corpus Scriptorum Muzarabicorum* 1, Madrid, 1973, pp. 314–15.
17. Jahiz, *Refutation of the Christians* 136: translation C. Pellat, London, 1969, p. 88.
18. S.H. Griffith, "Habib ibn Hidmah Abu Ra'itah, a Christian *mutakallim*", *Oriens christianus* 64 (1980): 161–201, p. 171.
19. A. Miquel, *La géographie humaine du monde musulman* 2, Paris, 1975, pp. 343–481.
20. Adomnán, *De locis sanctis* 1. 20. 20; 2. 12, 28. 3. 3: translation D. Meehan, Dublin, 1983, pp. 69, 83, 99 and 111.
21. Boniface, *Letter* 19 [27]: translation E. Emerton, p. 56.
22. *Hodoeporicon of Willibald* 4, in T.F.X. Noble and T. Head, *Soldiers of Christ*, University Park, Pennsylvania, 1995, pp. 153 and 159 and C.H. Talbot, *Anglo-Saxon Missionaries in Germany*, London, 1954, pp. 162 and 170.

CHAPTER 12

1. J. Werner, "Der Grabfund von Malaja Pereščepina und Kuvrat, Kagan der Bulgaren", *Bayerische Akademie der Wissenschaften: Abhandlungen* N.F. 91, Munich, 1984; *The Age of Sutton Hoo*, ed. M.O.H. Carver, pp. 235–340.
2. Adomnán, *Life of Columba* 1. 1 and 12: translation R. Sharpe, Penguin, Harmondsworth, 1995, pp. 110–11 and 121.
3. Adomnán, *The Law of Innocents*: translation J.N. Hillgarth, *Christianity and Paganism*, pp. 125–31.
4. *The Martyrology of Oengus* Prologue 165–9: translation W. Stokes, London, 1905, p. 24.
5. Cogitosus, *Life of Brigit* 32: translation S. Conolly and J.-M. Picard, *Journal of the Royal Society of Antiquaries of Ireland* 117 (1981): 25–6.
6. Muirchú, *Life of Patrick* 13 and 29: translation A.B.E. Hood, pp. 88 and 98.
7. Tirechán, *Life of Patrick* 2. 3.2: translation L. Bieler, *Patrician Texts in the Book of Armagh*, Dublin, 1979, p. 123.
8. *Rule of Cormac* 1: translation J. Strachan, *Ériu* 2 (1908): 63.

9. Adomnán, *Life of Columba* 1. 23, p. 129.
10. Gerald of Wales, *Topography of Ireland* 2. 71: translation J. O'Meara, Atlantic Heights, New Jersey, 1982, p. 71.
11. *Life of Enda* 2 and *Life of Colman* 8, C. Plummer (ed.), *Vitae Sanctorum Hiberniae* 1, Oxford 1910, pp. 60 and 261.
12. K. McCone, "Werewolves, Cyclopes, *Díberga* and *Fiánna*: Juvenile Delinquency in Early Ireland", *Cambridge Medieval Celtic Studies* 12 (1986): 1–22.
13. *Senchas Már*: translation *Ancient Laws of Ireland* 3, Dublin, 1873, pp. 33–5.
14. Adomnán, *Life of Columba* 2. 41, pp. 194–5.
15. R. Sharpe, "Hiberno-Latin *laicus*, Irish *láech* and the Devil's Men", *Ériu* 30 (1973): 75–92.
16. K. McCone, *Pagan Past and Christian Present in Early Irish Literature*, An Sagart, 1990.
17. *Senchas Már*, pp. 31–3.
18. Bede, *Ecclesiastical History of the English People* 1. 22–33: translation B. Colgrave and R.A.B. Mynors, Oxford, 1969, pp. 69–117, also translation L. Sherley-Price, Penguin, Harmondsworth, 1955: see I.N. Wood, "The Mission of Augustine of Canterbury to the English", *Speculum* 69 (1994): 1–17.
19. Bede, *Ecclesiastical History* 1. 32, p. 113.
20. Bede, *Ecclesiastical History* 1. 25, pp. 73–7.
21. Bede, *Ecclesiastical History* 1. 30, pp. 107–9.
22. Bede, *Ecclesiastical History* 2. 5, p. 151; *Laws of Ethelbert*: translation D. Whitelock, *English Historical Documents* 2, Oxford, 1955, pp. 357–61.
23. Bede, *Ecclesiastical History* 2. 13, pp. 183–6.
24. Bede, *Ecclesiastical History* 2. 16, p. 193.
25. Bede, *Ecclesiastical History* 2. 5, p. 153.
26. Bede, *Ecclesiastical History* 2. 15, p. 191.
27. Bede, *Ecclesiastical History* 3. 6, p. 231.
28. Bede, *Ecclesiastical History* 3. 2 and 12, pp. 217 and 251.

CHAPTER 13

1. Bede, *Life of Cuthbert* 8: translation J.F. Webb, Penguin, Harmondsworth, 1965, p. 83.
2. *Letter on the Death of Bede*: translation B. Colgrave and R.A.B. Mynors, p. 585; L. Sherley-Price, p. 20.
3. Bede, *Lives of the Abbots of Wearmouth and Jarrow* 5:

translation D.H. Farmer, Penguin, Harmondsworth, 1983, p. 189.

4. Barhadbshaba Arbaya, *The Foundation of the Schools of Nisibis*, *Patrologia Orientalis* 4, p. 64.

5. D. O'Cróinín, "Mo-sinnu moccu min and the computus of Bangor", *Peritia* 1 (1982): 281–95, p. 286.

6. Braulio of Saragossa, *Renotatio*, *Patrologia Latina* 81: 16D.

7. Mahé, Quadrivium et cursus d'études, *Travaux et Mémoires* 10 (1987): 159 and 166–70. The contribution of one such travelling polymath, Theodore of Tarsus, archbishop of Canterbury, has now been revealed by B. Bischoff and M. Lapidge, *Biblical Commentaries from the Canterbury School of Theodore and Hadrian*, Cambridge, 1994 and *Archbishop Theodore*, M. Lapidge (ed.), Cambridge, 1995.

8. *Fourth Council of Toledo* (633), canon 2, Vives, p. 188.

9. *Fourth Council of Toledo* canon 75, p. 218.

10. *Chronicle of 754* 51: translation K. Wolf, *Conquerors and Chroniclers of Early Medieval Spain*, Liverpool, 1990, p. 130.

11. *The Tain*: translation T. Kinsella, Oxford, 1970, p. 2.

12. Eddius Stephanus, *Life of Wilfrid* 24: translation Webb, p. 156.

13. Eddius Stephanus, *Life of Wilfrid* 11, p. 144.

14. Bede, *Ecclesiastical History* 3. 25, pp. 295–309; Eddius Stephanus, *Life of Wilfrid* 10, pp. 141–2.

15. Cummian, *On the Easter Controversy* 107–10, M. Walsh and D. O'Cróinín (eds), Toronto, 1988, p. 72.

16. Eddius Stephanus, *Life of Wilfrid* 22, pp. 154–5; *Martyrology of Oengus* Prologue 193, p. 25.

17. *Laws of Ine* Prologue 1: translation D. Whitelock, *English Historical Documents*, p. 364.

18. *Laws of Ine* 4, p. 364; Altfrid, *Life of Liutger* 6, *Monumenta Germaniae Historica: Scriptores* 2, Hanover, 1829, p. 406.

19. *Laws of Ine* 4, p. 365; Bede, *Letter to Archbishop Egbert* 7: translation Hillgarth, *Christianity and Paganism*, pp. 161–2.

20. Bede, *Life of Cuthbert* 3, p. 76.

21. Bede, *Life of Cuthbert* 9, pp. 84–5.

22. *Penitential of Theodore* 1. 15.1, A.W. Haddon and W. Stubbs (eds), *Councils and Ecclesiastical Documents* 3, Oxford, 1871, p. 189.

23. Bede, *Commentary on Acts* 4. 22: translation L.T. Martin, Kalamazoo, Michigan, 1989, p. 51.

24. Boniface, *Letter* 2 [10]: translation E. Emerton, p. 27.

25. Bede, *Ecclesiastical History* 4. 11, p. 367.

26. Bede, *Ecclesiastical History* 5. 12, pp. 489–99.
27. *Life of Guthlac* 46: translation B. Colgrave, Cambridge, 1956, p. 143.
28. Bede, *Ecclesiastical History* 4. 23, p. 409.
29. Bede, *Ecclesiastical History* 4. 24, pp. 415–22.
30. *The Dream of the Rood*: translation S.A.J. Bradley, *Anglo-Saxon Poetry*, pp. 160–3; *The Ruthwell Cross*, B. Cassidy (ed.), Princeton, New Jersey, 1992.

CHAPTER 14

1. *The Regions of the World* 42: translation V. Minorsky, Oxford, 1937, p. 157.
2. A. Cameron and J. Herrin, *Constantinople in the Early Eighth Century*, Leiden, 1984.
3. *Second Council of Nicaea*, G.D. Mansi (ed.), *Sacrorum Conciliorum nova collectio* 13: 345A: translation D.J. Sahas, *Icon and Logos*, Toronto, 1988, p. 161.
4. *Life of Leo V, Patrologia Graeca* 108: 1028 and 1032.
5. *Letter of Michael II and Theophilus to Louis the Pious*: translation C. Mango, *The Art of the Byzantine Empire*, Englewood Cliffs, New Jersey, 1972, pp. 157–8.
6. John of Damascus, *On the Divine Images*: translation D. Anderson, Crestwood, New York, 1980; Nicephorus, *Discours contre les iconoclastes*: translation M.J. Mondzain-Baudinet, Paris, 1989.
7. *Life of Symeon the Younger* 118, C. Mango, p. 134.
8. H. Maguire, "Magic and the Christian Image", *Byzantine Magic*, H. Maguire (ed.), Washington, D.C., 1995, pp. 51–71.
9. *Council in Trullo* 73: translation H.R. Percival, *Library of the Nicene and Post-Nicene Fathers* 14, p. 398.
10. *Council in Trullo* 82, p. 401.
11. John of Damascus, *On Images* 1. 22, pp. 30–1.
12. V. Déroche, Léontios de Néapolis, *Apologie contre les juifs, Travaux et Mémoires* 12 (1994): 43–104.
13. *Qur'an* 26: 71–4; see S.H. Griffith, Theodore abu Qurra's Arabic Text on the Christian Practice of Venerating Images, pp. 66–8.
14. O. Grabar, *The Mediation of Ornament*, Princeton, New Jersey, 1992.
15. M. Rosen-Ayalon, "The First Mosaic discovered in Ramla",

Israel Exploration Journal 26 (1976): 104–19.
16. M. Piccirillo, *The Mosaics of Jordan*, Amman, 1993, pp. 41–2.
17. Dionysius of Tel-Mahre, *Chronicle* 89: translation A. Palmer, pp. 169–70.
18. [Iconoclast] *Council of Hiereia* (754), cited at *Second Council of Nicaea* 260A: translation D.J. Sahas, p. 90 and C. Mango, p. 166.
19. *Council of Hiereia* 264C, D.J. Sahas, p. 93 and C. Mango p. 167.
20. Pseudo-Dionysius, *The Celestial Hierarchy* 2. 1: translation C. Luibheid, London, 1987, p. 148.
21. *Life of Andrew the Fool* 17. 132, *Patrologia Graeca* 111: 780C; Barsanuphius, *Correspondance* 416: translation L. Regnault, p. 290.
22. *Second Council of Nicaea* 240C and 252BC, D.J. Sahas, pp. 75 and 84.
23. Photius, *Homily* 17. 6: translation C. Mango, *The Homilies of Photius*, Washington, D.C., 1958, p. 295 and *Art of the Byzantine Empire*, p. 190.
24. John of Damascus, *On Images*, Testimonies, p. 39.
25. *Second Council of Nicaea* 256C, D.J. Sahas, p. 88.
26. Zosima the Deacon: translation G.P. Majeska, *Russian Travellers to Constantinople in the Fourteenth and Fifteenth Centuries*, Washington, D.C., 1984, p. 182.
27. *Libri Carolini*, L. Bastgen (ed.), *Monumenta Germaniae Historica: Legum Sectio 3; Concilia* 3, Hanover, 1924; selections translation C. Davis-Weyer, *Early Medieval Art*, Toronto, 1986, pp. 10–103; see W. von der Steinen, Karl der Grosse und die Libri Carolini, *Neues Archiv* 39 (1931): 207–80, pp. 250–1.

CHAPTER 15

1. Gottschalk, *Responsa* 168–9, C. Lambot (ed.), Louvain, 1945, p. 168.
2. *Annals of the Frankish Kingdom*: translation P.E. Dutton, *Carolingian Civilization*, Peterborough, Ontario, 1993, pp. 11–12.
3. A. Miquel, *Géographie humaine du monde musulman* 2, p. 360.
4. Arbeo of Freising, *Life of Saint Emmeran* 41, *Monumenta Germaniae Historica: Scriptorum rerum merovingicarum* (ed.) 6, Hanover, 1913, p. 518.
5. J. Werner, *Das alemannische Fürstengrab von Wittislingen*, Munich, 1950: *Life of Corbinian* 16 and 29, *Scriptorum rerum*

merovingicarum, 6, pp. 579 and 595.

6. Bede, *Ecclesiastical History* 5. 10, pp. 481–3; *Life of Saint Lebuin* 6, translation C.H. Talbot, *The Anglo-Saxon Missionaries in Germany*, London, 1954, p. 232.

7. Aethicus Ister, *Cosmographia* 2, O. Prinz (ed.), Munich, 1993, pp. 115–16.

8. *Life of Saint Amandus* 13–21: translation J.N. Hillgarth, *Christianity and Paganism*, pp. 143–6.

9. Fredegar, *Chronicle* 4. 68 and 74: translation J.M. Wallace-Hadrill, Oxford, 1960, pp. 56–7 and 63.

10. Alcuin, *Life of Willibrord*, in T.F.X. Noble and T. Head, *Soldiers of Christ*, University Park, Pennsylvania, 1995, pp. 191–211 and in Talbot, *Anglo-Saxon Missionaries*.

11. *Life of Wulfram* 8–9, *Monumenta Germaniae Historica*; *Scriptores rerum merovingicarum* (ed.) 5, Hanover, 1910, p. 667.

12. F. Thieuws, "Landed property and manorial organization in North Austrasia", *Images of the Past*, N. Roymans and F. Thieuws (eds), Amsterdam, 1991, pp. 299–407 and M. Costambeys, "An Austrasian aristocracy on the north Frankish frontier", *Early Medieval Europe* 3 (1994): 39–62.

13. Boniface, *de grammatica*, R. Rau (ed.), Darmstadt, 1968, pp. 360–8.

14. Boniface, *Letters* 22 [30], 53 [65] and 62 [78]: translation E. Emerton, pp. 60, 121 and 136; a selection of Boniface's *Letters* is also in Talbot, *Anglo-Saxon Missionaries*.

15. Boniface, *Letter* 36 [46], p. 75.

16. Boniface, *Letter* 85 [105], p. 178.

17. Boniface, *Letter* 15 [23], pp. 48–50.

18. Boniface, *Letter* 51 [63], p. 115.

19. Boniface, *Letter* 51 [63], p. 116.

20. Boniface, *Letter* 52 [64], p. 120.

21. Willibald, *Life of Boniface* 8, *Soldiers of Christ*, p. 136 and Talbot, *Anglo-Saxon Missionaries*, pp. 57–8.

22. Boniface, *Letter* 70 [86], pp. 158–9.

23. Boniface, *Letter* 16 [24], p. 51.

24. Boniface, *Letters* 54 [68] and 64 [80], pp. 122 and 144.

25. Willibald, *Life of Boniface* 6, *Soldiers of Christ*, p. 124 and Talbot, p. 42.

26. Willibald, *Life of Boniface* 6, *Soldiers of Christ*, pp. 126–7 and Talbot, *Anglo-Saxon Missionaries*, pp. 45–6.

27. Boniface, *Letter* 64 [80], p. 147; see J. Carey, Ireland and the

Antipodes, *Speculum* 64 (1989): 1–10.
28. *Roman Synod of 745* in Boniface, *Letter* 47 [59], pp. 101–2.
29. *Roman Synod of 745*, p. 103; Jonas of Bobbio, *Life of Columbanus* 1. 6, E. Peters, p. 75.
30. *Roman Synod of 745*, pp. 103–4.
31. *Roman Synod of 745*, p. 101; *Hodoeporicon of Willibald* 1, *Soldiers of Christ*, p. 146 and C.H. Talbot, p. 155.
32. *Roman Synod of 745*, p. 101; Bede, *Life of Cuthbert* 9: translation J.F. Webb, p. 84.
33. *Roman Synod of 745*, p. 101.
34. Boniface, *Letter* 40 [50], p. 82.
35. Boniface, *Letter* 40 [50], p. 79.
36. *Index of Superstitions*: translation J.T. McNeill and H.A. Gamer, *Medieval Handbooks of Penance*, New York, 1990, pp. 419–21.
37. *Hodoeporicon of Willibald*, preface, *Soldiers of Christ*, p. 144 and C.H. Talbot, p. 153.
38. *Capitulary concerning the parts of Saxony* 7, 8 and 11: translation H.R. Loyn and J. Percival, *The Reign of Charlemagne*, London, 1975, p. 52.
39. I.N. Wood, "Missionary Hagiography in the Eighth and Ninth Centuries", *Ethnogenese und Überlieferung*, K. Brunner and B. Merta (eds), Vienna, 1994, pp. 189–99.

CHAPTER 16

1. Einhard, *Life of Charlemagne* 13: translation L. Thorpe, Penguin, Harmondsworth, 1969, p. 67.
2. Alcuin, *Letter* 8 [121]: translation S. Alcott, *Alcuin of York*, York, 1974, p. 11.
3. *Liber Pontificalis* 98. 23–4: translation R. Davis, Liverpool, 1992, pp. 190–1 and H.R. Loyn and J. Percival, pp. 24–6; *Royal Annals*, H.R. Loyn and J. Percival, pp. 41–4.
4. Einhard, *Life of Charlemagne* 22, pp. 76–7.
5. Einhard, *Life of Charlemagne* 31, p. 84.
6. M. McCormick, "The Liturgy of War in the Early Middle Ages: Crisis, Litanies and the Carolingian Monarchy", *Viator* 15 (1984): 1–23.
7. *Capitulary of Herstal* (779) c.16, *Monumenta Germaniae Historica*: *Legum Sectio* 2: *Capitularia* 1, Hanover, 1883, p. 51 translation P.D. King, *Charlemagne*, Kendal, Cumbria, 1987,

p. 204; *Capitulary of the Missi at Aachen* (810) *c*.11 and 17, *Capitularia* 1, p. 153.

8. *Royal Annals (Vienna Manuscript)* AD 802, H.R. Loyn and J. Percival, p. 45.
9. *2 Chronicles* 34: 30.
10. Alcuin, *Letter* 125 [244], p. 132.
11. Alcuin, *Letter* 29 [19], p. 40.
12. Alcuin, *Letter* 128 [295], p. 134.
13. Alcuin, *On Scribes*: translation P. Godman, *Poetry of the Carolingian Renaissance*, London, 1985, p. 139; see D. Ganz, "The Preconditions of Carolingian Minuscule", *Viator* 18 (1987): 23–43.
14. *Admonitio Generalis* (789) *c*.72, *Capitularia* 1, p. 60, P.D. King, p. 217.
15. *Admonitio Generalis*, preface, *Capitularia* 1, p. 54,   P.D. King, p. 209.
16. *Admonitio Generalis c*.78, *Capitularia* 1, p. 60, P.D. King, p. 218; J.G. O'Keefe, Cáin Domnaig, *Ériu* 2 (1905): 189–214.
17. *Annals of Fulda* AD 847: translation T. Reuter, Manchester, 1992, pp. 26–7.
18. *Council of Tours* (813), canon 17, *Monumenta Germaniae Historica: Concilia* 2, Hanover, 1906, p. 288.
19. *General Capitulary for the missi* (802) *c*.2: translation H.R. Loyn and J. Percival, pp. 74–5.
20. Ghaerbald of Liège, *Second Diocesan Statute*, C. de Clercq (ed.), Louvain, 1936, pp. 357–62; see J. Lynch, *Godparents and Kinship*.
21. *Council on the Danube* (796), *Concilia* 2, pp. 172–6.
22. Alcuin, *Letters* 56 and 57 [110 and 111], pp. 72–4.
23. Charlemagne, *Letter to Ghaerbald*, *Capitularia* 1, p. 241.
24. *Frankish and Old Saxon Baptismal Oaths*, H. D. Schlosser (ed.), *Althochdeutsche Literatur*, Frankfurt-am-Main, 1970, p. 212; on the ever present danger and social basis of pagan revivals, see E.J. Goldberg, "The Saxon *Stellinga* Reconsidered", *Speculum* 70 (1995): 467–501.
25. C. Edwards, "German vernacular literature", *Carolingian Renewal*, R. McKitterick (ed.), Cambridge, 1994, pp. 141–70.
26. Agobard of Lyons, *On Hail and Thunder*, *Patrologia Latina* 104: 147–58 and L. Van Acker, *Corpus Christianorum: series medievalis*, Turnhout, 1981, translation P.E. Dutton, *Carolingian Civilization*, pp. 189–91.
27. Agobard, *On the illusions of miracles* 11, Van Acker, p. 242.
28. See C. Chazelle, "Matter, Spirit and Image in the *Libri Carolini*",

Recherches augustiniennes 21 (1986): 163–84; T.F.X. Noble, "Tradition and Learning in Search of Ideology: the *Libri Carolini*", *"The Gentle Voices of Teachers"*: Aspects of Learning in the Carolingian Age, R.E. Sullivan (ed.), Columbus, Ohio, 1995, pp. 227–60.
29. von den Steinen, *Neues Archiv* 39 (1931): 246.
30. *Libri Carolini* 1. 15, Bastgen (ed.), p. 35.
31. *Libri Carolini* 4. 21, p. 213.
32. *Libri Carolini* 2. 30, p. 93.
33. *The Wish of Manchán of Liath*: translation K.H. Jackson, *A Celtic Miscellany*, Penguin, Harmondsworth, 1971, p. 280.
34. *Libri Carolini* 2. 30, p. 98.
35. *Libri Carolini* 4, 5 and 40, pp. 181 and 211.

CHAPTER 17

1. S. Coupland, "Money and Coinage under Louis the Pious", *Francia* 17: 1 (1990): 23–34.
2. Paschasius Radbertus, *Epistolae variorum* 12; see I.N. Wood, *Christianization of Scandinavia*, pp. 64–6.
3. Greenlanders' Saga 4: translation G. Jones, *The Norse Atlantic Saga*, Oxford, 1986, p. 196.
4. *Norges Inskrifter* 5, Oslo, 1960, no. 449, see *Christianization of Scandinavia*, pp. 73–4.
5. Ermoldus Nigellus, *The Paintings at Ingelheim* 261–84: translation P. Godman, p. 255.
6. Rimbert, *Life of Anskar* 30: translation C.H. Robinson, London, 1921, pp. 98–100.
7. Ari Thorgilsson, *Book of the Icelanders* 7: translation Ithaca, New York, 1930, p. 66.
8. D. Dumville, "The Anglian Collection of Royal Genealogies", *Anglo-Saxon England* 5 (1976): 23–50.
9. *Lebor Gabála Erenn: The Book of the Taking of Ireland*: translation R.A.S. Macalister, Dublin, 1941, p. 165.
10. Einhard, *Life of Charlemagne* 29: translation L. Thorpe, p. 82.
11. *Anglo-Saxon Chronicle* AD 757: translation D. Whitelock, *English Historical Documents* 1, p. 163; see D. Whitelock, *The Audience of Beowulf*, Oxford, 1951.
12. R. Frank, "Germanic Legend in Old English Literature", *Cambridge Companion to Old English Literature*, M. Godden and M. Lapidge (eds), Cambridge, 1991, pp. 88–106.

13. Rudolf of Fulda, *Translatio Sancti Alexandri*, *Monumenta Germaniae Historica: Scriptores* 2, Berlin, 1829, p. 673.
14. *Sturlunga Saga* 31: translation J. McGrew, New York, 1970, p. 108.
15. Snorri Sturluson, *Saga of Olaf Tryggvason* 64, *Heimskringla*: translation L. Hollander, Austin, Texas, 1964, p. 204.
16. *Eirik the Red's Saga* 3: translation L.W. Jones, p. 214.
17. Burchard of Worms, *Corrector* 5. 65: translation J.T. McNeill and H.M. Gamer, *Handbooks of Penance*, p. 330.
18. *Vienna Spell*, H.D. Schlosser (ed.), *Althochdeutsche Literatur*, p. 260.
19. *Aecerbot: For Unfruitful Land*: translation S.A.J. Bradley, *Anglo-Saxon Poetry*, pp. 545–7.
20. Muirchú, *Life of Patrick* 29, A.B.E. Hood, p. 98.
21. *The Tain*: translation T. Kinsella, p. 2.
22. *Táin Bó Cúalnge from the Book of Leinster*, C. O'Rahilly (ed.), Dublin, 1970, p. 272.
23. *Beowulf* 1347–1352: translation M. Alexander, Penguin, Harmondsworth, 1973, p. 93.
24. *Book of Monsters*, M. Haupt (ed.), *Opuscula* 2, Leipzig, 1879, p. 223; see Whitelock, *Audience of Beowulf*, p. 46.
25. *Beowulf* 104–10, p. 54.
26. Ananias of Shirak in J.R. Russell, "Dragons in Armenia", *Journal of Armenian Studies* 5 (1990/91): 3–19.
27. Moses Khorenats'i, *History of the Armenians* 1. 61: translation R.W. Thomson, Cambridge, Mass., 1978, p. 204.
28. *Lorsch Spell*, Schlosser, *Althochdeutsche Literatur*, p. 260.
29. *Revue des études anciennes* 3 (1901): 273.
30. F. Harmer, *Documents of the Ninth and Tenth Centuries*, Cambridge, 1914, pp. 13–15.
31. *Life of Constantine the Philosopher* 10, F. Grivec and F. Tomšić (eds), Zagreb, 1960, pp. 116–17.
32. D. Obolensky, *The Byzantine Commonwealth*, London, 1971, pp. 69–101 and 134–63; I. Ševčenko, "Religious Missions seen from Byzantium", *Harvard Ukrainian Studies* 22/23 (1988/89): 6–27.
33. *Russian Primary Chronicle*: translation S.H. Cross and O.P. Sherbowitz-Wetzor, Cambridge, Mass., 1953, p. 111.
34. Nicholas I, *Answers to the Bulgarians* 59, *Patrologia Latina* 119; 1002 AB; compare Photius, *Letter* 8, D.S. White and J.R. Burgess, *The Patriarch and the Prince*, Brookline, Mass., 1982, pp. 39–79.

Selected Bibliography

CHAPTER 1

Barrett, J.C. et al. (eds), *Barbarians and Romans in North-West Europe*, Oxford, 1989.
Collins, R., *Early Medieval Europe*, New York, 1991.
Hedeager, L., *Iron Age Societies. From Tribe to State in Northern Europe, 500 BC to AD 700*, Oxford, 1992.
Pohl, W., *Die Awaren. Ein Steppenvolk in Mitteleuropa, 567–822 n. Chr.*, Munich, 1988.
Todd, M., *The Northern Barbarians, 100 BC–AD 300*, Oxford, 1975.
Whittaker, C.R., *Frontiers of the Roman Empire: A Social and Economic Study*, Baltimore, 1994.

CHAPTER 2

Bagnall, R., *Egypt in Late Antiquity*, Princeton, 1993.
Brown, P., *The World of Late Antiquity. From Marcus Aurelius to Muhammad*, London, 1971; 1989.
Cameron, A., *The Later Roman Empire*, London, 1993.
Lane Fox, R., *Pagans and Christians*, New York, 1987.
Mitchell, S., *Anatolia. Land, Men and Gods*, vol. ii. *The Rise of the Church*, Oxford, 1993.
Strobel, K., *Das Imperium Romanum im "3. Jahrhundert." Modell einer historischen Krise?*, Stuttgart, 1993.

CHAPTER 3

Barnes, T.D., *Athanasius and Constantius. Theology and Politics in the Constantinian Empire*, Cambridge, Mass., 1993.
Brown, P., *Power and Persuasion in Late Antiquity. Towards a Christian Empire*, Madison, 1992.
Brown, P., *Augustine of Hippo*, London, 1967.
Cameron, A., *Christianity and the Rhetoric of Empire. The Development of Christian Discourse*, Berkeley, 1991.
Elm, S., *"Virgins of God." The Making of Asceticism in Late Antiquity*, Oxford, 1994.
Fögen, M.T., *Die Enteignung der Wahrsager. Studien zum kaiserlichen Wissensmonopol in der Spätantike*, Frankfurt, 1993.
Fowden, G., *Empire to Commonwealth. Consequences of Monotheism in Late Antiquity*, Princeton, 1993.
Markus, R., *The End of Ancient Christianity*, Cambridge, 1990.
McLynn, N.B., *Ambrose of Milan. Church and Court in a Christian Capital*, Berkeley, 1994.
Sivan, H., *Ausonius of Bordeaux. Genesis of a Gallic Aristocracy*, London, 1993.
Stancliffe, C., *St. Martin and his Hagiographer. History and Miracle in Sulpicius Severus*, Oxford, 1983.
Thélamon, F., *Paiens et chrétiens au ive. siècle*, Paris, 1981.

CHAPTER 4

Cameron, A., *The Mediterranean World in Late Antiquity:* AD *395–600*, London, 1993.
Drinkwater, J. and Elton, H. (eds), *Fifth Century Gaul. A Crisis of Identity?*, Cambridge, 1992.
Hillgarth, J.N., *Christianity and Paganism, 530–750. The Conversion of Western Europe*, Philadelphia, 1986.
Lyman, J.R., *Christology and Cosmology*, Oxford, 1993.
Mathisen, R.W., *Ecclesiastical Factionalism and Religious Controversy in Fifth-Century Gaul*, Washington, D.C., 1989.
Muhlberger, S., *The Fifth-Century Chronicles. Prosper, Hydatius and the Gallic Chronicle of 452*, Liverpool, 1990.
Pelikan, J., *The Emergence of the Catholic Tradition (100–600)*, Chicago, 1971.
Rousseau, P., *Ascetics, Authority and the Church in the Age of Jerome and Cassian*, Oxford, 1978.

CHAPTER 5

Lebecq, S., *Les origines franques, ve.–ixe. siècle*, Paris, 1990.
Munro-Hay, S., *Aksum. An African Civilisation of Late Antiquity*, Edinburgh, 1991.
Thomas, C., *Christianity in Roman Britain to* AD *500*, Berkeley, 1981.
Wood, I.N., *Merovingian Kingdoms, 450–751*, London, 1994.

CHAPTER 6

Brown, P., *The Cult of the Saints. Its Rise and Function in Latin Christianity*, Chicago, 1981.
Goffart, W., *The Narrators of Barbarian History (*AD *550–800)*, Princeton, 1988.
Klingshirn, W.E., *Caesarius of Arles. The Making of a Christian Community in Late Antique Gaul*, Cambridge, 1994.
Les fonctions des saints dans le monde occidental (iie.–xiiie. siècle). Collection de l'École française de Rome, 149, Rome, 1991.
Nie, G. de, *Views from a Many-Windowed Tower. Studies of Imagination in the Works of Gregory of Tours*, Amsterdam, 1987.
Rousselle, A., *Croire et guérir. La foi en Gaule dans l'Antiquité tardive*, Paris, 1990.
Van Dam, R., *Saints and their Miracles in Late Antique Gaul*, Princeton, 1993.
Wood, I.N., *Gregory of Tours*, Bangor, 1994.

CHAPTER 7

Binns, J., *Ascetics and Ambassadors of Christ. The Monasteries of Palestine, 314–641*, Oxford, 1994.
Flusin, B., *Miracle et histoire dans l'oeuvre de Cyrille de Scythopolis*, Paris, 1983.
Frend, W.H.C., *The Rise of the Monophysite Church*, Cambridge, 1972.
Hirschfeld, Y., *The Judaean Desert Monasteries in the Byzantine Period*, New Haven, 1992.
Harvey, S.A., *Asceticism and Society in Crisis. John of Ephesus and the Lives of the Eastern Saints*, Berkeley, 1990.

Honoré, T., *Tribonian*, London, 1978.
Palmer, A., *Monk and Mason on the Tigris Frontier*, Cambridge, 1990.
Roueché, C., *Performers and Partisans at Aphrodisias in the Roman and Late Roman Periods*, London, 1993.
Tate, G., *Les campagnes de la Syrie du Nord du iie. au viie. siècle*, Paris, 1992.

CHAPTER 8

Brown, T.S., *Gentlemen and Officers. Imperial Administration and Aristocratic Power in Byzantine Italy* AD *550–800*, Rome, 1984.
Chadwick, H., *Boethius. The Consolations of Music, Logic, Theology and Philosophy*, Oxford, 1981.
Dagens, C., *Grégoire le Grand. Culture et expérience chrétienne*, Paris, 1977.
Markus, R., *From Augustine to Gregory the Great*, London, 1983.
O'Donnell, J.J., *Cassiodorus*, 1979.
Straw, C., *Gregory the Great. Perfection in Imperfection*, Berkeley, 1988.
Wickham, C., *Early Medieval Italy. Central Power and Local Society, 400–1000*, London, 1981.

CHAPTER 9

Clarke, H.B. and Brennan, M. (eds), *Columbanus and Merovingian Monasticism*, Oxford, 1981.
Frantzen, A.J., *The Literature of Penance in Anglo-Saxon England*, New Brunswick, 1983.
Muschiol, G., *Famula Dei: Zur Liturgie in merowingischen Frauenklöstern*, Münsten, 1994.
Paxton, F.S., *Christianizing Death. The Creation of a Ritual Process in Early Medieval Europe*, Ithaca, 1990.
Riché, P., *Éducation et culture dans l'Occident barbare, vie.–viiie siècles*, Paris, 1962: English translation, *Education and Culture in the Barbarian West*, Columbia, South Carolina, 1976.

CHAPTER 10

s.v. "Christianity", in Yarshater, E. (ed.), *Encyclopaedia Iranica*, vol. v, Costa Mesa, Calif., 1991.

Garsoian, N. et al. (eds), *East of Byzantium: Syria and Armenia in the Formative Period*, Washington, D.C., 1982.
Garsoian, N.G., *The Epic Histories Attributed to P'awstos Buzand*, Cambridge, Mass., 1989.
Izutsu, T., *God and Man in the Koran*, Tokyo, 1964.
Kister, M.J., *Studies on Jahiliyya and Early Islam*, London, 1980.
Monneret de Villard, U., *Le Leggende orientali dei Magi evangelici*, Rome, 1952.
Wolska, W., *La Topographie chrétienne de Cosmas Indicopleustes*, Paris, 1962.
Yarshater, E. (ed.), *The Cambridge History of Iran*, vol. III. *The Seleucid, Parthian and Sasanian Periods*, Cambridge, 1983.

CHAPTER 11

Cameron, A. and Conrad, L.I., *The Byzantine and Early Islamic Near East*. vol. I: *Problems in the Literary Source Material*, Princeton, 1989.
Gervers M. and Bikhazi, R.J. (eds), *Conversion and Continuity. Indigenous Christian Communities in Islamic Lands*, Toronto, 1990.
Griffith, S.H., Theodore abu Qurrah's Arabic text on the Christian Practice of Venerating Images, *Journal of the American Oriental Society*, 105, 1985.
King, G.R.D. and Cameron, A. (eds), *The Byzantine and Early Islamic Near East*, vol. II. *Land Use and Settlement Patterns*, Princeton, 1994.
Putman, H., *L'Église et l'Islam sous Timothée I (780–823)*, Beirut, 1975.
Raby, J. and Johns, J. (eds), *Bayt al-Maqdis. Abd al-Malik's Jerusalem*, Oxford, 1992.
Rosenthal, F., *The Classical Heritage in Islam*, Berkeley, 1975.

CHAPTER 12

Bassett, S. (ed.), *The Origins of the Anglo-Saxon Kingdoms*, London, 1989.
Campbell, J. (ed.), *The Anglo-Saxons*, Oxford, 1982.
Carver, M.O.H. (ed.), *The Age of Sutton Hoo. The Seventh Century in Northwestern Europe*, Woodbridge, Suffolk, 1992.

Hauck, K., *Die Goldbrakteaten der Völkerwanderungszeit*, Munich, 1985.
Hughes, K., *The Church in Early Irish Society*, London, 1966.
MacNeill, M., *The Festival of Lughnasa*, Dublin, 1982.
Mayr-Harting, H., *The Coming of Christianity to Anglo-Saxon England*, University Park, Penn., 1991.

CHAPTER 13

Blair, J. and Sharpe, R. (eds), *Pastoral Care before the Parish*, Leicester, 1992.
Collins, R., *Early Medieval Spain. Unity in Diversity*, London, 1983.
Fontaine, J., *Isidore de Séville et la culture classique dans l'Espagne wisigothique*, Paris, 1983.
Henderson, G., *From Durrow to Kells: The Insular Gospel Books*, New York, 1987.
Hillgarth, J.N., *Visigothic Spain, Byzantium and Ireland*, London, 1985.
Hodges, R. and Whitehouse, D., *Mohammed, Charlemagne and the Origins of Europe*, Ithaca, 1983.

CHAPTER 14

Belting, H., *Bild und Kult. Eine Geschichte des Bildes vor der Zeitalter der Kunst*, Munich, 1990: English translation, *Likeness and Presence: A History of the Image before the Era of Art*, Chicago, 1994.
Brubaker, L., Byzantine art in the ninth century: theory, practice and culture, *Byzantine and Modern Greek Studies*, 13, 1989.
Cameron, A., The language of images: the rise of icons and Christian representation, in Wood, D. (ed.), *The Church and the Arts. Studies in Church History* 28, Oxford, 1992.
Haldon, J.F., *Byzantium in the Seventh Century. The Transformation of a Culture*, Cambridge, 1990.
Herrin, J., *The Formation of Christendom*, Princeton, 1987.
Maguire, H., *Earth and Ocean. The Terrestrial World in Early Byzantine Art*, University Park, Penn., 1987.

CHAPTER 15

s.v. "Christentum der Bekehrungszeit," in Hoops, J. (ed.), *Reallexikon der germanischen Altertumskunde*, vol. IV, Berlin, 1981.
Lebecq, S., *Marchands et Navigateurs du Haut Moyen-Âge*, Lille, 1983.
Schaferdiek, H. (ed.), *Kirchengeschichte als Missionsgeschichte*. vol. II. *Die Kirche des fruhen Mittelalters*, Munich, 1978.
Wallace-Hadrill, J.M., *The Frankish Church*, Oxford, 1983.

CHAPTER 16

Banniard, M., *Viva voce. Communication écrite et communication orale du ive. au ixe. siècle en Occident latin*, Paris, 1992.
Bullough, D., *The Age of Charlemagne*, New York, 1965.
Chelini, J., *L'Aube du Moyen Âge. Naissance de la Chrétienté occidentale. La vie religieuse des laics dans l'Europe carolingien (750–900)*, Paris, 1991.
Lynch, J.H., *Godparents and Kinship in Early Medieval Europe*, Princeton, 1986.
McKitterick, R. (ed.), *The Uses of Literacy in Early Medieval Europe*, Cambridge, 1990.
McKitterick, R. (ed.), *Carolingian Culture: Emulation and Innovation*, Cambridge, 1994.
Wright, R., *Late Latin and Early Romance in Spain and Carolingian France*, Liverpool, 1982.

CHAPTER 17

Flint, V.I.J., *The Rise of Magic in Early Medieval Europe*, Princeton, 1991.
Gurevich, A., *Historical Anthropology of the Middle Ages*, Chicago, 1992.
Obolensky, D., *The Byzantine Commonwealth*, London, 1971.
Richter, M., *The Formation of the Medieval West. Studies in the Oral Culture of the Barbarians*, Dublin, 1994.
Sawyer, B., Sawyer, P. and Wood, I. (eds), *The Christianization of Scandinavia*, Alingsas, 1987.
Wormald, P., Bede, "Beowulf" and the conversion of the Anglo-Saxon aristocracy, in Farrell, R.T. (ed.), *Bede and Anglo-Saxon England*, Oxford, 1978.

Chronologies

ROMAN EMPIRE

238–270+ Crisis in Roman empire
258 Execution of Cyprian of Carthage
284–305 Diocletian
303 Great Persecution
306–337 Constantine
312 Battle of Milvian Bridge
325 Council of Nicaea
327 Foundation of Constantinople
337–361 Constantius II

WESTERN EMPIRE, GAUL

335–397 Martin of Tours
342–411 Melania the Elder
354–430 Augustine
        387 Conversion
        395 Bishop of Hippo
        397 *Confessions*
        413+ *City of God*
355–431 Paulinus of Nola
360–435 John Cassian
363–425 Sulpicius Severus
        396 *Life of Martin*
400 Honoratus founds Lérins
400–470 Hydatius
406 Major raids in Gaul
407–437 Germanus, bishop of Auxerre
410 Sack of Rome
413+ Pelagian Controversy

415	John Cassian at Marseilles
	420 *Institutes*
	426 *Conferences*
416	Orosius, *History against the Pagans*
418	Visigoths settled at Bordeaux
429–439	Vandal conquest of Africa
430–449	Hilary, bishop of Arles
443	Burgundians settled at Vienne
451	Attila raids Gaul
455	Hydatius, *Chronicle*
460+	Perpetuus, bishop of Tours
430–480	Sidonius Apollinaris
	470 Bishop of Clermont
481–511	Clovis
	486 At Soissons
490+	*Lex Salica*
	500+ Baptism
502–542	Caesarius, bishop of Arles
	512 *Rule* for Caesaria
506	Alaric II issues *Breviarium*
	Council of Agde
507	Battle of Vouillé
520–587	Radegund
	561 Founds Sainte Croix at Poitiers
538–594	Gregory of Tours
	573–594 Bishop of Tours
566/7	Venantius Fortunatus comes to Gaul
590–610	Columbanus at Luxeuil
603–645	Burgundofara
623–638	Dagobert
641–660	Eligius, bishop of Noyon
641–684	Audoenus, bishop of Rouen
658	Death of Gertrude of Nivelles
670+	Rise of *sceattas* as coinage
679	*Vision of Barontus*
680+	Amandus preaches to Basques
687–714	Pippin of Herstal, mayor of the palace
690	Willibrord comes to Francia
698	Willibrord founds Echternach
714–741	Charles Martel, mayor of the palace
716	Wynfrith/Boniface comes to Francia
733	Battle of Poitiers
741–768	Pippin (III)
	751 Anointed king
743	*Index of Superstitions* for Frankish council
745	Condemnation of Aldebert and Clement
754	Pope Stephen comes to Francia: re-anoints Pippin
	Death of Boniface
768–814	Charlemagne
774	Conquest of Lombards
778	Battle of Roncevalles
782	Alcuin comes to court
789	*Admonitio Generalis*
793	*Libri Carolini*
796	Palace built at Aachen
800	Charles acclaimed "Emperor" at Rome
802	Issuing of Laws at Aachen
813	Council of Tours
814–840	Louis the Pious
817	Einhard, *Life of Charlemagne*

BRITISH ISLES

406	Roman armies leave Britain
420?–490	Patricius
520+	Gildas, *On the Ruin of Britain*
522–597	Columba
	565 Founds Iona
540+–615	Columbanus
558	Last Feast of Tara
561	Battle of Cúl Drebene
560–616	Ethelbert, king of Kent
570+	Saxons enter Bath
597	Augustine comes to Kent
600+	Ethelbert's *Laws*
	Aneirin, *Y Gododdin*
614–680	Hild of Whitby
619	Paulinus comes to Northumbria
628	Conversion of Edwin of Northumbria
628–690	Benedict Biscop
	653 First travels to Rome
628–704	Adomnán
630–687	Cuthbert
630	Cummian writes on Easter Dating
633	Death of Edwin
634–709	Wilfrid
634–642	Oswald of Northumbria
635	Lindisfarne founded
642–671	Oswy of Northumbria
650+	Cogitosus, *Life of Brigid*
658–739	Willibrord
664	Council at Whitby
671–685	Egfrith of Northumbria
672–735	Bede
	731 *Ecclesiastical History*
674	Wearmouth founded
675–714	Guthlac
675–754	Wynfrith/Boniface
680/700	Muirchú, *Life of Saint Patrick*
688/693	Ine's *Laws*
697	*Cáin Adomnáin*: "Law of Innocents"
700+	*Dream of the Rood*
	Codex Amiatinus produced
720	*Senchas Már*
750	*Book of Kells*
757–796	Offa, king of Mercia

ITALY, SPAIN AND CENTRAL EUROPE

434–453	Empire of Attila
440–461	Pope Leo
454–482	Severinus in Noricum
476	Romulus Augustulus deposed
476–493	Odoacear rules Italy
480–524	Boethius
	524 *Consolation of Philosophy*
493?–526	Theodoric rules Italy
495	Celebration of *Lupercalia*
511	Eugippius, *Life of Severinus*
529	Benedict at Monte Cassino
490–583	Cassiodorus
	550 *Institutes*
533–540	Justinian reconquers Carthage, Rome and Ravenna

547   Benedict dies
560–636   Isidore of Seville
                    636   *Etymologies*
568   Lombards enter Italy
540–604   Gregory the Great
                    579   At Constantinople
                    590–604   Pope
                    593   *Regula Pastoralis*
                    594   *Dialogues*
589   Conversion of the Visigoths from Arianism to Catholicism
698   Arabs conquer Carthage
711   Arabs conquer Spain
751   Lombards conquer Ravenna
755–756   Franks invade Italy
774   Charles conquers Lombard kingdom
778   Battle of Roncevalles

CENTRAL EUROPE AND SCANDINAVIA

685–719   Radbod, king of Frisians
745–784   Viergil of Salzburg
751   Boniface founds Fulda
772   Charles sacks Irminsul
782   Massacre at Verden
785   *Capitulary on Saxony*
792   Avar War

                    826   Baptism of Harald Klak
                    800–865   Anskar
                    870+   Settlement of Iceland
                    950–986   Harald Bluetooth in Denmark
                    995–1000   Olaf Tryggvason in Norway
                    1000   Conversion of Iceland
                    1122/33   Ari Thorgilsson, *Book of the Icelanders*
                    1179–1241 Snorri Sturluson

EAST ROME AND THE MIDDLE EAST

154–
*ca.*222   Bardaisan of Edessa

                    224   Rise of Sasanian Empire
                    216–277   Mani

250–356   Anthony, hermit in Egypt
                    270   Goes into desert
250–336   Arius
263–340   Eusebius of Caesarea

                    298–330   Trdat III, king of Armenia

296–373   Athanasius of Alexandria
325   Council of Nicaea
327   Foundation of Constantinople
350–428   Theodore of Mopsuestia
356   *Life of Anthony* appears
363   Defeat and death of Julian
376–395   Theodosius I
378   Battle of Adrianople
385–466   Shenoute of Atripe
391   Destruction of Serapeum

                    400+   Creation of Armenian alphabet

396–459   Symeon Stylites
408–450   Theodosius II
412–444   Cyril of Alexandria
428–431   Nestorius, patriarch of

	Constantinople		
431	Council of Ephesus		
438	*Theodosian Code*		
		439–457	Yazdkart II, king of Persia
444–451	Dioscorus of Alexandria		
451	Council of Chalcedon	451	Battle of Avarair
465–538	Severus of Antioch		
470–547	Barsanuphius of Gaza		
		470+	P'awstos Buzand, *Epic Histories*
		470–496	Barsauma, Nestorian bishop of Nisibis
			Rise of Nestorian Academy of Nisibis
489	Closing of school of the Persians		
	at Edessa		
491–518	Anastasius		
500+	Ps.-Dionysius the Areopagite		
518–527	Justin		
527–565	Justinian		
507–588	John of Ephesus		
		519–531	Ella Atsbeha, king of Axum. Origin of *Kebra Nagast*
		523	Martyrs of Najran
529	Closing of Academy in Athens		
	Codex Justinianus		
		530–579	Khusro I Anoshirwan, king of Persia
532	*Nika* Riot		
533	*Digest* and *Institutes*		
537	Hagia Sophia completed		
		540–552	Mar Aba, Nestorian patriarch
540–628	Wars between Persia and east Rome		
542–543	Plague begins		
542–578	Jacob Baradaeus establishes		
	independent Monophysite church		
553	Condemnation of the *Three Chapters*		
550+	Slavs penetrate Balkans		
		570–632	Muhammad
580+	Formation of Avar empire		
		591–628	Khusro II Aparwez
610–641	Heraclius		
		610	Muhammad begins to receive *Qur'an*
		622	*Hijra* of Muhammad from Mecca to Medina
		632	Death of Muhammad
634–650+	Arabs conquer Syria, Egypt and		
	Persia		
		635–638	Nestorians at Hsian-fu
660	*Qur'an* written down		
		665	Ananias of Shirak, *K'nnikon*
675–753/4	John of Damascus		
680	Arculf visits Holy Places		
685–705	Abd al-Malik		
692	Dome of the Rock		
699	Arabic replaces Greek in		
	administration		
717	Defeat of Muslims at Constantinople		
717–741	Leo III		
726	Iconoclasm begins		
		740–825	Theodore abu Qurra
741–775	Constantine V		
754	Iconoclast Council of Hieria		
759–826	Theodore of Studios		
		762	Foundation of Baghdad
		762	Uighurs adopt Manichaeism
		780–823	Timothy I, Nestorian patriarch
787	Iconodule Council of Nicaea		

		788–803	Harun al-Rashid
802–814	Krum, Khan of the Bulgars		
810–893	Photius		
815–843	"Second Iconoclasm"		
818/820	Nicephorus, *Antirrheticus*		
		820	Uighur inscription of Karabalghasun
		840+	Translations of Greek into Arabic
843	"Triumph of Orthodoxy"		
863	Constantine and Methodius in Moravia		
864	Conversion of the Bulgars		
		873	Hunayn ibn Ishaq dies
987	Conversion of Kiev		

Index